Early Settlers and Indian Fighters

OF

Southwest Texas

BY

A. J. SOWELL

AUTHOR OF "TEXAS RANGERS" "BIG-FOOT WALLACE," ETC.

FACTS GATHERED FROM SURVIVORS OF FRONTIER DAYS

Southern Historical Press, Inc.
Greenville, South Carolina

This volume was reproduced
from a personal copy located in
the Publishers private library

All rights reserved. No part of this publication may be reproduced,
stored in a retrieval system, transmitted in any form, posted
on the web in any form or by any means without the
prior written permission of the publisher.

Please direct all correspondence and book orders to:
SOUTHERN HISTORICAL PRESS, Inc.
1071 Park West Blvd.
Greenville, SC 29611

Published 1900 by:
  ISBN #978-1-63914-632-1
Printed in the United States of America

ED. WESTFALL.

E. D. WESTFALL.

Came to Texas in 1845.

Edward Dixon Westfall was born in Knox County, Indiana, on the 22d day of December, 1820. His father, Abraham, was a Virginian by birth, but went to Indiana with his parents when quite young. His grandfather, Isaac, was a surveyor, and followed that profession for several years in the new State. When the Indian war broke out and General Harrison fought the battle of Tippecanoe young Abraham wanted to go with the soldiers and take part in the battle, but his father made him stay at home and went himself.

In 1841 Abraham Westfall moved with his family to Jasper County, Illinois.

In 1843 Edward Dixon left Illinois and came over into Missouri, but being of a roving disposition soon moved on, and arrived in Hopkins County, Texas, in 1845. In the following year he came on to San Antonio.

By this time the Mexican war had broken out and he joined the company of Capt. John Conner, Bell's regiment of mounted riflemen. The lieutenants in the company were — Jett and — Patterson. Col. P. H. Bell, who commanded the regiment, was afterwards Governor of Texas. As to the service of Mr. Westfall in Mexico, suffice it to say he made a brave and gallant soldier, never shirking duty or danger at any time.

After the war was over the regiment returned to Texas and was discharged at San Antonio.

Mr. Westfall, although educated and a well-informed man, had a natural love for the solitude and romance of the wild woods, and like his erstwhile boon companion, Big Foot Wallace, delighted to roam over a new country, shoot game, and camp out. At this time no country afforded a more inviting field for a man of that turn than Texas, and he soon cut loose from the companionship and habitation of civilized man and built a cabin on the banks of the Leona River, in the dense solitude of the great southwest, distant more than 100 miles from San Antonio. The only settlement then west of San Antonio was the colony of Henry Castro, and he was far in advance of them. Soon after Westfall settled on the Leona, Fort Inge was built on the same stream about thirty miles above. This induced others to come, and in a few years a settlement was made at the present town of Uvalde, four miles above the fort. This was about 1852.

Westfall soon became familiar with the surrounding country and the ways and customs of the Indians, who then held sway in all this vast country. He became a noted man on the frontier as Indian fighter, guide, and trailer for soldiers, rangers, and settlers. Hardly an expedition went out without him or the two other famous guides in the west, Big Foot Wallace and Henry Robinson, being along. They looked to either of these three men to pilot them through mountains, canyons, and cedar brakes, or the devious windings through chaparral and prickly pear.

Just before Fort Inge was built the Lipan Indians came down from the mountains and raided the country east in the vicinity of where Big Foot Wallace lived, and carried off some of his horse stock and others of the settlement. Wallace waited until the Indians thought no one was going to follow them, as he conjectured, and then came after Westfall. These two hardy leaders came back to the Wallace ranch, and gathering about thirty men went on a hunt for the Lipans, who were found in camp at a place now called the Frio waterhole, on the divide at the head draws of the Frio River. A battle ensued in which ten of the Indians were killed, and about 200 mules and horses taken which had been carried off from the settlements. The Indians were completely surprised and made a poor fight, none of the settlers being killed. Wallace was riding a fine mare, and she fell with him just as they were charging into the Indian camp, and he went over her head but lit on his feet. Wallace killed one Indian with the only shot he got with his rifle. He had a flintlock, and the flint in the holder burst. One old squaw and a daughter of the chief were left in camp. The old squaw had nails on her fingers an inch long. She tried to scratch Wallace in the eyes when he stooped to look in her face after the fight. Some one wanted to shoot her, but Big Foot prevented them.

Westfall and Wallace were conspicuous figures in the fight. Wallace had black curly hair, dark eyes, 6 feet 2 inches in height, and weighed 240 pounds. Westfall had nut-brown hair, blue eyes, 6 feet 3¾ inches in height, and weighed 190 pounds. From the battleground it was a long, tedious route over the rough country, without roads, to drive the horses back to the settlements, but it was finally accomplished, and Westfall, bidding farewell to his friends, went back to his ranch.

As the country began to settle stock was brought in, and Westfall, having located a considerable tract of land and having plenty free grass and water, also commenced raising stock. To do this successfully he needed neighbors for mutual protection for stock, especially horses, as they drew raiding bands of Indians around a ranch. Having this in mind, he went to San Antonio and made an offer to anyone who wished to come that he would give each 100 acres of land. Several accepted and went, but the majority soon tired of frontier life and went back. Two, however, remained—James Hammock and a man named Blanchard. They opened up a farm and lived in the house with Westfall. In 1850 they planted a crop of corn. There was no provisions to be had except wild meat, and deer at this season of the year were poor. Thinking this was not substantial enough to make a crop on, Hammock got Blanchard and another man who was there to go with pack mules to San Antonio and bring back some bacon, flour, and salt, and he would cultivate the crop. Three months passed away, and nothing was seen or heard of the two grub-hunters. Hammock made the crop, living on deer meat, and as farmers say, "laid it by." Westfall, who took all of these things philosophically and never complained at anything, now proposed to Hammock that they take a hunt to the Espantosa Lake and get a supply of venison and honey. This was very agreeable to the despondent farmer, who had complained a great deal and would have said hard things about his long-absent partner if he had been certain he was not killed by Indians.

They arrived at the lake all right and found everything to their hands—fat deer and plenty of wild honey. Hammock was in high spirits and enjoyed himself. He had made a crop on poor venison without salt, and said now he did not care if they never come back from San Antonio. Soon after the return to the ranch, however, their absent friends also arrived. They had a tale of woe to tell of incessant rains, high water in creeks and rivers, which caused many delays. All they returned with was a little bacon and coffee. The flour and salt had all been spoiled by the rain.

Long and impatiently they now waited for the corn to get hard enough to grit or grind. When the shucks began to dry they gathered some, and by exposing it to the hot sun soon had it dry enough to shell and grind on a steel mill which Westfall had. Some was ground that looked sufficient for four men to eat at one meal, but Jim Hammock said grind some more; that he wanted a good bait while he was at it. When the corndodgers were cooked and put on the table the men were mistaken in how much they could eat. There was plenty left. They had done without bread so long it did not taste natural, and they soon got enough of it.

Westfall now proposed to take another hunt with Hammock. Jim, however, objected this time, saying it would turn out disastrously. He was always predicting dire calamities, and said he had been warned not to go on this trip. Westfall laughed at these things, and said he thought it was a fine time to go. Hammock finally, with a long and sad face, began to get ready and said he would go and risk it. They intended to stop this time on the Nueces River, not quite so far out as before, and where there was also plenty of honey. Deer were everywhere. On the way out they stopped to noon in a shady elm grove, not far from a lake. Hammock was to get dinner, while Westfall went to kill a deer for the purpose of casing the skin to put the honey in. No sooner had Jim raised a smoke than it attracted a large band of Indians passing, who at once came and attacked him. Hammock saw them in time to make a run and fired at them as he went. At the lake he threw his rifle down and sprang in, with the Indians in pursuit, yelling and shooting at him. He had no time to mount a horse, as they were both staked out. By diving almost continually as he swam he avoided the arrows which cut the water around him, and arrived safely on the opposite bank. The Indians did not attempt to follow him, but went back to plunder the camp. He continued his flight through the brush for some distance until he got out of the valley and ascended rising ground. Then he looked back to see if the Indians were following. He was very uneasy about Westfall, and what was his consternation now to see his friend running at full speed almost into the Indians to succor him, thinking he was being killed by the

Indians in camp. The distance was too great for his voice to reach him in assurance of his safety, and with a heavy heart he sped on, not wanting to see the horrible sight of his noble companion butchered. His purpose was to get to the ranch somehow, and get help and come back after his body.

Westfall was a quarter of a mile or more from camp when he heard the rifle shot, but at first supposed Jim had shot a deer or turkey. He had stopped for an instant and was about to resume his walk when the loud yelling of Indians suddenly burst upon his hearing. "Indians!" he exclaimed. "My God, they will kill Jim; I must go to him," and wheeling with his gun in his right hand he sped back towards camp. He ran about 600 yards before stopping, and was getting somewhat winded when he approached the camp. The grove was literally swarming with Indians, but he could nowhere see his friend. While stopped in plain view getting his wind back the Indians discovered him, and they came yelling in crowds, on foot. They were coming in on a raid and had no horses. Westfall was willing to risk his life to save his friend, but not to throw it away if it was too late to help him. He now yelled and called the name of his companion, but getting no response, and thinking and almost knowing it was all over with him, turned and ran, followed by a flight of arrows and the Indians who were shooting them. There was an open flat around the grove of several hundred yards in extent, and across this he had to run to cover. The Indians saw he was fast, and sent one of their number who was on a mule to cut him off from the chaparral. Westfall watched him, intending to kill him if he came too close or was about to run around him, but he beat the mule to the brush too far to talk about. He also left the foot ones far in the rear. Almost exhausted, he made his way to about the center of the thicket and lay down. Besides the load in the rifle he had a large single-shot pistol. He knew Indian nature well—that they dreaded a concealed foe. Here he was, besieged by the whole band, it seemed from the noise they made, until night. They whooped and yelled, beat the brush, and shot arrows into it. At times they would come part of the way in, making the brush rattle as much as possible, like they were going to charge over the spot where he was, hoping he would get scared and run out. He stood all this, however, and kept his rifle ready, knowing if they did come he would get one or two, and he had just as soon be killed in the brush as out in open ground. This was not the first time he had been in a thicket from Indians.

On this occasion, when the Indians finally hushed their jargon and demoniac yells, and the dark mantle of night closed down on hill, dale, and chaparral, Westfall came forth slowly and cautiously, stopping and listening at the slightest sound, sometimes with one foot raised and bated breath, as the distant bark of a coyote was heard or the bushes rustled by some prowling nocturnal animal gliding away from his presence. In this way, step by step and many halts, he approached their noonday camp, determined not to leave until he found out the fate of his companion if possible. Poor Hammock! Where was he now, at whom he laughed only that morning about his warnings and bad omens? All of these things passed through Westfall's mind as he passed among the trees. Every dark object on the ground was examined or touched. A white something appeared at his feet. His heart sank within him. It might be the body stripped and mutilated. He slowly stooped and touched it, and a breath of relief came. It was the ashes where the fire had burned out that Jim had made that day at noon to boil their coffee and roast their meat. His search was of course fruitless, as at this time Jim was tearing through the brush and pear, lacerating himself at every step, trying to get to the ranch in the dark.

Horses, saddles and everything were gone. With noiseless tread of his moccasined feet he searched the open ground around the mott. He might have ran a distance before being killed. Finally, however, he gave it up and was about to start on his journey to the ranch, when he thought of his spurs. Surely the Indians did not find them hung up as high as he could reach among the thick leaves of an elm tree. When he felt for them they were gone, too. There was nothing left now for him to do but to return to the ranch and report Jim killed and get Blanchard to come back with him after the body. With shouldered rifle and long, steady strides he commenced his dark and lonely journey through the pathless woods.

Long after the turn of the night, when the cock had crowed twice, Jim Hammock, torn by thorns, wet and full of prickly pears, startled the inmates of the Westfall ranch by knocking at the cabin door and announcing his name. Explanations soon followed after he entered. He told of the attack by the Indians and flight of himself across the lake, and then from elevated ground beheld his noble companion going in a run to his rescue. Being almost in among the Indians when he last saw him, it was almost certain that he had perished. Winding up, he said, "Yes, boys, Westfall is gone. The Indians got him this time, and no mistake."

"No they haven't, Jim. Here I am!" came a voice from out the darkness near the cabin door, which at that instant opened and the tall form of Westfall stood before them. The reader can imagine the joy and explanations that followed. Westfall was just about to announce his presence and the death of Jim when he saw a light in the house and heard the voice of his companion telling the others of his death.

Although Hammock had nearly half a day the start of Westfall, the latter came near beating him to the ranch on account of his better knowledge of the country and coming straight.

Soon after this the men all left Westfall, and he was alone once more except for the companionship of his dogs and horses. He was greatly attached to one of his dogs, whom he called George Washington. Jim Hammock wanted to see some of the country still further west, and when Big Foot Wallace obtained the contract to carry the mail to El Paso he got in as one of the stage guards. Before starting on his first trip, however, he again predicted evil and said he would never come back. This time, as before, his words seemed prophetic, for he was killed at a fandango in El Paso by a Mexican.

The Indians learned to know and dread Westfall, and tried many times to kill him. On one occasion he went on foot to take a short hunt, and the Indians came in his absence and laid an ambush for him. They saw his trail where he had left the cabin and crossed the river on a foot log which he had placed there by chopping a tall tree across it for convenience when wishing to pass to the opposite side on foot. Here at this log the Indians waited concealed. One, however, exposed himself, and the keen eye of the settler discovered him when he returned, and he hastily went back, knowing there was an ambush there. The Indians left cover and followed, and he took the brush on them in a dense thicket and stopped, lying flat on his stomach, so that he could see to some extent under the brush. Here he awaited developments. Presently the Indians commenced a great yelling all on one side of the thicket, like they were coming in. Westfall turned a little and listened at them, but without getting up. Soon a stick cracked in the other direction, and his attention was directed there. With his face almost to the ground and rifle ready he waited. A bush moved. A dark object was seen, which finally developed into the face and black head of an Indian as he slowly, inch at a time, moved into view looking for the white man. Only a moment it was seen there and the crack of a rifle was heard. The brush around Westfall for a few moments was enveloped in smoke and he lay still in the position he occupied, with his pistol ready for an emergency if any others were close behind. All was still, and he hastily reloaded his rifle. The Indians outside of the thicket quit yelling. When the smoke cleared away Westfall saw that he had got his Indian. He could see his hair spread out on the leaves. All the balance of the evening he stayed here, but could hear nothing more of the other Indians. About sundown he crawled to where his dead Indian was and looked at him. He was shot between the eyes. His hair was about two feet in length and very thick. His bow was strung and one arrow in his hand ready to shoot. The Indians evidently sent this fellow in there to crawl up on Westfall and shoot him while they attracted his attention by their yelling in the other direction. When their man did not return after the report of the rifle they knew what his fate was, and left without any further investigation. When night come Westfall cautiously left the thicket and made his way back to his cabin, but not by way of the foot log; he avoided that and crossed lower down. When he did not wish his dogs to follow he left them in the cabin, and they were there on his return. Although the Indians had been near they had not approached the house.

Westfall went several trips with Wallace as stage guard, but not liking this business soon quit.

One of the relay stations for Big Foot Wallace was at Fort Inge, and on one occasion just before arriving there he discovered the track of the Big Foot Indian where he and six of his followers had crossed the road. Wallace had often trailed this Indian on the Colorado, had seen him three times, but never fired at him. His track was fourteen inches in length as measured by Wallace on one occasion near Austin. On arriving at the fort Westfall was there, and Wallace told him of the presence of Big Foot and his band, and furthermore, if the Indians made a raid in the vicinity and cleaned up the horse stock, that he would leave his relay of mules on the Frio, and if he needed them to follow Big Foot with, to go and get them. As Wallace expected, all of the horses were taken and the mules were sent for, and three or four men and one boy mounted and set out on the trail, led by Westfall. The Indians went up Nueces Canyon to its source, and then crossed over into the head draws of South Llano. Here they went into camp in a dense cedar brake and proceeded to rest and cook a small bear which they had killed. Thinking they had got all the horses, they did not fear pursuit. The soldiers at the fort had gone on a scout.

About sundown of the second day of the pursuit the camp of the Indians was located by their smoke. Westfall now camped, but without building any fire, and awaited morning for the attack. At daybreak he went to reconnoiter their position, taking the boy, whose name was Preston Polly, with him. The other men were told if they heard his gun to come quickly. At first he descended into the bed of a gorge which skirted the foot of a hill to the right of Big Foot's camp, which was on this elevation, but back in a cedar brake, as before stated. Following up the gorge to a point opposite the place where smoke was seen the evening before, a trail was discovered which led down the hill to a pool of water fed by seep springs, and below it was very rank, coarse grass. Westfall had halted in this grass for a few moments looking at the trail and was about to follow it, when he saw the legs of a horse and an Indian under the bushes following the trail coming towards the pool of water. He now instantly cocked his gun and stood in readiness, and when the Indian came into full view the heart of the pioneer beat quickly, for Big Foot, the scourge of the southwest frontier, was before him. Silently motioning for the boy to be still who stood behind him, he slowly and steadily raised his gun. At this time the horse discovered the presence of the ambushed marksman and snorted. Big Foot turned quickly to look at him and was for a moment stationary, presenting a fair side view, and—bang! Night came down on the burly chief. He fell in his tracks, shot through the heart. The last object his eyes rested on was a white man's horse. He belonged to Adolf Fry, and was taken near Fort Inge. The other men now came quickly and a charge was made up the hill, past the body of the dead chief, into the camp. The other Indians, however, were gone, being alarmed by Westfall's gun, which no doubt they thought boded no good for their chief, as no shout or call came from him. The stolen horses were all in camp except those ridden off by the fleeing Indians. It was evident they were about to leave, and the chief was going to water his horse. The hungry men ate a good portion of the bear meat, which was fat and well roasted. Among other things left in camp was a shield and quiver of arrows. The big chief was 7 feet in height and would weigh about 300 pounds. He had such a grip on the halter by which he was leading the horse that the animal could not pull away from him or move him out of his position as he lay. He made several efforts to do so, when the gun fired and the Indian fell. Also in one hand the chief clutched a bow and some arrows, and his fingers had to be opened with force to release them, as was also the halter in the other hand. He had a broad, rough face and powerful arms and legs, and his hair was about a yard in length. It was not in the nature of Westfall and Wallace to scalp their victims, as many did. Westfall had promised Wallace to bring him the moccasins of Big Foot if he killed him, so these were taken off for that purpose. One of the men wished to wear them back and pulled them on over a heavy pair of boots, and then they were too large. On the Indian's right knee was the sign of Tom Green's bullet, where he wounded him near Austin in 1839. This was Gen. Tom Green in the civil war, and he was killed at the battle of Blair's Landing, La., in 1863.

When Westfall and his men returned to Fort Inge the moccasins were left there for Wallace, but he never goth them. A man there obtained possession of them with a promise to deliver them to Wallace at San Antonio, but he never did, and went on to the States with them.

When Big Foot Wallace quit the mail service he was commissioned by Gov. P. H. Bell to raise a company of rangers for frontier defense. The company was raised, with Westfall as lieutenant.

The hardest fight they had during this service was on the Todas Santos (All Saints) Creek, at a place called the Black Hills, sixteen miles from the present town of Cotulla, in La Salle County. There were eighty Indians and nineteen rangers, and one of them named Jackson was very sick, and had to lie on a blanket under a mesquite tree during the combat. It was hot, dry weather, and the rangers had been three days without water. It was in August, 1854, and the rangers were fighting to get at a waterhole which was in the possession of the Comanches. Captain Wallace knew where all the waterholes were, and had led his men over the hot, desolate hills and valleys, through prickly pear and catclaw bushes, to this watering place, and found the Indians there, and a desperate battle ensued of an hour or more. The Indians were finally driven away, leaving twenty-two of their number dead on the ground, among whom was the chief. Captain Wallace killed him with a large rifle which once belonged to Col. James Bowie. The mesquite tree behind which Wallace stood was struck by many bullets. Westfall did some splendid shooting, and more than one Indian went down under his fire. Several of the rangers were wounded, some severely, and they were carried on stretchers to Fort Inge. None were killed.

After the company was disbanded Westfall returned to his ranch and once more took up his hermit life. The Indians still tried to get him, but were foiled many times.

In 1855 a Frenchman named Louie came down from Fort Inge and wanted to live with Westfall. This was agreeable, and a day was set to return to the fort to bring his effects down to the ranch. When the time arrived Westfall said it was best to wait until night to make the trip, as there were Indians in the country. He had been out to kill a deer and saw their signs. This was the 30th day of June, 1855. At 3 o'clock Westfall went out to the hand mill and ground some corn. Everything looked quiet and serene, but at this moment a band of Indians were secreted near by and watching his every movement. When his back was turned and he started back to the house with the meal on his shoulder, an Indian left cover, and making a quick run gained a position behind the corn crib near the cabin. When Westfall arrived at the door of his house he turned, as was his custom before entering, and took a look around. At this moment the Indian behind the crib, who had his gun in position, fired and badly wounded him in the right breast. The ball entered high up near the collar bone and ranged a little down, going through the upper part of the right lung and passing on out through the body. He did not fall, but carried the meal in the house, and getting his gun and pistol started to go out to fight the Indians, who by this time were yelling and shooting at the house. Thinking he could not recover from the wound, his intention was to try and get as many of them as they did of him, or more if he could.

The Frenchman held Westfall back, and said that he would fight the Indians. Being now very weak from loss of blood, he yielded and fell back on the bed, but protruded the muzzle of his rifle through a crack between the logs of the cabin, from which he had torn a board for that purpose. The brave Louie kept his word. He took up a shotgun loaded with buckshot, and throwing open the door fired one barrel and killed the Indian at the crib. A great shout was now set up by the Comanches, and many balls hit the house, mostly coming from across the open ground.

The Frenchman was greatly excited and raved and swore, going to the door again to get another shot, against the advice of Westfall, who admonished him to keep still and watch a chance to shoot. As he presented himself in the open door he was struck by a ball that went through his body and fell in a tin pan sitting on a table behind him. He turned quickly and looked at the ball as it rattled in the pan, and then put his gun down and told the almost unconscious Westfall that he was killed, too. He then sat down in a chair, pulled off his boots, called for water, and fell over dead on the floor. The door was still open and Westfall was not able to get up and shut it. The dog, George Washington, who was in the house, now sallied forth when Louie fell, and attacked an Indian who was approaching the house. He pulled the rigging off the Comanche, even the quiver from his back, and bit him badly, but was mortally wounded by a lance, and returning to the house went in and died beside the Frenchman. Westfall now gave up all hope. He was too weak to make a fight, and expected every moment his foes would be in upon him, who would have paid any price almost for his scalp. This was the only time they ever had him in their power and unable to defend himself, and would have got him if they had known the situation. Not knowing this, they finally took their departure and left him alone.

The wounded man stayed all night in the cabin on the blood-covered bed, part of the time unconscious. When daylight came his head, neck, and eyes were so badly swollen he could not see, and only knew when daylight came by the birds singing. He had been expecting some men down from Fort Inge to fish and hunt, and now looked to them to help him, expecting them to come that day. The day passed off and they did not come, and he passed another night alone and in darkness on the bed, and his dead companion and dead dog on the floor. The only chance to get help was for him to go to the fort himself. He was a man of powerful strength, courage, and will power, and on the third day determined to make the effort. The swelling in his eyes had abated to some extent, so that he could see his way. Not wishing for the dead man and dog to decay in the house, he had a hard time in getting them out, but was finally successful. He was not able to carry his rifle, and hid it in the weeds. A pistol, gourd of water, and some ground coffee and tin can to make it in was carried along. He also aided locomotion with a stick. The first day only five miles were made. When he became exhausted he would make a little very strong coffee and drink it. On the third night, as he was slowly and painfully making his way along the Fort Inge road, he was met by the party whom he had been expecting at his ranch to hunt. They were traveling at night to avoid Indians. One of the party, named William Luckey, came near shooting him for an Indian. They helped him to get on to the fort, and he was put under the post surgeon there.

About three days after Westfall left his ranch Big Foot Wallace and two other men come on the scene. At first sight of the dead man in the yard Wallace said, "Hello! the Indians have killed Westfall." On coming nearer and seeing the discolored face and black hair of the Frenchman, he again exclaimed, "No; Westfall has killed an Indian." Further inspection revealed the truth of the situation, and Wallace then went to look for his friend, believing he was either dead or wounded somewhere near by. By his knowledge of woodcraft he soon found the trail of Westfall, and came back and told his companions, who had never been on a frontier before, that Westfall was wounded and gone to Fort Inge. and described all the circumstances of his having his pistol and gourd, walking with a stick, and had no gun, etc.

Wallace now took the trail, expecting to find the wounded man on the road, but late in the night met a party who were coming down to bury Louie. They went back to the fort together, and told Wallace the particulars as they went along. After staying a while with Westfall, Wallace went back with a party and buried the Frenchman and also the dog. Westfall had two horses tied in the brush when he was wounded, and thought the Indians had got them, but they were found by Wallace and taken care of. They were nearly starved. The two men who came with Wallace first to the ranch were planters from the Colorado, hunting for runaway negroes. They went back to San Antonio from the fort. Westfall had a hard pull for his life. Big Foot Wallace came often to see him, and brought books and papers for him to read while convalescing.

This episode in the life of Westfall caused him to think of laying up something for a "rainy day." After his recovery and return to the ranch his brother Abel, who had been informed of his situation, came from the States and lived several years with him, and assisted in the management of the stock. During the civil war the stock was removed to Nueces Canyon and located near Camp Wood, another military post which had been established. Here he stayed nine years, and during that time acted as guide and trailer for citizens, rangers, and soldiers. The Indians knew him and Henry Robinson so well they painted their pictures on a rock—Robinson with his shotgun and Westfall with his rifle.

In 1874 he sold all of his cattle, and in 1877 moved to Bexar county and settled fifteen and one-half miles southeast from San Antonio, on the west bank of Calaveras Creek. In 1881 he sold his Leona ranch and went farming. In the same year, June 5th, he married Miss Josephine Susan Dillon. He lived on the farm here until his death, which occurred on the 12th day of June, 1897. He had been in bad health for some time, and on Thursday, the 10th, before his death, was taken in the middle of the afternoon with cholera morbus, which terminated fatally on Saturday. He died easy and without a struggle. Those who stood around his bedside in his last hours besides his wife were his brother, Abel Westfall, William Boykin, Lemuel Mays, and D. H. Dillon, a brother of Mrs. Westfall. In the cemetery at Elmendorf, on the Aransas Pass road, the great frontiersman was buried. He left no family except his wife. He had a brother-in-law, John Reinbold, who lives in San Antonio. Had also two neices and one nephew there. One brother, Isaac, died in Grayson County, Texas. Henry, another brother, died near Mumfordville, Ky., during the civil war. Mrs. Westfall has a knife which her husband carried for many years, and which originally belonged to his old friend and companion, Henry Robinson. It has "H. R." cut on the handle, done by Robinson himself. The following is the will of Westfall, as copied by the writer from the San Antonio *Express,* bearing date of June 26, 1897:

"The last will and testament of the late Edward Dixon Westfall, who died June 12th, 1897, has been filed for probate. All of the deceased's property, valued at $5000, is bequeathed to his wife, Josephine Susan Westfall. The will provides that after her death the property shall be invested in the city of San Antonio in trust to be converted into cash and applied to the establishment of a free public library, to which whites and blacks shall have access on equal terms, but separate reading rooms."

At the request of many friends of Mr. Westfall in the West, the writer made a journey of more than 100 miles in February of 1897 to interview him and write a sketch of his eventful life, not knowing he had passed away. His wife and brother furnished most of the data for this sketch. He thought a great deal of Big Foot Wallace, and said that while he was the most cautious man he ever saw, that when the test came his courage never failed him, nor his presence of mind, and that his judgment was never at fault.

HENRY BRUCKS.

Came to Texas in 1846.

Mr. Henry Brucks, the subject of this sketch, and one of the pioneers of Southwest Texas, was born on the 16th of February, 1838, in Westphalen, on the Rhine, and came to Texas with his parents and brother in 1846 as a Castro colonist. The ship in which they sailed was the Medina, and the first port touched was Galveston, Texas. The objective point, however, from which to make their start on the overland route to the Castro settlement was Port Lavaca, but in attempting to land at this place the ship was blown off by a norther and had to land at Corpus Christi.

In writing up the early history of the West there is bound to be more or less repetition and the same ground gone over again to some extent, where different individuals are interviewed who participated in the same events described, but in getting the statements of more than one, new facts are brought out. Every one does not have the same experience, and often in giving the details of battles or settlements one will remember an incident that escaped the recollection of another who was present.

From Corpus Christi the Brucks family after many hardships arrived at Castroville. Other colonists who had preceded them had already commenced a settlement under the management of Henry Castro, and their future town named. This was on the Medina River, twenty-five miles west from San Antonio. After staying a month at this place the Brucks family, with others, went further west about ten miles and commenced a settlement on the Quihi Creek, at the famous lake of the same name. Quihi means eagle in Spanish, or one certain kind which Americans call a Mexican eagle, or buzzard. They are not a buzzard, however, but an eagle. They have white heads, brown bodies, white tails, and tips of wings white. They were quite numerous in this country at an early day.

A town had been laid off at this place by Castro, and each settler received a town lot besides his regular grant of farming land. There were no roads out to this place, and the journey with women and children and heavily loaded carts and wagons was slow and tedious. The start was made on the 2d day of March, 1846, and at sunset of the same day they arrived on the ground. Each man's lot was numbered on a stake driven in the ground. John B. Brucks, father of Henry, had a lot near the lake and succeeded in finding his number before dark, and camped the first night on his possession. Night came on so soon after arriving that many could not find their numbers, and they camped as convenience suited them for the night, building many bright and cheerful looking fires up and down the creek. Mr. Brucks distinctly remembers how the bright fires looked on that first night. Next day the people all found their lots and occupied them. As there was no chance to build houses for some time to come, the people had to live in tents. The colonists divided, part of them settling one mile below the lake. Of this party was the old man Boinkhoff, his wife, one married son and his wife, one single son about 10 years of age, and a grandson about the same age. All of these were living in one tent. About 12 o'clock at night of the eighth day of the new settlement, a man who had been a cook on board the ship in which they sailed for America came up from the lower settlement, where he lived, and told the elder Brucks that the Indians were in the lower settlement and were killing all the people down there. On being awakened and told this startling news Mr. Brucks hastily arose, and, donning his garments, went and aroused every man in the colony who had been a soldier in Europe, and organized them into a squad to fight the Indians. Those who had not been soldiers were not allowed to go with this crowd, but were left with the women and children. A man named Deides was detailed to ring a bell which hung on a mesquite tree near Mr. Brucks' tent. This bell had been sold at auction on board the ship and bought by Mr. Brucks. Captain Brucks now formed his men and ordered them to fire off their guns and reload them, so as to be sure they were in good condition. They now marched down to the scene of the trouble. They were not used to Indian warfare, and talked loud as they marched along. On arriving at a point about half way to the lower settlement a voice came out of the brush and darkness asking if Mr. Brucks was in the crowd. On being answered in the affirmative, the voice said, "Come out here to me and pull these sticks out of my head." Mr. Brucks at once went to the man, and found it was old man Boinkhoff with two arrows in his forehead. With some difficulty they were extracted, and the wounded man went on up to the upper settlement. Brucks and his men went to the tent and found that the two women were dead and scalped in front of it. Another voice now came out of the darkness about thirty yards away, calling for Mr. Brucks. On going out there young Boinkhoff was found to be mortally wounded, shot through the bowels with a bullet. He begged the men to kill him, and died before daylight. He told them before he died that they heard wolves, as they supposed, that night close by, but paid no attention to it. After a while a shot was fired, and the ball came through the tent and struck him. He knew nothing about Indians, and supposed it was a man named Bruckman shooting turkeys, which he had been doing several nights. The turkeys roosted in the timber on the creek not far from the tents. He told his wife to go and tell Bruckman not to shoot any more, as he had already hit him. Both of the women went out of the tent to do so and were met by the Indians almost in the door of the tent, who at once began to lance them. They screamed and tried to escape, but soon fell and expired under the terrible thrusts. The old man now went out under the tent and got behind a tree and looked around it to see what was going on, and received two arrows in the forehead. Young Boinkhoff also crawled under the tent and went to the brush while the Indians were killing his wife and mother. The man Bruckman, who was supposed to be shooting the turkeys, lived in a tent near by.

After the two unfortunate women were slain the Indians went into the tent and began to plunder it. In the tent was a large box which had been brought from Europe, and which contained clothing and guns, the latter being at the bottom and hard to get at, and had never been taken out. By this time the alarm had been raised above, bell ringing, guns firing, etc. The Indians only took a few things, not getting down to the guns, which were left, and they commenced their retreat, carrying the two boys with them. The wounded man in the brush could hear his son calling, "Help me, father; help me!" but his cries soon ceased, and the father thought that they had gone out of hearing; but the Indians had killed him to stop his cries. His body was found next morning not far away. It was lying inside of what is now the yard of Lienber Boele. Next day the news of the raid was carried to Castroville, and men came and followed the Indians, but could not find them.

In about six months news came that the boy who had been carried off was in Fredericksburg, having been brought there by an Indian agent, and old man Boinkhoff went there on foot to bring him home. Mr. Henry Brucks was with the boy a good deal after he was brought back, but he would not talk much, and very little could be learned about his captivity. He said, however, that the Indians traveled three days after the raid before they would stop and make a fire. They then camped on a bold, running stream, where were many pecan trees. This must have been the South Llano. They stayed here some time, and the Indians painted the boy. As soon as he got a chance he washed it off, and was whipped by the squaws for it. The boy and the old grandpa both died in less than a year after the boy's return.

Not long after this first rude shock of the western savage the settlers built a large brush fence near the lake and fronting on it. Here the people lived inside of the inclosure and called it "the yard." Many of them took the fever, however, and here old man Boinkhoff and the captive boy died.

The next thing to happen was the capture of a boy named Henry Snyder by the Indians. He and Baptiste Nuspaum, a grown man, were herding cattle to keep them out of the crops, as they had no fences at that time. Baptiste and the boy separated, and no one saw the Indians when they captured him. He was never recovered. In 1847 the elder Brucks went to hunt cows for Baptiste Nuspaum, who had no horse. Mr. Brucks went down the Quihi Creek beyond where 'Squire Charobiny now lives, and ascending a hill so as to see over into the valley, discovered six Indians dismounted and standing by their horses. At sight of the white man the Indians mounted to chase him. Brucks, having no gun, turned and fled towards the settlement, followed by the yelling savages. The chase led through what is now the yard of 'Squire Charobiny, down the steep hill, then into Quihi Creek, and across the open flat now inclosed in the Charobiny farm. The Indians, seeing they could not catch him, stopped on the bluff and fired their guns at him as he ran north of the creek. The faithful horse who was carrying his master safely away was struck by a ball and mortally wounded. He held up, however, and kept his speed until out of sight of the Indians, and then fell dead in a liveoak grove. After the death of his horse Brucks continued his flight on foot and safely reached the settlement. Next morning he and others went back to the dead horse and removed the saddle. The bullet had passed through him. Nothing was seen of the Indians.

After Meyer was killed and Mrs. Charobiny captured, an Indian was taken in a fight out west and was brought to Quihi by Tom Rife and a man named Allen, and some others. They wanted to see if Mrs. Charobiny could identify him as one of those who had captured and badly wounded her. All Indians, she said, looked alike to her, and she could not tell. There was a family who kept a barroom or a barrel of whisky at Quihi, and would sell to anyone who wanted it. To this place the men who had the Indian went and stayed all night and drank whisky, and during the time some of them killed the Indian. Next morning a man put a rope around the dead Indian and dragged the body half a mile, and left it for the hogs to eat. A field covers the place now. The Indian was killed where Rolhf's blacksmith shop is now, or was. Some of the old settlers that live at Bandera think the Indian that was killed here was "Old Delaware Bob," a friendly Indian, or had been at least.

On the 14th of March, 1867, the Indians killed old man Hiram Gerdes, about two and a half miles southeast of Quihi. At this time Henry Brucks was a guard for the United States mail from Fort Clark to Fort Stockton. Holiday was boss of this part of the line, and Cook of the other. One would start from Stockton and the other from Clark and pass on the route. At this time the Indians had captured and robbed the Cook outfit. They went into camp on Liveoak Creek, above Fort Lancaster, intending to rest the mules three hours and then go on. A man was sent with the mules to water a short distance from camp, and the Indians made a rush and got them. The men stayed in camp all night, and next morning saw the Indians coming in all directions to attack them. There were only ten men in Cook's party, but they fought the Indians for some time and then began a retreat through the roughest part of the country, fighting as they went.

There was a Mexican in the crowd called Big Joe, who got into a hole in the side of a hill and watched the Indians rob the mail and burn the stage. When Brucks and his party came on they met Big Joe just beyond the Painted Cave, on Devil's River, and he told the men not to go on, as they would all be killed. The party, however, said they must go on with the mail, and would do so and deliver it or die in the attempt, and told Joe he had better go with them. He got in the stage and rode a short distance, but then jumped out, and said, "I can't go; you will all be killed, boys; they have done killed our men." Near Camp Hutson a halt was made to rest and feed the mules. Mr. Brucks, who had just been relieved from guard duty, heard someone talking on the road in English, and it was soon discovered that it was Cook's men. They were glad to get with the others, and were hungry and tired. They told about the fight, and said they tried hard to save the stage but were compelled to abandon it, not, however, until their ammunition was nearly all gone. They retreated into a gorge full of cedar, and the Indians did not follow them any further. The Mexican, Joe, they also said, left before they did and watched the Indians burn the stage, and supposed they were all killed, as he did not see them when they commenced their retreat. The Cook party were all on foot and went on to Fort Clark, and the Brucks party to Lancaster. There were two roads. One went down a steep hill, but cut off eight miles. The Cook party went the long route by Liveoak Creek, but Holiday's men went down the steep hill so as to get to the fort as soon as possible. At 12 o'clock in the night they saw fires and were almost sure there were Indians, but saw none. Passed the Pecos and stopped two hours at Pecos Springs. They got to the fort all right and stayed there three days, so as to give Cook's party time to go down. The Indians thought the stage was coming back at once, and laid a trap to capture it at Howard's Wells, but left when they saw it was not coming. When the men did come on with the stage they saw signs of a large crowd of Indians at the wells. They went by and examined the place where Cook's stage had been burned. The ironwork of the coach was seen in the ashes, and portions of the mail scattered around. These Indians went on down to Bear Lake on Devil's River, and then went towards the head of the Nueces and Frio rivers and raided below the mountains. Mr. Brucks thinks these were some of the Indians who killed old man Gerdes, as it was done about the same time.

Mr. Brucks was a member of Captain Richarz's company of rangers, and did good service on the frontier. He now lives in Quihi, near the place where he settled with his father fifty-four years ago. In regard to the bell which was rung that night during the Indian raid, it was carried to D'Hanis and used for a church bell. A sister of Mr. Brucks married Mr. Nick Ney and moved to D'Hanis, and that is the reason why the bell was carried there. This was the first bell brought to that country. When a new church was built and they wanted a better bell they sent the old bell to the foundry and used it in the construction of the new one with the other material. The people thought a great deal of the old bell, and this one, composed of the old and the new material, is still at D'Hanis.

HERMAN HUEHNER.

Came to Texas in 1846.

Five miles east of Castroville, on the San Antonio road, lives a quiet, unassuming farmer named Herman Huehner, and anyone seeing him at his daily labors as he toils for an honest living on his farm, and hears him speak in his soft, low voice, never alluding to what he has done as frontiersman or soldier, would be led to infer that he had never been fifty miles from his little farm since coming to this country and settling, and that nothing of passing interest had occurred in his quiet home life to ruffle the even tenor of his way. On the contrary, however, this pleasant, sociable old gentleman has passed through some stormy scenes in his life—fought Indians on the Texas frontier, Mexicans in Mexico, and on several occasions followed the fortunes of the famous "Mustang" Grey.

Mr. Huehner was born in Switzerland, but his parents were German. His father was of delicate constitution and went to the mountains of Switzerland for his health, spent several years there, and finally died there. Herman was born there in 1825. His mother also died there, and then he made his way back to Germany. In 1846 he come to Texas with one of his uncles, sailing from Bremen. The ship on which they sailed was the Louise Fredericke, commanded by Captain Knigge. On board were 103 immigrants, sixteen crew, and two mates. The vessel was one of the fastest on the line, and made the trip without incident in forty days. One ship left two weeks before this one, but was seven days behind when the Louise arrived at Galveston. The names of some of the colonists who came on the ship were Louis Moehnig, George Leisburg, John Leisburg, Keiser, Esanhauer, and Frederick. The uncle of young Huehner was named Herman Fernan. When the ship landed at Galveston our subject obtained a job of helping to unload it, which took several days. The final start for the west was made from Port Lavaca, and they came direct to Castroville. Supplies were short in the colony, and cornmeal had to be brought from Austin, the capital of the State, distant about 100 miles.

On one occasion Mr. Keiser and Mr. Keller went to Austin in an ox cart after meal, and stayed so long fears were entertained for their safety. The delay, however, was caused by an overflow in the Guadalupe River. They remained a long time on its banks, but as it went down slowly and they were consuming their meal, finally gathered logs and made a raft, on which they crossed their cart and oxen. It was a long, slow, and tedious trip through the black prairie mud to Castroville, and when they finally arrived there they only had a pint of meal apiece for each member of the two families.

After arriving in Castroville Mr. Huehner only remained there ten days, and going to San Antonio in search of work found a job of cutting pickets for Mr. Nat Lewis on the Leona, ten miles west of San Antonio. He worked at this ten days, making money enough to buy a horse, when he joined a company of Texas rangers commanded by Capt. John Conner. They were stationed at the San Lucas Springs, between San Antonio and Castroville. Their lieutenant was William Jett, and Mr. Huehner says he was a splendid man. A great deal of scouting was done by this company, but not many encounters were had with the Indians. On one occasion, however, Mr. Huehner participated in his first fight while in this service. The rangers were scouting on the Seco, and late in the evening were just preparing to camp two miles above the present town of D'Hanis, when they were attacked by the Lipan Indians. The rangers had all dismounted, but their horses were still saddled. Taken by surprise, but not dismayed, the rangers met the charge on horseback, having mounted at the first yell. The numbers were equal, being twenty-five on each side, and the combat did not last long. The Indians went back after the first charge and scattered, leaving two dead near the rangers, and some went off wounded. Old Castro, the Lipan chief, led the Indians. The rangers camped on the ground and kept vigilant guard through the night, but nothing further transpired. Next morning the rangers took the bows and shields of the dead Indians and a pistol which one had in a belt around his waist, and left, but did not scalp them.

The war with Mexico now being on hand, Captain Conner's company was mustered into the service of the United States on the 23d day of September, 1846, and joined General Taylor's army at Monterey. They were placed in the regiment of rangers commanded by Col. Jack Hays, and did picket duty outside of the city, and the regulars stayed inside. Many Mexicans were killed here and there by the pickets. Captain Conner had four Indian scouts in his company. One, a Choctaw, was called Captain Williams; Bill Chism, another, was a Cherokee, and Merrell was a Tonkaway. The other's name is not remembered. The Tonk was the best runner; no horse could catch him in the brush. The road into the city of Monterey was lined on each side with brush and Spanish daggers, and the Mexican cavalry would conceal themselves here near the road and rope any of the regular infantry who happened to be caught out and drag them in. The rangers were always mounted, and the Mexicans never tried to rope any of them.

During the movement of supplies for the army up from Camargo a large train was attacked by the Mexicans between Monterey and Seralvo, near a large ranch called Santa Maria. The Mexicans ambushed them beside the road in the brush, and a terrible massacre of teamsters ensued. The escort was small and soon put to flight, and most of them were killed. Behind this train four days was another large one of 300 wagons and 400 men as an escort. Two companies of regular infantry, with two cannon and two companies of mounted Texas rangers composed the force. The rangers were commanded by Capt. John Conner and Mustang Grey. Mr. Huehner was still with the former command. They heard of the capture of the train at Camargo, and Captain Grey called for volunteers to go on ahead and bury the dead teamsters. Sixty volunteered, among whom was Mr. Huehner, and they set out rapidly for the scene of the massacre. When they arrived at the place they first began to find the dead teamsters scattered along the road in a little valley, and then on both sides of the road. Towards the last they were badly scattered, where they attempted to escape. Many were found in the brush some distance from the road, where they were overtaken singly and killed by the Mexican cavalry. Some were lying in the road where they were shot dead from their mules when first fired on. The bodies were badly mangled on account of the wagons in the rear running over them during the terrible panic of yelling Mexicans and running mules as they dashed along the road with the wagons and without drivers. Wild animals and buzzards had torn the bodies of the Americans badly but had not touched the body of a Mexican, twenty-two of whom were killed in the fight and had also been left where they had fallen. The teamsters and escort were greatly outnumbered, but put up a good fight, as the dead bodies of the greasers that lay among them attested. Forty Americans were found and buried. Mustang Grey was furious, and when the last sad rites to the dead were finished, took his men and captured the village of Pana Maria and burned it, killing twenty-five Mexicans there. He was satisfied, he said, that Mexicans from this place helped to capture the train.

Mr. Huehner went on to Monterey with Captain Grey, and his men came later. A lot of Mexican women came on from Pana Maria and reported to General Taylor of the raid on their village, and pointed out Mustang Grey as the captain who with his men did it. Grey sat very unconcerned and said nothing while the women were pointing their fingers at him in accusation. General Taylor looked at the ranger captain a few moments, and then, laughing, turned away. The Mexican women had to return without seeing the "mucho diablo Tehanas" shot, as they foudly hoped to see.

Another train was now coming up from Camargo on a new road which ran by the town of Catarina, and General Taylor was told that a body of 500 Mexican lancers were going to attack it. One hundred and fifty rangers and two companies of regulars were at once sent to protect it. Conner's and Grey's companies composed the ranger force, and they were very anxious to proceed in a hurry. Catarina was the place where the attack was supposed to be made. The line of march was taken up at 10 o'clock p. m., with Grey's men in the lead. Next came the regulars, and Conner's men brought up the rear. The regulars went slowly, and Grey, who was anxious to reach Catarina by 4 o'clock in the morning, became very impatient at the slow progress. The officer in command of the regulars gave orders through the night in a loud voice to "Slow up in front." Grey finally said he would go on with his men, and if the rangers in the rear wanted to go with him to come on, and if the regulars did not get out of their way to run over them. Conner's men now divided and ran on both sides of the regulars until they got ahead of the line and went on with Grey. At daybreak the rangers arrived at the town and saw Mexicans running from it in all directions. Grey would not go in at once for fear of a large force there, but he had accomplished what he intended—to arrive in time to succor the train if necessary at this place. The sun was high up when the regulars got there, and the officer in command wanted to enter the town in regular battle order, with the rangers in the rear. Mustang Grey said, "No, sir; I was here first, and I am going into the town first." A quarrel now ensued, and Grey cursed the officer in fierce language, and said that he and his men would go into the town as they d——d please, and wound up by drawing his pistol and threatening to shoot. Lieutenant Jett, of Conner's company, now went to Grey and persuaded him to come away. When the start was made into town the rangers took the lead. A great disappointment, however, met them—no Mexican soldiers were there. The Americans were very hungry, and soon found plenty to eat, and took everything they wanted. Some of the Mexicans treated them well, and Grey put guards around their houses and would not allow anything of theirs to be molested. They went on from here and met the train and escorted it safely through.

After the return to headquarters there were so many complaints made to General Taylor of the insubordination of the rangers he thought best to send the most of them back to the Texas frontier, as the fighting was now about over in Mexico. The general liked Grey for his vim and unquestionable courage, but thought he should keep his men under better control. He sent for him when it was decided to send the rangers back, and said: "Grey, your rangers are rough, ready, and rugged, and you can take them back to Texas to fight Indians."

Most all of the rangers were sent back at this time except the spy company of Ben McCulloch. Many of them, however, went back to Mexico again and participated in some battles under General Scott. Grey's and Conner's men separated on the Rio Grande, the former going to Corpus Christi. Mr. Huehner was mustered out of the service in November, 1847. He intended to join the company of Big Foot Wallace, whose captain, Ad. Gillespie, was killed at Monterey, and he was raising a company to go back, but at this time was taken sick and did not get off. Mustang Grey and his men had a fight on the Nueces with the Comanche Indians before they got to Corpus Christi, and were badly used up, but not whipped. Grey was wounded and his horse killed, besides quite a lot of his men. Mr. Huehner heard that Grey was killed in the fight, and never knew any better until he met him one day in San Antonio. He says Grey was tall, handsome, well made, and had light hair and blue eyes. His given name was Mabry, and he was a native of Tennessee.

While in Mexico one of Conner's men named Adolph Gusman owned a fine gray horse, which took the fancy of General Taylor, who wanted him to match one he had, and a trade was made. This horse lived to be very old, and died near Baton Rouge, La., during the civil war.

On one occasion Mr. Huehner and Jim Brown followed some Indians who had stolen horses, and came upon their camp ten miles above Castroville. Only two Indians were in camp with the horses, and they crept within eighty yards of them, each selecting an Indian, and fired at once. The Indian Brown shot yelled once, although hit in the head. Mr. Huehner shot his in the breast, and he fell over without uttering a sound. The horses were gathered up and brought back to the settlement.

When Nat Lewis built a mill in San Antonio in 1850 Mr. Huehner was married and living there, and boarded the hands that built the mill.

To give an idea how many rattlesnakes there were in southwest Texas in the early days, Mr. Huehner said that on one occasion he and Bill Adams came out from Castroville on the San Antonio road and stopped to camp about sundown, two miles from Castroville, at the first creek, near where Fisher's farm is now. They dismounted under a mesquite tree and took off their saddles, but had to kill seven rattlers before they could spread their blankets for the night.

INDIAN FIGHT IN SABINAL CANYON.

1848.

In the above named year a company of rangers were stationed on the Seco two miles above D'Hanis, in Medina County. Gillette was first captain of this company, but he being promoted, Captain Warfield was in command at the time of which we write.

The time of enlistment for this company was about to expire, but one more scout was made up for a trip into the Sabinal Canyon, then unsettled, and distant from the ranger camp about twenty-five miles. The rangers anticipated a fine time killing bear if no Indians were found. The scout was composed of thirteen men as follows:

First Lieutenant Knox, in command; Second Lieutenant Kaisey, John Saddler, Doc Saddler, Jim Fell, Doc Huffmann, Rothe, Heynard, John Wesley Deer, Josiah Cass, Rothe Reinhard, John Eastwood, and Harrison Daugherty. Also one visitor who accompanied the scout.

The men passed out through what is now the pastures of the Rothe brothers, John Reinhart, and Mrs. Donoho. They went into camp in a pecan grove somewhere not far from the present village of Utopia, and had fine sport for several days. It was in the fall of the year; pecans were plentiful, as were also bear, and very fat. One evening Indians were seen on a mountain some distance off, and that night the usual guards were placed, but as the weather was cold a fire was made and some of the men lay down near it. After the turn of the night Wesley Deer was put on guard and he stood his time nearly out, but being very cold came to the fire and kicked together the smouldering chunks and made a blaze. Now at this time a band of Indians, having located the ranger camp by the light of their fire, were cautiously creeping upon them as young Deer stirred up the fire. A single shot was fired from the darkness, and the young ranger fell backward shot through the heart. His head struck the pallet of Lieutenant Knox and Josiah Cass. The Indians at once charged after the shot with loud yells, thinking to put the balance to flight, but the rangers met them bravely and a fierce fight commenced. John Saddler received an arrow in the breast as he sprang up and fired his gun at an Indian near the fire and killed him, supposed to be the one who killed Deer. The fight was not of long duration. The rangers poured in such a deadly volley from rifles and pistols that the Indians were beaten back and disappeared in the darkness. The arrow was taken out of Saddler, and a strict watch was kept until morning, but no more Indians appeared. Daylight revealed eight Indians dead around the camp. Doc Huffmann had an arrow shot through his hat, which was hanging up in camp or on the horn of his saddle. Deer was the youngest of the party, and had never seen an Indian. He was lashed to his horse and conveyed to camp and buried. Saddler recovered.

Lieutenant Knox was afterwards sheriff of Bexar County.

Josiah Cass is the only one known to be alive now of the men who were in this fight. He now lives at Somerset, Atascosa County.

"DOKE" BOWLES.

Came to Texas in 1849.

Among the early settlers of Uvalde County were the Bowles family. They were bold, fearless men, and aided materially in settling up the country and fighting the numerous bands of Indians who made desperate efforts to drive the border men back on the settlements east.

W. B. Bowles, better known as "Doke," was born in Allewamby County, Tennessee, October 22, 1835, and came to Texas with his father, John Bowles, in the winter of 1849, and settled on the Lampasas River, in Bell County, four miles from Belton. John Bowles helped to organize Bell County in 1851. He was born in Virginia in 1802, and went to Tennessee with his parents when quite young. When the war of 1812 was in progress and General Jackson was raising volunteers, his father joined and was killed at the battle of New Orleans. He was hit twice, and died of the wounds. There were thirteen children in the family of John Bowles—seven girls and six boys. At the time the Bowles family lived in Bell County a large band of Kiowa Indians were in the country and camped three miles from the Bowles home, on the spot where the beautiful little town of Salado is now. There were but few settlers in Bell County at that time, and they had been on friendly terms with these Indians, and let their horses, which were few in number, run on the prairie, which was covered with fine grass and nothing fenced. Game was abundant, and the Indians spent most of their time in the chase. Things went on this way for some time, but finally the settlers began to miss horses off the prairie, which by the most diligent search could not be found, and suspicion pointed to the Indians as having something to do with their disappearance. A consultation was held among the white settlers, and it was determined to drive the Indians away. So accordingly eight men went to their camp and gave them orders to leave at once, or a strong force would be brought against them. These men were John Bowles and some of his sons, Doke being one, and a man named Blair and his sons. The Indians, when they heard the demand of the white men, stood in silence a few moments and then commenced singing and preparing to leave,—saddling horses, packing others, until all were ready,—men, squaws, and children. Five or six of them would leave, and when they were fairly on the way another band would go, until all were gone, stretched out across the prairie, headed north. The settlers went home relieved, as the presence of the Kiowas had been a menace to the whites ever since they pitched their camp on the banks of the Salado.

About ten days after the departure of the Indians every horse on the prairie and the forks of Little River was stolen, supposed to have been done by them in revenge for having to leave. About four months after this some of the settlers were at a trading post up the country, and saw some of the horses, which had been brought in by the Kiowas and traded off.

John Bowles came to Uvalde County with his family in 1855, and settled on the Sabinal River, in the Patterson settlement, six miles below the present Sabinal station. At this time the Indians were numerous and hostile, and it was only by constant watching that a horse could be kept. Mr. Bowles had brought some good horses to the country, and in 1856 established a ranch on the west side of the river and built a house. This place was below the settlement, and was somewhat more exposed to Indian raids. Mr. Bowles built a strong pen in front of his house, and one of the boys or himself stood guard almost every night, especially during light moons. The horses were put in this pen and a blind made for the guard to stand behind, so that he could not be seen and make a target for an Indian. Some one has said that "eternal vigilance is the price of safety," and it seems to hold good under all dangerous circumstances; but men will get careless even on an exposed frontier, and it always happens that at that time the savages strike their blow. One night they failed to mount guard at the Bowles ranch, and the first thing anyone knew the horses were all out of the corral and in a dead run. All arose, grabbed their guns, and went in pursuit. The course of the horses could be followed by the rattling of a bell on one of them. Mr. Bowles and his sons followed in their night clothes and without their shoes, and soon became scattered. The old man caught up with the horses first and saw one Indian leave them, but fearing it was one of the boys did not fire at the moment, and soon it was too late. The horses were now driven back and put in the pen, and Doke got in the blind to stand guard the balance of the night. The father said he would go and sit under a hackberry tree on the east bank of the river, near a trail, with his shotgun and six-shooter, and watch there. The moon was just up, and Doke had not been long on guard when he heard the report of his father's gun, and the boys all started in a run towards the spot, but before getting there heard the old man fire six shots from his revolver. Thinking he was having a close fight, the boys ran with the utmost speed, and when they arrived at the scene saw their father rising up from a prostrate Indian with a scalp in his hand, and remarked to them, "Hog my cats, if I haven't got one of them." This was about the only byword Mr. Bowles ever used. He never swore or allowed his boys to do so if he could prevent it, especially in the presence of himself or their mother. Mr. Bowles said there were three Indians, and he first discovered them about fifty feet off in the trail, one behind the other, and when they came close, not more than thirty feet distant, he fired one barrel of his gun, and one of the Indians fell and the other two disappeared. The one who fell raised up to a sitting position and attempted to shoot an arrow at Bowles, but he fired the other barrel at him and then emptied his pistol before he fell over. While Bowles was scalping him he raised one hand feebly three times towards the knife. There was a gray horse standing not far from the Indians, and he was hit in the shoulder by some of the buckshot. While looking around a groan was heard near by, and the men bunched together and commenced a cautious search, and a dog that was along struck a trail. They soon heard him baying and started to him, but met the dog coming back with an arrow in him. The party now all went back to the house and a runner was sent to the settlement to give notice of the raid, and several got to the Bowles ranch before day and had a jolly time over the dead Comanche. By daylight next morning a party went to the spot where the dead Indian was, and about thirty steps from him lay another dead one, shot through the bowels with three buckshot. The first one had an arrow grasped in his hand with which he was about to shoot Bowles when he received the second shot. His bow also lay near him.

Another bloody trail was found leading from the spot where the Indians were fired on. This Indian was followed four miles but not found at that time. It was he who shot the dog when overtaken. The groans and strange noise heard came from the one found dead next morning. The Indian who made his escape at the time was afterwards found one mile from where his trail was lost or abandoned. All three of the Indians received mortal wounds from the first shot from the gun. Doke Bowles was a quick, wiry man in those days, a good shot with rifle or pistol, and was guide and trailer on many occasions after Indians.

In 1856, after the fight in Sabinal Canyon in which Leakey and Barrymore were wounded, old man Bowles joined the scouts who went in pursuit and was in the massacre of Indians on the Leona, an account of which is given elsewhere. In 1859 John Bowles moved and settled on the Leona, near where they had this fight. This was a very exposed place, no one else living near. Westfall had lived down there but was gone. At this time Doke, who was married, had a ranch on the Blanco where the Wish ranch is now, and no other settlers were near.

On the 28th day of October, 1859, happened one of those sad frontier tragedies which so often threw the settlers into great excitement. This was the killing of John Bowles and John Davenport by the Indians. On the day before Doke Bowles and his wife took a horseback trip to the mountains, several miles away to the north, and returned late in the evening. On the way home they passed their herd of horses, which were quietly feeding, and they passed on to the house. The horses they had ridden were hobbled out, and they went jumping up the creek to join the others, about 300 yards or more away. About sundown Mr. Bowles picked up a rope and started to get a horse near by to go after the others, but changed his notion and came back. This surprised his wife and she asked the cause, and he said he did not know, but it seemed his legs refused to go any further, and that he was very uneasy from some cause, he could not tell what. About this time he looked up the road towards the settlement and saw a man coming on horseback. He was glad to see the man, and started to intercept him and have a talk, but the horseman turned himself and come towards the house. It was Tom Wall, who lived in Frio Canyon, and was on his way home from San Antonio by way of Uvalde. He told Doke he was sick, and wanted to stay all night. "All right," said Bowles, "I am glad to have you stay, for I feel greatly depressed about something." By the time Wall's horse was staked out it was getting dark, and in a few minutes the stock horses came running in and the two saddle horses were not with them. The others stood about the yard the balance of the night. About daylight John Davenport rode up driving a yoke of oxen. He lived on the road at Rancheros Creek. This was the main road that ran from San Antonio towards Mexico. Davenport said to Bowles as soon as he came, "There are Indians around here. Did you know it?" Bowles replied, "I thought so." There was a large train encamped about 300 yards from the house on the way to Mexico, and some of these men had just told Bowles that the Indians had been around all night trying to get their mules, and succeeded in getting one horse and one mule which had strayed off with drag ropes on. Davenport had started before day to get his oxen, as he knew where they ranged, and was now starting home with them and soon proceeded on his way. After sunup twelve men come from the Frio on the trail of the Indians. This was October 28th. These men said the Indians had come near getting some one on the Blanco, near the foot of the mountains, the evening before, but they had left their camp before the Indians got there. This was Doke and his wife, where they ate their noonday meal on their trip to the mountains. The Indians had followed them and caught their two hobbled horses after they returned.

Mr. Bowles joined the Frio scout and took the trail of the Indians, leaving a guard at his house. About 11 o'clock the scout rode to a hill between the Blanco and Sabinal and looked over towards the Patterson settlement. Doke was in the lead on the trail and saw a man running his horse in their direction, and when in speaking distance he said the Indians had made a raid in the Patterson settlement and killed John Bowles, Doke's father, but the body could not be found. This was a severe blow to Doke, and a surprise, too, as he supposed his father was at his ranch on the Leona, many miles away to the southwest. This news was hardly told before another man was seen running his horse on the San Antonio road. He was signaled by the waving of hats, and when he came he said the Indians had killed John Davenport between the Sabinal River and Rancheros Creek. He was on his way from Doke's ranch, and was still driving his

THIS STONE MARKS THE SPOT WHERE JOHN BOWLES WAS KILLED BY INDIANS.
FROM A PHOTO BY MISS EDITH DILLARD.

oxen. This man said the Indians had gone northwest towards the mountains after killing Davenport, and that John Bowles was missing and all were satisfied he was killed. Doke told him to go back and tell all of the connection to look for the body of his father, and he would follow the Indians. He led the scout, and went to John Kennedy's, on the Sabinal, where there was a little store, and laid in a supply of provisions, which were packed on a mule, and then sent a runner to Lieut. W. B. Hazen, who was in command of Fort Inge, asking him to come with all the men he could spare and meet his scout at the mouth of Frio Canyon. Doke and his party took the trail of the Indians where they killed Davenport, and followed it to the foot of the mountains on the Blanco, and here the Indians had made a halt, and here also Doke made the discovery that beyond a doubt his father was killed, and also aroused a spirit of revenge which made him furious to overtake the Indians and give them battle. This certain proof of his father's death was the finding of his shoes, covered with blood. When dark came the settlers lay down on the prairie and spent the night without water. On the 29th the trail was again taken up and followed to the Frio road, and kept that on out through the pass. On the way they come across some men who had seen the Indians in the distance, but thought they were the scouts. Lieutenant Hazen and his men now got with them, and also part of a minute company of citizens from Uvalde numbering ten men. Hazen had thirteen, and these combined with the force under Bowles made forty-two in all. Among the settlers there were John Q. Daugherty, John Kennedy, James McCormick, Ben Pulliam, Clabe Davenport, William Thomas, Frank Isbell, Nobe Griner, Arnold, Arnette, Everette, Williams, and others whose names are not now recalled. Daugherty was in command of the minute men, with Everette as second, and Lieutenant Hazen was in command of the whole. He told Daugherty to take the lead on the trail and follow it to the jumping-off place, and when they came upon the Indians he would take command and lead. Williams was selected as trailer, and all moved forward at a good speed. Doke Bowles asked permission to consult with Williams and help trail, and it being granted, these two took the lead. The trail led across the canyons and sides of the mountains until the settlements were passed, and then it kept the beds of the creeks. They camped that night on the river, and on the 30th the trail lead out to the head of the Main Frio. Here the Indians had left a bunch of horses as they came down on the raid, and which they now collected and carried along with them. They had been hobbled and left in a little valley, rough on all sides, so they could not get out. From the signs there were about fifty head of these, and this accession made the trail much plainer. Noon was made at the Frio waterhole, and a dry camp that night on the plains.

The trail now led across the prairie. Being plain, it was followed fast, and seventy-five miles were covered that day, no halt being made at noon, and the horses a good deal of the time in a gallop. Passed two fires where the Indians had stopped and cooked meat, the first since they commenced their retreat from the settlement. This day's trailing was very exciting. The prairie was in rolling swells, and as each crest was crossed all were eager to get to the next to look over, expecting each time to sight the Comanches. This long stretch of prairie was finally crossed, and they came to low hills and cedar brakes. Daugherty said halt. The water had given out, and had been for half the day. The men lay down and made a dry camp, too thirsty to eat. Daugherty said, "Boys, we are close upon them, and they have not discovered us yet." Bowles asked permission for himself and Williams to take a scout and see what was ahead. This was granted, and the two trailers went about two miles in the direction the trail pointed at dark, and then climbed a cedar tree, hoping to see their fire, but could see nothing and returned.

At daybreak the trail was again taken up, and when they arrived at a point half a mile beyond where the trailers had climbed the tree the Indians were discovered in camp nearly a mile away, in a glade near a small cedar brake, and were saddling their horses. Williams suddenly exclaimed, "Yonder they are, boys." The citizens were in front and the soldiers next, led by Hazen; they traveled in this manner during the pursuit. When the alarm of Indians was raised in front Hazen came forward and at once ordered a charge, himself leading the way. It was a wild and disordered charge. Soldiers, settlers, and pack mules all went together with a terrible clatter, and everything was soon badly scattered and making the rocks and brush fly. The Indians were taken by surprise and ran, but tried to carry the horses along with them. Being pressed for time, all were not able to mount a separate steed, and sprang behind others. One Indian tried to rope horses for those afoot, and another went off with just a loop over the nose of his horse. During all of this time the terrible charge was sweeping towards them and the Texans had begun to yell. The foremost ones soon closed in on the rear of the Indians. Bowles came close to one and jumped down so as to get a good shot at him, but before he could do so the Indian tumbled from his horse, hit by a volley fired from the left. At this time Arnette came up to Doke, riding a race horse called "Fuzzy Buck," and proposed to exchange with him, as Bowles' horse was not as fast as his. He had agreed to do this if it was a running fight, so Doke could have a chance to kill an Indian.

Bowles now mounted "Fuzzy Buck" and set out again after the Indians, who were now 200 yards ahead. Lieutenant Hazen was ahead now on a fast horse, holding his pistol in his hand, and came close to an Indian, who turned with pistol also in hand and charged the lieutenant. Both fired together and at close range. The ball from the Indian's pistol struck Hazen in the right hand, knocked the pistol from his grasp, and then penetrated his breast and lodged against the backbone. His horse reared and fell backward, and then sprung to his feet and ran off, leaving his rider on the ground. The white men were badly scattered, and only those who rode the fastest horses could get into the fight. The Indians, although outnumbered by the whites, were game, and knew how to scatter their enemies and fight them in detail. A part of the Indians had left this bunch and gone another way. Bowles was coming up behind Hazen when he was shot from his horse, and as the Indian turned his horse to run again saw where the lieutenant hit him, but it was too low down, and he went on waving his pistol and yelling. The Indian who rode the horse without bridle or saddle ran to the left, and was pursued by John Kennedy and William Thomas. Kennedy fired and hit the Indian in the back of the head, and he came tumbling from his horse. In the meantime Bowles had dismounted by Hazen and turned him over, and feeling the bullet in his back, said, "There is one dead man, sure," and remounting went on in the chase and soon came to the front again, and saw four Indians in sight. The second lieutenant of the minute men, Everette, was ahead of Bowles, and attacked the Indian who had just shot Lieutenant Hazen. Both had pistols, and when the Indian turned to face him the muzzles of the revolvers almost touched and both fired at once. Everette fell from his horse, with the hammer of his pistol shot off and wounded in the hand and mouth, all done with the same bullet. Two of his teeth were knocked out, and the ball lodged in his left temple. The Indian wheeled his horse, waved his pistol, and went on yelling. Bowles halted at the body of this second fallen man, and seeing blood running from his mouth again exclaimed, "Another dead man!" The horse of Everette went on in the charge.

There were now ahead of Bowles Ben Pulliam, William Thomas, and Arnold, and just ahead of them were two Indians on the same horse and all going at a breakneck speed. In crossing a deep ravine the hindmost Indian fell off in it, and as Ben Pulliam, who was in the lead, dashed in the Indian shot him in the back with an arrow after he passed. Pulliam fell from his horse and the Indian was killed by Arnold, who was coming close at hand, with a shotgun. The Indian died with his bow and another arrow in his hand. This was the finest-looking Indian in the lot. He was young, nearly white, and had fine, soft, black hair, and was profusely ornamented with beads, rings, and silver plates. He had John Davenport's pistol belt on, fastened to which hung the scalp of John Bowles.

When Pulliam fell and Arnold shot the Indian, Thomas, who came next, dashed up the bank in pursuit of the mounted one and soon came alongside of him, and both commenced firing with pistols hand to hand. Thomas fired once and the Indian twice in quick succession, his balls glancing the thigh of Thomas and going into the front of his saddle not more than two inches apart. Thomas went out of sight in another gulley, and the Indian went on yelling and waving his pistol. "Another dead man," said Bowles, who saw it all as he came charging on. The Indian who shot the two lieutenants covered the retreat of the balance. He did the most of his bloody work that day with Davenport's pistol. When it was empty he threw it away and used arrows, and it was recovered. This Indian had been fired at more than a hundred times, and was now stripped completely naked and was bloody from head to foot, as was also his horse, but he continued to yell defiance to his foes and wave his pistol. He still carried his shield and had three pistols, all of which he emptied. When his pursuers would come close he would wheel his horse and make many motions with his pistol before firing, and keep the men dodging. The white men in the chase would only come up with the Indians two or three at a time, and so the fighting that was done was evenly matched. The horses of the settlers at this time were nearly all run down, and there were three Indians still in sight. Bowles now got a shotgun from Arnette, and leaving all behind chased the Indians alone, thinking he could run up close and kill two of them. He had emptied and reloaded and emptied his revolver several times, firing many shots at the noted Indian in the rear. When he came up close to the rear Indian with the shotgun all three were in line. Attempting now to fire, the gun snapped. There were no caps on the gun, and having to stop now to adjust some the Indians made a good spurt ahead. "Fuzzy Buck," however, soon overhauled them again, and the Indians in sheer desperation plunged down a steep bluff. Bowles came up and looked over and saw that it was about fourteen feet down, but not exactly perpendicular. He waited until some more of the men came up and they said it was too steep to go down on horses, and fired their guns at the Indians across the valley, but they were out of range.

Bowles said where the Indians could go white men could, and plunged down, landing safely. Frank Isbell, Nobe Griner, and Williams followed, and these four went on after the Indians. In three miles Doke overtook and once more commenced the battle with them, firing both barrels of the shotgun. The Indians stayed together and sent arrows back, and yelled continually. The other men could not catch up. Bowles would stop and wait for them and get loaded pistols, and then on the racehorse come up with them again. In this way he fought them many miles. Williams had a very long-winded horse, and finally caught up and they both charged together. Doke fired the last load from the shotgun, and only had one in his pistol. The bloody Indian now turned back and charged Williams, who was coming towards him, and he dismounted to fight him with a pistol. The Indian also dismounted and faced him with bow and arrows, no longer having any loaded pistols. The fight commenced at six yards. Williams only fired one shot and received an arrow in the breast. He turned towards Bowles, and the Indian continued to drive them into him. "I'm killed, Doke," he said as he passed, and Bowles saw arrows sticking in his back. The Indian now charged Bowles, who leveled his pistol at him and fired his last load, and then had to turn back and commence dodging arrows, as the Comanche still advanced. The Indian himself was in a terrible plight. He was covered with wounds, and the strap shot from his shield which held it in place, and it was gone. When he left Bowles and went back he mounted the horse of Williams and rode off yelling. Doke counted nine bullet holes in his body as he rode away, and his horse and saddle looked as if they had been dipped in blood. Fourteen bullets had hit the horse on the side that Bowles rode on and fired during the long chase. The Indian lay low on his horse while being fired at, and that accounts for the animal being hit so much. On this horse, which the Indian left standing nearly ready to sink to the ground when he mounted that of Williams, were the saddle rope and bridle of Doke's father, but his horse was still ahead, ridden by another Indian.

The Indians could tell when Doke's loads were out, and would then turn and run him back, but being on a fast horse they could not catch him. Williams lost one of his pistols, which was on the horn of the saddle, when the Indian got his horse.

Bowles watched the three Indians until they got to the top of a hill, where two of them dismounted and laid down, and it was afterwards learned from an Indian on a reservation that they died there, and the third one had a broken arm. Williams was put on a horse and carried slowly back. It was twenty miles back to where the fight commenced, and men were scattered all the way,—here and there a dead Indian and wounded white men. Most of the soldiers stopped with Lieutenant Hazen. The heavy cavalry horses of those who went on soon gave out, and none but the toughest Texas ponies could keep in sight of the Indians. No one had any water, and the wounded men nearly perished for it, but were finally relieved on the way back by men who were met on the trail with some. It was 12 o'clock when Bowles and the others started back with Williams. The bullet was cut out of the temple of Lieutenant Everette with a pocket knife. All the men hit were badly hurt, but none died. Judge James McCormick, who was in the fight and took a conspicuous part, volunteered to go to Fort Clark, a distance of eighty miles, after surgical assistance for Lieutenant Hazen. In the meantime a camp was established and a guard left with Hazen, and the balance of the men drifted back home. McCormick made the trip all right with the surgeon, but had a race with Indians before arriving at the post. It took three days and nights to get back to the spot with a hack. He pulled spikes out of some of the men with his bullet moulds. It was found on examination of Lieutenant Hazen that the ball did not go directly through his body, but struck the breast bone and ranged round. He was first carried to Brackett, and then in about three weeks back to Fort Inge.

During the chase Mr. Bowles noticed an Indian throw something under a cedar tree which he thought was his father's scalp, not knowing at the time that the fancy Indian killed at the ravine had it. Doke hunted for it on the way back, and found that it was an old-fashioned reticule with a drawstring to close it up, that women used in those days, and that it contained four children's scalps, paint, poison, etc.

On the way back, ten miles from where the battle commenced, a bunch of horses was discovered in a cove, standing still, about a mile away. Williams being wounded, Bowles was in charge as guide, and said they were Indians, and at once made preparations to charge them. About this time also a large bear put in an appearance, and four of the men were detailed to charge the bear and the balance to charge the Indians. The men were very hungry, and did not want the bear to escape. The bear was fat and large, and was ample to last the men all the way back, they eating it without bread or salt. The horses taken to be Indians were brought back by Captain Daugherty and his crowd, who charged the supposed Indians. They were some of their own that had broken away from the battle. The paint horse which was ridden by one of the Indians, and which was wounded so many times, belonged to a man named Wheat, of Medina County, who was killed off of him by Indians on Black Creek. The settlers also got Wheat's coat, and the holes in it showed where the Indians shot him. His sons came to Uvalde when the men returned and claimed the property. One of them, Ira, was for long time sheriff of Edwards County.

The body of John Bowles was found at a place called Guide Hill, six miles below where Sabinal station now is. He had come over the day before from his ranch on the Leona to hunt stock, and that night his horse was taken out of an inclosure by Indians. Thinking the horse had got out himself, he procured another at the place where he was stopping in the Patterson settlement, and went to hunt him without his gun. The trail of the horse led toward Guide Hill. During part of this time he rode in company with a frontier preacher named H. G. Horton, who was going up the country, and he was the last white man that saw Mr. Bowles alive or talked to him. After parting company with Rev. Horton Mr. Bowles went to Guide Hill, and from close observation of signs afterwards seen, the Indians had tied the horse in the brush on the side of the hill, but where he could be seen from the valley below, and secreted themselves near him and awaited for some one to come after him. They shot Mr. Bowles at ten steps distant with three arrows at once, which all struck near the left nipple, not more than an inch apart. This fact was ascertained by Doke finding his father's vest in the chase after the Indians, and the holes in it showed where the arrows struck.

The Indians got his horse after he fell from him. A stone now marks the spot where he fell, with date of birth, death, manner of death, etc.

Doke was an inveterate Indian hater, and trailed and scouted and fought them until 1879, when they made their last raids on this part of the frontier. The fight above described took place in the head draws of North Llano, in the edge of the plains, 200 miles from Uvalde.

This fight caused the rapid promotion of Lieutenant Hazen in the army, and he wore the shoulder straps of a general in the Union army during the civil war, and was connected with the signal service department after its close. He died in the early 90's, and in the fall of 1899 his widow married Admiral George Dewey, while the laurel was still green on his brow after his famous victory over the Spanish fleet in Manila Bay.

W. M. BRAMLETT.

MEXICAN WAR VETERAN.

Mr. Bramlett has been in southwest Texas ever since 1849, and has had the experience of all other frontiersmen—Indian fights, alarms, trailing, and scouting.

In 1846, when the war with Mexico broke out, Mr. Bramlett was at his home in Virginia, and there enlisted for the war in the company of Capt. Montgomery Coarse, Company B, First Virginia Volunteers. Colonel Hamtinmoch commanded the regiment. Lieut.-Col. Thomas Randolph, of Virginia, was second in command. He was related to the noted John Randolph, of Virginia. The command went round by water, and Mr. Bramlett says they sailed by the coast of Cuba, and it was the greenest looking country he ever saw. The grass came down to the water's edge, and beautiful green hills and prairies could be seen far back from the coast. The portion he saw was unsettled, no houses being seen.

In Mexico they went to the army of General Taylor, and Mr. Bramlett participated in the battle of Buena Vista, being under the command of Col. Jefferson Davis, and was in many desperate charges during the all-day battle, and saw many men killed and wounded. During one severe fire Colonel Davis ordered the men into a ravine and came in himself on horseback. Mr. Bramlett noticed that one of the colonel's feet was partly shot off, and some of the men called his attention to it, but he said it was only a scratch, and then dismounted. He could hardly stand, and suffered a good deal with it. Colonels Clay, of Kentucky, and Yell, of Arkansas, were both killed, and after the battle Mr. Bramlett helped to bury them. They were buried in one grave. Both had gray hair, and wore the same kind of uniforms, and were buried in them, wrapped up close together. When they were taken up to be carried to their respective States to be reinterred, Mr. Bramlett helped to take them up, and thinks it likely a mistake was made. He is certain that Clay was put on the north side and Yell on the south. There was a controversy as to which body was on the north side, and he thinks it might be possible that Clay was sent to Arkansas and Yell to Kentucky. Both were shot and lanced.

Mr. Bramlett passed over the ground where the train was captured by Mexicans and nearly all of the escort and teamsters killed. Many signs of the conflict were there. Here his command killed the largest rattlesnake he ever saw. It was lying across the road, and its body was as large around as a man's leg and about seven feet in length.

On one occasion, while himself, Calvin S. Turner, and others were on a scout they discovered six Indians camped in open ground, and charged and killed all of them before they could get to cover. Two got into the edge of a thicket.

Mr. Bramlett came from Mexico after the war and settled in southwest Texas, and has been there ever since. After Big Foot Wallace got too old to live alone he lived with Mr. Bramlett in Frio County, near Big Foot postoffice.

TWO FIGHTS BETWEEN RANGERS AND INDIANS.

1851.

Some time in the month of March, 1851, While Lieutenant Walker, of Capt. John S. Ford's company of rangers was scouting with a few men on the Arroyo Gatto (Cat Creek), about sixty miles southeast from Laredo, they came upon a band of hostile Indians fifteen in number. The rangers at once charged them, and in the first onset four of the Indians were killed and the others ran and were pursued for some distance, and two more killed. The Indians made a poor fight, and the rangers suffered no loss. They captured sixty-nine head of mules and one pony. Among the men along were Robert Rankin, Vol. Roundtree, David Steele, John Walker, Andrew Gatliff, Marvin E. McNeill, Albert Gallatin, — Brown, and others not now remembered.

Now, about this time Lieut. Ed Burleson was on his way from San Antonio with a scout of rangers going to Laredo, and came upon this same band of defeated Indians on the following day and had another fight with them about twenty-five miles from Laredo. This time, however, the Indians made a most desperate fight, and the rangers had all on their hands that they could manage. They were evenly matched as to numbers—nine Indians and nine rangers. The names of some of the rangers besides the commander were Baker Barton, William Lackey, James Carr, Alf. Tom, Warren Lyons, and a German whose name was something like Mille.

The Indians were on the open prairie, and when the rangers charged them they did not run, and a hand-to-hand fight commenced. Pistols, rifles, arrows, and lances got in their deadly work at close quarters, and for a time it seemed as if the rangers would be defeated. The Indians would yell and charge the rangers whenever they would get scattered in the fight by their horses running or rearing in fright. The terrible conflict ended in a drawn battle. The rangers held the ground, but all of their men were killed or wounded except two. The Indians finally rode away, leaving four of their warriors dead on the ground and all the others wounded. Of the rangers, Baker Barton was killed, William Lackey was killed, and Lieutenant Burleson, Alf. Tom, James Carr, Warren Lyons, and the German were wounded. Lyons had once been a prisoner among the Indians. He was captured near Lyonsville, in Lavaca County, at an early day. The rangers who were able to do anything had a hard time getting their dead and wounded to Laredo.

Alf. Tom was wounded in the leg by an arrow, and when it was withdrawn the spike remained, but was not noticed at the time, as the man who pulled it out threw it down without looking at it. The wound would never heal, and two years after it was sore and running corruption. He got his brother, Capt. John Tom, to examine it, and the spike was discovered and cut out. The wound then healed all right.

CAÑON DE UVALDE.

The above was the original name of the beautiful valley now known as Sabinal (Cypress) Canyon. It is situated about ninety miles a little north of west from San Antonio and is partly in Uvalde and Bandera counties, the northern half being in the latter. It is about twenty-five miles in length and from three to eight miles in width. The Sabinal River runs through its center, skirted on both sides with pecan, cypress, cedar, and other timbers. The land is black and very productive, yielding fine crops of corn, cotton, oats, wheat, potatoes, etc. Occasional severe droughts is one great drawback to farming. Utopia, the principal village, is situated about midway of the valley, twenty-two miles from Sabinal station, its nearest railroad point, and forty miles from Uvalde, the county seat.

This beautiful valley was once the home of the Comanche Indians. Long before the white man made his appearance they lived here, had numerous villages, and roamed at will over the mountains in pursuit of game, or fished and bathed in the clear waters of the river. Numerous mounds and stone arrow-heads tell the tale of their presence.

The question has often been asked how the county of Uvalde obtained her pretty musical name. I will say that it was named for Colonel Uvalde of the Mexican army, who defeated the Comanche Indians in a great battle in this valley. Long before the white man came near enough from the east to meet the rude shock of the western Indians the Mexican pioneers along the Rio Grande had to contend with them. The town of Laredo was founded in 1757, and ranches were extended between that place and the Nueces, and during the last quarter of the century above mentioned many herds of cattle, horses, and sheep grazed there. The first ranch on the Rio Grande was that of Barrego, at a place called Dolores, twenty-five miles below Laredo. These settlements and fat stock attracted the attention of the roving bands of Comanches, and numerous raids were made from these mountain strongholds and the stock driven off. To check these raids and to punish the Indians, Colonel Uvalde of the Mexican army was ordered by his government to take a large force and follow these marauding bands to their strongholds and drive them out with fire and sword. Uvalde was a brave and energetic officer, and at once set out to carry his orders into effect. With expert scouts and trailers a band was pursued across the country towards the Sabinal mountains, and it is likely that Uvalde and his men passed over the spot on which is now situated the town of Uvalde, then across the Frio and Uvalde prairie to the mouth of what is now Sabinal Canyon, where is situated a dense cedar brake. Here information was received that the Indians were in large force in the canyon and had many villages and much stock. Uvalde's force consisted of about 600 or 700 men, and the Indians were capable of bringing 1000 warriors into the fight. The Mexican commander pushed on, and instead of trying to conceal his movements began to fire the villages which he first found on passing the cedar brake and entering the canyon. These, however, had been deserted. The first one was at a place now called the Blue waterhole, on the west bank of the river, at the extreme entrance of the south end of the canyon. No Indians were as yet in sight, but they were concentrating further up the valley, where the greatest confusion prevailed. Crowds of squaws and children were fleeing north up the canyon, and warriors were coming south from the upper villages to meet and fight the invaders. There has been some doubt as to where the final battle was fought. There was a tradition among the early settlers of the valley that it occurred below the present site of Utopia, along the brakes of the river, across the land now owned by Mr. Tampke. On one occasion a young man named Harly Martin told the writer he believed he had found a place where a battle had been fought. I asked him why so, and he said on account of the numerous bullets he had found there. I examined the balls and found there two sizes—the large ounce ball and buckshot. This was the kind of ammunition used in those days by the Mexican soldiers, and they fired them out of a short musket called an escopet. They were done up in paper cartridges, and called "buck and ball" by the Americans. The ounce ball was in front and three buckshot behind it. The Mexicans used the same kind of cartridges when they fought the Texans at the battle of San Jacinto. Also a few copper balls were found. I at once associated this place with Uvalde's battleground. It is situated four miles below Utopia on the west bank of the river, several hundred yards from the stream, on a low hill which is the extreme south end of the divide between Salt marsh and the river. It is now in the pasture of Mr. John Kincaid, of Uvalde. Five hundred yards north of this ridge is another higher hill, part of the same divide, with a timbered valley between. Here also bullets were found, but not so many as on the first hill mentioned. On towards the river and across the field of Mr. Tampke other signs of the battle were seen—bullets, arrow-heads, etc. I made a close examination of these places in company with my brother, Mr. P. S. Sowell, of Seguin, and concluded beyond a doubt that this was the famous field of strife. My son, Lee, who was also along, found a human tooth.

Here then the fierce, painted warriors assembled to try issues with their no less dusky foes. It was a fine position to make a stand, for the view to the south was unobstructed to the mouth of the canyon, six miles away. The Indians could see the smoke of the burning villages below and the advancing Mexicans. When Uvalde's men arrived at the point of the hill and commenced the assault the battle must have been long and fierce. Thousands of musket balls must have fallen like hail on the hill, from the amount of them found there at this late day. Of course those that fell in the flats have long since been covered up by decaying vegetation. After a hard rain is the best time to find the balls on the hill, for they are moved out of place and sometimes are found lying clearly exposed on flat rocks. This first hill was finally carried, and the Comanches retreated across the flat and made a stand on the next ridge, but evidently not of long duration, for not many bullets are found here. The rout of the Indians being now complete, they broke away from here and went down the steep bluff on the north side of the hill and scattered along the banks of the river.

Uvalde pursued the Indians relentlessly for twenty miles, in fact until he drove them out of the canyon and on to the rocky divide along the brakes of the Llano, burning all of the villages and taking all the stock that could be secured. The squaws and papooses were scattered for many miles through the brakes and gorges.

At this time the Apaches lived in the Medina valley and their stronghold was around the Bandera Pass, as it is now called. A force sent out from San Antonio under General Bandera defeated and drove them away.

After Uvalde's fight the canyon was called by his name. I saw a deed to some property in Utopia which read, "Being and situated in the Canyon de Uvalde, in the town of Montania." Montania was the name of the place until changed to the one it now bears. When the country settled the name of the valley was changed, but the county and county seat retained it.

JAMES BOWIE'S OLD FORT.

Attacked by a Band of Comanche Warriors—"Nigger" Jim's Perilous Trip for Water—A Texan's Deadly Rifle Shot.

There is a place on the divide between Dry and Main Frio where is a circular pile of rocks resembling an old fortification. These rocks had been placed there at an early day by the hand of man. The fort, which I call this rude structure, was built on the south side of the hill which slopes towards the Main Frio. It makes a complete circle except a gap at the lower end which had been left for a place of entrance. Some of the stones are very large and would have required the united efforts of a dozen men to put them in place. The height of the rock wall when first built would have covered a man to the neck, and would have been an admirable place to stand off a band of Indians, which no doubt was the purpose for which it was constructed.

When the writer first discovered this place many years ago, although it was known to the old settlers years before that, I made a critical examination of the surroundings to see if I could determine the cause for building this rude fort in such an out of the way place. I half suspected it had been done by gold or silver hunters, and soon this fact was verified. I noticed the entrance to the fortification was on the lower side toward the foot of the hill and opposite a small cedar brake, as if men would come from that point to enter it in case of danger. As soon as I entered the cedar brake above mentioned the problem was solved at once. I saw an immense pile of soil banked up, and near it a shaft. It was near the base of the hill, not a hundred yards from the fort, near the head of a ravine. It was an old mine, either of gold, silver, or lead, and had been worked many years before. The entrance into the shaft was down a flight of ten steps cut in the soil, which time and the action of water pouring into it during heavy rains had not effaced. At the bottom of the steps the excavations extended west under the hill upon which the fort was built. I did not penetrate it far, on account of having no light. A great deal of the soil which had been taken out had washed into the ravine, which run east towards the Main Frio. On the mound of soil near the entrance to the shaft grew cedar trees as large as a man's body, indicating a period prior to the advent of the Texas pioneers into these mountains, when the country was full of hostile Indians. The fort on the side of the hill commanded all approaches to the mine, and a signal from the lookout which I suppose was kept there would bring the workmen into the inclosure in a short time.

BOWIE'S BATTLE.

In surmising in regard to who worked this mine I at first concluded it was Spaniards or Mexicans, but finally connected this place to my own satisfaction with the famous Texan, Col. James Bowie, and the time about 1831. I recollected hearing my father tell of a circumstance which he heard Colonel Bowie relate in Gonzales, in substance as follows: That on one occasion about the time of the above date, while prospecting for gold or silver in the mountains west of San Antonio, he had sunk a shaft where there were indications of silver. He had about thirty men with him, and anticipating attacks from Indians, they fortified their camp by piling up large rocks. Their position commanded every approach to their camp and shaft, and also a spring of water something more than a hundred yards distant at the foot of the hill. While engaged here working in this shaft they were suddenly attacked one morning by a large body of Comanches. Bowie and his men at once took refuge in their fortification, and the battle commenced with great fury. The Indians, however, were soon driven to cover in the ravines and among the rocks by the deadly fire of Bowie's men. The fight lasted all day, each party firing as opportunity offered. During the day, however, Bowie's men drank up all their water, and began to suffer very much with thirst. The Indians, from their position in the ravines and rocks, commanded the spring, and it was almost as much as a man's life was worth for anyone to venture near it. If the men all sallied from the fort they would be overpowered by the superior force of the savages; but something must be done to relieve their thirst, if possible.

A NARROW ESCAPE.

Now, Colonel Bowie owned a strong young negro man named Jim, who was now with him.

"Jim," says Bowie, turning to the negro, who was keeping his head below the level of the fortress, "I want you to take the canteens and bring us some water from the spring."

"No, sar, Mars Jim; couldn't think of sech a ting. Dem ole Injuns is a layin' dar in dem rocks and bushes an' dey can git up from dar an' kill dis nigger fo' you could say scat twice, and befo' I could half fill dem canteens. No, sar; can't go."

Bowie looked at the negro with his keen, piercing eye, and said: "Jim, which are you the most afraid of, me or those Indians?"

"Well, now," says Jim as he caught the meaning of the eye and question, "if you 'sist on me goin', ob cose I'll go, if de boys is bound to have some water befo' dey can whip de Injuns, an' you 'sist on me goin' den I'll voluntare my service. Hunt up dem canteens. I'm off."

Bowie now told Jim he need not fear, as they could protect him with their rifles from the fort while he was getting the water. It seems the Indians were not expecting anyone to make an attempt to get to the water, and evidently did not see him when he left the inclosure; in fact, they had to keep well hid themselves, as the least exposure of their person brought a whizzing rifle ball from the fort. The negro advanced to the spring, filled the canteens, and was starting back before the Indians discovered him. They now, however, set up a terrible yelling and commenced shooting at him, which also drew the fire from the fort, as several of the Indians had shown themselves. Jim now commenced running as best he could with the canteens dangling about him and several Indians in pursuit, notwithstanding several of their number fell before the deadly aim of Bowie's rifles. All ran back except one burly savage, who dropped his empty gun and pulling his tomahawk ran close to Jim, intending to strike him down with that.

Jim now began to get thoroughly frightened and sang out, "O Mars Jim, shoot dis Injun here! He gwine to hurt somebody here d'rectly."

A DEAD SHOT.

Bowie's gun was empty, but he was rapidly ramming a ball, when a rifle cracked from the lower edge of the inclosure and the Indian fell back so suddenly his feet flew up in the air. Jim, who was running and watching the Indian at the same time, again shouted out, "Never mind now, Mars Jim. Mars Bob done knock his heels higher'n his head."

The negro soon arrived safe in the fort, puffing and blowing, but unhurt, and bringing all the canteens with him.

"Now, Mars Jim," he said between breaths, "make dis water go fur as possible. It won't take much mo' dis kind a work to be one nigger less in dis big wide world. De wool lacked a flew dat time. All dat kept dat big, ugly debbil frum puttin' dat hatchet on my head cause Mars Bob hold him load back and make de bullet cum straight. Ha! ha! ha! You orter hear him grunt when dat piece lead took him kerchug."

The "Mars Bob" to whom Jim here alludes was Robert Armstrong, one among the bravest and best rifle shots of the men that followed the fortunes of Bowie. The negro either knew the crack of his gun or saw him when about to fire, as he kept turning his head alternately from the fort to the Indian as he ran and called for help. It was Armstrong who shot the Indian through the head as he was attempting to fire the grass around them during Bowie's terrible fight in the San Saba hills while in search of a gold mine up there in the following year.

This negro lived for many years after the death of Colonel Bowie in the Alamo, and went by name of "Black Jim Bowie."

On this present occasion the Indians withdrew when night came, and nothing more was seen of them. This place is 100 miles west of San Antonio.

Since the writer visited this old mine parties have been at work there opening up the old shaft, which had been greatly filled up by the washing in of soil and small rocks. They brought to light twelve more of those steps alluded to, and then come to the top of a cedar ladder. When the bottom of this was reached it was found to be twenty feet long, and at its foot lay a pick. It was short and heavy and was made on an anvil, as the hammered spots indicated. It is not known if any thing in the way of paying ore was found.

EARLY HISTORY OF GUADALUPE COUNTY.

Guadalupe County was originally a part of Gonzales, which latter was settled by colonists from the United States under Green De Witt, who contracted among others with the Mexican government, who then owned the country, to bring and settle a given number of families at various places which were assigned them.

These contractors were called empresarios, or emperors on a small scale, and the magistrates of the towns were called alcaldes. For their services in bringing and settling the families the contractors received fifteen leagues and two labors (labores) each, or 66,774 acres of land. Each immigrant who was the head of a family received one league and a labor of land, which was called his headright. A league of land contains 4428 acres, and a labor contains 177 acres. Each head of a family could make his own selection for a place to locate his headright.

De Witt selected a spot on the Guadalupe River one mile below its confluence with the San Marcos River to plant his first colonists and build a town. In 1825 the first colonists arrived with the surveyor James Kerr, and went to work. Among these were.— Berry, Edward Morehouse, Henry S. Brown, Elijah Stapp, John Wightman, — Durbin, and Erastus Smith, afterwards known as "Deaf" Smith, the famous spy and scout of the Texas army. This first installment was broken up by the Indians, and Wightman killed and Durbin severely wounded. By the year 1830 the settlement was firmly established, and in 1832 the town named Gonzales, for Raphael Gonzales, Provisional Governor of Texas, as was also the county, which at that time extended to the line of Bexar, including all of the territory of what is now Guadalupe County.

Among the families which came in 1829 were those of John Sowell, grandfather of the writer, and his son-in-law, Humphrey Branch. As most of the best land in the vicinity of Gonzales had been taken up, these two came on up the Guadalupe River in search of a location, and passed over the spot where Seguin is now in 1831. At the mouth of the Comal River they turned back.

Branch located his league and labor on the spot where Seguin is now situated, and John Sowell located his league in the bend of the river below, now known as the Stuart Bend, but reserved his labor and located it at the mouth of what is now called Sowell's Creek, where it empties into the Guadalupe, six miles below town.

The next fall or winter they both moved from Gonzales and settled on Sowell's Creek and commenced clearing land. Their nearest neighbors were at Gonzales, and no white family lived west of them.

In 1833 the Sowell boys—Andrew, William, Louis, John, and Asa—raised the first corn ever raised by white men within the present limits of Guadalupe County. It was planted between the creek bottom and the river, in what is now the Lay farm, and about forty bushels per acre were gathered.

Other colonists came in during the year and settled on the river above the mouth of Mill Creek, among whom were Dickinson, Baker, Tomlinson, Montgomery, and others. In this year also Humphrey Branch moved up and settled on his league. His house stood on the spot now known as the Neill place, but was called by him "Elm Spring Hill."

At this time the prairie stretched away from the river without a bush to obstruct the view as far almost as the eye could reach, dotted here and there with small motts of liveoaks. At times vast herds of buffalo could be seen crossing the prairie north and coming towards the river. At times they would stampede, and the noise of their running resembled an approaching hurricane. Walnut branch at that time was a rushing torrent fed by a large spring at its head, which sent a perfect sluice of water to the river.

The settlers in the meantime at the mouth of the two creeks were doing well and thought they were settled in permanent homes. Some had milk cows, game was in abundance, and living cheap. The country also abounded in dangerous wild animals, such as bears, panthers, Mexican lions, and tigers. Often on moonlight nights grandfather's family could see bears crossing the open flats between the creek and river bottom. On one occasion Mrs. Baker was coming up the river to a neighbor's house when she was suddenly confronted in the trail by a ferocious-looking animal. The woman was badly frightened, and after setting the dogs upon it which were following her, turned and ran back. The dogs were badly whipped, and one of them killed. The next morning James Tomlinson killed a large tiger near the carcass of the slain dog. On another occasion a large bear ran through grandfather's yard in daylight, but did no harm except to give the small children and women a scare, the boys being gone. A panther also came one night and took a pig out of a pen in the rear of the house, but the boys and dogs gave him such a hot chase he was compelled to drop it and take to a tree in the creek bottom, where he was killed. One morning a settler went out to hunt and was never seen or heard of again. His dog come back on the following day, badly torn and mangled. About this time two of the Moore children were lost, girls eight and ten years of age. They went out in the evening to drive up the cows, but never returned. Diligent search was made for them many days but without success. Andrew Sowell hunted sixteen days for them. On York's Creek he found a small bit of the dress worn by one of the girls, which had been torn off by a thorny bush. At the time the little girls disappeared an old blind horse on the place was also missing, and it was believed the children had managed to mount this horse to search for the cows and had lost their way. This old horse was also found by Andrew Sowell on York's Creek, near the "Big Thicket." Whether they were carried off by Indians or perished in the woods no one could ever tell.

For some time after the settlement commenced at Sowell's Creek no signs of Indians were seen, but one day a hunter came in and reported that Indians were in the vicinity, for that day he had crossed the trail of a red man. This news caused some uneasiness, and the settlers were ever on the alert. Things went on in this way for some days, when suddenly a band of Indians boldly entered the settlement. They professed friendship and camped and hunted several days on the river, but when they departed two horses were missing out of the neighborhood. It was believed that the Indians got them, and Andrew Sowell, James Tomlinson, Montgomery, and two others armed themselves and went in search of the missing horses. At the mouth of Mill Creek in the river bottom they found the horses in the possession of two Indians. They were disarmed and taken into custody and carried to the house of Dickinson, near the spot where the farm house of Thomas D. Johnson afterwards stood, on the west bank of Mill Creek. Here the settlers who had captured the Indians proposed to try the Indians and come to some understanding as to what disposition to make of them. Dickinson was not at home, and after some consultation these men passed a law among themselves that the punishment of all horse-thieves, whether white or red, should be death, and at once carried the Indians off to execute them. Mrs. Dickinson implored them not to kill them near her house. It was then decided to carry them across a ravine to a grove of timber on elevated ground. As they walked along Montgomery was on the right of the largest Indian. They knew what was in store for them, and commenced conversing in a low tone in the Indian dialect. Andrew Sowell was closely watching them as they talked, and was satisfied from their actions that they were going to make a desperate attempt to escape, and although disarmed, warned Montgomery not to walk too near the big Indian. By this time they were nearing the place of execution.

"All right," said Montgomery, in answer to the warning; "I am watching him, and if he makes a move I will plug him." These words had scarcely left his lips when the Indian, with a motion almost as quick as lightning, drew a long knife from somewhere about his person and plunged it to the hilt in Montgomery's breast, who sank to the earth without a groan, and expired in a few moments. Both Indians now made a quick leap and ran. Three shots were fired almost together, and the big Indian, the one who killed Montgomery, fell dead before he had gone a dozen yards; but the men in their hurry and confusion shot one of their own number, wounding him severely in the leg. The other Indian was not hit and was about to escape, when one of the men snatched up the dead man's gun and at a distance of more than one hundred yards shot the Indian dead in his tracks. This occurred in the timber south of the widow Patterson's farm.

After this occurrence the Indians did not show themselves, but prowled about the country and their tracks were frequently seen. One evening as two of the youngest Sowell boys, John and Asa, the latter being the youngest and father of the writer, were out after the cows they saw an Indian secrete himself ahead of them, evidently with the intention of killing or capturing them. Terror lent wings to their feet, and they soon arrived at home and told the news. Search was made for the Indian, but he could not be found.

There were no mills of any kind in the settlement, and John Sowell made a mortar to pestle corn in. This was a heavy liveoak log (short) with a cavity chiseled in the end of it sufficient to hold several quarts of corn. It was set on end and the corn beaten into coarse meal with a wooden pestle, having nails driven thickly in the end of it. Years afterwards, when this property came into the possession of Mr. Wilson Lay, this old mortar was still to be seen there. Mr. Mitty Lay told the writer that he remembered seeing it many times. An attempt was made by some of the younger Sowells to recover it in after years as a relic, but it could not be found.

On account of Indians and trouble brewing with the Mexicans this settlement was broken up, and by the year 1835 they were all back at Gonzales. Branch left his place and came to Sowell's Creek and they went back together, and for several years no human being crossed the spot where Seguin now stands except it were Indians or fugitive Mexicans from the battlefield of San Jacinto.

The Mexicans commenced the trouble by sending a company of men to demand a small cannon which was in the possession of the settlers at Gonzales. They refused to give it up, with the excuse that their alcalde was absent, and the matter would be referred to him on his return. This was done to gain time, although the chief magistrate was absent. That evening eighteen men assembled under arms, runners were sent to other settlements for reinforcements, and a boy named John Gaston ascended a tall tree to watch the Mexicans. This gallant boy was killed the following year in the Alamo when it was stormed by the Mexican army, as was also Almon Dickinson, one of the first settlers in the present limit of Guadalupe County.

We will not go into the details of the war for Texas independence, the flight of the settlers before Santa Anna, and the great victory at San Jacinto, which is a matter of Texas history, and is mentioned incidentally in some of the sketches of old veterans in other parts of this work. I will here, however, give the names of those who had gotten back to Gonzales up to 1838, many of whom were citizens of Guadalupe County after it was made such, to wit: Judge McClure, Mr. Havens, the Lockharts, the De

Witts, Simon Bateman, Ben Duncan, the Hodges, Colonel King, J. D. Clements, Widow Rowe (husband killed in Alamo), — Fraiser, Geo. W. Davis, Almon Cottle, the Berrys, Daniel Davis, John Clark, I. J. Good, Eli Mitchell, Matthew Caldwell, James Patrick, Adam Zumwalt, Ezekiel Williams, E. Bellinger, Miles Dikes, the Sowells, the Darst and Nichols families, Wm. A. Matthews, Dr. John T. Tinsley, Widow Fuqua (husband killed in the Alamo), Maj. V. Bennett, Henry and Ben McCulloch (brothers), John McCoy, Wilson and Barney Randle (brothers), Arthur Swift, the Smiths, Kings, Days, V. Henderson, James H. Calahan (escaped from Fannin's massacre), John S. Saump, Baskes and Rhodes, Mitchell Putnam, — Kinkennon, William Morrison, Aulcy Miller, Kit Ackland, Clem Hines, Eli Hankins, Nathan Burkett, Simon Cockerell, — Wolfin, — Cooksey, — Hoskins, George Edwards, Arch Gibson, John Archer, Arch Jones, Josh Threadgill, W. B. Hargess, — Grubbs, — Baker, R. Miller, John Miller, — Killin, C. C. Colley, — Fraiser, Pony Hall, and Robert Hall. All of these did not live in the town of Gonzales, but in the colony in and around the town, and many of them were in the battle of San Jacinto.

By this time the settlers had again pushed out towards the west, and the smoke from the white man's cabin once more floated over the green liveoaks on the spot where Seguin now stands. As we have before stated, Humphrey Branch built a house here in 1833. The next one was built by Robert Hall six years after. It stood on Walnut branch, not far from the spot where Judge Doc Douglas afterwards settled. Humphrey Branch sold his league of land here and never returned any more. In 1838 three Mexican families lived in the vicinity of Seguin. Manuel Flores and Jose M. Cardinus lived on the south side of the river and had large ranches on the property afterwards owned by Gen. William Saffold. Antonio Navarro and Luciano Navarro had ranches north of town on the San Geronimo Creek, where Ewing Springs is now. Before any settlements were made here Ben McCulloch was in command of a company of rangers and stationed at Walnut Springs, now almost in the heart of the city of Seguin, for the defense of Gonzales County against Indians.

Guadalupe County takes its name from the Guadalupe River, which derived its name from a shrine in Mexico, "Maestro Dona de Guadalupe" ("Our Lady of Waurloopa"). Most of the early settlers called the river "The Warloop." The county was not organized until 1846, and was up to that time known as Gonzales County. It is bounded on the north by Comal, Hays, and Caldwell; Wilson on the south, Gonzales on the east, and Bexar on the west. The first Americans who settled in the county after the battle of San Jacinto were Henry and Ben McCulloch, Andrew Neill, Colonel Young, Andrew Sowell, John Sowell, Asa Sowell, John Nichols, James Nichols, Tom Nichols, Soloman Nichols, Milford Day, Soloman Brill, James H. Calahan, William S. Turner and his sons, William, Calvin, Hardin, and John. Then there were the Mays, Johnsons, Smiths, Olivers, Toms, Jones, Wilson Randle, Hopple, T. N. Menter, Boyds, Kings, Henderson, and others. The first families were few in number, and drawn closer together by their isolation. They were sociable, free-hearted, and respected, and were ever ready to aid and assist those who needed it. They depended on each other in time of danger. Soon after the first settlers many others came and occupied the rich bottom prairie lands.

The county seat of Guadalupe County was laid out in 1838. Its first document is dated "the 12th of August, 1838, Gonzales County, Republic of Texas." Henry and Ben McCulloch, Arthur Swift, J. A. Martin, Matthew Caldwell, and James Campbell were instrumental in laying out the town on the eastern half of the Humphrey Branch league, situated on the north side of the river, half way between the town of Gonzales and the city of San Antonio, being thirty-six miles to each. This tract of land was divided into four classes of lots, which were located in the center of the tract from east to west. It was first laid off into fifty-six blocks two hundred feet square, with a seventy-foot street between each block; the second center blocks were designated as a public and market square, and the blocks fronting this square were divided into ten lots, the remainder of the blocks were divided into eight lots. Outside of these blocks was a tier of blocks of one-acre lots, and that portion of the tract fronting the river was laid off into five-acre lots. The northern being much the largest portion of the tract, it was laid off into twelve-acre lots and called farm lots, and the said lots were then divided in forty-four shares. J. S. Martin, then being the owner of the land, reserved ten shares, and the remainder were sold to the following parties: Arthur Swift, W. W. Killen, H. P. King, Barney Randle, John R. King, Wilson Randle, P. E. Beall, Abe Roberts, P. Martin, W. Clinton, J. Roberts, J. A. Swift, Milford Day, Andrew Neill, W. A. Hall, Matthew Caldwell, M. Cody, W. Cody, A. S. Emmett, John Russell, Miles Dikes, G. W. Nichols, J. W. Nichols, Cyrus Crosby, French Smith, H. G. Henderson, R. St. Clair, Andrew Sowell, W. S. Beebe, Kelley Matthews, and Robert Hall.

On the 22d of September, 1838, the shareholders met, and after arranging the preliminaries, proceeded to draw their lots, which was done by placing the number of shares on slips of paper, and the lots were arranged in the same manner, and these were placed in a hat and drawn out by Asa J. L. Sowell, then a youth 17 years of age. The names of the shareholders were then called out after the drawing. The town was then named Walnut Springs, taking its name from the many walnut trees which grew along the margin of the spring branches.

The lots were to be sold for $50, and each shareholder was to build a house in the town and settle either in person or by proxy. Some of the shareholders failing to comply with the terms of contract, their shares were sold to others on the 23d of February, 1839.

On the 25th of February, 1839, another council was held, at which they changed the name of the town. Seven voted it be called Tuscumbia and eighteen Seguin, in honor of Col. Juan N. Seguin, a Mexican, who was at that time a fast friend of the Americans and fought with them for the independence of Texas, and commanded a small company of his countrymen at the battle of San Jacinto. Some years later, for some fancied or real grievance, he turned traitor to Texas and moved with his family to Mexico, and returned with the invading army of General Wall and fought against the Texans at the battle of Salado.

As soon as the settlement commenced at Seguin it attracted the attention of the hostile bands of Indians who roamed in the wilds of the great West. The leading Indian fighters at that time were Ed. Burleson, Jack Hays, Henry and Ben McCulloch, Matthew Caldwell, and James H. Callahan.

Grandfather John Sowell died at Gonzales soon after returning at the close of the war with the Mexicans. William was killed there in a difficulty, Louis died there, and Andrew, John, and Asa, his boys, came and settled on their league below Seguin.

Soon after the settlement was made at Seguin Capt. Matthew Caldwell raised a company of minute men for its protection and kept scouts out, especially west of the setltement. About this time Gen. Vincent Cordova, a disaffected Mexican who lived at Nacogdoches, left there with a motley crowd of Mexicans, runaway negroes, and Biloxi Indians, and started to Mexico, stealing horses as they went and committing other depredations. Their trail was discovered at the crossing of the Colorado by the scouts of Gen. Ed. Burleson, and he went in pursuit with his rangers. Cordova was overtaken in Guadalupe County, five miles east of Seguin, on Mill Creek, at a place now called Battle Ground Prairie. The impetuous charge of the rangers soon broke the formation of the enemy and they ran, firing as they went. Night put an end to the pursuit two miles south, in the edge of the Guadalupe bottom. How many were killed could not be ascertained. Three rangers were wounded, but none killed. Citizens of Seguin, among whom was the father of the writer, came out to the battleground next morning. The grass had been set on fire by paper wads from shotguns of some of Burleson's men, and had burned all over the country, exposing plainly to view several dead bodies. The fight commenced at the head of a ravine around which the Seguin road now runs near the Handley place. Here were the bodies of two dead Mexicans. About one hundred yards from these further south in the prairie lay two negroes, and an Indian with his head cut off was under a mesquite tree on the rising ground south of the road.. The Mexicans and others of the band in their flight passed over the spot where now is the farm of Mr. Clay Butler. One old negro was captured and carried to Seguin, but was there shot on account of statements he made of killing white women and children. A young wounded negro was also taken.

Cordova's band traveled up the west bank of the river after crossing, and at daylight came upon the Seguin scouts, members of Captain Caldwell's minute company. They were Milford Day, Tom Nichols, and David Runnels. This was near Young's ford. The scouts made a fight, but were forced to leave their camp, losing everything, including horses and saddles, and Milford Day was badly wounded. His comrades, however, bore him to the river and secreted him under a bluff, and Tom Nichols then swam the river and went to Seguin after assistance. A cart was sent back strongly guarded, and Day brought in. Cordova was pursued to the Nueces River by citizens and rangers, but was not again overtaken.

In 1840 the Comanche Indians, about 500 in number, made a raid through Texas and burned the town of Linnville, on the coast, a trading point on Lavaca Bay. Among the victims of this raid were Dr. Gray, Mr. McNuner, Vartland Richardson, Pinkney Caldwell, Major Watts, Mr. O'Neill, Dr. Bell, one Mexican, four negroes, and the infant of Mrs. Crosby. Besides those slain they carried off Mrs. Crosby, Mrs. Watts, and a negro girl as prisoners. Men rallied from every point to fight them on their return, and the battle took place at Plum Creek, now in Caldwell County. Among the Guadalupe (present limits) County men who helped to win the victory were James Nichols, Ben and Henry McCulloch, Ezekiel Smith, French Smith, Andrew Sowell, and Milford Day. James Nichols was wounded. During the battle Henry McCulloch and others rescued Dr. Switzer, who was surrounded by Indians and was helpless, on account of having one arm pinned to his side with an arrow.

Among the men in the fight from other places were Gen. Ed. Burleson, Gen. Felix Houston, Jack Hays, Gen. Matthew Caldwell, Clark L. Owens, Thos. W. Ward, W. B. Dewees, Col. John H. Moore, Monroe Hardeman, W. J. E. Wallace, Dr. Brown, Judge Clint C. De Witt, Aulcy Miller, Maj. A. S. Miller, Judge Bellinger, Dr. Switzer, Rev. Z. N. Morrell, Rev. R. E. B. Baylor, Rev. T. W. Cox, Ben Highsmith, Tom Galbreath, John Jenkins, and many others.

At the commencement of the fight the Indians attempted to kill their prisoners. Mrs. Crosby was shot in the breast and soon expired, but not before her husband had dismounted by her side and soothed her last moments. Mrs. Watts was also shot in the breast, but the arrow, striking a steel corset which she wore, glanced and gave her a painful but not fatal wound. Her screams attracted Z. N. Morrell, the pioneer Baptist preacher, to the spot, who dismounted and attempted to withdraw the arrow, but was at first unsuccessful on account of the wounded lady holding on to it as if not being able to withstand the pain of having it withdrawn. About this time Dr. Brown of Gonzales came upon the scene, and while the preacher held the hands of Mrs. Watts the doctor removed the shaft. The Rev. Morrell then spread his blanket under a liveoak tree for her to recline upon, and she soon became composed. Near by was the body of the negro woman, who had also been killed.

On one occasion, while Seguin was in the incipiency of its settlement, a band of Indians were running buffalo on the prairie north of town. The herd became scattered and one turned towards the river, pursued by several Indians. Now, Seguin was a small place at this time, and almost obscured from view under the liveoak trees along the spring branches, and probably the Indians or buffalo were not aware of its existence. Be this as it may, however, they ran the buffalo into town, and one of them shot it with such force with an arrow that the spike came through the hide on the opposite side, having passed between the ribs. The Indians made no halt, but dashed on and crossed the river south of town. At this time there were no houses around the square, but the noise of the running brought several citizens out where they could see what caused the commotion, and beheld the Indian when he bent his bow, and with the spike almost touching the side of the buffalo sent the arrow into him. Before a pursuit could be organized the Indians made their escape into the sandhills. The wounded buffalo ran around in a circle a few times, and then fell and died near where the courthouse now stands, and was cut up and divided among the citizens.

On September 11, 1842, the Mexicans under Gen. Adrian Wall very unexpectedly to the Texans advanced from Mexico and captured San Antonio. The district court was in session, and the members were taken prisoners, among whom were Col. Andrew Neill, of Seguin, and Rev. Gustav Elly, the latter a resident of the county for many years, and who died at Seguin at a very advanced age. The news was carried swiftly from settlement to settlement, and once more the call to arms was sounded along the border to repel Mexican invasion. This call was, as ever, promptly obeyed by the brave pioneers of the Guadalupe, San Marcos, and Colorado valleys. Once more the gallant Hays, Caldwell, and others rallied their chosen scouts and rangers around them. Seguin was the place of rendezvous, and all night long before the start on the following morning men were busy making preparations to meet once more the dusky sons of Mexico on the field of battle. There was a scarcity of horses among the citizens of Seguin on account of a recent Indian raid, and men gave high prices for common Spanish ponies that would carry them to San Antonio. All through the night men were coming from the east. Rifles were cleaned and bullets moulded. Those that had no horses were trying to make trades for them, offering land or anything else almost three times the value of them. Two men fought over a stray horse which happened to be in town, until neither one was able to go. Enough of Guadalupe County men, however, got off to count in the news of the battle, which, as has been stated in other places, was fought on the Salado near San Antonio. The following men from Guadalupe County participated: Henry E. McCulloch, James H. Calahan, Ezekiel Smith, French Smith, Soloman Brill, Calvin Turner, William Turner, Hardin Turner, Andrew Sowell, T. N. Menter, Wilson Randle, Andrew Erskine, John P. Erskine, William King, John King, Milford Day, and probably some others who can not now be recalled. After the departure of Caldwell and his 200 men, when a sufficient time had elapsed the people at Seguin began to look anxiously for messengers from the scene of action. Only six years had elapsed since nearly that many had perished in the Alamo, and they had left home as light-hearted and as confident as those now under Caldwell. Once more the mothers and wives of the Guadalupe valley had to watch and wait, every minute expecting the messenger of death to dash in upon them bringing the sad news of defeat and slaughter like that which befell Travis and Fannin. They thought these fears were realized when Aulcy Miller rode into town, bareheaded, his horse covered with foam, a fugitive from Dawson's battlefield, and bringing the news of a most desperate fight, that nearly all of Dawson's men were killed, and that he and one other alone made their escape by hard and desperate riding. He knew nothing of Caldwell's men. They heard heavy firing in the direction of the creek, and were hurrying rapidly to their assistance, when they were surrounded by the whole Mexican army and cut to pieces.

The father of the writer stood by Miller's panting horse and heard him tell the sad tale of Dawson's defeat. The Indians had stolen father's horse, and he could not go. Miller was badly

MASSACRE OF DAWSON'S MEN.

sunburned, and father took a fine Mexican hat from his own head and placed it on that of Miller as a present.

Nicholas Dawson was a lieutenant in the battle of San Jacinto, and fought in the front where men fell thick, and rejoiced with his comrades over the victory and the independence of Texas, and when the messenger came announcing another invasion, he rallied his neighbors around him and met his fate at the hands of his old enemies. On the way from Fayette County to join Caldwell, Dawson made his last camp on Nash's Creek, in what is now the lower edge of Guadalupe County. Here he met Caldwell's messenger urging every one forward, and hastened on, making an all-night ride.

Here are the names of those who fell with him: Lieutenant Dickinson, Zodack Woods (80 years of age), — Church, Harvey Hall, Robert Barclay, Wesley Scallorn, Eliam Scallorn, Asa Jones, Robert Eastland, Frank Brookfield, George Hill, John W. Pendelton, J. B. Alexander, Edmond Timble, Charles Field, Thomas Simms, — Butler, John Dancer, and a negro man belonging to the Mavericks. This negro was sent out by Mrs. Maverick to communicate with his master, who had been captured while attending court at San Antonio. He was faithful to his trust and fought bravely in the battle, dying by the side of Captain Dawson.

The bones of these brave men now rest on Monument Hill, opposite La Grange, in Fayette County. The gallant patriots from the Colorado valley were ever ready to peril their lives in defense of their country, and there was hardly a battle fought in Texas where their blood did not stain the soil, and on this occasion, when the fiery Dawson came among them calling on them to rally to the defense of the "Lone Star," they seized their rifles and told him to lead the way, and rushed day and night to their death.

Wilson Randle, of Seguin, killed General Cordova in the battle on the Salado. Cordova had returned from Mexico with the army of General Wall to help chastise the Texans for his defeat at Mill Creek. Calvin Turner was the only man hurt from Seguin in the battle. He had a glancing shot from a musket ball on the side of the head.

In 1843 Captain James H. Calahan raised a company of minute men for the protection of Guadalupe County, which was constantly harassed by Indians and Mexican horsethieves. Now, before this time a Mexican named Flores had raised a band of robbers, and after committing some depredations between Seguin and San Antonio went on towards northern Texas to incite all the Indian tribes to make war on the Texans. The career of this freebooter, however, was short. He was pursued by Lieut. James O. Rice, of the rangers, and overtaken on the San Gabriel, about twenty miles from Austin.

In the battle which ensued the Mexicans were defeated and Flores killed. Rice captured 300 pounds of powder, a quantity of lead, shot, and balls, and about 100 head of mules and horses.

On the person of Flores were found papers and letters showing the grand scheme of the Mexicans of arousing and inciting all the border Indians to aid them in the war with Texas.

Flores had messages from General Canalizo, of Matamoros, to the chiefs of the Caddoes, Seminoles, Biloxis, Cherokees, Kickapoos, Brazos, Tehuacanas, and others. By concert of action, at the same time the Mexican army marched into San Antonio, the Indians were to light up the whole frontier with the flames of Texas dwellings and cause the very air to resound with cries of women and children. It was well for Texas at this time that she had a Hays, a McCulloch, a Burleson, a Caldwell, a Calahan, and a James O. Rice on her borders to hurl defiance to her thousands of foes, and who dared to lead where any dared follow.

While Calahan was operating in Guadalupe County with his company, Jack Hays was on a scout in the Sabinal and Seco mountains with his men, and finding a large force of Comanches, sent for Captain Calahan to come and help him to fight them. Calahan took a portion of his men and went at once. He found Hays in the mountains at the head of the Sabinal River, and the Indians strongly posted on a high, rough mountain. Captain Hays and his men had one fight with them in the valley, in which sixteen of the Indians were killed, and they had retreated up the mountain. The combined force of the rangers assaulted their position and drove them off. The only casualties on the side of the white men was one of Hays' men wounded. Calahan, Ben McCulloch, and Andrew Sowell from Seguin were in the fight. McCulloch had a very long range gun, and did good service in picking off Indians from the crags and high places that others could not reach.

Mr. H. G. Henderson, a resident of Guadalupe County, while in San Antonio soon after this learned that a band of horse-thieves had a hiding place near Seguin. He lost no time in communicating the same to the ranger captain. The best scouts were sent out from time to time to get trace of them, but for some time were unsuccessful, but finally Milford Day, who was a good trailer, located them in a dense thicket on York's Creek, about eight miles northeast from Seguin. This thicket was cut through by a deep gully near which was the camp of the robbers.

Captain Calahan and a portion of his men approached on foot through the underbrush, often crawling upon their hands and knees, and succeeded in surprising them. The Mexicans, after hastily firing their escopets, scattered into the brush, and most of them escaped, the rangers only getting one fire at them. Two or three were killed and several wounded. The rangers returned to Seguin, but in a few days came back again to look around, and found a wounded Mexican at a spring. He was killed by one of Calahan's men. Near the place was a round, rocky hill, with a grove of liveoaks growing on its crest, and there the Mexican was buried by the rangers, and to this day it goes by the name of the "Rogue's Grave," and the place where they fought is called "Rogue's Hollow."

Soon after this two more Mexican horse-thieves were caught and brought in. By a vote they were condemned to be shot. They

MILFORD DAY, ONE OF THE FIRST SETTLERS OF GUADALUPE COUNTY.

were executed and buried under some liveoak trees in the western portion of town, near the General Jefferson place. The members of Calahan's company who were present besides himself were Milford Day, Calvin Turner, Andrew Sowell, John Sowell, Asa Sowell, John Nichols, and some others, likely. Calvin Turner was one of the four who did the firing. The Mexicans were made to dig their own graves by Captain Calahan. This fearless ranger captain saw the fearful butchery of Texans at Goliad, saw his comrades shot down right and left after they had surrendered,— men who had stood shoulder to shoulder with him and had fought as men seldom fight, and for nine long hours in an open prairie held an army at bay.

During these years the Lipan Indians, then friendly, came

from the Colorado valley and made their camp at the Walnut Springs by permission of the settlers. They went on many hunting trips and often came in contact with the Comanches, their bitter enemies. On one occasion, while the tribe was camped here, one of their hunting parties had a fight with the Comanches up the river near where New Braunfels is, and defeated them, killing four. They returned with the scalps, and that night had a scalp dance in their camp at the springs, and invited the citizens of Seguin to witness it, which many of them did.

At the time of which we write Castro was head chief of the Lipans and Flacco was second chief. The latter delighted to accompany Jack Hays (one of the most famous Texas rangers that ever lit a camp fire on the frontier of Texas) against the Comanches, and fought bravely by his side on several occasions.

Captain Hays was early identified with the people of Seguin, marrying a daughter of Major Calvert of this place, and was brother-in-law to Col. Thomas D. Johnson and Alfred Shelby of this place, who also married daughters of Major Calvert. One night in 1844, while a dance was in progress at the house of Milford Day, near the Walnut Springs, a band of hostile Indians made a raid in the vicinity and attempted to carry off some horses. They were discovered by John R. King, who was on guard, and he fired on them. One of the Indians returned the fire, and then they all retreated. The alarm was soon given, and the dance came to an abrupt termination. The men at the dance all had their guns, and a party was soon mounted and in pursuit. They were William King, Henry King, John R. King, Andrew Sowell, Anderson Smith, Paris Smith, and Milford Day. The night was dark, and the settlers, after riding through the prairie for some time, and finding no clew to the whereabouts of the Indians, repaired to the Three-mile waterhole. By this time a drizzling rain had set in, and they sat under the liveoak trees and held their horses by the bridles until morning. As soon as it was light enough they again set out in quest of the Indians, and found their trail near Plum Ridge. It led up the river, and the men followed rapidly and soon came upon them, as the Indians were on foot and twelve in number. The place was near Twelve-mile Spring in the prairie. Only one of the Indians carried a gun, and he dropped down in the grass and attempted to fire at William King and Anderson Smith, who were riding close together. His gun failed to fire, and he was instantly killed, shot through the head by William King. A curious fight now commenced. When the balance of the settlers attempted to fire all of their guns failed, and the Indians commenced yelling and shooting arrows, but they fell harmless, having no force. The trouble was that the rain during the night had spoiled the caps on the guns of the white men, and had also wet the bowstrings of the Indians and they had relaxed, being made of sinews, and an arrow could not be sent with any force. It was not far to the river, and the Indians soon ran in that direction, followed by the settlers, who put on fresh caps as they ran, and tried in vain to fire on them, but the tubes were stopped up from the damp friction of the inferior caps of those days, and it was no go. The Indians would turn and make a weak discharge of arrows when the white men came too close, but no one was hurt. They could be warded off with arm, hat, or gun barrel. When the Comanches came to the river they plunged in and commenced swimming across, and the whack, whack, whack of snapping locks could be heard on every side as the settlers still continued to try their pieces. Presently bang went one gun, and an Indian sank, shot in the back of the head. William King had reloaded his gun, and coming up at this time had fired and killed another. The balance all got over safely and soon disappeared in the bottom. The dead Indian in the prairie was scalped and his gun taken, and a return to Seguin was made.

In 1845 Prince Solms Braunfels arrived at Seguin with German immigrants for Fisher and Miller's colony, but the Indians being so numerous and hostile in the country where the first intention was to settle (within present limits of Gillespie County), a large tract of land was purchased on the west bank of the Guadalupe River, at the mouth of the Comal, at the foot of the mountains, and here the colony was settled and their town named New Braunfels. This colony was not harassed as much by Indians as those further west, but they suffered all the privations and discomforts of subduing the wilderness and building up homes. Many of them were poor and had a hard struggle to succeed, but did so. Some became wealthy and all prospered, and there are no more thrifty people now than those of Comal County.

From Seguin there was no road leading to the place of destination of the colony, it being northwest from the San Antonio road up the river. All was prairie and grass. It was necessary to have a guide from there on, and Asa Sowell and Calvin Turner were employed by Prince Solms to pilot them through. They were acquainted with the fords of the Guadalupe, and could go straight across the prairie to the mouth of the Comal. Ferdnand Weyel, who lives on the Santa Clara, is one of the pioneers of that colony, his father having built one of the first houses in New Braunfels.

Guadalupe County was organized in 1846. The first officers were H. G. Henderson, chief justice; Thomas H. Duggan, county clerk; Asa J. L. Sowell, district clerk; Milton Osborne, sheriff, and William G. King, assessor and collector of taxes.

The first term of the district court was held in September, 1846, at the residence of Mr. Paris Smith, afterwards known as the Rust place. Hon. William E. Jones was judge, Asa J. L. Sowell district clerk, John A. Green district attorney, Milton Osborne sheriff. The sitting of the grand jury was in the liveoak grove now inclosed in the yard of G. W. L. Baker. The following are the names of the first grand jury: Paris Smith, foreman; Sam Towner, John F. Tom, S. R. Miller, Col. French Smith, G. W. Lonis, John W. Nichols, C. A. Smith, John Sheffield, Soloman G. Nichols, I. H. Turner, John N. Sowell, John R. King, Matthew A. Doyle, and Andrew J. Sowell, Sr.

The first bill found was State v. William Baker, charged with theft of a hair brush. His sentence was to be publicly whipped in the square. This sentence was only partly carried out, so some of the old settlers say, by Col. French Smith coming on the scene when about five licks were struck, and picking up a rock, told the man who was laying them on to desist.

One of the grand jury, George Washington Lonis, was a veteran of San Jacinto, and was severely wounded in the breast on that occasion, as was also John F. Tom, who had a leg broken by a musket ball there. John Sowell, another one, was also in the battle of San Jacinto, and loaned a pistol to a man to shoot Santa Anna. Matthew Doyle was one of James Bowie's men in his terrible Indian battle near the San Saba gold mines.

The first petit jury was as follows: Solomon W. Brill, foreman; Joseph Zorn, Jacob Eckstein, John Lowe, P. Medlin, W. B. Pinchard, William C. Winters, E. P. Forest, ― Baker, William Turner and W. Clark.

In March of the previous year the Indians made a raid in the vicinity of Seguin and killed a Mexican named Verimendi near Ewing Springs. Most of the citizens were in Gonzales attending court. A severe norther and sleet came up soon after the killing and the settlers followed the trail of the Indians but a short distance, as they were forced to return on account of the cold.

Cottonwood Creek, which empties into the Guadalupe about three miles below Seguin, on the south side of the river, was known to the first settlers as "Shawnee Creek." It received this name from a circumstance which happened there before the white settlers came into the country. At that time the Comanches were very numerous in the Guadalupe valley above the forks, and the Shawnee Indians, a friendly tribe, lived in the white settlement near Gonzales. They often came up the river on hunting expeditions, and on one occasion encountered the Comanches, their bitter enemies, on the little creek now known as Cottonwood, about three miles above its mouth. A battle ensued, in which the Shawnees were defeated and two of their chiefs killed. In their retreat they carried off the bodies of the chiefs and buried them on a point that fronts on the river, a little below the mouth of the creek. White hunters from the settlement below also came up in here hunting and knew of the circumstance above mentioned, and called the place "Shawnee Creek."

In 1847 a contract for building the first courthouse was let to Thomas D. Spain. It was a two-story frame building 30x50 feet. The upper room was to be used as a courtroom; the lower part was divided into four rooms, for the chief justice, county and district clerks, and sheriff.

Mrs. Mildred P. King was one of the noble pioneer women of Guadalupe County, and lost a son (William) at the storming of the Alamo. When General Wall captured San Antonio and the settlers there were hurrying to the front to repel the invaders, Lieut. H. E. McCulloch, of Hays' rangers, was riding night and day through the settlements notifying the settlers and urging everyone forward that was able to go. When he came to the house of Mr. King he said to him, "I know you are too old to go, but is there not some one on the place who could go?"

His only son old enough to bear arms was standing by impatient for the answer, as the father hung his head in deep emotion. Mrs. King spoke up: "John might be spared from home a few days very well." The old man's eyes filled with tears as he said, "We lost William in the Alamo. Can we see John go, too?" The mother said with a firm voice: "'Tis true, William died in the Alamo, and we have no son to spare, but we had better lose them all than our country." He went, and like a true son of the noble mother who had offered him, if need be, upon the altar of her country, he stood amidst the clash of arms and din of battle side by side with the descendants of the heroes of the Alamo and other citizens of the country, till victory perched upon the banner of the Lone Star on the bloody field of Salado.

In 1855 the Indians made their last raid into Guadalupe County. They came along the western edge down the Cibolo valley and first stole some horses near the residence of James F. McKee. From there they went to the ranch of Mr. Robert Hellmann, passing around his field near where New Berlin is now. The first victim at their hands was a negro belonging to Mr. Elam. Next they came across Mr. Pendleton Rector and Doc McGee, a young son of the Rev. John S. McGee, a Methodist preacher. They attempted to save themselves by flight, but the animal Mr. Rector rode fell with him and he narrowly made his escape into a thicket, the Indians getting his mare and saddle. Young McGee was riding a mule and fell an easy prey. He was roped, dragged to the ground, lanced and scalped. Mr. Rector got to the setlements and gave the alarm, and a runner was sent to Seguin. Capt. H. E. McCulloch called for volunteers to follow the Indians, and a general panic ensued among the people. Twenty-eight men rallied to McCulloch, among whom were John Ireland (afterwards Governor of the State), Rus. Hudson, D. C. Bledsoe, Sam Calvert, Frank Marshall, Nat Benton, and others. The Indians had a long start ahead, and were not overtaken.

Not long after this raid Capt. James H. Calahan got up an expedition into Mexico to chastise Indians over there who depredated on Texas. They had a hard battle and were compelled to cross the river. (See full account of this in another place.) Among those who went from Guadalupe County were Capt. Nat Benton, his son Eustus, Wesley Harris, Hughes Tom, John King, Henry King, and others. Captain Benton, Eustus Benton, and Henry King, Seguin men, were wounded.

Some time after Calahan's expedition a freebooter named Cortinas invaded Texas with several hundred men and committed depredations along the Rio Grande. Captains Herron (from Seguin), Tobin (from San Antonio), and others raised companies and marched against him. Among the Guadalupe men along were De Witt Petty, Luke Mayfield, John Mayfield, Hez. Williams, and others. Cortinas was defeated near the Rio Grande and driven back into Mexico. At one point where the Mexicans had planted a cannon a sharp fight ensued. When the cannon was captured, De Witt Petty, from Seguin, mounted it, and, standing erect, clapped his arms to his side and crowed.

Guadalupe County has had her statesmen. Arthur Swift and Ben McCulloch were in the Congress of the Republic in 1839 and in the Legislature of 1845; Henry E. McCulloch in the Legislature of 1853 and in the senate from 1855 to 1859; Thomas H. Duggan in the senate previous to this; John R. King in the Legislature in 1855; I. V. Harris in 1857; W. H. Burges in the senate in 1882; M. D. Anderson of prior date; Middleton Dunn in the Legislature in 1866, as was also Captain Wm. M. Rust.

At a later date P. S. Sowell was in the Legislature and Joseph B. Dibrell in the senate; James Greenwood, also in the Legislature; John Ireland, twice elected Governor of the State—1882 and 1884.

Guadalupe County has had her military men. Ben and Henry McCulloch were both generals in the Confederate army. William P. Hardeman, known in the army as "Old Goch," lived in this county for many years. He commanded a company, and greatly distinguished himself at the battle of Val Verde, in New Mexico, and arose to rank of general in the Louisiana campaign. Capt. Nat Burton raised a company, arose to the rank of colonel, and lost an arm at the battle of Blair's Landing, in Louisiana. John P. Bane raised a company and arose to rank of colonel. John Ireland commanded a regiment, and John P. White a company.

LIST OF MEN KILLED, WOUNDED, AND DIED FROM GUADALUPE COUNTY DURING THE GREAT CIVIL WAR.

Col. John P. Bane, severely wounded at Gaines Mill.
Thomas Cox, wounded at the second battle of Manassas.
Andrew Herron, killed at Gettysburg.
George Buttler, killed at Gettysburg.

Levi Maddox, captured at Missionary Ridge, and died in the Rock Island prison.

Dolf Allen, died in a hospital on the Potomac.

James Buttler, killed at Sharpsburg.

Paris Smith, wounded at Gaines Mill.

Julius Glazier, severely wounded with a ball and bayoneted at Chickamauga.

Fritz Glazier (brother), killed at Chickamauga.

R. J. Burges, desperately wounded with a grape shot at Manassas; same discharge killed Lieut. Ig. Johnson; R. A. Burges, wounded at the battle of the Wilderness.

W. H. Burges, wounded at Sharpsburg.

Lot Calvert, wounded at Gaines Mill, and died.

James Campbell, died in service near Richmond, Va.

John Davidson, killed at Gaines Mill.

Tom Ewing, wounded at Gaines Mill, and died.

Hat Franks, wounded at Chickamauga.

Isham Fennell, killed at Gaines Mill.

William Erringhaus, wounded at Gaines Mill.

Middleton Dunn, wounded at Gaines Mill.

Alonzo Gordon, wounded at Gaines Mill, and died.

Scott Green, wounded at Gaines Mill and killed at Gettysburg.

Andrew Erskine, killed at Sharpsburg.

Albert Green, wounded at Gaines Mill.

Fred Glazier, killed at Gettysburg.

Austin Jones, wounded at Gaines Mill. (He was the man that turned General Lee's horse around and led him back from the front at the Wilderness.)

R. H. Jones, wounded at Manassas.

John R. Jefferson, Jr., wounded at Manassas.

James King, died in service.

William Davis, killed at Sharpsburg.

James Whitehead, killed at Manassas.

Lieut. Tom Holoman, killed at Gaines Mill.

Napoleon Dimmit, wounded at Gaines Mill.

James Dimmit, wounded at Gaines Mill.

John Young, killed at Gaines Mill.

James White, wounded at Gaines Mill and in several other engagements.

William Harris, wounded at Cold Harbor.

Nelson Mays, killed at Gettysburg.

Lieut. Henry McClaugherty, severely wounded at the Wilderness and at Chickamauga.

Frank Saunders, wounded at Gettysburg.

Steward Sanders, died in the hospital at Fredericksburg.

James Herron, died on the Potomac.

John Smith, died on the Potomac.

John Dibrell, died on the Potomac.

John Miller, died in service.

Ben Terrell, wounded at Sharpsburg.

Reason Lackey, killed at Gaines Mill.

John Baker, wounded at the Wilderness.

Rainey Brooks, died in prison at Springfield, Ill.

Lewis and William Smith, brothers, died in prison in Springfield, Ill.

Abe White, killed at Chickamauga.

Alex. Ochiltree, killed at Chickamauga.

William Moltz, wounded in Georgia.

John Donegan, wounded at Franklin, Tenn.

—— Hale, wounded at Jonesborough.

Adam Saunders, wounded at Chickamauga.

Capt. Ed Thompson, killed at Franklin, Tenn.

Zeke Smith, died at Richmond, Va.

Tom Smith, died in service.

Capt. Dudley Jeffries, wounded at Manassas.

Lieutenant Richards, killed at Gaines Mill.

Leonidas Millett, killed at Gaines Mill.

Alex. Wilson, wounded at Gettysburg, the Wilderness, and at Chickamauga.

W. W. Wilson, wounded at Gaines Mill.

Mike Rogers, died at Fredericksburg, Va.

John King, wounded at ———.

Henry King, wounded at ———.

Frank Newton, wounded at Chickamauga.

——Glawson, killed at Chickamauga.

Tom Watson, killed at Chickamauga.

A. J. Cody, killed at Chickamauga.

—— Dovie, killed at Chickamauga.

George White, wounded at Val Verde, N. M.

Henry Many, wounded at Val Verde.

Colyer Allen, died and was buried at "Dead Man's Hole," in the edge of the Staked Plains.

George Turner, died at Albuquerque, N. M.

Pendleton Francis, killed at Franklin, La.

Aaron Ferguson, wounded at Cheyneville, La.

Martin Rogers, wounded at Franklin, La.

William Ferguson, wounded at Val Verde, N. M.

Robert Ferguson, killed at Mansfield, La.

Austin Ferguson, wounded at Mansfield, La.

James Sowell, accidentally wounded after Yellow Bayou fight, in Louisiana.

Bud Pearman, died near Fort Thorn, N. M.

Col. Nat Benton, severely wounded at Blair's Landing, La.

Fritz Suchart, leg torn off at Atlanta or Peach Tree Creek, Ga.; same shell killed Bates, Pace, and Alfred Alexander.

Henry Roemel, died in prison at Springfield, Ill.

——Swan, died in prison at Springfield, Ill.

Sawney Calvert, killed at Blair's Landing, La.

Lochard Arbuckle, wounded at Saline Creek, Ark. Marlin Heflin passed by where he was lying wounded with others under a tree, and gave him his blanket and $5 in money.

Lieut. Norvel Cartwright, killed in Louisiana.

Henry Nicholson, died at Ringgold Barracks, on the Rio Grande.

Dr. George Francis, died at Galveston.

George Sanders, died in Virginia.

Victor Stein, wounded at Corpus Christi, Texas.

Joe Francis, killed at Gaines Mill.

Sam Herron, wounded at Stone River.

Gustav Werner, killed at Blair's Landing.

Henry Brands, died at Jones' Bayou, La.

William Scull, killed at Murfreesboro, Tenn.

Most of these men belonged to the famous Fourth Texas, and followed Hood in all of his battles. They were the flower of the country and the bravest of the brave.

MASSACRE OF THE PEDDLERS AND BATTLE OF EL BLANCO.

From the year 1832 to 1835, while numerous disturbances were going on in eastern Texas, and collisions taking place between Mexican and American settlers, especially around Velasco and Nacogdoches, and the war cloud just then visible in the east, but which was soon to spread from the Sabine to the Rio Grande, or vice versa, leaving desolation in its path, De Witt's colony at Gonzales on the Guadalupe River had just begun to flourish. Numerous accessions of settlers had arrived and the population largely increased in and around the town. Indians were hostile and numerous in the west, and committed many depredations. Some of the colonists had settled a considerable distance west of Gonzales, and bore the same relation to people in town as the advance guard to an army. As the Indians generally came in from the west, these isolated settlers received the first blow, and then on swift horses alarmed the people further east of the approaching raid. Some had settled as far west as the present town of Seguin, but had returned, not being able to sustain themselves so far out. In the spring of 1835, or about that time, as near as we can get the record now, there lived an outside settler named John Castleman. His ranch was fifteen miles west from Gonzales in the Guadalupe valley, on the south side of the river.

One evening just before sundown there stopped at his house a French merchant or peddler named Greser, accompanied by ten Mexicans as guards. He had a large lot of costly goods which he was going east to sell, probably having purchased them in Mexico. Castleman lived on what was called the "Old San Antonio road," the main traveled route from San Antonio to eastern Texas. The merchant in question inquired of the settler as to a good camping place for the night, where there was wood and water. Castleman informed him that there was a large pool of water not far from the house, and pointed towards it, but at the same time remarking, "You had better camp here by my yard. I have plenty of wood and water, and you can get all you want. The Indians are very hostile now, and they might attack you before morning; there is no telling. You will be safe here, for my house is surrounded by strong palisades, and in case of danger you can come inside, and I will help to defend yourself and property." The Frenchman thanked him very politely for his proffered hospitality and protection, but declined, saying his men were well armed, and would go down and camp by the pool of water.

Castleman made everything secure for the night and retired. Just before daylight next morning he was awakened by the firing of guns and the yelling of Indians in the direction of the Frenchman's camp. He instantly sprang out of bed, hastily clothing himself, unbarred a small window, and looked out. Day was just beginning to dawn, and by this time the fight was raging at the peddler's camp. The Mexicans seemed to be making a stout defense. The loud reports of their escopets continually ringing out on the morning air mingled with the yelling of the Comanches. The sun arose, but still the Mexicans kept them at bay. Castleman stood at the window with his long rifle and several times expressed an intention of trying to get to them and aid in the battle, but it was too hazardous, and he could only watch and wait and see how it would terminate. The Indians would make a charge, but being repulsed each time with loss, would fall back and wait some time before renewing the contest. The Mexicans had made breastworks of their carts, saddles, bales of goods, etc. This accounts for the length and obstinacy of the battle, considering the numbers engaged, for the Comanches had seven to one of the Mexicans. At this time there had been no rupture between the Mexicans and De Witt's colonists, and Castleman would have risked his life in their defense, as the Comanches were the foes of both Mexican and Texan. The latter was hid from view during the fight, but the Indians could be plainly seen, being between the house and the encampment. The fight was going on at the base of the elevated ground on which the settler's cabin stood. The pool of water was near a mott of timber, in which the Mexicans were posted. The Indians often changed their position, and were very numerous.

About one hundred and fifty yards from the house, at the foot of the hill, there stood a large tree upon which Castleman had tacked a piece of white paper to serve as a target when he felt disposed to rifle practice. This paper caught the eye of an Indian as he was scouting around, and he came to the tree for the purpose of seeing what it was. The settler saw him and at once raised his rifle, as this was too good a chance to lose of killing an Indian. His prudent wife, however, laid her hand on the gun and begged him to desist, saying the Indians might go away and not molest them if he would not take a hand. The Indian did not long remain a target for the pioneer, for as soon as he discovered several bullet holes in and around the paper on the tree a revelation came to him, and he turned and looked towards the house, and seeing Castleman at his window beat a hasty retreat, using the tree for cover as he went.

The fight lasted until about 10 o'clock, and by that time the Mexican force seemed to be greatly reduced or else their ammunition was failing. Only an occasional shot could be heard. The Indians now assembled their whole force and charged on three sides at once and entered their position. Castleman could tell this from their great yelling and the direction their voices came from. The position the Mexicans occupied could be located by the smoke from their guns, which drifted above the treetops. Evidently a short hand-to-hand conflict took place, then all was still for an hour or more. The Indians were then discovered in long single file coming towards the house. It was a trying time for the lone pioneer, not knowing what their intentions were, but he consoled himself, like many had done before him and since, with the grim satisfaction of knowing that if they attacked him he would get as many of them as they did of him. The Comanches, however, had enough fighting for that day, and rode slowly past the house and shook their lances at it. There were eighty of them, and they had their own horses and those of the Mexicans which had not been killed or crippled in the battle, laden with the Frenchman's goods. The bloody scalps of the slain men were also visible. They had no firearms, it seemed, except those taken from the Mexicans, and likely no ammunition for them, as none of these were used in the battle which followed with the settlers from De Witt's colony. They had bows and lances.

As soon as Castleman was satisfied they were gone he went and examined the battleground. The Mexicans had arranged their carts in a circle and piled up goods and saddles and chunks of wood in the spaces between carts and wheels and spokes, and here in a small compass the eleven bodies lay horribly mutilated and drenched in blood. Many arrows were in the trees and carts, and several broken guns were there. The Indians evidently lost heavily, as the blood stains on the ground away from the carts indicated, but they had thrown their dead in the waterhole.

When Castleman returned to his house he mounted himself and family on ponies and hastened to Gonzales with the news. It spread rapidly, and before morning twenty-seven men were in their saddles and on their way to the Castleman ranch. From Mr. David Darst, of Gonzales, who was a boy at the time and saw them start, I obtained the following names of the men whom he remembered were present: Gen. Matthew Caldwell ("Old Paint"), James C. Darst, Dan McCoy, Ezekiel Williams, B. D. McClure, John Davis, Tom Malone, — White, Jesse McCoy, Washington Cottle, Almon Dickinson, Dr. James Miller, Andrew J. Sowell, Sr., and John Castleman. The balance of the names can not now be ascertained.

B. D. McClure was elected captain, and the party, pushing rapidly forward, soon arrived at the scene of the massacre. Only a short halt was made here and the trail taken up, which led up the Guadalupe valley on the south side of the river. Ten miles west the Indians turned north and crossed the Guadalupe River at a place afterwards known as "Erskine's Ford," in the present limits of Guadalupe County, and distant about twelve miles below the present town of Seguin. After crossing Darst Creek about twenty-six miles from Gonzales, just below where the ranch of Col. French Smith afterwards was, the Indians amused themselves by unwinding spools of thread across the level flats, likely tying the ends to their horses' tails. They did not seem to apprehend pursuit.

After passing through this part of the country they bore to the northwest, passing out near the head of Mill Creek and crossing the York's Creek divide. The pursuing party would camp as soon as night came, and then be off again as soon as it was light enough to see the trail. The Indians were traveling slower than the white men on account of their heavily loaded horses, but they moved on sometimes in the night, and thus had the advantage, as the settlers could only trail in daylight. Two ravens followed in the wake of the Indians, picking up the offal from their camps, and would fly up and follow on at the approach of the white men.

One night when the trailers were camped near the York's Creek divide Andrew Sowell, who was a good scout and trailer, left the camp and went some distance and remained alone on a ridge, listening, and while doing so his quick ear caught a far-off sound like Indians singing. The captain was informed of this fact and went out and listened, but could hear nothing, and supposed it was coyotes.

By daylight next morning they were again on the trail, and in about two miles came to the Indian camp, in the midst of which stood a pole. The camp was on a high ridge, south of and overlooking the present town of San Marcos, in Hays County. The grass was tramped down around the pole in a circle where the Indians had performed the scalp dance the night before. As they always sing when engaged in this merry-making, it proved beyond a doubt that the scout was right in his assertions that he heard Indians singing. The sound of the voice in their frenzied screechings would float a long distance on the still night air.

From here the Indians went to the foot of the mountains and entered them, and the pursuit was still continued. The trailing was now more difficult, and that night Captain McClure and his men camped in the brakes of the Blanco River. Next morning was foggy, and they moved with great caution. The signs indicated that they were close upon the Indians. As they were going down into the valley of the Blanco the fog lifted, and soon the yelling of an Indian was heard on a mountain across the river. He had been placed there as a spy, and was giving the alarm of the approach of the white men to his comrades in the valley below. Captain McClure, knowing that he was now discovered, ordered a rapid advance, but they soon entered such a dense cedarbrake that they were compelled to abandon their horses and proceed on foot. Almon Dickinson and James Darst were sent ahead to locate the Indians, and the others slowly followed in single file, stooping and crawling as they went. Finally they came out into an opening near the river where three or four could walk abreast, and at this instant bang! bang! came the sharp report of two rifles and the yelling of Indians near at hand. "Charge up, boys!" shouted McClure, as he sprang in front. "Here they are!". The two scouts were now seen running back, closely pursued by several Indians, who were pulling arrows and adjusting them to their bowstrings. The captain and others raised their rifles, but could not shoot without endangering the lives of Darst and Dickinson, who were directly between them and the Indians. They saw this, and sprang to one side, and gave them a chance to fire. Captain McClure shot first and killed the foremost Indian. John Castleman shot the next one and he fell across the body of the first, being directly behind him. Several shots were fired, and a third Indian had his bow stick shot in two while in the act of discharging an arrow. Andrew Sowell attempted to fire with a flintlock rifle, but it flashed in the pan. He had stopped up the touch-hole to keep the powder dry in the fog, and had forgotten to take it out. The other Indians now ran back towards the river, yelling loudly. By this time most of the men had gotten clear of the brush and charged with McClure across the open ground.

Near the river they met about fifty Indians, and the fight became general. The yelling of the Comanches almost drowned the report of the firearms, and echoed far up and down the Blanco valley. The Indians soon gave way and commenced crossing the river. Some had been engaged trying to cross the goods over while the fight was going on, and partly succeeded. They had camped here near the water on the east or south bank the previous night. Another fight took place at the river, some of the Indians stopping in the water to shoot, but they soon retired before the rifles, and all went across and disappeared in the brake beyond. Andrew Sowell killed one after they got over. He tried to cross lower down than the balance, and came in contact with a steep bank on the opposite side which he could not hastily climb, and was discovered and shot. He rolled back to the edge of the water. None of the white men crossed the river.

None of the settlers were killed, and those wounded with arrows were not badly hurt. The Indians made a very poor fight and seemed badly rattled at the very commencement, shooting wild and running at every volley from the whites. They had evidently exhausted most of their arrows in the fight with the Mexicans. Those killed had but very few in their quivers, and some even had none.

A return was now made by the settlers back to their horses, which were found all right, except one which had gotten away and gone on the back track out of the valley, but was recovered. One man was also missing, and a search was made for him, thinking he was killed somewhere, but without success. Finally he came to them, as one of them afterwards expressed it, "looking as wild as a buck." He had neither hat, gun, nor shoes, and seemed to be perfectly bewildered, and could give no rational account of himself. He said he could not stand the firing and yelling, and ran and kept running until it was all over. He could give no account of his gun or shoes. The latter were found at the river, almost in the edge of the water, below the battleground. The gun or hat could not be found.

The settlers carried their horses back to the river and loaded them with goods, but could not take them all, and left the remainder piled up on the bank of the river, with bows, shields, blankets, and buffalo skins. The return to Gonzales was made without further incident. A party afterwards went back to bring away the balance of the goods, but they were badly damaged by rain.

Matthew Caldwell took part in many battles. He was a member of the Santa Fe expedition in 1843, and was captured with his son Curtis and others and carried to Mexico and confined with the Mier prisoners. Caldwell County was named for him. He was called "Old Paint" on account of his having gray spots in his black hair. Almon Dickinson was the Lieutenant Dickinson that perished in the Alamo with Travis, and father of the famous character known in Texas history as the "Babe of the Alamo." She was an infant in her mother's arms in the fort during the terrible conflict.

OLD SETTLERS OF D'HANIS.

In 1897 the writer, while circulating around the old historic place of D'Hanis, found many interesting old settlers. Among these were the Kochs, Saatoff, Enderle, Wolf, Richarz, Judge, Miller, Neys, Rothes, Fingers, and many others.

The Ney family, who came here at an early day, are related to Napoleon's great field marshal of that name. John Ney, grandfather of the younger ones here, was present at the battle of Waterloo. On the morning of that famous battle Marshal Ney was sitting on his horse listening to the roll call and heard the name of Ney, and a man answered to it in the ranks. He at once rode up and asked the man where he was from and who his people were. On the information being given, the marshal said, "You are my nephew." This was John Ney, ancestor of the Neys who now reside in Medina County. John Ney was in all the desperate fighting that day at Waterloo, and charged repeatedly with the troops led by the marshal. Of the large company to which Mr. Ney belonged, and with whom he fought that day, only seventeen came out alive. They were engaged from early in the morning until about 3 o'clock in the evening, when Marshal Blucher came upon the scene with 50,000 fresh troops to the aid of the English commander, Lord Wellington. The French army then went to pieces, and the rout commenced.

The Waterloo veteran, John Ney, had three sons—Joseph, John, and Nicholas—and two daughters, Elizabeth and Angelina. Elizabeth married Mr. Zurcher, and Angelina Mr. Herbert Weynand. Of the boys, John was killed by Indians on Black Creek, in Medina County, and Nicholas died at Fort Lincoln, on Seco, two miles from D'Hanis. Joseph Ney had four sons—Joseph, John, Antone, and Henry. Joseph is now and has been for many years sheriff of Medina County, and lives at Hondo City, the county seat. John lives at New D'Hanis, and Henry at the old town of the same name. The writer was shown a bronze medal by Johnnie Ney which was given to their grandfather, John Ney, by the French government on account of his relationship to their great field marshal, and for services at Waterloo. On one side of the medal is an image of Napoleon, and the date of his death on the other. This medal is prized very highly by the Ney family. The Ney boys, except the sheriff, are engaged in farming, stock raising, etc. John has a gin at D'Hanis, and Antone is on a ranch in the mountains on Parker's Creek.

Another old pioneer of D'Hanis is Mrs. Caroline Brotze. She was born in Wurtemburg, Germany, and came to America, landing at New York in 1849. The trip across the ocean was very slow, consuming six weeks. She came to Texas in 1850, and first lived on the Cibolo and then on the Salado, coming to the Seco in 1856 and settling where she now lives, about a mile north of New D'Hanis. Mrs. Brotze has had some interesting experiences on the frontier. Many times has she moulded bullets for her husband and other men to fight the Indians, and prepared narrow strips of greased cloth to patch the bullets with. Her husband was a ranger, and on one occasion captured an Indian girl and brought her to Fort Lincoln and gave her to the commander, Captain Oakes. Many times the people suffered for bread, and her husband, who died several years ago, went to Mexico after flour. The flour was high-priced, dark, and hardly fit to eat, and Mrs. Brotze does not believe it was made from wheat. It tasted, she says, like it had cinnamon bark in it.

On one occasion the men caught up with a band of Indians who had stolen a lot of horses, and recaptured them and returned to D'Hanis, putting the stock in a pen in the rear of Ney's saloon for the night. The Indians followed the settlers, and during the night succeeded in getting the horses again and carrying them off. They were again pursued, stock retaken, and brought back; but this time a stricter watch was kept over them.

Old Fort Lincoln, which has been referred to several times in these sketches of the pioneers, was not named for President Abraham Lincoln, as many might suppose, but for General Lincoln, of Revolutionary fame, who took a prominent part in the battle of Monmouth and many other engagements. He was an able officer and had the respect and confidence of General Washington. The fort was erected long before Abraham Lincoln came into any prominence. It is built of rock, and is still standing. Many young officers have been inside its walls while on duty in the Southwest, who espoused different sides when the great civil war burst upon the land, and fought each other.

HISTORY OF THE SETTLEMENT OF D'HANIS.

Settled in 1846.

There is in Medina County, near the line of the Sunset, or Southern Pacific Railroad, fifty miles west from San Antonio, a very interesting and historical place called "Old D'Hanis," settled in 1846 by German colonists. Among the very few now left of the first settlers is Mr. Christian Batot (pronounced Bah-do), who was young at the time and can tell many stirring incidents of that time, being well informed and having a bright and retentive memory. He was born in Alsace, near the town of Colmer, capital of Upper or Northern Alsace, in 1838. This country at that time belonged to France.

In 1846 Henry Castro came through that country representing an immigration company for America. The land upon which the colony was to be planted was in the wilds of western Texas. Each immigrant who was head of a family was to receive 320 acres of land, and each single man was to receive 160 acres. The conditions were that each colonist was to pay 260 francs from fifteen years and upwards, and those under that age half price. For this sum per head the company agreed to deliver them at their destination, food, etc., furnished. To these hardy Germans who dwelt in Alsace and other parts of the adjacent country this seemed to be a fine opening to secure good homes at small cost. That amount of land in the country where they lived would be a small fortune, and it was worth the attempt to brave the dangers of the ocean and all other hardships to obtain it. Castro was very successful in his mission, and soon obtained three shiploads of colonists, amounting to about 1000 persons of all ages. The vessels set sail from Antwerp on the 1st day of August, 1846, and many long and last looks were cast back at the fast receding shores of the old country. The time consumed in crossing the ocean was ninety-two days, and on the 10th of December they landed at Galveston, Texas. The ship in which Mr. Batot came was the Herratzes.

The colonists had paid their fare to Castroville, another colony of Henry Castro which had preceded them and had made their settlement on the Medina River, twenty-five miles west from San Antonio.

The land of this second colony had not yet been surveyed or their town of D'Hanis laid off, so they had to remain at Castroville until a surveying party could go out and do the work. When the time came for the lots in town to be drawn, old man Batot, father of Chris, went out, and being satisfied with the situation, drew his lots, which consisted of one building lot and one twenty-acre farming lot. When Mr. Batot came back to Castroville he said to his family, "Well, I am going out to our land now to fix a home, and will take Chris along to cook." When everything was ready the old man took his provisions, bedding, and tools on his back, and Chris took a pick, and they walked from Castroville out to the new town, the distance being about thirty miles, with no road except the trail of the surveyor's wagon through the high grass. The town was laid off on a high prairie about two miles east of the Seco Creek, on a bold-running but small creek. The land was black, very rich, and covered with rank sedge grass. One drawback which confronted the men who were trying to build homes for their families was the want of building material. The only chance was short mesquite pickets, which grew in the valley near the Seco. Some of these were six feet long and some only four feet. These were set in an upright position, making a pen, and others tied together at the top and slanting both ways, so as to make the frame for a roof, and then covered with the long grass of the prairie. For a door a kind of framework was made of small poles, and then the grass worked in and out to close up the spaces, and then fastened to one end of the shanty. In constructing these rude shelters it was all done without a nail or any kind of metallic substance in its structure. Some only slanted the roof one way, letting the ends of the poles rest on the ground, and then digging a hole inside to make the roof high enough so that a man could stand erect inside of it.

Of all the vast throng who started from the old country to obtain a home here, only twenty-nine families succeeded in arriving and finally settling. They were scattered from the coast to Castroville, some stopping in San Antonio and various other towns and settlements. When the families came out they had poor transportation, and came out slowly from Castroville. They came by the surveyor's trail through the high grass across the prairie, and saw many deer and wild mustang horses. The families did not all come out at once from Castroville, and up to the 19th of March six families were still behind. The lack of provisions was keenly felt in this far-away frontier country, and the colonists had no money. On the day of the above date the colonists were surprised and somewhat frightened to see seventy-two painted Comanche Indians ride into the settlement. They carried a white flag, however, and the little German children and women stood and looked in wonder and astonishment at the strange, painted men. The Indians all carried shields, bows, and arrows, and each one had two horses, making quite a formidable appearance. These Indians brought a letter from the Indian agent at Fredericksburg, stating that they were not enemies to white people. They also said if they were Mexicans they would not let them settle here. These Indians showed their friendship and good will to the white men by taking all the provisions the poor colonists had, which was not much, and then taking their departure.

After they had gone old man Batot said to his son, "Chris, here is a little meal left; make some mush and we will eat it up." While the mush was making the Indians came back, and some of them stood around Batot's fire and watched the mush cook. Finally one of them took out a little sugar which he had robbed a settler of, and putting it into the mush stirred it up. Mr. Batot thought the Indian was going to fix it up good for him and Chris, but when it was cooked sufficient, the Indians lifted it from the fire and ate it all themselves. The colonists had placed a white flag on the D'Hanis hill to the south, near the settlement, to guide any lost settler back home, and the Indians finally all went up there to look at it. From this elevated position they discovered some immigrant wagons coming containing six families, the last of the original twenty-nine families which composed the first settlers. The Indians now turned east down the hill and met the wagons and stopped them, but did not molest anyone. In this party was Mrs. Batot, who up to this time had remained in Castroville. When the Indians rode up to the wagons there was a young woman in one of them named Josie Rutinger, who was dying, having been taken sick by the way. This family had a hard time of it. One of their horses gave out, and they had to unload their wagon at a place now called "Finger

Hill." The load which they had to leave consisted of trunks containing all their earthly possessions of value, and they left one of the Rutinger girls only 14 years old to watch them. The wagons then slowly moved on, trying to get to the setlement with the dying girl. Three miles further the team gave out entirely, and they had to send to the settlement and get the Castro oxen, as they were called, as they had been furnished by him for their use. When the oxen were brought and hitched in, the wagon moved on again, and about midnight arrived at their destination, and just as they did so the sick young lady died, and was the first one buried at D'Hanis.

Can anyone imagine the feelings of the little sister left alone six miles back on the prairie with the trunks? Night soon closed down around her. The range of mountains to the north faded from sight. One by one the stars came out and commenced their ceaseless twinkling. The night wind stirred the tall grass around her, and anon the distant bark of the coyote was heard. Alone on the prairie, far in advance of civilization, with roving bands of Comanches not far away! No doubt her mind as she kept the solitary vigils of the night went back to the old home across the ocean,—the preparations to embark; the talk of the new home in the far distant country; the long, tedious voyage, and the joy at sight of land, the place where they were to find a beautiful home; the disappointment on landing; the long distance yet to go by land towards the setting sun, most of the way on foot, following the slow, heavy-laden wagons, and on and on to the present night,—nearly there, but left alone, and her sister dying in the wagon ahead. This is no overdrawn picture. Next morning a party came back with a wagon and got the trunks and little girl and brought them on to the settlement, and that evening the dead sister was buried.

The place where the little girl was left, called "Finger Hill," was named for Mr. Joseph Finger, who camped there and cut grass to cover his house. It is near the present town of Hondo City. The little girl lived to be an old lady, and died at D'Hanis in 1893.

We can hardly realize now what these early settlers had to endure while trying to subdue the wilderness and build up and provide homes for their families. They had no money, and here they stayed six months alone, cut off from the rest of civilization,.

not a house west of them in Texas, and none for many miles east. Corn was $6 per bushel, and no mills to grind it on except by hand. The turfy soil was hard to subdue with insufficient plows and teams. Game was plenty, but these people were not hunters. They had no guns suitable to kill large game. Some few brought small bird guns from the old country, and those that had guns that they could kill a deer with soon exhausted their ammunition, which was high, and they had no money to buy any more. They deserve more credit than the American pioneers. The latter came from States where they were used to hunting game, brought good rifles with them, and were at home in the forest or on the plains. On the other hand, the Germans came from towns and thickly settled districts, and knew nothing about camp life or living in the woods and shooting wild game.

At last, however, relief came. One evening a band of Texas rangers arrived in the settlement and went into camp on the Seco two miles from town. They were commanded by Capt. Tom Rife, and were sent here to protect these isolated settlers, as Indian friendship did not last long. The rangers had good guns and plenty of ammunition, and not only gave them ample protection, but killed game of various kinds and brought to them. The Delaware and Lipan Indians also came and traded with them until the latter became hostile. The Delawares lived over in the Guadalupe valley, near where Comfort is now, but there were no settlers there then. The Lipans were on the Francisco. One day a discharged ranger named Sam West came to D'Hanis from below and got some men from the rangers and went to the Lipan camp and arrested some of them, stating that they had killed a man in Quihi, a new settlement of Germans fifteen miles below, and had robbed him and carried off a girl 16 years old. The girl got away before they carried her far, and that night got back home. West found one camp of the Lipans at the Comanche waterhole and carried them to Quihi to see if the young woman could identify any of them, which some say she did. A pointed out one, and the men killed the Indian and carried the balance to San Antonio and turned them over to the authorities. This young girl, as the ranger West called her, was Mrs. Charobiny, and she had been married three months. The man killed was her brother, Blas Meyer.

In 1849 a company of United States regular troops came and

went into camp in tents two miles from D'Hanis, and good times began to come to the colonists. The rangers had been ordered elsewhere or disbanded before the regulars came. Mr. Batot speaks highly of the Texas rangers, and says if it had not been for their timely assistance he believes the colony would have broken up. With the soldiers came employment for the men of D'Hanis. They could get $1 per day for cutting tender grass to furnish hay for the cavalry horses and many other things they required to be done.

In 1850 Fort Lincoln was built and Captain Oaks put in command of it. The building of the fort, barracks, hospital, quartermaster department, and many other things gave employment to the D'Hanis men at $1.50 per day and board. By the time the government contracts were all finished crops began to be raised in the settlement and times were good. In 1857, however, crops began to fail and the Indians became hostile, especially when settlers began to go further west, and the D'Hanis people saw hard times again.

These people were so completely cut off from the outside world that they could only get their mail once a month. Big Foot Wallace had a contract to carry the mail from San Antonio to El Paso, and it was only when he stopped at their settlement going west that they obtained their mail.

On one occasion Mr. John Grocenbacher and his daughter Barbara became lost while out from the settlement, and wandered about fourteen days. During this time they lived on bird eggs and a young fawn which they caught. They first sucked the blood of the young deer and then carried the body along, which they partook of from time to time, even eating the hide. They were found by a band of friendly Indians and brought to the settlement. This girl, Barbara Grocenbacher, lived many years, and was the mother of the Leinweber boys, who now live at Hondo City.

Mr. Batot relates an incident of one of his escapades at D'Hanis when a boy. A stray steer came into the settlement, having both horns sawed off, and he gave the people a great deal of trouble by depredating upon their crop. He was also a fighting steer, and would run anyone who would come to put him out of a field. These honest people finally concluded to kill the steer and cut out the brand on the hide and take care of it, so that if anyone came there making inquiries about stock in that brand they would pay him for the slain animal. When the steer was killed a square piece of hide was cut out, containing the brand, and placed in the care of old man Batot for him to keep secure in case it was ever needed. Now this brand and piece of hide on which it was imprinted was the prime factor in getting Chris into trouble and causing him to run away from home. The old man placed the piece of hide in the roof of the house between the grass cover and a rafter over the bed upon which Chris reposed at night. In time the piece of hide became full of hairy worms, and often would fall upon Chris at night. This made the boy mad, and he arose in his wrath one night, and seizing the offending thing hurled it out into the darkness. The old man had all this time kept an eye on it, and when it was missed asked Chris what had become of it. He denied any knowledge of it whatever, but the old man had an idea that he was concerned some way about its disappearance and sprang at him to chastise him, but Chris ran, followed by his father, who threw things at him, but could not catch him. The old man was very much afraid of the law. The boy was afraid to come back home, so he took the road and traveled east until he came to Sutherland Springs. He was now footsore and nearly starved. He was afraid to stop at any of the settlements further west, for fear his father would find him. This place was a new settlement, and the property owned by Dr. Sutherland, who had a hotel. Here Chris stopped and applied for something to eat, which was given, and then the doctor employed him. His business was to wait on table, and his compensation was $2 per month and board. Chris thought this was fine, living at a hotel, and enjoying himself very much. For fear he might be found out, he told the doctor his name was Joseph. One night the Indians came into the settlement and stole some horses, and next morning the doctor and some of his neighbors followed and had a fight with them about thirteen miles from there, over in Karnes County. They killed three of the Indians and brought their scalps and shields back. Chris finally went back to D'Hanis and got on good terms with the old man again.

In 1858 they had their first trial at D'Hanis. A bachelor who lived in the lower part of town stole a pumpkin from Mr. Strausser, and he was tried for the offense before Justice Marrell, who found him guilty and assessed his punishment as follows: He was to have the pumpkin strapped securely between his shoulders on Sunday, and march from one end of the town to the other, followed by the jeering populace. Mr. Herbert Weynand, an old settler, and who still lives, was at one time justice of the peace in the early days.

In 1861 a band of hostile Indians came in near D'Hanis and stole a lot of horses. Before the people knew they were in the country an old man named John Schreiber went out in the morning on a mule to hunt a yoke of oxen. Some time in the day the mule came back with an arrow in him. Great excitement prevailed in the settlement, as all were satisfied the old man was killed. A large crowd assembled at D'Hanis to search for the body and fight the Indians if they came upon them. These people were very particular about adhering strictly to the letter of the law in all of their proceedings, and thought best to hold an inquest over the body when found. At this time they were without a peace officer, but their school teacher was an educated man and they thought he could hold the inquest as good as anyone. His name was Schalkhausen. When all this was agreed upon a wagon and team were procured. The teacher was placed in the wagon with the driver, and the balance of the men went on horseback in search of the missing man. When they arrived near the place where they supposed the old man had been killed they separated to hunt for the remains, and it was understood that the successful one should let it be known by hallooing. A man named Decker first came upon the body of the unfortunate settler and gave the signal. The searchers came together on the spot, and Mr. Batot was sent to inform Mr. Sauter, son-in-law of the dead man, of the fact of the finding and how to come with the wagon, as he was the driver. The wagon had passed the spot where the body lay and had been stopped to await developments. They had now to turn back and go up a ravine, near which the dead man lay, in order to cross the gully. This was back towards D'Hanis, and Mr. Batot told Mr. Sauter how to go, and said "You can see us when you get opposite the place" (where the crowd had now assembled awaiting the wagon and school teacher). Mr. Batot now rode back, crossing the ravine and going a nearer route, and told the men the wagon would soon be there. The horses had not been unhitched, only the bridles removed, and when these were adjusted the wagon was turned up the ravine. In the meantime, however, the teacher had left the wagon and followed Mr. Batot, saying he too would go the near way on foot. Mr. Batot looked back and saw him leave the wagon and follow on after him, but as the distance was not great paid no attention to it and hurried on, thinking he would come in a few minutes. When the wagon arrived the men were around the body ready to hold the inquest, but the teacher had not yet arrived. After waiting a short time two men were sent to see what had become of him. They were gone about twenty minutes, then returned, and reported that they could not find him. Fifteen men now set out on horseback and scattered in various directions, shouting and shooting for six hours, but no response came. By this time a cold norther had sprung up, and the men, being without coats, were compelled to abandon the search and return to D'Hanis. The dead body was placed in the wagon and carried back, where it was buried without the inquest being held. The body was lanced and scalped, but had neither been shot with bullet nor arrow. The wounded mule must have dodged into a thicket and the limbs and brush dragged the old man off, and he fell an easy prey to the lances without being shot. The mule came in with the saddle and bridle on.

After returning home the men got their coats and some provisions and returned to the scene of the killing to look for the lost man, and there searched in wide circles for three days, but without success. It is surmised that the Indians who killed Mr. Schreiber were concealed near by and watching the party, whom they were afraid to attack, and seeing this man alone and on foot captured and carried him off, as he was not armed and could make no resistance. If he had been killed some remains of some kind would certainly have been found of clothing, etc. He was a man 60 years of age, had a good school, and it was not reasonable that he would absent himself without letting some one know it. There were plenty of Indian signs in the vicinity, but these could have been made by those that killed the other man. Be this as it may, he was never heard of again by the people of D'Hanis.

Six months after this the man Deckard, who found the body of Mr. Schreiber, was killed by Indians under almost similar circumstances six miles below. He was also out ox-hunting and was not armed. A searching party went after him and hunted several days before he was found. He was killed on a ridge, in some liveoak timber, and the coyotes dragged the body down into an open flat, and there it was discovered. Only the skeleton remained, and it was put in a sack and brought to D'Hanis and buried. It could only be identified by shoes and some other things.

Mr. Batot was in Castroville one day when Big Foot Wallace brought an Indian in there whom he had captured. A crowd gathered around Wallace and the Indian, among them being a county officer who proposed to take charge of the Indian. Big Foot refused to give him up, and said to the man, "If you want an Indian, go and catch one. This is my Indian; I caught him." There was a general laugh over this—the idea of the officer out trying to catch an Indian. Wallace took the captive to San Antonio and turned him over to the agent there.

In 1870 Mr. Batot joined a company of rangers commanded by Captain Richarz. They were stationed at Fort Inge. During this year the Indians invaded the west like they were going to take the whole country, and part of Captain Richarz's company had a desperate battle with them, the particulars of which are given elsewhere.

There is a vast difference now in the looks of the country around "Old D'Hanis" and when the first settlers came there. It is grown up in mesquite and other kinds of brush, and the little creek which ran so clear and bold is now dried up. There are still many of the grass-covered houses standing, but they are used for outhouses, cribs, stables, etc. There are but few of the original picket shanties left. These grass-covered ones here now, though old, were once comfortable, being built of rock at a later day. The old grass covers still shed the water as good as shingles. The old town is one mile east of the new.

Mr. Batot furnishes the names of all he can remember of the original settlers, as follows: Old man Finger, — Hagemueller, Donnel French, Whipf, Batot, Carr, John Ney, John Rieddemann, John Schreiber, Antone Ludwig, Joseph Wollehker, Antone Strausser, Frank Biell, John Nehr, Joseph Rudinger, J. B. Deckard, Dr. Marrell, John Schumaker, Ben. Grocenbacher, Rissmann, Kaufmann, and Joseph Echtile. Frank Biell was killed by Indians on the Medina, above Castroville.

OLD SETTLERS.

Thirty-three miles southwest from San Antonio is the flourishing little city of Devine, in Medina County. It was named for Judge Devine, of San Antonio, long before the whistle of a locomotive was heard in this country. The pioneers had erected their cabins here and commenced that long and desperate struggle with the savages for the mastery, in which civilization in the end was destined to triumph.

Now, instead of the yell of the Comanche, Lipan or Kickapoo, is heard the scream of the steam engine, and the trail of the redman is covered along the graded track by the right of way. In a radius of twelve miles of this place, covered by portions of Frio and Medina counties, many bloody encounters took place. Nearly every hill, valley, branch, creek, or mott of timber is historic; and many graves are shown here and there, and the traveler is told "they were killed by Indians." Many of these old settlers still survive who escaped the arrow, bullet, lance, or tomahawk, and among these at the time of which I write (1897) were Tom Galbreth, Lon Moore, Sam McCombs, Gip Tilley, Bee Tilley, J. W. Winters, Big Foot Wallace, Thomas A. James, John Craig, Tobias Long, James Long, West Davidson, Holly Laxon, George Crawford, James Crawford, Mrs. Amanda Long, Aunt Peggy Halsel, Mrs. Minerva Laxon, Rev. Newton, Reese Moore, W. M. Bramlett, Mrs. Anna Burch, Mrs. Sarah Smith, George McCombs, and many others. Nearly all of these have been here from thirty-five to fifty years; the first one to come being Big Foot Wallace.

The writer, in company with an old friend, Tobias Long, set out from Devine in April, 1897, about the 20th, to his ranch and farm twelve miles south of Devine. The country is very sandy in places, which makes locomotion slow, but the soil is very good for corn, cotton, melons, and potatoes. We arrived at Mr. Long's place about sundown, and the writer received a hearty welcome from Mrs. Long, who was an old acquaintance of other days in Guadalupe County, but she could not see me, having been blind for many years. Her first husband, James Winters, was killed by Indians, and during my stay I was shown the three arrows which were pulled from his body, and which she had carefully preserved for nearly forty years. The Indians in scalping him had taken the hair off so close but little was left on the head, and the grief-stricken wife could only procure a small bit just above the ear to keep as a memento. The opposing forces consisted of six white men and twenty-five Indians, and a full description of the battle is given elsewhere. Mrs. Long, before her first marriage, was Amanda Davidson, and the daughter of "Aunt Peggy" Halsel, by Mrs. Halsel's first husband.

In this settlement the writer met two old schoolmates of forty odd years ago, Mr. West Davidson and Mrs. Minerva Laxon, son and daughter of "Aunt Peggy" Halsel. This old pioneer mother, who still lives, was born in Alabama in 1812. Her father, Tobias Long, was a soldier under General Jackson, and was in the battle of "Horse Shoe Bend."

While taking a drive through the country with the family, consisting of Mrs. Halsel, Mrs. Laxon and her husband, Holly Laxon, the writer was shown an old road which was washed out into gullies where it emptied into Cesquadara Creek, at the mouth of Elm, and was told that here a boy's horse fell with him while he was making a desperate run from the Indians. The name of the boy was Simon Fraiser. He was out in the woods near Sand branch when he discovered a band of Indians. The horse young Fraiser was riding was a mustang, which had been caught when a colt and was a rather awkward pacer and not noted for speed. It was two miles home, and the boy turned for the nearest house, only half a smile away on Cesquadara, and made the best time he could, with the Indians in pursuit, three of them on good horses. So confident were they of their little victim that one of them fixed his rope as he ran to throw over Simon's head when he came up beside him. The boy used every effort to urge his mustang to his utmost speed in this run for life, but at first the pony only went in an ungainly pacing gallop. The three Indians were mounted on races horses which they had stolen from settlers, and soon shortened the distance between them and the seemingly doomed boy. Two of these fast horses belonged to Than. Terry, and one noted for speed was called Cornet. The other one belonged to Lon Moore. When the Indians came near they began to utter loud, keen whistles to terrify the lad, but this likely saved his life, as the mustang became badly frightened and at once began to get his legs under him in proper shape and to run level and at a terrific speed. In vain the Indians tried to flank him, two running on each side and one in the rear. When the bank of the Cesquadara Creek was reached the boy's horse plunged down and fell, throwing his rider over his head, and then rising dashed away, leaving Simon to take care of himself as best he could. Near by, however, was a family living at the old James Winters place, and thither he made his way in safety. The horse passed this place and went on to Mr. Trout's and was there caught by Miss Louisa Trout. They had been listening to the noise of the running horses across the creek, but were not aware of the presence of Indians in the country, but now realizing the situation, thought sure young Frasier was killed. The Indians came close to the house, trying to get the horse after he threw the boy, for they saw he had wonderful speed, and they wanted him very much, but were prevented by Miss Trout catching and tying him near the door, and the Indians would not come within gunshot of the house.

The boy Simon Fraiser had a brother killed by Indians. His name was Henry McCulloch Fraiser, and he was named for Gen. Henry McCulloch. This boy was out near the house hobbling a horse, and as he raised up an Indian grabbed him around the waist, and pulled a knife from Henry's belt and stabbed him with it, and then stripped him of his clothing. The boy succeeded in getting to the house in this bloody and naked condition and lived long enough to tell how it was done. The Indian who did this was supposed to have put on the boy's shirt, as one was killed shortly afterwards by Montel's rangers who had on a hickory shirt, the sleeves of which were very much too short for him. This killing of Henry Fraiser was a short time before the Indians gave his brother Simon such a chase.

While being shown several places of interest by Mr. West. Davidson, we came upon a small elevated place near Sand branch, where was a lone grave in a mott of liveoak trees. The man buried here was a Texas ranger and had been killed near this place in a battle with the Indians in 1845. The rangers on this occasion, twenty in number, were coming back from a scout to their camp, which was at the Garcia crossing on the Medina. It was nearly night, and the rangers were going up Sand branch to a spring, where they intended camping for the night. Eighty Indians were already encamped at the water, and their spies had discovered the rangers approaching. The Comanches met them near this grove and a battle ensued. The rangers took advantage of the liveoak timber along the branch and opened a severe fire from their rifles. The Indians did the same, and many shots were exchanged, during which one of the rangers was killed, and night coming on the Indians went back to the spring, carrying away their dead, and the rangers camped on the battleground, and that night buried their dead comrade and attended to others who were wounded. Next morning the Indians attacked them again, but soon drew off. The rangers went on to their camp, and getting additional force returned and trailed up the Indians and completely routed them and captured many head of horses and other property. On the way back from the scout the rangers stopped and built a pen of poles around the grave of the dead ranger. When the settlers began to come into this part of the country the grave attracted their attention, and a Mr. Woodward who lived near Pleasanton gave Mr. Davidson the history of it, for he was one of the rangers in the fight. The grave is now marked by a mesquite stake about four inches in diameter driven into the ground. The pen first placed around it by the rangers in time rotted away, and this stake was put here by "Aunt Peggy" Halsel many years ago, and has thus far preserved the site of the grave from being lost. Mr. Davidson could not tell me the name of the ranger or his captain, but thinks the latter was Walker. The old ranger who gave the account is now dead. If the writer could learn the name of this dead defender of the Texas frontier who has now lain for fifty-four years in this lonely liveoak grove, a stone suitably inscribed should be placed over it. The spring mentioned is now filled with sand and used to be known as the "Toola waterhole."

Mr. Tobias Long was one of Montel's rangers, and also served under Capt. Ed. Burleson, and has had much experience on the frontier, and has eaten horse meat with Big Foot Wallace while nearly starving on the plains.

Byrd Smith, an old Texan near Devine, was born in Gonzales County in 1845. One of his ancestors, after whom he was named, was a soldier under General Jackson in the Indian wars and fought in the command of General Cocke. Just before one battle he told General Cocke that he would be killed in the fight, and while it was raging came up to the side of the general and was killed by a rifle ball in the forehead. After the war General Cocke named one of his sons Byrd Smith Cocke.

Y. P. OUTLAW.

Came to Texas in 1848.

In the summer of 1898, while the writer was hunting for old settlers in the vicinity of Moore's station, between Pearsall and Devine, he was fortunate enough to find an old friend from Guadalupe County, Mr. Y. P. Outlaw, who lives near Moore, with whom a most agreeable night was spent, as he is an old Texan and has many interesting things to relate. He was born in Manuel County, Georgia, in 1817. and when quite young served against the Creek Indians, in which he experienced a great deal of hard service during the bloody war with this fierce tribe. He was in many battles with small bands, but passed through them all without receiving a wound. In 1836 he entered the service in the war with the Seminoles in Florida, and carried arms for the troops from middle Georgia to where the army was operating in the Everglades. This service lasted until 1837 and was marked with many hardships for the soldiers in that swampy and brush-covered country.

In 1848 Mr. Outlaw came to Guadalupe County, Texas, and settled near Seguin and successfully farmed and raised fruit for many years.

When the Civil war broke out he served the Confederacy in the regiment of Colonel P. C. Wood, Company D, Capt. W. L. Foster. He was in the battles of Blair's Landing, Yellow Bayou, Marksville, and many others. At the battle of Blair's Landing he was near Gen. Tom Green when he was killed. They were in plain view of the Federal gunboats and in a very exposed position. General Green was anxious to make an attack, and remarked that he thought the gunboats had grounded. Colonel Majors, who was present, said: "No, that is a trick; they are only anchored." General Green said he would make the attack anyhow, if he got the top of his head shot off. The charge was made all along the bayou. and General Green rode his horse close to the gunboats under a terrific fire and dismounted, holding his bridle on one arm. Many of the men by this time were being hit by the rifle fire and grapeshot from the boats, and one of the latter struck General Green on top of the head and he fell to the ground. Mr. Outlaw was so near that blood flew all over him, but he at once went to the prostrate general, and with the assistance of Nathan Busby and Schram tried to carry their slain commander off the field under a heavy fire. General Green kicked a good deal while they were trying to carry him away. Mr. Outlaw received several severe kicks from him. The grape shot which struck the general carried off the top of the skull, exposing the brain, but without breaking the membrane that inclosed it. The fire became so severe that the brave men were compelled to abandon their commander for the time being and seek shelter in the brush and cane further back. Busby caught the general's horse and mounted him, and Mr. Outlaw got on behind him, and thus they left the field. The blood of the slain general remained on the clothing of Mr. Outlaw until it wore off. During this short time of attempting to carry off the body of General Green, Mr. Outlaw was wounded three times, but none of the wounds were severe, and two balls passed through his hat. Capt. Eugene Millett went back with a squad of men and succeeded in bringing off the body. In 1867 Mr. Outlaw married Mrs. Celes Little, widow of Mr. W. W. Little. The maiden name of Mrs. Little was Grinage, one of the old settlers of Guadalupe County.

In 1882 Mr. Outlaw moved from Guadalupe County and settled at Moore's station in Frio County. He has a nice home there and carries his eighty-three years well, and takes a lively interest in all of the main issues of the day.

MRS. NANCY KELLEY.

Came to Texas in 1850.

While we record the deeds of the heroes of the frontier and tell of their prowess in verse and prose, we must not forget our heroines. In following the tracks of the pioneers in later years when the country is no longer a frontier, we only see the signs which they have made. Here and there are decaying log cabins with a few acres around them which were once cultivated but now grown up in brush, and the picket or brush fence rotted down. Old roads are seen which were cut through the brakes; lone chimneys rudely built of rock standing like sentinels, the cabin gone, crumbled into dust, and many other things tell of their presence in the long ago and which mark the footsteps of the pioneers. Scattered through the country, and often in close proximity to these old ruins, stand nice ranch houses, strong pasture fences, schoolhouses, churches, and farms. Where are the pioneers,—the first white settlers of this fair land? We ask ourselves this question as we gaze around. How did they live and die; where and when and under what circumstances? What were their names and where did they come from? Perchance we ask a man who lives here now and has for many years, and he willingly gives us all of the information that he is possessed of. He might tell you that the man who built that cabin which is now crumbling to decay was killed by the Indians—went out one morning to get his horse or oxen, and not coming back search was made and his body found full of arrows and scalped. He is buried in that grave over there. "Come and I will show you his grave." Almost covered by weeds and briars we see a sunken mound; a rude stone marks the head, and by pulling the shrubbery back can make out the date of his death some thirty, forty, or fifty years ago. Some of the first settlers moved on when crowded, as they called it, and no one here knows what became of them. Some met death in violent ways, and some naturally. Many stopped in the country and settled permanently and now live in good houses near the old cabins where they unloaded their wagons under the trees fifty years ago and made their first rude shelters. Many of these places and graves were shown to the writer while traveling over the counties of the southwest.

During all of these exciting frontier times frail women were there and nobly did their part in the desperate struggle for the mastery in the west. While nearly every State in the Union has had experience with Indians in settling up the country, none has equaled Texas in combats with the savages. Kentucky, the "dark and bloody ground," can not compare with the Lone Star State in the number of her battles with Indians. Boone, Kenton, and Logan with their men fought some bloody and most sanguinary battles, such as "Blue Lick" and Point Pleasant, but Texas fought four to their one. One reason of this was the extent of the Texas frontier—600 miles across—and the numerous tribes of Indians which infested the border and roamed across the vast plains,—Comanches, Apaches, Lipans, Kickapoos, Cheyennes and others, besides Mexicans, who for years invaded Texas with large armies.

Among the pioneer women of Southwest Texas who deserve a chapter in the history of early settlers is Mrs. Nancy Kelley, wife of Mr. Chris. Kelley, an early settler of Uvalde County, who died some years ago. Mrs. Nancy Kelley was the daughter of Milton Williams and was born in Perry County, Illinois, in 1833. Her grandfather, Robert Williams, was a soldier under General Washington and took an active part in the War of the Revolution.

When quite young Mrs. Kelley came to Arkansas and was married there to Mr. L. C. Kelley in 1847, in White County, near Siercy. She came to Texas in 1850 and lived two years in Kaufman County, and then in 1852 moved to Sabinal Canyon, Uvalde County. Mr. Kelley built his house in a beautiful and romantic valley on the west prong of the Sabinal River, now called the Anglin prong after Mr. Aaron Anglin, another early settler, now deceased. This house was near the present ranch of Mr. Sam Harper. Here they lived in peace and quiet for more than a year before any trouble with Indians was experienced. It was not long, however, before these painted and feathered nomads discovered the new settlement in the mountains, and then the trouble commenced.

To the question asked by the writer if she had ever seen an

Indian, Mrs. Kelley said: "Oh, yes, and heard them yell, too." When the Indians commenced raiding they killed and carried off Mr. Kelley's horses and cattle, and it was very dangerous to hunt stock or even do the work about the house away from shelter. Mrs. Kelley often went with her husband to the field and held her baby and his gun while he pulled fodder or did other work.

On one occasion Mr. Kelley and other settlers followed the Indians, and the women and children of the settlement congregated and all stayed at one place until the return of the men. Some of the women were timid and fearful, but Mrs. Kelley was calm and serene, telling the others to trust in a higher power and all would be well. The Indians often came near Mr. Kelley's house, and one one occasion went through his field.

Mr. Kelley finally concluded to go to California with his stock, and moved his family to Uvalde for safety. Uvalde was a small place then, just starting, but had the protection to some extent of soldiers and sometimes rangers who were stationed at Fort Inge, three miles below.

In the winter Mrs. Kelley went back to the canyon, forty miles distant, to kill her hogs, which had been left on the range at the ranch, but before arriving there had a narrow escape from Indians. Her party consisted of her two boys, Robert and Joseph, and three smaller children. George Spencer and Jesse O'Bryant, two young lads, were mounted on horses, and Mrs. Thompson, who lived in the canyon, was in the wagon with Mrs. Kelley and the children. The wagon was drawn by two horses. When near Nolton Creek in the Uvalde prairie they came upon a fresh trail of Indians going west. Mrs. Kelley was traveling northeast. A mounted Indian spy was now discovered on a hill, watching the wagon. He had one led horse, which he tied and then came towards the wagon as if about to make an attack upon it. A less courageous woman than Mrs. Kelley would likely have turned back and been pursued by the Indian, whose yells would have brought others, and the whole party would have been massacred. She, however, put on a bold front and resorted to a frontier strategy in order to fool the Indian, who was too far off to make out exactly what they were doing. She told her two boys, Robert and Joseph, to get out of the wagon and get a stick each, and then mount the horses hitched to the wagon and put the sticks on their shoulders. The two other boys, Spencer and O'Bryant, were told to tie their lariats to the tongue of the wagon in front of the other horses, and then to proceed at a fast gait along the road. The Indian had stopped and was watching all of these proceedings, and no doubt was under the impression that the sticks were guns which had been taken out of the wagon and that there were four men ready to fight. He came no nearer and the party made their trip in safety.

Mr. Kelley stayed two years in California with his cattle, and Mrs. Kelley managed as best she could under the circumstances, aided by her boys, and they had many experiences with Indians. She moved to Frio Canyon to get the benefit of a school there, and had another frontier experience while making the journey. She saw some white men over a hill with a wagon, and not being able to see them distinctly thought they were Indians, as they were out of the wagon, moving about loading wood, and she could only see their heads. Not wishing to turn back she again resorted to strategy. There was one man along whose daughter was in the wagon going over to attend the school, and the girls all had new hats but did not have them on, but were now requested to put them on and sit up straight so they could be seen good. Her two boys were in the wagon with hats on, and the man on horseback rode up where he could be seen, and altogether they presented a rather formidable appearance. Five men at least, it seemed, and they now awaited developments. The other party soon discovered them and the identity of each was soon realized, and they made the trip without further incident. The children in the wagon were very much frightened, but Mrs. Kelley told them to trust the Lord and all would be right.

When Mr. Kelley came back from California he made a trip with his family to Sabinal Canyon, but camped on the way at a place called the Blue waterhole. That night the Indians got his horses and he had to leave his family there in the mountains near a cedarbrake in dangerous proximity to the Indians, and go on foot to the settlement ten miles above to get a team to bring his wagon and family on.

Mr. Kelley afterwards settled at this place, and one morning he mounted his horse and went to look for his oxen. Not finding them at the place expected he kept on around the foot of the mountains until coming to the mouth of Blanco Canyon, he turned up that. He soon discovered where some horses had passed along, but thought they were ridden by cowmen, who he knew intended to camp over there. The men, however, had not as yet arrived, and the trail he saw was made by a band of Indians who had come over from the Guadalupe valley and were at this time encamped on a mountain overlooking the valley. This place is now called Lone Tree Mountain, and John Davenport has a ranch at its base.

The Indians had two captives, a little white girl 8 years of age and a negro boy about 12. One Indian came down the mountain to get water and saw Mr. Kelley coming, and at once gave a peculiar howl to inform the others of the fact. Mr. Kelley heard this, but thought it was a wolf. The negro boy afterwards said that as soon as the other Indians heard this howl they grabbed their guns, seven of them, and went down the mountain to where the one was who gave the signal. It was Mr. Kelley's intention to go to a spring he knew of and get a drink of water, and that was where he was making for when the Indians came down, and placed seven of their men near the spring in ambush and awaited him, while the eighth was stationed close to the trail beyond to get him if the others failed. Mr. Kelley changed his mind and kept on by the spring on the high ground, thinking he would soon come to the camp of the cowmen and get water there without dismounting and having to go into the ravine after it. As soon as the Indians discovered by the noise of the horse's feet that the white man had passed the spring they went up on the bank and all aimed their guns at him and fired, he being only thirty steps away with his back towards them. Not a ball touched him, and he thought it was the cowmen firing to scare him, which it did, coming so sudden and close, and he turned his head towards them quickly and exclaimed, "What in the hell are you doing?" In making this quick move his hat fell off, and at the same moment he made the discovery that it was Indians, and at once put the quirt to his horse and dashed up the trail, but ran upon the Indian who had been placed there to kill him and had his gun up ready to shoot.

Mr. Kelley had pulled his Winchester from the scabbard, but the Indian was on the wrong side to shoot him easy and he had to bring his gun around with a swing, and as he did so, fired, and the Indian did the same, but both missed. When Mr. Kelley again looked ahead his horse was about to run under a low limb with him, and he was compelled to abandon the horse to keep from being knocked off. He now turned towards the mountain on the east side of the creek on foot and succeeded in eluding the Indians in the thick brush and rocks, and made his way on up the mountain towards home. The balance of the Indians came on the scene, and he heard them yell loudly when they caught his horse, thinking he was near by badly wounded or killed. The first fire the Indians made at him at the spring the balls cut the limbs and twigs all around him. He had killed a deer and had the hams and hide tied to the saddle. On the way up the mountain Mr. Kelley began to suffer very much with thirst and stopped in the head of a little gorge and raked up snow and ate it to quench the thirst. There had been quite a snowfall a few days before, and there was still some in the gorges where it was protected from the sun. While here, looking to the west across the valley, he saw the Indians on the mountain beyond, packing up to leave camp. He thought there were eleven Indians and some pack horses. What he took to be packs on some of the horses were the captives, no doubt. Mr. Kelley was very much exhausted, but after resting and quenching his thirst his strength returned and he succeeded in getting home about sundown. Mrs. Kelley was expecting him back at dinner time, not knowing he had extended his ox hunt over into the Little Blanco country, and when he failed to arrive at the time expected the children began to express their fears as to his safety. Mrs. Kelley felt distressed but prayed all evening for his deliverance. Mr. George Dillard, his future son-in-law, was at his house when he returned, and saw Mr. Kelley before he got to the house. Being on foot and his hat gone, Mr. Dillard knew something was wrong, and said to Mrs. Kelley: "Here comes your old man and the Indians have been after him." She ran to meet him and could hardly be convinced that he was not wounded as he was very tired and was bracing one hip with his hand as he walked.

Next morning Mr. Kelley and Mr. Dillard went back to the scene of the ambuscade and found the deer hams where they fell from the saddle, but of course the horse and hat were gone. The distance where Mr. Kelley and the Indian exchanged shots when he abandoned his horse was found to be ten steps. The account of the fight which the Frio men had with these Indians, in which they recovered the captives and Mr. Kelley's horse and hat and gun scabbard, has been given elsewhere.

At one time Mr. Kelley owned a very fine horse, which he kept for his own use, and which was very fast and long winded. He loaned this horse, however, on one occasion to a man who lived on the Medina to ride home, and he started the horse back in the care of two boys, or young men, named Alf and James Watson. They camped on the road, and that night the Indians stole all of their horses and the young men had to walk to Sabinal Canyon. Mr. Kelley was very much distressed at the loss of his favorite horse, and at once raised a squad of men and went in pursuit of the Indians, who went west. The trail was closely followed, and in the Frio Canyon the settlers came upon the body of Young Henry Robinson, whom the Indians had just killed. They caught up with Indians, who had stopped and dismounted, but at the sight of the white men they again mounted and made off. The chief was mounted on Mr. Kelley's horse, but was thrown as soon as they started, but he held on to him and mounted again, and this time stayed with him and made his escape. Mr. Kelley ran after him for some distance, but knew it was hopeless, for he was familiar with the speed of both horses. The Indian actually played along ahead of them, out of gun shot, and made the horse prance, and would sometimes turn him around in a circle. He had on a fine bridle, with silver ornaments, which would glisten in the sun very brightly when making the turns. The men finally gave up the chase and came back home.

In 1880 Mrs. Kelley lost her eyesight and has been hopelessly blind ever since. Mr. Kelley died in 1888.

Mrs. Kelley was the mother of twelve children, four of whom died in infancy. The oldest of those alive (Sarah) married Mr. George Dillard. Joseph married Miss Ida Crank. Robert is unmarried and lives with his mother. Emma married Mr. John Davenport and lives on Little Blanco, near the spot where her father made such a narrow escape from the Indians. Zeno was killed by a horse falling on him. He had been married six months. Edward married Miss Lela Martin, daughter of Judge William Martin, of Kerrville. Florence married Mr. Henry McBride, merchant of Sabinal. Albert is unmarried.

Mrs. Kelley is a member of the Christian church and bears her affliction with calm patience and has a kind word and gentle greeting for all with whom she comes in contact. She has great faith in the Lord and looks earnestly to the time when somewhere in the great heavenly kingdom of God she will see the Savior whom she has trusted all her life.

MRS. MAHALA JONES.

Came to Texas in 1850.

Mrs. Mahala Jones, one of the early pioneers of Bandera County, was born in Granger County, Tennessee, in 1825, and came to Texas from Missouri in 1850. Her grandfather, Joseph Yaden, was a revolutionary soldier and was present at the battle of Bunker Hill as a drummer boy, and lustily beat his drum while the British troops were advancing to assault the American works. Mrs. Jones now lives at Indian Spring, on Myrtle Creek, six miles north of the town of Bandera, coming to this place in 1863 with her husband, John A. Jones. About three years after settling here, one day at noon, just as the family were sitting down to dinner, Mr. Tom Click dashed up to the yard fence and called for Mr. Jones. He was bare headed, and his horse was breathing heavily and panting. Mr. Jones thought that Mr. Click had been on a bear chase from all appearances, but soon discovered that he had been chased by Indians and was badly wounded. He was coming from the Guadalupe valley and was ambushed at the Bandera pass and had a desperate run for his life, leaving the main road and taking the road to Jones' ranch, three miles away. The Indians shot many arrows at him, one of which struck him in the back. One Indian came so close that he tried to catch the bridle, but the fleetness of the nag he rode eluded the grasp of the savage, and to this fact Mr. Click owed his life, as he was not armed. He pulled the arrow out of his back as he ran, and had it in one hand and a sycamore switch in the other when he arrived at the yard gate of Mr. Jones. During all of this long, exciting chase the dog kept close to his master, and was not hurt. After Mr. Click was assisted into the house he was unable to remain still on account of the great misery he was in, and walked the floor incessantly, and finally took a severe chill. He called for a pipe to smoke, but when it was prepared for him was deathly sick and unable to smoke it. A negro was placed on Mr. Click's horse and sent to Bandera after Dr. Fitz Gibbons. In the meantime Mrs. Jones with a pair of scissors clipped the shirt from around the wound, stopped the flow of blood, and put hartshorn on it. Mr.

Click was not frightened and remembered everything distinctly in regard to the chase, and said that a hackberry limb had torn a piece out of his shirt, and that there were twelve Indians. He also said that he could find the last arrow they shot at him, as he saw where it struck in a bunch of bushes, a little to one side and ahead of him. All this was found to be the case afterwards, the bit of shirt on the hackberry limb and the arrow in the bunch of bushes. When the doctor came and made an examination of the wound it was discovered that Mr. Click had been wounded with a poisoned arrow, which was the direct cause of his intense suffering. The pain was like that which ensues after being bitten by a rattlesnake, for the spike was poisoned by venom from one of these most deadly reptiles. The doctor gave strychnine until the water in which he gave it was colored like milk, to counteract the poison. Mr. Click finally, after months of suffering, recovered, but a large piece of the flesh rotted out around the wound.

Soon after the Civil war Mr. Joseph Moore was living near where Medina City is now, and one Sunday he went visiting in a wagon drawn by a yoke of oxen, having his wife and four children with him. One of his children, a boy, had been left at a neighbor's house. In the evening, while returning and near home, Mr. Jones got out of the wagon in order to drive carefully down a steep hill into the bed of a deep ravine or small creek. A band of Indians was lying in wait here, aware that some one was coming by the noise of the wagon coming over the rocks. The first intimation that Mr. Jones had of the presence of the Indians was the exclamation from one of his little girls, "Papa! Papa! There is some men!" The Indians had just raised up from their concealment near the wagon, and one of them aimed a gun quickly and fired, and gave Mr. Jones a fatal wound. The stricken father attempted to get back into the wagon, but was not able to do so, and after holding onto the wagonbed a few moments sank down and died. The Indians now fired again and killed Mrs. Moore, who was in the wagon with the children. One Indian then got into the wagon and began to lance the terror-stricken and screaming littles ones. One little boy jumped out and succeeded in making his escape to the house of John Walker. The other three children left in the wagon were all wounded, but none of them died. One little girl had the baby in her lap and displayed great presence of mind and courage. Instead of throwing the child down and trying to make her own escape she held on to it and jerked it first one way and then the other to keep the Indian from getting his lance through it, which he would have done but for her quick movements of the child when he would make his thrusts, and it only received glancing wounds. One circumstance, however, which saved the lives of the children finally was the fact that during this time the oxen were running away with the wagon towards Mr. Walker's house, and when nearing that place the Indian jumped out and ran back.

One of Mr. Moore's boys, the one who had been left at Mr. Walker's, was in the cowpen at the time, helping to milk, and when he heard the guns remarked: "I expect that is Indians killing papa and mamma." As soon as the situation was known Mr. Walker armed himself and went to the place of the killing, but the Indians were gone. The bodies of the dead pioneers were buried, and Mr. Walker took the orphan children to his house and cared for them.

A brother of Mrs. Moore lived at Boerne, in Kendall County, and he came and carried the wounded children to his home as soon as they were able to travel. On the way back the uncle camped for noon with the children near Mrs. Jones' house, and she carried some milk to them. She tried to get him to come to the house with them and eat dinner there, but he said they had plenty to eat and that he only wanted milk for them. The children looked pale and thin.

Not long after the Indians killed Mr. Moore and his wife they made another raid and killed his mother. The old lady was going to see Mrs. Curtis, who was sick, and she was killed near the house of Mr. Walker. Mr. Walker armed himself when he heard her screaming, and ran to the spot, but the Indians were gone and Mrs. Moore was lying on her face, lanced to death.

On another occasion, above where Medina City is now, about where the Crockett place is, Mr. Joe Sheppard was riding along alone, and was shot by an Indian with a gun, who was hiding behind a big cypress stump. Sheppard saw the Indian just before he fired and thought it was a bear. When the ball struck him he sprang from his horse and ran behind a drift near the river and waited with his gun ready to shoot, not knowing how many Indians there were, and supposing they would follow him. No Indians came, however, but soon a man named John Henning came upon the scene in a wagon and helped Sheppard to get into it and lie down. The ball hit him in the side, and he was badly hurt. Henning carried him to a doctor called the French doctor by the people, but he could not find the ball and said it must have dropped out while jolting in the wagon, or else dropped inside of him, as he was unable to find it. After a hard struggle Sheppard recovered.

In 1867 the Indians made another raid into Bandera County and were followed with a small squad of men by Capt. Bob Valentine. One of the trailers in this chase was Andy Jones, son of Mrs. Mahala Jones. During the time that Captain Valentine and his men were on the trail of the Indians John Scott and one of his boys were at work in the field, and the Indians were just preparing to kill them when the trailers came upon them and they rapidly stampeded, leaving some of their paint sacks and one horse. These same Indians got together again and killed a Mexican on Pipe Creek. The scouts kept after them and found the body of the Mexican. He was at work on a fence, and when shot ran and took refuge in an old chimney, which was standing alone where a cabin had stood, and there squatting down presented his pistol and died in that position. The Indians, not knowing he was killed, did not assault his position and went on, but Captain Valentine could never bring them to battle, and finally had to abandon the chase.

Mrs. Jones has a fine ranch and a good deal of stock and lives with her brother, Mr. Capps, and some of her children, her husband having died some years ago. The brother, Mr. Delaney Capps, has no family. He came to Texas in 1850, and in 1851 cut hay near Seguin, Guadalupe County. The first work he did in Texas was for Gen. Ed Burleson. He put up a house for his son-in-law, Felix Kyle, at Sink Springs. He knew Gen. Sam Houston and heard him make two speeches. During the Civil war he served the Confederacy under Gen. H. E. McCulloch. He also knew Capt. Jesse Billingsly and heard him say that when he was a member of the Legislature he furnished his own grub, slept on his own blanket, and wore a buckskin suit that he took from a Comanche Indian whom he killed in a battle.

L. C. DAVENPORT.

Mr. L. C. Davenport (Clabe) came to Texas at an early day from Missouri, and in 1853 settled in Sabinal Canyon, Uvalde County. In 1856 he lived on Ranchero Creek, when the Indians made the raid, in which they killed his half brother, John Davenport, and also John Bowles. At the time of this raid Mr. Clabe Davenport was at work on the ranch of Dr. Isbell, which was situated on the Frio at the foot of the mountains. This ranch is now called the Annadale, and is owned by Judge Florea. The Indians came near this ranch and were followed by Mr. Davenport and three others, one of whom was Frank Isbell. The trail was followed south down Blanco Creek, through the prairie to the Eagle Pass crossing, on the main road from San Antonio to Mexico, and then it turned towards the Patterson settlement on the Sabinal. The settlers continued to follow, and during the day learned from other settlers who had discovered the presence of the Indians and were gathering, that they had killed John Bowles near Pilot Knob, and John Davenport six miles north towards the mountains. The scout now went to where Davenport was killed, and getting more men took up the trail of the Indians, which led back in a northwest course. Some citizens from Uvalde and soldiers from Fort Inge joined them the next day. Among the citizens from Uvalde were James McCormick, Doke Bowles, Ben Pulliam, and others. The Indians made several halts and had a wounded one with them evidently, from the bloody rags which were found where they dressed his wounds. They also found where grass had been pulled for this one to lay on. It was also supposed that the Indian died in camp, but his body could not be found. They could smell it, but it was in a cave or under rocks, and not a great deal of time was spent in searching for it.

The Indians were overtaken in a hilly country, near the head of North Llano. The men were badly scattered and could only ride in single file on account of the nature of the country. Word was passed back to the rear that the Indians were in front and to keep still. The Indians, however, soon discovered the white men and commenced hastily leaving their camp, two of them mounting on one horse. A charge was ordered, and shooting soon commenced. In the pursuit the Indian who rode behind the other one on the same horse was killed and fell off into a ravine. At this time Ben Pulliam, Clabe Davenport, and two others were in front. Pulliam dashed into the ravine and was shot by the wounded Indian, who was not yet dead, but had a mortal wound. The arrow struck Pulliam in the back as he passed the Indian. The Comanches did not remain together and many shots were fired in the long running fight. One Indian did splendid riding and shooting. He shot Lieutenant Hazen from his horse and also a man named Williams, and got his horse, which he was riding the last seen of him. Mr. Davenport got some close shots and thinks he hit several Indians. Three Indians were killed and all of the balance wounded, and among the killed was the one who had John Davenport's pistol. Another one of the dead Indians had John Bowles' scalp. It had been stretched around a hoop made of a switch and nicely dressed. The scalp of Davenport could not be found and was no doubt carried away by one of those who made their escape. The Indians killed had been hit many times.

After the chase was over the men went into camp and stayed several days with the wounded men, and a messenger was sent to Brackett for surgical aid. Some of them came on with Ben Pullium, but when they arrived at the head of the Frio River he requested the men to stop and make an examination of his wound, as it was paining him very much and something was wrong with it. On examination it was found that the spike had struck the backbone and twisted around it like a fishhook. He had pulled the arrow out himself when it struck him and threw it down, but the spike remained, hence the trouble. He was now placed on his stomach on the ground, the wound pressed open until the spike was revealed, and then a man with a pair of bullet moulds caught it and pulled it out. The wounded man suffered excruciating pain, but it had to be done. Mr. Davenport also thinks a man named Everette was wounded.

On another occasion the Indians made a raid and stole about fifty head of horses belonging to Dr. Isbell and drove them along the divide between the Frio and Sabinal, the roughest place they could find, and many colts were killed by having to jump down bluffs and steep rocky places. Mr. Davenport and other citizens and a few soldiers from Inge followed them to the head of the rivers and overtook them on the divide in an open postoak country with small cedarbrakes interspersed. The Indians ran, but were pursued so closely they dismounted and made breastworks of their horses, and the fight commenced. There was a good deal of shooting done, and two horses were soon killed. The Indians had large guns of some kind, and one of them was aimed at Mr. Davenport and fired, but the ball struck the ground at his feet and went skipping and bouncing beyond him. The Indians, seeing the whites about to surround them, once more ran and made another stand in a small cedarbrake. The white men now dismounted and commenced shooting into the brake, and the Indians saw their only chance was to charge, which they did, coming close to the white men, and a hard fight ensued. One Indian especially was very brave and was hit many times, and finally couched down on his knees, and a soldier, taking good aim at him, shot him through the head. Mr. Davenport was so close to him he saw the smoke from the hot brains as they flew out of the top of his head. The Indians now ran back into the brake and went on through in a desperate attempt to escape. The men followed and fought them for several miles. John Leakey followed one and shot at him many times, and got close enough to him once to strike at him with his gun, but could not bring him from his horse. It was now nearly night, and the Indian getting into the cedarbrake, Leakey left him and went back. One Indian turned on a man, who dismounted and aiming his gun fired, but missed, and the Comanche crowded him so close he left the horse, not having time to mount, and the Indian mounted him himself and rode away, carrying a pistol, overcoat, and other things which were on the saddle. The stolen horses were all retaken except a few and carried back to the ranch. Years after the skeleton of an Indian and a horse were found under a tree near where Leakey left his wounded Indian. It is supposed the Indian, when clear of his pursuer, dismounted and tying his horse to the tree lay down and died and his horse starved to death.

On one occasion in 1862, when Mr. Davenport was living on Ranchero Creek, he and Ambrose Crane went out towards the Comanche waterhole to look for some horses and came upon the trail of a shod horse, and wishing to ascertain who it was, went on the trail at a gallop and found that it was John Ware coming back home from the war on a furlough. Crane went home from there, but Davenport went on towards the waterhole, although his horse was well jaded by the long gallop. Arriving at the place he ascended a hill to see if he could discover the horses he was looking for, and saw six men coming around the brush towards the water, driving some horses, but they stayed partly in the brush so that he could not make out who they were until they came close, and he then perceived that they were Indians, and they charged him. A desperate race now commenced, and Davenport had to make a circle to get home, as the Indians were coming from that direction. He ran over one hill and then made for another which had brush and liveoak on it, and which was about half a mile away. In making the run across the flat between the two hills he passed through a bunch of sheep and looked for the herder, thinking he would make a stand with him and fight them, but not being able to see him anywhere he kept on to the hill, which he ascended, and then stopped as his horse was nearly run down, being tired when the chase commenced. While halted here he heard a terrible yelling among the Indians and knew they were killing the herder, whose name was Shockhouse, and was a brother-in-law of Captain Richarz of D'Hanis, who owned the herd of sheep. Mr. Davenport, being uneasy about his family at home, six miles away, again ran. When he arrived at home he found his people all right, but he had killed his horse, the faithful animal dying soon after the saddle was pulled off. Next morning Mr. Davenport went back and met some men, who told him that Shockhouse was killed. There was a little house at the sheep camp, and two of Captain Richarz's children were at it at the time, but their uncle not coming back they went to D'Hanis in the night, five miles distant, and informed their father.

When the Indian raid was made in which Wolf and Huffman was killed, Mr. Davenport was in the cowpen milking, and heard Indians yelling at Ross Kennedy's ranch, and at once went to the house and told the family that the Indians were killing some one at Kennedy's ranch. The ranchman himself soon came and said the Indians had run his Mexican herder to the house and killed him. Men were raised and the pursuit commenced, Mr. Davenport being one of the number. The Indians were heard of on the Sabinal, and some more men being raised the pursuit was continued, and on the river not far from the present home of Mrs. Nancy Kelley a gray horse was found shot in the hip with an arrow. The trail was here scattered a good deal, showing a fight had occurred, and soon a dead Indian was found under a tree with his shield, bow, and quiver hanging near him. Not knowing who had the fight, the party went on and came upon the Indians camped in the edge of a cedarbrake on the Big Blanco. They had killed a muley cow, and setting a brush pile on fire were cooking the meat while their horses stood tied near by. When they saw the white men close upon them they ran and left their horses. Mr. Davenport had a good shot at two Indians running close together, but was prevented from shooting by General Knox, who said: "Let the Indians go and save the horses." He had charge of a train, and his mules being stolen, thought these were the ones and wanted to save them. The horses and saddles of the Indians were all captured, and the men went back home that night, arriving there when it was nearly day. Next morning they went back and found the bodies of Huffman and Wolf near where they saw the dead Indian in the tree. The two white men had made a stand at a liveoak tree which was full of arrows, but had run from there and were killed in the flat one hundred yards away. The Indian was also killed there, for the blood was on the ground where he fell, and also the sign where the other Indians had dragged him to the tree.

Mr. Davenport had lost many head of stock from Indian raids, but still has plenty and lives on a fine ranch at the mouth of Dry Frio Canyon.

His son Sidney also had a narrow escape from Indians when a small boy. He had been sent down the road to notify the people of an Indian raid, and the Indians crossed the road just ahead of him, and his horse reared and wanted to run back when he smelled the trail across the road.

Mrs. Della Davenport, wife of Sidney, is the daughter of Mr. Joe Kelley, of Sabinal Canyon, and has been raised on the frontier. She can remember seeing the Indians running off their horses and her father getting on his horse with his gun and following the Indians to get his horses back.

SECO SMITH.

Came to Texas in 1856.

There is no name along the Texas border, comprising the counties of Uvalde, Medina, Bandera, and others, that is better known than that of Seco Smith. While not in as many Indian battles as some others, he was a splendid scout and trailer and knew all of the country for hundreds of miles around. He could lead a band of frontiersmen through all of the dense brakes and dangerous defiles in the mountains, and was never at fault as to his bearings. He was strong and wiry, of a jovial disposition, and had many friends, even among the police of San Antonio, although he handled them very rough at times when they interfered in his little games of sport when on a trip with the boys down there. He would yell when the spirit moved him, and no two of them could carry him to the calaboose. They finally got so that when they heard his warwhoop they would smile and say "That is Seco Smith; he won't do any harm if they will let him alone."

W. D. Smith (Seco) was born in Mississippi in Copiah County, October 24, 1836. In 1849 he took a trip to California by way of Salt Lake City, Utah, arriving there in 1850. He stayed there six months and then came overland to Texas by way of El Paso, Fort Thorn, and Quitman, and arrived in San Antonio, June 26, 1856. They had no trouble with the Indians on the trip until near Fort Davis, and there one night the Indians stampeded the horses and ran them over the guards, but the men followed and rounded them up in a cove and put out guards again, and held them there until morning, so the Indians failed to get any of them. Seco was one of the guards, and before day was certain he saw an Indian. He leveled his gun and fired, but it proved to be a Spanish dagger. His aim, however, was good, and he put a hole through it, as daylight revealed.

From San Antonio he moved out to Olmos Creek, six miles from town, and commenced ranching. The Indians, however, soon found him out here and stole all of his mules and horses. A crowd of men were gathered to follow them, among whom were John Jones, Henderson McCoy, Grant Bennett, Dave Bennett, Jim Bennett, Amos Jones, Robert M. Smith (father of Seco), and Oliver Bacon. The Indian trail led out towards the head of the Cibolo, and thither it was followed by the trailers, and when arriving at the head of the creek the trail led directly through a large patch of wild plums, and it being in season for them the fruit almost covered the ground where the ripe ones had fallen off. Here a rather strange thing happened, somewhat out of the ordinary. The trail of the Indians was lost on account of bear tracks. It seems that all of the bear in the country had been there after the Indians passed, eating plums, and completely obliterated the trail, and the settlers turned back after a fruitless effort to locate it again.

In 1859 Seco moved further west and settled on Seco Creek, and hence his familiar nickname. Stock-raising was the main pursuit, from a financial standpoint, of the settlers, and many cow hunts and Indian scouts were participated in by Mr. Smith.

On one occasion, while out on a cow hunt, George Redus won thirty yearlings from Lon Moore shooting with a pistol. Seco then bantered Redus to shoot with him for yearlings, and the challenge being accepted, he won all of the yearlings back and returned them to his friend and boon companion, Moore.

In 1862 Mr. Smith joined the Confederate army and served in the Louisiana campaign against General Banks, and was in many battles and skirmishes. The hottest place was in the fight at Cheneyville, where they fought in a lane almost hand to hand, and fought with revolvers, both Federals and Confederates.

In 1866, while Seco and John Elam were building a house at some stockpens on Seco Creek, old man Miller, father of Jack Miller, a well known settler, came down there with provisions for his son Jack and other hands, who were engaged in branding cattle. Mr. Charles Richter started to go back home with the elder Miller, but in a short time they came running back and said the Indians were up the creek with a large drove of horses. The men at the pens mounted their horses in hot haste and went after them, the party being composed of George Johnson, Ambrose Crane, Seco Smith, Isaac Elam, Charles Richter, and William Fritz. The Indians were soon overtaken and found to have forty head of horses belonging to Judge George Harper, who lived on the Hondo. The Indians scattered, as was supposed, for a great dust arose and objects could not be seen very plainly. Seco Smith says that he did not see but one Indian and took after him. Others said they saw another one, but he fled at great speed when the charge was made. Seco soon ran close to the Indian he was after, who was poorly mounted on a mare belonging to Judge Harper. During the chase the Indian ran into a thicket and Seco closely followed, shooting at him with a revolver. When the Indian got through the thicket he dismounted and crawled on all fours to a mott of liveoak timber. By this time Smith had fired eleven shots at him and the other men were also shooting and made quick work of the lone warrior. Seco wounded him the first few shots in the arm and he dropped his bow, not being able to shoot it, and threw rocks at Seco. After he was dead an examination of the body was made, and five bullet wounds were discovered in the back and one in the arm. He was a very fine, stout looking Indian, and appeared to be about forty-five years of age. During these troublesome times a family named Long lived on Blanco Creek, east of the Frio, and the Indians made a raid in that vicinity, and killed Sam Long, who was out herding cattle. One of his sisters who had been to a neighbor's house that day was seen by the same Indians as she was returning home and they galloped around her in a circle and one of them taking her by the hair pulled her from her horse, at the same time pulling a good deal of her hair out. They now lanced and scalped the unfortunate girl and left her for dead on the prairie. Life, however, was not extinct, and she was found and conveyed home, and by careful attention recovered and afterwards married Seco Smith. She died a number of years ago, leaving a family of several children. Seco Smith still survives and lives at Medina City, in Bandera County.

JACOB HABY.

Came to Texas in 1844.

Mr. Jacob Haby, who now lives on the Medina River above Castroville, is one of the old pioneers of southwest Texas and one of those large connection of Habys who made a record as brave men and Indian fighters on the frontier. He was born in Alsace on the 16th of October, 1833, and started to Texas with his parents the 19th of March, 1844. Of his family on the ship was his father, Jacob Haby, one brother, Louis, a sister named Paris, and his mother. His mother was a Kempf, and some of the connections are still in Medina County. August Kempf is clerk of Medina County and lives at Hondo City, the county seat. One brother, Nichalus, had preceded the balance of the family to Texas. One other brother was named George. He served as a captain on the frontier.

The ship the Habys were on first landed at Galveston, but went from there to Port Lavaca and made the start for Castro's colony. They were one month on the road from the coast and arrived in San Antonio in July, but did not go on to the settlement of the present town of Castroville until October of 1844. They first settled in the town and stayed there four years and then moved up to what is now now called the Haby settlement, and where Jacob and others still reside.

The Lipans and Delaware Indians lived along the Medina River at that time and were friendly. The Comanches, he said, were not so good and would not come about the settlement much, remaining further west. On one occasion, however, a large body of them came close to town and the people were very uneasy. Capt. Jack Hays was in town, and he was informed of the proximity of the Comanches. Captain Hays at once mounted his horse and set out for San Antonio, distant twenty-five miles, where his company of rangers were stationed, and when daylight came next morning the people were surprised to see his men camped in the edge of town and their guards scattered around it. These tireless guardians of the frontier, on being notified by their captain of the danger to the settlement by the presence in the near vicinity of the Comanches, mounted their horses and sped away in the darkness, and while the inhabitants of the little village slept, silently placed their guards around them and watched and waited, ready to risk their lives in their defense.

No wonder that these old men of Castro's colony revere the name of Jack Hays and his rangers and never tire of sounding their praise. The Comanches no doubt had their spies out, and knowing the situation dared not attack the place while their dreaded foes, the rangers, who had so often defeated them, were there. Captain Hays said he believed the intention of the Indians was to burn Castroville and kill and drive the people away. Mr. Haby told the writer that Jack Hays was one of the best Indian fighters that was ever in the west, and that the people always felt safe when he was around. Haby and others were in the Bandera Pass in 1856 and saw many signs of the battle there fought by Hays and his men some years before. There were graves of rangers and bones of horses and Indians killed in the fight. He says that in a fight which Captain Hays and the rangers had with Indians, one Alsace man was killed who was a ranger under Hays. His name was Peter Fore and he was from Strasburg.

While Mr. Haby was in San Antonio in the summer of 1844 he saw two of Jack Hays' rangers who were badly wounded by Indians in a fight on the Nueces. He says they were both shot in the face and were under the doctor's care when he saw them; that they lay in a room back of the large mercantile establishment now run by Mr. L. Wolfson. No buildings, however, were there then except the small house in which the wounded rangers lay. He does not remember their names, but the writer will say that they were Kit Ackland and Rufe Perry.

Mr. Haby has not been in any Indian fights, but saw four men once who had been killed by Indians, the account of which and the names are given in the sketch of Mr. Nichalus Haby.

Mr. Jacob Haby did not travel about the country much, but stayed at home and helped his father work. His father died in 1853. One night when all of the Indians had become hostile and left the country a band of them came back on a raid, and first struck the Haby settlement above town. The alarm was given and all kept a sharp lookout that night for their horses.

Mr. Haby chained his horse close in front of his open door and lay on a bed where he could watch the horse, with a new six-shooter in his hand. The moon was full and shining brightly. Late in the night the horse became uneasy, snorted, reared, plunged, and stood on his hind feet. Mr. Haby knew an Indian was near, and expected every moment to see him approach the horse, when he was sure he could kill him. While intently watching he saw a curious thing close to the door facing, and at first could not imagine what it was, but as it came a little further into view and grew larger and more distinct he discovered that it was the feathered end of a quiver of arrows on an Indian's back. The Indian was inching slowly so as to get one eye around the door facing and see if Mr. Haby was asleep, being afraid to approach the horse until assured of that fact. The wide awake settler at once cocked the pistol to shoot him, but the new weapon clicked loudly and the Indian vanished like a ghost and nothing more was seen of him. Mr. Haby said he made a mistake in not having the pistol ready to fire, and could then have got him. The writer was shown the old cabin near Mr. Haby's more substantial residence where this occurred.

HENRY SHANE.

Came to Texas in the 40's.

Six miles south of Sabinal station, on the east bank of the Sabinal River, lives Henry J. Shane, one of the old pioneers and Indian fighters of Uvalde County.

Mr. Shane was born in Berlin, Germany, in 1836, and came to America with his mother and other members of the family in the late forties. They first landed in New York City. The father had preceded them and sent back for the family. They stayed some time in New York, not knowing where the elder Shane was, as he had gone from there to Texas. During this time he was with the American army in Mexico and knew not of the arrival of his family.

After the war with Mexico was over the family learned from returning soldiers that Mr. Shane was at Laredo, Texas, on the Rio Grande. Thither the family started by way of San Antonio, Texas, and joined him in 1850. He still belonged to the army, and his regiment was ordered to Arizona soon after the arrival of Mrs. Shane. The family now went back to San Antonio. From here Henry went back to Laredo and took a trip with Colonel Ruggles to El Paso as a soldier. Here he quit the command on account of a severe affliction of the knee, which rendered him unfit for the service. He then went to Fort Clark with David Vanderburg and hired to Major Baredon to take charge of a sheep camp. The major was quartermaster for the troops at the fort and also owned a sheep and goat ranch on Pinto Creek, twelve miles from the fort. To this place young Shane was sent to oversee the Mexicans there and to keep supplies, etc. Deer were plentiful, and being fond of hunting he killed a great many of them for use at the ranch. One day while out he killed a deer and laid his gun down to skin it without reloading. He was soon after surrounded by Indians who had been attracted to the spot by the report of his gun.

It was no use to make any resistance, and as they did not seem disposed to kill him, he surrendered. The first thing they did was to give him a severe whipping with a pair of hobbles.

They then placed him on a mule and started off briskly towards the northwest. They had not proceeded far, however, when they were joined by nine more Indians, making fifteen in all. They traveled all that day and part of the night and then stopped to rest and eat something. Here they whipped their captive again, but for what cause he could not tell, as he had given them no trouble whatever. For his repast they gave him a small piece of burnt meat with the hair on it. The Indians then lay down and rested until nearly morning, and then started again, moving rapidly until 9 o'clock in the forenoon, when they again halted to eat and rest.

In the meantime the Mexican herders had raised an alarm about the Indian raid. They heard Shane's gun when he killed the deer, and when he failed to put in an appearance at the expected time they went in search, finding the slain deer and the trail of the Indians. They knew he was killed or captured; the latter they supposed, as his body could not be found. News was at once carried to the fort, and a squad of soldiers was ordered out to follow the Indians, guided by "Old Roka," a Mexican who had been with the Indians many years and was a good guide and trailer. The camp of the hostiles was near a cedarbrake, and the soldiers came upon them while they were eating. The Mexican guide had taken advantage of the cedarbrake when the camp was discovered and led the soldiers upon them unawares. Shane was not aware of the presence of the soldiers until they were among them and firing.

The Indians, although taken by surprise, made a fight with the soldiers, and things were lively for a few minutes. Bullets and arrows were both flying, and Shane concluded he would run out of it into the cedarbrake near by. It is a custom with Indians when they have captives to kill them when attacked, so when Shane started an Indian shot at him with an arrow, which went through his arm and remained fixed there. After getting into the brake he stopped, and breaking the arrow below the spike so he could pull it out, threw it down and listened. The fight was still going on, the Indians yelling and the carbines in the hands of the soldiers still continuing to pop. Some of the Indians seemed to be trying to make their escape into the same brake where Shane was, and he continued his flight, intending now to make his way back to the fort without waiting for the soldiers.

He saw four Indians fall before he left the scene of the battle. He came to a creek, which he followed all of that day and saw many wild animals, tigers, bears, panthers and Mexican lions. When night came he was nearly exhausted and climbed into a tree to spend the night for fear of wild animals. He obtained some sleep by getting into the fork of a tree so that he could not easily fall out when he could no longer keep awake. When daylight came he resumed his journey and arrived at the fort that day. He was forty-eight hours without food except the little piece of burnt meat the Indians gave him. After the fight the soldiers looked for Shane, but not being able to find him, returned.

Mr. Shane remained here at this fort until the Civil war broke out, and then joined Captain Gibson's command, Company B of the Eighth Texas Cavalry, Col. Rip Ford's regiment. He was in several fights with the bands of Cortenas and had to guard the river all the time. At one ranch, about thirty miles above Brownsville, the troops had a sharp fight, and many of the Mexicans jumped off the bluff into the river and were drowned. Captain Dunn of the Confederate force was killed and several others were killed or wounded. The fight took place in a very brushy place and some of the men killed were not found. Mr. Shane was in the last battle of the war between the North and South. It commenced, as near as he can remember, near the old Palo Alto battleground and lasted all the way to the Federal ships, ten miles away. About 100 prisoners were taken, and among this number was a man called Paddy, who had been with Shane on the frontier, but had joined the Union forces when the war broke out. He recognized Shane when brought in a prisoner, and ran to shake hands with him, but was stopped by a soldier, who raised his gun to strike him. Shane now interfered and prevented him from getting hurt.

After the war Mr. Shane settled on the Chicon creek, thirty miles east from Eagle Pass and sixty miles west from Uvalde, at the foot of the Anna Catchi mountains. While living here on one occasion he started to the Cameo ranch, but on the way had to pass the San Miguel ranch. This was an old-time Mexican ranch with a rock wall all around it, with an entrance through a gate. When he arrived at this place he could see no one stirring and the gate was open. He dismounted and went in, but could see no signs of life except a little dog, which barked at him. On a smooth piece of sheet iron which lay upon two rocks were several cakes of bread which had not been turned and were burned on the under side, and the fire still burning under them. Shane thought there was something wrong, but as he could see no one, proceeded on his way. About 300 yards from the ranch he had to cross Sauce Creek, and here he found a dead Mexican. That he had been killed by Indians was evident, as the body was full of arrows, and near by was his horse, which had also been killed. It could be seen that the Mexican was trying to get to the ranch, pursued by the Indians, who first killed his horse and then killed him. When Shane got out of the Sauce bottom and up on a ridge he discovered a horse tied some distance off. By this time he had learned enough about Indians not to approach the horse, but went around him and continued his journey. Before he lost sight of the tied horse he saw an Indian near him and soon five others came into view and came in pursuit of Shane, but he was on a good horse and made his escape from them. He now came to a ranch where there was a crowd of excited Mexicans, some of whom were from the ranch where lay the dead Mexican. This man, they said, was away from the ranch when it was attacked, and they cut him off and killed him when he made a run to get inside the walls. After the Indians left these people also left and came to this ranch.

In 1866 Mr. Shane moved from the ranch on the Chicon and settled at the Presidio crossing of the Frio. Next year he moved up the Frio to the Adams ranch. In March of the next year he had a sheep camp half a mile from Adams, and there he had another experience with the Indians. There was no house of any kind at the camp, but the tent was surrounded by a brush fence. One night Shane was sitting with his back to this fence, parching coffee, and was not aware that the Indians were in the country, but at this time they were prowling around his camp, and even noticed his position while roasting the coffee. One of them slipped up on the opposite side of the fence with the intention of poking his gun through the brush and shooting Shane in the back. In getting the muzzle of the gun through, however, the Indian made too much noise breaking twigs, and Shane heard him. Turning to his Mexican herder, Felipe Flores, he said: "What is that?" The Mexican replied: "It is a rat; I saw one go in there." About this time the Indian attempted to shoot, but his gun snapped and hung fire, and Shane jumped, but the gun went off as the Indian attempted to jerk it back through the brush, and the ball went through the rim of Shane's hat. The Indian ran before a gun could be got to shoot him, but was seen as he ran off and went into a thicket. Next morning Shane went up to the Adams ranch and found that the Indians had been there and carried off twenty-five horses. A few men were raised to follow them, and by the time they got to Rhiner's ranch on the Blanco the force had increased by accessions on the route to thirteen men, and the Indians were overtaken on the west prong of the Nueces. They were in camp, but saw the white men as they came up a mountain, and ran away, carrying the horses with them. The trailers saw the Indians going through a gap in the mountains, and at once charged and crowded them so close they dropped seven head of the Adams horses. These were recovered, but they got no shots at the Indians. The men were very hungry and went back to the Indian camp and did justice to the fat beef which was on the fire cooking. The camp was on a mountain a mile from water, and the Indians had two beef paunches up there filled with water. The horses were down in the valley. So sudden was their flight they left some shields and headdresses. The settlers had water along with them and did not sample any of that in the cow paunches.

After leaving the Indian camp the men came back to the chalk bluff on the river and camped for the night. Next morning Mr. Shane, being anxious to get back, saddled up first and started back home, as the scout was now over. A Mexican named Leal, who was boss at the Knox ranch, also went, and they traveled on together about two miles, when suddenly and very unexpectedly they met a band of Indians in the road driving a bunch of horses. When the Indians saw Shane and Leal, they turned the horses away from the road and kept on. Shane said to his Mexican companion: "We should go back and tell the other men here is a chance to fight Indians." Leal said no, he was going home, and continued on his way, while Shane hurried back to the other party, who were still in camp at the bluff, but had their horses saddled and were about to start when Shane returned. On hearing the news some of them mounted quickly and set out, anxious for a fight. These men were Ben Pullium, Nubb Pullium, Capt.

Bill Adams, Ed Downs, Henry Shane and a Mexican named Antonio Lopez. When the men overtook them the Indians ran and waved their blankets and fired on the white men, who ran among them and passed a few shots at close quarters. During this close firing Shane had a piece shot out of the horn of his saddle, and two Indians were killed, but their horses carried them into the brush. The Indians finally made a stand on a round top mountain, but ran again when the white men charged them, and left three saddled horses. There were nine of the Indians when the chase commenced, and when last seen going up a mountain there were but seven, and some of these were wounded. The white men got thirty head of horses and seven mules belonging to Chapman, who lived on the Frio. All the men on this trip were not in the fight, but only those whose names are given. The others were slow in getting off from camp, and only came up as the pursuit ended. They followed and picked up shields, blankets, etc.

In 1870 Mr. Shane still lived near the Adams ranch, engaged in the sheep business, and one of his brothers, named Constance, lived with him and helped with the sheep. One morning Constance was about 200 yards from the house with a bunch of sheep, near the creek bank, and heard horses' feet knocking the rocks under the bluff. He stepped up to look over, thinking it was cowmen coming, but it was a band of nine Indians with the chief in the lead. Just as Constance looked over at them they rode up the creek bank in a cow trail. It was steep and they came rapidly, almost running against young Shane as they came out. The chief had a heavy quirt in his hand, with which he struck Shane a stunning blow over the head which knocked him down, and then dismounted and stripped him. The Indians now all collected around the naked and stunned captive. Henry Shane saw the Indians from the sheep camp, and getting his gun went to the corner of a fence and stood and watched them, not knowing they had his brother there. When the Indians saw Shane with the gun they shot Constance with an arrow and then went off. Henry followed on after them to see which course they took, and then came back to the camp, still not aware that anything had happened to his brother. Not long afterwards Constance came in covered with blood and the arrow still in him, which he he was unable to extract. It had struck below the left shoulder blade and ranged downward, nine inches of the deadly weapon being hid in his body, and it was with great difficulty that Henry, who was a powerful man physically, could withdraw it. The Indian who shot him was on horseback, and that gave the shaft the downward tendency. Constance said there were eight bucks and one squaw, and that it was the squaw that shot him. It was evident the arrow penetrated part of the left lung, for he spit blood for six months, but finally recovered. Every one who looked at him said he was bound to die and would not live past the ninth day.

In 1871 Mr. Shane married a daugher of "Butch" Dillard, and they all lived on the Sabinal at the present ranch of Mr. Shane.

In January of the above mentioned date Henry early one morning went up the river, about one and a half miles, to the ranch of Joe Brown, who had a sheep vat and furnace. The ranch was vacant, Mr. Brown having moved to Uvalde. He had told Shane he could have the use of his vat and furnace for dipping sheep, and also his pens, etc. Shane intended to start a fire in the furnace for the purpose of boiling tobacco, which was used in dipping the sheep to cure them of scab or preventing them from taking it. A Mexican named Bernaldo, who was in the employ of Mr. Dillard, went with Shane to bring back some horses which were in a small pasture up there. Soon, however, the Mexican was seen running back from the pasture, whipping his horse with his hat. When Shane asked what the trouble was the Mexican was so excited he passed on without seeing or hearing him, although close by. Shane was not armed, something that seldom happened with him, as he rarely ever left the house without his gun, even for a short distance. Not wishing to raise a false alarm he went to the pasture on that side where he heard a commotion among the horses, bells rattling, horses running, etc. He soon discovered seven Indians in the pasture after the horses. When they saw him coming three of them left the inclosure and gave chase to him. Shane carried a long stick in his hand, which he used to punch up the fire in the furnace. He turned and ran, but the Indians, being mounted, soon came close upon him, and he pointed the stick at them as if about to shoot. Every Indian dodged and hunted the other side of his horse. This gave him a chance to make another run, and he now made for the ranch of John Patterson, who lived just above

Shane and nearer than to his own house. The Indians soon caught up with him again, but again he fooled them with the stick, and gaining a little more time finally reached Patterson's and jumped over the fence into the cowpen. The Indians shot some arrows at him and then turned backed and helped to get the horses out of the pasture. Shane told Patterson if he would go with him they would have the horses. This was agreed, and the two men sallied forth. Patterson gave Shane a rifle and he himself took a six-shooter. They soon met the Indians coming down the D'Hanis road, driving the horses, and the two men stepped to one side to ambush them. Shane got behind a large Spanish dagger, and as the foremost Indian came near took good aim at him through the dagger top and the gun snapped. The Indians had not as yet discovered the white men, and Shane turned to ask Patterson for the pistol, but he was not near enough to hand it to him. The Indians now discovered them and turned the horses out of the road and went south. About the time Shane got back to Patterson's, Mr. Dillard rode up on the horse which the Mexican had ridden when he gave the alarm of Indians, and having a shotgun said he would follow the Indians. Patterson and Shane had no horse and could not go with him. Dillard soon overtook the Indians, but they turned and chased him back, shooting at him, and he fired both barrels of his gun at them. They did not quit him until they came close to the house, and then turned back and went on with the horses. A party was now made up and mounted to follow them, consisting of the following names: Henry Shane, "Butch" Dillard, William Brown, and two Mexicans. They overtook the Indians where Pearsall now is, in Frio County, but the Indians had received accessions to their number and showed up about twenty-five. The attack was not made on them, and the settlers hurried across to Blackally's ranch and got him and his hands, and once more took the trail of the Indians, but so much time had been lost they could not come in sight of them any more, and the pursuit was reluctantly abandoned.

In 1872 Mr. Shane commenced a sheep camp about two and one-half miles from where he lived, and was down there one morning with a wagon, fixing it up, his Mexican herder being out with the sheep. The camp was under a forked liveoak tree, and Shane was adjusting a plank between the forks to serve as a shelf to place things on. His wagon was a dozen yards away from where he was at work, and in which was two guns. This was the situation when he was attacked by the Indians. At first only one Indian showed himself, and he came up behind the wagon on horseback and shot at Shane with a six-shooter, the ball striking the right hand fork of the tree and knocking bark into his face and eyes. The guns being in the wagon between him and the Indian, Shane had to face the leveled revolver of the savage to get to them. Being a cool and composed man under all circumstances, he went for his gun and received two more shots from the Indian before he could get to the wagon. He avoided these by stooping low as he went, and the balls passed over his head, the Indian having to fire over the wagon. The Comanche realized what the white man was after, and when he saw that his shots had failed to take effect wheeled his horse and ran off. Shane having secured a gun, fired a shot at him as he went and killed his horse, which ran some distance before falling. Eight more Indians now showed themselves and commenced yelling and charging, to fight the lone ranchman. The gun which he had just fired was a Mississippi yager, and he had no more balls for it. The other gun was a new, single-shot Ballard rifle, and he had only two cartridges for it, one in the gun and one in his pocket. In getting away from home that morning he had left his belt, which was full of cartridges for the Ballard gun. He now found himself in a very close place, but determined to make the best fight he could and not waste a shot. Using the wagon for a breastwork he awaited the onset of the Indians, and when they came near he raised his gun and aimed at them. They soon realized what kind of a man they had to deal with, and not knowing but what he had a repeating gun and plenty of cartridges, dodged and took shelter behind prickly pears and chaparral and mesquite bushes. From this cover they opened fire, hitting the wagon and the ground around it repeatedly. Several times Shane had fair opportunities to shoot, but held his fire. The wagon had been brought down the day before with camp equipage and provisions, and the herder had remained there with the sheep, and on this morning Shane had ridden a mule down there to arrange camp fixtures, as before stated. He had tied the mule ninety-four steps from the wagon, where he could eat grass. During the progress of the fight a daring Indian concluded to risk his chances and get the mule, and leaving cover advanced across open ground for that purpose. When Shane saw the Indian coming with his knife ready to cut the rope, he determined to risk one of his shots at him. He was a good shot, and knew he could kill the Indian if he did not dodge too quick. He took a quick but good aim and fired. The Comanche jumped three times high and then fell in a sheep trail and lay there. The other Indians set up a terrible howling when they saw this one was killed, and several of them ran quickly, and taking him by the hair dragged him out of sight behind the pears and bushes. The Indians did not show themselves any more, dreading to expose themselves to such marksmanship. The pioneer still remained and watched for them with but one shot left.

The Mexican herder heard the fight, and from the number of shots fired supposed his employer was killed and ran to the ranch on foot to inform Mrs. Shane of the fact. He knew it was Indians making the attack by their yelling. Mrs. Shane now sent two other Mexicans to the camp to see what was the fate of her husband. The Indians left before they arrived on the scene, and they met them on the way, but the Mexicans hid themselves and were not discovered. After the Comanches passed them they came on to where Shane was and found him still on the lookout, not knowing the Indians were gone. They informed him now of this fact, and also said the Indians had a dead one with them on a horse, wrapped up in a blanket. For the first time now Shane left the wagon and went to the spot where the Indian fell. There was plenty of blood there, so much so that it had run four feet in the sheep trail, the ground there being slanting or undulating. It seems the Indian was not dead when they carried him away from the place where he fell, and they had tried to doctor him. The ball went through the Indian and they had made a poultice for each bullet hole out of mashed prickly pears and bound them in place by a belt around the body. When the Indian died and they were fixing to leave they cut the belt and left it and the two bloody poultices lying on the ground.

These same Indians went in near where Sabinal station is now and stole horses from John Kennedy. They were followed by George Johnson, C. Pingenot, John Kennedy, several other white men and one negro. They overtook them and a fight ensued, in which the negro was killed, and the Indians getting the best of the fight went on with the horses. John Kennedy said the Indians still had the dead one with them which Shane killed.

When Shane returned home from the scene of his fight he found that his shepherd was in a very bad condition from over-exertion while carrying the news of his supposed death. His body and stomach were badly swollen and he was in great pain. Mr. Shane, wishing to do all in his power for the poor fellow, placed him in a wagon and carried him to San Antonio, a distance of eighty miles, and employed the best physicians there to attend him, but all of no avail; he died.

In January, 1874, Mr. Shane had a sheep camp three miles from his house at a place called Long Hollow. He had his old Mexican herder, Felipe Flores, with him. Early one morning Shane heard rocks rattling in the hollow, and he and Flores walked out a short distance from the tent to investigate. The Mexican said it was Mr. Dilliard, whom they were expecting to come and help hunt for some lost sheep. It was ten Indians, however, and they were up the bank on horseback, and after them before they knew what it was. Shane turned and ran to the tent after his gun, but Felipe was crowded so closely he ran backward with an Indian close upon him trying to thrust a lance into his body, and fell into the fire, which was away from the mouth of the tent. The balance of the Indians were all firing, trying to hit Shane before he could get his gun, and many balls hit the tent. Shane got in one shot at them and they retreated, but if he killed one the others carried him away. It was very brushy and they all soon disappeared. The fact of old Felipe falling over the fire likely saved his life, as the Indian nearly had the point of the lance against him when he went over. One saddled horse was left close by. Two Indians on the same horse were seen to ride behind a thick bunch of prickly pears, and only one was seen to pass on. Flores said the other Indian was still behind the pears, and was left there to shoot any one who should come out to look around. Shane aimed and fired at this bunch of pears, and sure enough routed an Indian, who ran off. When the spot was afterwards examined a bullet hole was seen in the pears and the Indian made a narrow escape when he stood behind them. At 9 o'clock Mr. George Dilliard came, and he and Shane followed the Indians, but did not overtake them.

In 1876 Mr. Shane and two Mexicans, Antonio Guerril and

Salizar, went down the river less than a mile from the ranch to a place called by some the "Weed Patch" and by others "Indian Crossing." They had with them a wagon and pair of mules and were out for the purpose of sawing up cypress logs to make boards or shingles. These logs had been left by an overflow against an elevated place in the river channel, and it was around this place where there were so many weeds, mostly cockleburrs, that gave rise to the name. They managed to get the wagon to this place, the bluffs being high on both sides. There was a crossing above, and they came down the hill there and drove the team to where the logs were deposited. They finished their work and loaded the wagon with cypress blocks and were about to start back home when Shane got into one of the closest places with Indians that he had as yet experienced. One of the Mexicans (Antonio) had a gun which had been resighted, and he wanted Shane to try it at a certain tree upon the bluff on the west side of the river before they started. Shane fired two shots, and then the Mexican went to see where he had hit. About this time there were forty Indians coming to the old crossing of the Sabinal above, as before mentioned, and heard Shane firing at the tree. Upon investigation they learned the situation and invested themselves in such a way that it seemed impossible for Shane and his party to escape. Half of the Indians came up on the bluff on the east side, opposite Shane and his men, and the balance went to the old crossing above so as to come around opposite them on the west side, having them between the two fires and their retreat cut off both ways. The first intimation they had of the presence of the Indians was the rattling of the rocks at the crossing. Antonio was still on his errand of investigation in regard to the accuracy of his gun and the marksmanship of Shane. The other Mexican mounted a stump so he could see the crossing, and said it was soldiers coming across the river. Shane now got on the stump to look, and said: "Soldiers, thunder! Those are Indians." The first Indians to get out of the channel of the river had only to turn down a short distance to be opposite Shane, and in doing this encountered Antonio and opened fire on him. He had discovered them and was trying to get back to Shane, but was hit by a bullet and badly wounded. He fell in the high weeds and lay there. The Indians on the east side now appeared and opened fire, and the brave settler saw that once more he had desperate chances against him and had to fight the battle alone. One of his men was already down, wounded, and was even now calling to him for help, and the other had crawled under a tree top until nothing but his feet were visible. The Indians dismounted and commenced a rapid fire with Spencer carbines. Shane took shelter behind a large cypress log and commenced the unequal battle, firing with unerring aim as opportunity offered, and the savages soon learned what manner of foe they had to deal with. The bullets came from both sides of the creek and kept a continual spattering on every side, hitting the logs, wagon, etc. Shane lay close and refrained from firing much, and it was evident the Indians were uncertain as to the force they were fighting and were afraid to come down into the bed of the river and fight at close quarters, for at this time on the border many of the settlers had cartridge guns. I will state here that the Sabinal River only stood in pools below the mountains, and there were long stretches without any water at times, but the channel was covered with rocks. The bluffs also were high. During the fight the wounded Mexican crawled to where Shane was, but left his gun, being too weak to bring it along. The fire from the Indians' guns made it smoky on both sides of the river like a regular battle, and must have nearly exhausted their ammunition. Finally they sent a warrior on horseback below where Shane was to come up the river channel through the high weeds to investigate and see if the white man's party were all killed, which they thought must be the case from the amount of lead they had fired into their position. Shane was on the alert, with watchful eyes, and caught the first motion of the weeds as the Indian approached. The balance of the Indians on both sides of the river had ceased firing and were all under cover and still. Shane held a large revolver in his hand as he lay close to the ground, watching around the end of a log as the fellow came in view, and at once aimed at his breast and fired. The Indian reeled and fell to one side of his horse, but clutched the mane of the animal, and he ran up the bluff with him, where he was headed by some of the other Indians. The horse ran around in a circle with the Indian still hanging to his mane. Shane could see all this from where he lay. This wound up the fight. The Indians held a short council and then mounted and rode off, both parties getting together before starting. They had to pass through some open country after starting and getting away from the brush along the river, and Shane left his position and got up on the bluff where he could watch them. He counted forty, but how many he hit besides the last one he could not tell. He took no time to investigate, but made preparations to leave. The signs of the battle which he noticed at the time was his Mexican with a broken hip, one bullet hole through his own bootleg, one through the top of his hat, two through his shirt, three in the wagonbed, and one of the mules wounded, besides many marks on the ground and in the cypress log where they struck. The side of the mound which had formed the drift where the logs had caught was also perforated in many places and balls were dug out of these afterwards. These balls flew high and came from the crowd on the east bank. The wounded mule was able to help pull the wagon home, so Shane placed Antonio in it with the help of the other Mexican, who crawled out of his hiding place when the battle was over. Bullets were found in the blocks when the shingles were made. Shane acted as surgeon for his wounded Mexican, cutting the bullet out and dressing the wound. The ball had gone in a little below the hip and ranged down, and was cut out below the kneecap. It took this course on account of the Indian who was on the bluff firing down at Antonio as he was running back. He recovered after many weeks of suffering. Shane raised a party and went back to the battleground and found one moccasin full of blood and one buckskin hunting shirt with two holes in it, one on each side, and very bloody. In the high weeds where he shot the Indian a six-shooter was found, and the distance from there to where Shane lay was sixty steps.

Mr. Shane was out one time with a wagonload of water barrels, hauling water to one of his camps, and was attacked by a band of Indians. It was in an open country, and he took refuge under the wagon after locking the wheels so that his team could not easily run away. His sharp fire soon drove the Indians off, and he suffered no inconvenience, except the shots from the Indians perforated his water barrels and let all of the water run out, and it almost drowned him as he lay under the wagon.

In the same year of 1876 Mr. Shane saw his last wild Indians. One evening in the winter he went down to a place called "Griner's bottom" to listen for turkeys to fly up to roost. He was not long there when he heard the sound of horses' feet, and looking around saw five Indians riding towards him, but unaware of his presence. There was no time to run, so he stood close behind the large liveoak tree, against which he was leaning, and the Indians passed on both sides of him, two on one side and three on the other. It was getting dusk, but had they looked back after they passed the tree they would have discovered him. He was not fixed for a fight, only having a muzzle-loading shotgun loaded with shot, and it sometimes missed fire. He stood very straight behind the tree while the Indians were passing.

Mr. Shane had two Mexican shepherds killed by Indians at different times, but as he was not with them could tell nothing about the circumstances, except that he found them and pulled the arrows out of them and buried them. One was killed with lances and bullets, and the other with arrows.

Mr. Shane once hunted twenty-four hours for a little girl that was lost. He passed her twice, but the child was afraid of him and hid. He finally came across a Mexican and told him he could trail the child to a certain place, but there always lost it and could not find it any more when it had passed a certain point, and she must be near there somewhere. The Mexican went with Shane to the spot, and the little girl came out of the brush to them. Her father had employed the Mexican at one time, and the child knew him and was not afraid of him.

Henry J. Shane is one of the solid citizens of Uvalde County, has many friends, and can be relied upon for any statements made of frontier days. He has a good ranch and is doing well.

KILLING OF JAMES WINTERS BY INDIANS.

1861.

In connection with the killing of Mr. James Winters by Indians, briefly mentioned in a previous article, the following by Dr. Thos. Speed is taken from an old copy of the San Antonio Herald, bearing date of November 2, 1861, and the article being as follows:

"INDIAN NEWS.

"FRIO COUNTY, October 24, 1861.—Messrs. Editors: Having partially recovered from my wounds, received in an encounter with Indians on Saturday, the 19th instant, at about 11 o'clock, and thinking a few lines from myself and comrades in defeat may be of interest to your readers, I endeavor to give you some of the incidents of the fight:

"At about 8 o'clock on the morning of this fateful day Mr. N. Kennard came to Mr. Hood's, near my ranch, and informed me that the Indians had passed near my house with a large caballado of horses, and that some of the neighbors were on the trail in pursuit. I instantly mounted my mule, then almost exhausted, I having been on his back some eight or ten days almost constantly, and the last four days riding in deep sand. I started home for my gun. I then happened to fall in with Mr. T. L. Ward, James Bishop, James Craig, and N. Kennard. We all started off on a long gallop to find the trail, which we came across near the divide between the south fork of Cesquadara and the waters of the San Maguel. We followed it as rapidly as we could in a gallop nearly all the time until we reached a high eminence overlooking the San Maguel valley, at which place I loaded my gun, not having taken time to do so up to that time. We then started on, and in a few jumps we saw Mr. James M. Winters and W. W. Davidson about one mile across the San Maguel on the high ground waiting for us. The boys broke off at a rapid rate, leaving me greatly in the rear, their horses being much fleeter than my mule. Upon coming up with them they informed us that the Indians were not more than two miles ahead. We all immediately started in pursuit, but did not go but a short distance before Mr. Davidson's horse gave out, being a 2-year-old colt, and he with much regret was compelled to turn back, which left but six of us. We did not delay. We had no organization or understanding, and at this time I mentioned to the boys that we must stay together, but upon the run I can not say whether they all heard me or not. We there struck the blackjack timber between the Maguel and Black Creek, in which Mr. Winters and I were thrown near together, when I again said we must all stay together. His reply I did not distinctly understand, but thought he said 'Certainly.' About four or five miles from where we overtook Winters and Davidson, and just as we came out of the thick blackjacks to the valley of Black Creek, Bishop said, 'Boys, there they are.' At this instant Winters and Kennard changed horses, Kennard's horse being the fleetest in the company. Again I said we must all stay together, and without anything further being said the boys pushed on as fast as their several horses could carry them without ascertaining the number of the Indians, and leaving me greatly in the rear, having to make a run of about a mile from where we first saw them. The Indians on discovering us began to assemble together and to string their bows. They stabbed a little negro boy they had with them, belonging to Mr. Marcellus French, in two places, and gave him some external bruises, none of which were fatal, and left him and also the horses in a large mott of timber, and ran up a hill. When overtaken by the boys they were out in open ground covered with tall grass and scrubby mesquite bushes, and then the fight opened. At this time they were all behind the liveoak mott. I could not see them. I must have been 150 or 200 yards behind, pressing on as hard as my mule could carry me. When I rounded the point of timber all the Indian warriors were on foot and their horses stampeding. Their number was about twenty-five, and they were yelling 'Charge,' as I understand the meaning of the word they used in English. They had been at this for some time before I came in sight of them from behind the timber. I then saw our boys in a state of confusion and disorder. Mr. Winters was down on one knee surrounded by the Indians. At about this stage Winters said to Ward, 'Come to me,' which Ward attempted to do until he had exhausted his shots and had to retreat. I, seeing his condition, made the charge to his relief, and when near enough fired a volley upon the Indians from a double-barreled shotgun which I had got from Mr. Davidson when he turned back. Not being in the habit of shooting such a gun I caught the wrong trigger, and before I could touch the other one an Indian shot my mule in the neck, which caused her to wheel around and commence pitching. This she continued to do for some twenty or thirty steps. The Indians, seeing me come up, commenced their charge on me. At this time I did not know where the other boys were, but when my mule stopped pitching saw all four on the retreat together, two on horseback and two on foot. Craig and Bishop were on horseback, going off the way we came. My mule again commenced pitching, turning to the right, and an Indian shot me in the back with an arrow, a glancing shot three or four inches deep, and I then went to the boys. Ward was wounded in the back. He had lost his gun and his pistol was empty. Kennard had also lost his gun and was wounded in the shoulder. Bishop and Craig were unhurt. Bishop had no pistol and only a single-barreled gun. Kennard's and Craig's pistols proved inefficient and were of no use. The four had but two guns and one pistol, and all empty. When I came up I gave Ward my shotgun, and Bishop got him up behind him, and Kennard mounted behind Craig. After traveling 150 or 200 yards to a clump of trees they got down to load their guns. I then discovered that Ward did not have the gun that I gave him. I asked him what he had done with it, and he said I did not hand it to him. Some of the boys now told him that I had done so. His wound had so paralyzed him that he was not cognizant of what had transpired for a time. His wound, though painful, was not dangerous. Kennard's wounds were slight. The Indians having left the horses and stabbed the little negro, and leaving behind them the large mott of timber of which they had complete possession, proves to me that they were willing to make their escape, but seeing the confused state of our boys in the charge they dismounted and commenced themselves to charge, the horses all stampeding except a few on which were squaws. Their whole number must have been from twenty-five to thirty. By not attempting to pursue us in our unarmed and disabled condition proves to me that the boys did good service with their shots, and when they went back after Winters there were five or six different pools of blood near where Winters lay dead. Ward says he shot one who fell from his horse and his horse kicked him. Their wounded and dead was the cause of their not following us. Had I been up in the charge and missed my shots, all would have been killed, for they quit the other boys and came after me and came near cutting me off from the others, of which I was entirely unconscious until my mule stopped pitching. At this point I looked back to see if I could be of any service to Winters. He was falling over, having made his last effort. My comrades no doubt did all in their power to save our unfortunate companion, but of no avail. None knew him but to admire him. He was in every sense of the word a gentleman, and as a neighbor, citizen, and frontiersman was all that he should have been. His bereaved companion has lost a kind husband, and his small children a faithful father. This was the second time he had pursued and overtaken the Indians. The first time he and his comrades did not charge them, their number being too small for the attack. After this time he had been heard to say the next time he saw the Indians he would make the charge and get some of them anyhow, and now I have no doubt he kept his word, for he never looked back after he commenced the charge to see where the rest of us were. The Indians must have had 200 horses or more, as they covered a large space of ground. We could not see them all for the bushes in the valley. About the same time of day five of our neighbors—Major A. Allen, Nathaniel Terry, D. Yarboe, J. W. Bennett, and R. Coode—coming on after us over the same trail, discovered a band of Indians going up the Chicon near the mouth of the Francisco and near where our trail had crossed the Maguel, those streams uniting to form the Maguel. As soon as they could assemble they made the run after the Indians, and who, when discovered, commenced to charge. The major and company dismounted, fastened their horses, and made a stand. The Indians before coming within range of the guns turned off. The number of the Indians was from fifteen to eighteen, but they finally left and the major and his party went on westward, riding in the direction where we had the engagement, distant about five miles. We learned at Mrs. Tomlin's that about twelve men from the Hondo were close on the trail, not more than two or three hours after us, where we were in the battle with the Indians, so if we had all kept together and kept them off from the horses, we had got all of the animals, or so engaged them until we had been reinforced by those twelve men. Monday morning twenty men started in pursuit six miles beyond D'Hanis, about eight or ten hours behind them, intending to keep the trail until they found out where they went or overtake them. That they were Indians of small stature there is no mistake. The little negro said they were all Indians except one, and he was a Mexican and had curly hair, and that there were three squaws among them. They also killed two grown negroes of Mr. French. They killed a man by the name of Herndon, wounded O'Brien and Anderson, and pursued another named Tucker in sight of Pleasanton, all below here. This is the fourth time they have been in this season, always going out near where we had the fight with them. There must have been fifty Indians in a space of five miles at the time we fought them. Respectfully yours,

"THOS. SPEED.

"We the undersigned corroborate the foregoing statement.

"L. T. WARD,
"JAS. BISHOP,
"JAS. CRAIG.
"NORVILL KENNARD."

[I will say that Dr. Speed was well and favorably known in the community where he lived, that he died a few years after the fight, and some think caused by the wound received there. Kennard was also a long time in recovering. Ward was wounded in another fight after this. The men he mentions as being on the trail at the time he wrote were led by Big Foot Wallace. They fought the Indians at the head of Seco in the mountains and captured 190 head of horses from them. Just before the fight the Indians killed the tax assessor of Bandera County.—AUTHOR.]

TRAILING INDIANS.

For quite a number of years after the Civil war the Indians continued to raid the settlers in West Texas. In the fall of 1876 they made their last raid through Sabinal Canyon. They first struck the settlers on Main Frio, and then came like a wave of destruction through this valley, and then made a circuit of many miles back towards the Rio Grande, sixteen persons meeting death at their hands during the raid. They came into Sabinal Canyon on the 10th of September, and stole quite a lot of horses, and then turned southeast below the foot of the mountains, palying havoc as they went.

The Sabinal men gathered quickly and were soon joined by the scouts from Frio Canyon, who were coming rapidly on the trail. The following are the names of the men from both canyons: From Sabinal were James Thigpen, Phil Hodges, Albert Harper, C. S. Jones, J. H. Simpson, James Watson, Jack Kelly, and a German schoolteacher named Lirch. From Frio were Henry Patterson, John Patterson, Riley Patterson, Joe Van Pelt, James Highsaw, Jack Grigsby, William Wall, John Kittenger, William Nichols, and Joe Richarz. Seeing the necessity of having a leader, the settlers elected Henry Patterson to fill that position, and they soon set out briskly on the trail, Phil Hodges and John Patterson being the trailers, taking alternate turns. For the first day and night the trail led southeast, and in this route the Indians killed a Mexican who was herding sheep for Henry Shane. He was literally shot to pieces and horribly mangled and scalped. He had made a desperate fight for his life and killed one of the Indians and wounded others; this was supposed from signs on the trail. On Squirrel Creek they killed and scalped another Mexican herder.

From the place where the Indians killed the herder they turned a south course for sixty miles, and while on this route killed six men in the lower part of Frio County—two white men and four Mexicans. The white men were out in a buggy looking for sheep when attacked, and as to the fight they made no one could tell, Their mangled bodies lay on the prairie; their buggy was torn to pieces, horses gone, and the harness cut into small bits. From this place back to the Rio Grande they completed the list of sixteen victims.

When the pursuit first commenced the schoolteacher, who had not been long in this country and knew nothing about trailing and fighting Indians, took quite a lot of provisions with him, and when the balance of the men run short divided with them, saying he would buy some more when they got to town, which he thought would be the next day. The boys helped to clean up what he had and then commenced joking him, saying he would do well to get back alive, as there were no towns. He then wanted to know how the Indians lived on these raids if they did not pass through any towns where they could get some provisions. The boys said they would show him how Indians lived before they got back.

By 3 o'clock the next day the men were very hungry, and also about this time they struck a flock of sheep. Captain Patterson told some of the men to go and get two or more muttons for the men to eat. Phil. Hodges and Joe Van Pelt went and asked the herder for the sheep, stating their business, how long they had followed the Indians, the hunger of the men, etc. The man informed them that they could not get them. It was generally understood on the frontier that men who were following Indians were welcome to kill stock of any kind to subsist on when in this business, and if the parties owning the stock refused to let it go the trailers played "old soldier" on them and conscripted it. The two men on being refused the sheep pulled their guns and killed three and dragged them to where the captain and the balance of the men were. Joe Van Pelt killed two of these sheep at one shot; the ball went through the first one and killed another thirty yards away. The horses were now unsaddled, so their backs could cool while they fed on the luxuriant grass. The hungry men built fires and commenced cooking and eating, calling the attention of the schoolteacher as they did so to take notice how Indians got something to eat on a raid. After the repast the horses were again saddled and the trail taken up, the men tying what meat was left to their saddles, which was very little.

After the trailers left this camp and kept on after the Indians it was found that they had turned in a northwest direction, and in two miles came upon the dead bodies of two white men who had been slain with bullets, no arrows being used. They were both lying together and had evidently been ambushed as they were traveling a road and met their death without warning or any chance to defend themselves. From here the trail led to Westfall's ranch on the Leona, and the Indians had been fought and defeated here by Henry Courtney and his hands who occupied the ranch attending to stock, Westfall at the time being absent. By this time, as the route had been long and tedious, the men were hungry again, and at once began to hunt for something to eat, Courtney telling them to help themselves to anything they could find that was eatable. A pot of cooked turkey and dumplings was soon found and the men went for it with forks, soon taking out all of the meat and leaving the soup and some of the dough condiments. Harper Simpson, being fond of thick turkey soup and having no spoon readily at hand, turned up the pot and proceeded to drink some of it out, but unfortunately the bail of the little pot dropped down over his head and around his neck, and he could not get it off. But the boys with shouts of laughter continued to fish in the pot with their forks for the dumplings on both sides of his head, despite his protest, and for a minute he presented quite a humorous spectacle, they not giving him any assistance in relieving him from the pot until the contents were all out.

From here the trail turned west to the Nueces River.

Captain Patterson now concluded that the Indians were a good distance ahead, and he would have to change his tactics to overhaul them before they reached the Rio Grande. Indians when being pursued had a great advantage over the pursuing party. When night came the trailers had to stop, while the Indians could keep on. This was one reason why so many raiding bands got out of the country without being brought to a battle. The captain now decided to try a night ride, thinking that if he would go straight west, guided by a bright star in that direction, it would throw him south of the trail, and then when daylight came turn north and intercept the trail of the Indians again. One reason why he thought this plan would work was because the Indians generally turned up the country and crossed into Mexico at the mouth of Devil's River. This time, however, the Indians acted the reverse and turned south, and the settlers failed to find the trail as they anticipated when daylight came. Finding the marauders had eluded them, the party now turned and went to Uvalde to procure fresh horses and more provisions, intending to strike the trail again and follow it into Mexico. Here eight of the men left and went home, including the schoolteacher in the party.

The company was now reduced to twelve men, and it was thought advisable to telegraph to Fort Clark for United States soldiers to meet them at some point west of the Nueces River. The soldiers were allowed to cross into Mexico after Indians, but citizens were not. There was at this time a frontier telegraph line from San Antonio to the Rio Grande. The place designated for the soldiers to meet them was the "Anna Catchi" mountains, twenty-five miles or more west of the Nueces. The men who remained to go in pursuit were Capt. Henry Patterson, John Patterson, Riley Patterson, Joe Van Pelt, Jim Highsaw, Jack Grigsby, William Wall, John Kittinger, William Nichols, Jim Thigpen, Albert Harper, and Phil Hodges. The commanding officer at Fort Clark responded to the call and sent Lieutenant Boyd with a detachment of soldiers, and they all got together at the place designated. Lieutenant Boyd had strict orders from General McKenzie about crossing the Rio Grande, and all had to act accordingly; but it was agreed that the citizens should cross as United States soldiers, but still be under the command of Henry Patterson. Everything being arranged, the party, forty-nine in all, set out for the Santa Rosa mountains in Mexico, as that was supposed to be the stopping place for all Indians when they crossed the river to avoid a battle with the Texans.

The soldiers had a Seminole Indian along for a guide and trailer, but the first night out he lost his horse and the men lost his services. The trailing then devolved on some of Patterson's men. The day before the command got to the river another large Indian trail came into the one they were following. A consultation was held, and it was decided to halt there, and Lieutenant Boyd would send down to Fort Duncan after more men, as the Indians now greatly outnumbered them and they would have to follow them into Mexico to chastise them. About twenty men came from Duncan, and it is supposed brought whisky along, for that night the soldiers got on a spree and one of their number was badly wounded by the accidental discharge of a gun. The man who did the shooting was tied up all night by the thumbs by order of the commanding officer, Boyd. The wounded man had to be sent back for treatment, and the balance went on to the river. Here, however, an insurmountable difficulty confronted them. The Rio Grande was badly swollen by recent rains and could not be crossed. Some of the men were so anxious to go over they made an attempt to swim it, but came near being drowned and had to desist. Among those who made the attempt was a daring man and good Indian fighter, Jim Thigpen.

The Indians had not long crossed over before the rise. Their place of crossing was opposite "La Villa Nueva" (new town), and they carried 200 head of horses into Mexico. Some of the men wanted to shoot across the river at some Mexicans who were standing over there watching them, but the officers said it would not do. A few shots, however, were fired by some of Patterson's men and the Mexicans beat a hasty retreat. The citizens went back as far as Fort Clark with the soldiers and from there home.

I have given rather a lengthy detailed account of this scout, that those who are not familiar with such things can form a clear conception of the difficulties which had to be encountered in the efforts of the settlers of southwest Texas to chastise the Indians who were continually depredating upon them and killing the citizens.

Henry Patterson, who led the settlers, was at one time sheriff of Uvalde County, and later tax assessor. Newman McCollum Patterson, father of Henry Patterson, was born in Alabama in 1825, came to Texas in 1845, and first settled in Smith County. In 1853 he came to Uvalde County, then very sparsely settled, and on the extreme frontier, and was in many fights with the Indians in the early days. He served Uvalde County as sheriff in 1860 and as tax collector in 1865, and as county judge two terms in the 80's. Before leaving Smith County he married Miss Lucy Dollihite. Judge Patterson still survives and lives on the Patterson ditch farm, in Frio Canyon, where he has a mill and cotton gin. He has three other sons living, William, Riley, and John.

M. C. CLICK.

Came to Texas in 1863.

While traveling through the mountain country of Bandera County hunting for frontier incidents, the writer had the pleasure of spending a night under the hospitable roof of Mr. M. C. Click, who lived at that time in the Hondo Canyon, about two miles south of the Bandera and Utopia road.

While Mr. Click is not one of the earliest settlers of this country, he came here before all of the Indians were gone, and has many true and interesting tales to tell of their daring raids and bloody deeds. He came from Arkansas to Texas in 1863, and to Bandera County shortly after. In 1875 he moved to Hondo Canyon, but there were already some settlers here and had been for some time. The following incident, which took place before he came here, is a fact which he was familiar with:

In 1866 David Cryer and a Mr. Foster, who lived in the canyon north of the Bandera road, went to the town of Bandera in a two-horse wagon, purchased supplies, and came back across the mountains through the pass, and saw no signs of Indians until arriving near a noted mountain called the Sugar Loaf, from its peculiar shape, which was near their homes, and distant from Bandera about ten miles. Here at the head of a ravine around which the road ran they were ambushed by five Indians who were on foot, and likely saw the white men when they came through the pass. The Indians were not more than thirty feet from the two settlers when they showed themselves and drew their arrows back to shoot. Mr. Cryer saw the Indians just as they were in the act of shooting, and hit the horses a sharp blow, which caused them to spring forward quickly, and at the same time the arrows came, one of which struck Cryer in the small of the back and he fell from the seat backward into the wagon bed. Foster was not hit, and at once took the lines and whipped the team into a fast run, followed by the Indians, who commenced yelling and still continued to shoot arrows. There was a gun in the wagon which Foster now secured and aimed back at his pursuers, but they sprang to one side and he would not fire for fear of a miss, and waited for a better chance. During this flight over a rocky road the wagonbed jolted up over a wheel, and the horses, not being able to run with it in that condition, began to slacken their speed. Although it was a most critical time, Foster stopped them, and getting out with great effort, lifted the bed back in place and then resumed his flight. The wounded man suffered untold agony during the wild ride, bouncing from one side to the other in the wagon with the arrow still in his body. It was not more than two miles home, and at the rate of speed the horses were forced into they soon arrived there. The Indians had long since abandoned the chase and went back. There was no doctor near to attend Mr. Cryer and he suffered great pain, as the arrow was deeply imbedded and could not be withdrawn by ordinary force or means. A man at Bandera named O. B. Miles had been a hospital steward and generally attended men who were shot by Indians or any other way, and he was at once sent for and came, but Cryer had received a mortal wound and died in three days. Miles did all he could for him, extracted the arrow and dressed the wound, but of no avail. Three or four men went back to the place of the ambuscade, but could see nothing of the Indians. Many arrows were picked up along the road.

The writer drove around the foot of Sugar Loaf Mountain, inspecting it, and indeed it is of peculiar shape and location, rising abruptly and alone out of the valley and towering high in a conical shape, and being almost perfect in symmetrical formation, except near the base, where it terminates in rough spurs and small gullies. The place of the ambush was also visited. The road is the same as at that time, coming round in a curve as it crosses the ravine near its head. There is a fall here of about six feet, over which the water pours during a freshet, but dry at other times. It is all solid rock, and the action of the water in time has scooped out a basin underneath in which a dozen men could secrete themselves and not be seen by any one traveling the road unless they stepped out into view. In the few moments the writer spent here recalling and pondering over this sad frontier tragedy and gazing down on the very spot where the savages stood and sent the fatal shaft into Cryer, he could almost, it seemed, see their upturned, painted faces, and hear the twang of the bowstrings as with brawny and sinewy arms they drew the arrows almost to the head and let them fly on their mission of death to a pioneer.

In the fall of 1866 Thomas B. Click, brother to M. C., was killed by Indians on the Medina River. He lived in Bandera, and was on his way up the river to see a man named Huffmann, who lived six miles west of town, and who was going to move away. Mr. Click started in the early part of the night and was riding a mule. When arriving at a point three miles from town at the fork of the road the Indians attacked him. He had no gun, and it was supposed from the sign that he turned and attempted to make to the Medina River, 300 yards away. An Indian on a big horse (from the tracks) cut him off from there and turned him back to the road, where he was killed by a lance thrust, done evidently by the Indian, who ran around him, as the mule and horse track indicated they were close together. The slain man fell in the road, but the Indians dragged him out and left the body about fifteen steps away. Mr. Click had on a fine pair of buckskin breeches, which the Indians stripped him of and carried away with them. Next morning M. C. Click and D. A. Weaver started to Bandera, from about where Medina City is now, to attend to some business, and came upon the spot where the unfortunate man lost his life the night before. Mr. Click saw his brother's blood in the road, and stopping his horse said to Weaver, "Some one has killed a maverick here." About that time, however, his eyes rested on a small butcher knife in the road, and he dismounted and picked it up, recognizing it as belonging to his brother. This discovery made him feel uneasy, and a short search, for the grass was high, revealed the body by following the trail where it had been dragged. Officers in town were notified and an inquest held over the body, after which it was taken back and buried in the cemetery at Bandera. A party took the trail of the Indians, but they scattered and nothing could be done with them. The Indians also got the mule and saddle.

In 1867 Rufus Click, another brother, while coming from Kerrville to Bandera, was ambushed by Indians at the Bandera Pass. He had a dog with him, and when they got into the pass the dog raised his hair and got behind Mr. Click. This looked suspicious, but being on a fast horse he rode on, and was soon fired on both with bullets and arrows. The frontiersman leaned forward on the horse's neck and the race for life commenced. There were two parties of the Indians, some on both sides of the road, and he had to run the gauntlet between them. A bullet hit his mare in the neck above the windpipe, and an arrow struck him below the shoulder blade and ranged up as he was leaning forward. The speed of his nag saved him, and he made it to the ranch of Mr. John A. Jones, three miles distant. He had to be assisted into the house, and a negro was sent to Bandera after Dr. Fitz Gibbon. He came and said Mr. Click was shot with a poisoned arrow, and he would have to give strychnine to counteract it, as it was the only chance to save him. He got well, but was never stout again. The poison was that of a rattlesnake. The Indians afterwards made a raid and stole the mare that Mr. Click rode that day and killed her below Bandera, stretched her hide on the ground and cut lariats out of it, commencing in the center.

In the winter of 1875 Jack Phillips, who lived six miles above Bandera on Winin's Creek, started to Sabinal Canyon on business for his brother-in-law, Buck Hamilton, who was sheriff of Bandera County. There was no wagon road over the mountains then to the canyon after leaving the settlement in Hondo Canyon; only a horse trail from there on. Phillips ate dinner with Mr. Click, then living in Hondo Canyon, and then went on his way. When he arrived at the pass which leads into Seco Canyon he was attacked and killed by Indians. This trail was above where the main road now runs. Mr. F. L. Hicks had made a pasture fence across the trail, and in lieu of a gate had common draw bars through which to pass. Phillips got through this and the Indians came down a point to the right and made their attack upon him. He ran back the way he came and succeeded in getting through the bars again, but was closely pursued. It was a long chase of half a mile, the Indians firing, and the horse was finally shot through the shoulder with a ball and fell into a ravine. The doomed man now took down the ravine on foot, but was soon overtaken and killed. If he made any fight with them it could not be told.

At this time Mr. William Felts and Miss Josephine E. Durban were on their way from Sabinal Canyon to Bandera to get married, and came upon the body shortly after the Indians left. They first saw the horse, which was lying in sight of the trail, and went to him. Here they discovered the tracks of Phillips, where he ran down the ravine, and following these about fifty yards came to him lying face downward. They now hurried to the ranch of Mr. Click, told him the news, and stayed at his house that night. Next morning Click, Weaver and others went after the body, and Felts and Miss Durban went on to Bandera and carried the news over there. When Mr. Click and his party arrived at the scene of the killing the horse was still alive but unable to get up, and was shot by Dave Weaver. The body of Phillips lay face downward, stripped and mutilated. The Indians took the saddle off the horse and carried it away. The body was brought to Joel Casey's, the nearest Hondo settler, but off the main road, and Mr. Click went to Bandera that night and had a coffin made. Mr. Phillips was a Mason and was buried by them at Bandera. Mr. Click is also a Mason of long standing.

The Indians were followed by Hondo men, but not overtaken. The shoes of Phillips were found on the trail. A scout of Texas rangers was on the trail of these same Indians, but their horses gave out and they were just turning back on Wallace Creek, fifteen miles away north, at the time the Indians were killing Jack Phillips, as it was afterwards learned. Dr. J. C. Nowlin, of the Guadalupe valley, was with the rangers on this occasion, and said they followed the Indians from North Llano, about where Junction City is now.

Mr. Click was a Confederate soldier, and was in many battles during the Civil war.

LAST INDIAN RAID IN FRIO CANYON.

1882.

In 1882 the Indians struck their last blow at the settlers in Main Frio Canyon. For more than thirty years they had made constant raids and many whites were slain, and in this last two more victims fell,—Mrs. Kate McLauren and Allen Lease, a youth who lived with the McLauren family.

John M. McLauren, husband of the murdered woman, was born in North Carolina and came to Texas in 1857. In 1871 he married Miss Kate Ringer, at Lockhart, Caldwell County, Texas. They soon after came to Frio Canyon and first settled below the town of Leakey, but moved in 1880 seven miles above, and were the outside settlers at that time. Here they lived two years without being molested.

On April 19, 1882, Mr. McLauren left home and went down to Cherry Creek, below the Leakey settlement. It was a wild, gloomy looking place where the McLauren family lived. The canyon was narrow, and just below the house was almost a shut-in. The sides of the mountains next to the river were high rock bluffs, and in time many huge boulders had become detached and went plunging into the river below. Just above this narrow place is an elevated spot on which the house stood. There was a garden spot between the house and the river east. Above, north and west, the valley widened and the mountains curved around and terminated in the huge cliff fronting the river. At the time McLauren left home that morning a band of Indians came around on top of the mountains and stopped on the cliff which overlooked all the valley and house, and no doubt saw the settler when he left home. The family at home consisted, besides the mother and boy Allen, of Maud, 6 years old; Alonzo, 3 years, and Frank, the baby in arms. The eldest daughter, Mary, was away boarding with the family of Richard Humphreys, near Leakey, and going to school.

After dinner Mrs. McLauren took the children and went down to the garden to work. During this time Mr. John Thompson, who had been up the river horse-hunting, passed back and saw the woman in the garden; but no signs of Indians at that time. He carried a Winchester, and no doubt the Indians saw him from their elevated position. They could keep concealed from view by the rocks and cedar with which the mountain top was covered. About 2 o'clock the Indians came down the mountain north of the bluff where it was not so abrupt, and going to the cabin commenced to plunder it. Mrs. McLauren had sat down on a blanket to rest and nurse her baby, and the balance of the children were sitting down around her. The Indians made a noise at the house, which was not more than sixty yards away, but back from the brow of the hill at the base of which the garden was situated. Thinking hogs were doing some mischief there, Mrs. McLauren told Allen Lease to run up there and scare them off. The boy did so, and almost ran into a crowd of Indians in the yard. Uttering a cry of fright he ran back, pursued by an Indian with a Winchester, who fired at him just as he reached the foot of the little hill. The ball hit Allen in the back of the head and came out at the nose, and without uttering a sound he fell forward on his face dead. By this time Mrs. McLauren had sprang to her feet and the Indian fired a shot at her, hitting her in the breast. She fell to the ground, but at once arose and started to run, with the baby still in her arms. The Indian now fired again, and she was wounded in the right arm, but kept on towards the garden fence next to the river. The murderous rascal kept on shooting, and before getting to the fence the poor woman was wounded three times more, twice in the right leg and once in the hip. Before this time she had told the children to run, and Maude was over the fence. The now badly wounded woman handed Maud the baby, which she still clung to despite the fearful shots she was receiving, and tried to get over herself, but another whizzing ball came and struck her again in the hip, and she fell to the ground on the outside of the fence and was unable to rise. The Indians did not follow them and continued to rob and pillage the house, and now occurred an incident that has but few equals in frontier annals. Mrs. McLauren was lying with her head on the bare ground and rocks, writhing and moaning, covered with blood, and little Maud was weeping beside her. The child conceived the idea that her mother could rest better with a pillow under her head, and in her devotion and solicitude lost all fear, and crossing the fence ran swiftly across the garden, past the dead body of Allen and through a crowd of Indians into the house, seized a pillow, and running back tenderly placed it under the dying mother's head. Strange to say the Indians made no attempt to molest her. Did not this innocence and devotion call forth the Divine power which stayed the bloody hand of the savage?

The mother now told her daughter that if she could get help she might live, and the brave little Maud set off at her utmost speed down the river towards the settlements. Now, at this time Mr. George Fisher was not far down the river fishing, and the child soon came upon him. He heard her breathing hard on the bank just above him, and looked up and said, "Is that you, Maud?" "Yes," she said, excitedly; "is that you, Mr. Fisher?" and at once sprang down the bank to where he was. In broken accents she told him that the Indians had killed Allen and shot her mother, and wound up by saying, "Mamma says for you to come quick." Mr. Fisher lived a mile below, and Mrs. McLauren had told Maud to go to his house first, as it was the nearest place. He, not believing that he was able to cope with the Indians alone, carried the child to his house and then informed his neighbors—James Hicks, Henry Wall, and Mrs. Goodman—of the fearful tragedy. Mrs. Goodman wanted to go back to the wounded woman at once, but no one would accompany her, the men scattering with the news and gathering a force to fight. Before doing this, however, they carried Little Maud and Mrs. Goodman to the house of another neighbor, named David Thompson. James Hicks came on down the river to John Leakey's, who as soon as he learned the news took two Mexicans who were in his employ and set out rapidly on foot for the McLauren place. Before he went far he saw McLauren coming behind him in the road, and stopping told him the news. He had, however, already ran his horse down going back home, having a presentiment that all was not well. At J. B. Johnson's he found Mr. Fisher and they went together, having obtained a fresh horse from Mr. Johnson. Mrs. McLauren was still lying where she fell when they came to the spot—alive, it is true, but that was all; the last spark of life was flickering. She faintly asked for water. McLauren went to the river a few yards away and brought some in his hat brim. This she drank, and died in three minutes after. The baby was lying on the ground by her side, and little 3-year-old Alonzo was sitting beside it.

It was now sundown, and who can tell what that poor woman suffered from 2 o'clock until this time with wounds and thirst, expecting each moment when sufficient time had elapsed for some one to come and assist her. Then likely the thought would occur that something had happened to 6-year-old little Maud, and that she had never reached her destination, and still no one knew of their direful distress. Allen Lease was still lying at the foot of the hill where he fell, but the hogs had eaten his face off. The bodies were taken down to the lower settlement and buried in the Leakey cemetery. Great excitement prevailed. It had been a long time since an Indian raid, and the people had begun to think that the days of Indian alarms were over. Twenty men assembled to follow and fight the Indians, if possible to overtake them. The trail was taken up at the McLauren ranch, and it led back up the mountain the way they had come down. Among the pursuers were W. J. McLauren, captain; Tobe Edwards, James Hicks, — Coryell, H. T. Coston, Henry Wall (better known as "Boy" Wall), Frank Pollard, George Leakey, M. V. Pruitt, John Thompson, and Frank Sanders. John McLauren, husband of the slain woman, was not of the party, the reason of which he says was his horse running into a stooping tree the day of the killing and nearly putting his eyes out, so that he could hardly see for several days. The trail led a western course, and was followed with such vigor and over such a rocky country that many of the horses gave out, and at Kickapoo Springs all turned back except W. J. McLauren, Tobe Edwards, H. T. Coston, and Coryell. These went on to the last slope that turns into the Rio Grande valley, and then they turned back. Coryell left them where the trial crosses the road that runs from Brackett or Fort Clark to Howard's Well, and went to Fort Clark and informed Lieutenant Bullis, who commanded the Seminole scouts, of the raid, and where they last saw the trail, which he was satisfied led into Mexico. Bullis at once took his scouts, and getting on the trail followed it out of Texas and five days into Old Mexico to a place called by the Seminoles "Horseshoe Bend." Here the Indians were in camp in a little valley on a creek, thinking they were now safe from the vengeance of the Texas settlers. Bullis had two guides—one Seminole buck and a Lipan squaw. The

Indians being followed were Lipans, and when the squaw learned from something found on the trail that it was her people they were following, she tried to decoy Lieutenant Bullis and his party off another way on a cold trail, where some Indians had passed some time before. The Seminole guide, however, said she was wrong, and that they were on the right track. When the squaw perceived that her directions were not to be followed she got on the warpath and had to be tied on her horse. She was the wife of one of the Seminole scouts.

Lieutenant Bullis located the hostile camp with the aid of a spyglass three miles away, from a hill top. Dividing his men, he left half with the horses and belligerent squaw, and taking the others surrounded the camp at night and awaited the dawn. At daybreak the chief came into view, smoking a pipe, and was instantly killed by some shots from the ambushed scouts. A general charge was now made on the camp, and some were killed before they got up from where they were lying, and others as they ran. When the fight was over five Indians were dead on the ground—four bucks and one squaw. One buck ran off, pursued and fired at many times, but jumped off a bluff twenty feet high, and the last three men to shoot at him after he jumped off said streams of blood were running from his wounds. That he survived these shots is not likely. One wounded squaw with a hand shot off was captured and brought back.

John McLauren met Bullis at Fort Clark on his return and identified several things that were taken from his house, and there is no doubt that the right Indians were punished. The wounded squaw acknowledged they were the ones, but claimed leniency from her captors, stating that she kept the bucks from killing the children. Some might say now that it was the Indian squaw that saved the little girl's life when she went after the pillow, instead of Providence, but God makes wicked and bloody men sometimes the instruments to carry out his behest. The heart and mind of the wild, painted Indian squaw could be used the same way. The wounded squaw was sent to the Fort Sill reservation.

About two weeks before the killing of Mrs. McLauren and Allen Lease one morning McLauren was telling a dream he had the night before of something horrible, and could see streams of blood running, etc. His wife said, "O, don't tell those scary dreams; I don't like to hear them." Allen then put in and said, "Don't tell it before breakfast; it might come to pass." Mrs. McLauren had an uncle killed in the Alamo. His name was Galbreath Fuqua. McLauren's father was a gunsmith, and he showed the writer a gun barrel which he made and which was used in the Seminole war in Florida. He also had an Indian tomahawk which was washed up out of a ravine. It had a long, thin blade.

Mr. John Thompson showed the writer over the ground where Mrs. McLauren and Allen Lease were killed. Some remains of the house are still to be seen. Young Lease only lacked one day of being 15 years old.

AMASA CLARK.

VETERAN OF THE MEXICAN WAR.

Came to Bandera County in 1852.

Mr. Amasa Clark was born in Schoharie County, on a creek of the same name, in the State of New York, in 1828. In 1846, when the war with Mexico broke out, Mr. Clark was in Albany, and volunteered from that place. He enlisted for the war in company I, commanded by Captain Chandler, Third United States infantry, Major Alexander commanding the regiment, Twigg's division. The first lieutenant was named Whistler. The regiment joined General Scott at Vera Cruz, and here Mr. Clark, then a youth, saw his first battle when the city was bombarded. The troops landed in surfboats before the war vessels opened fire. The Mexicans would not surrender, and General Scott gave permission for all those who wished to abandon the place before a shot was fired. The troops on land had a good view of all that was transpiring on the war vessels in front of the city. There were three foreign warships there, and the men on them watched the American vessels with great interest. These ships were British, French, and Spanish. The officers were on deck and the men in the rigging. The American army landed in three divisions some distance from the city. Just before the bombardment commenced, and while the American army was landing, the bands of the different regiments played "Yankee Doodle," "Hail Columbia," and the "Star-Spangled Banner." After the firing commenced it was kept up at intervals for three weeks. Seven thousand shells were sent into the city. The troops on land watched the shells with great interest, especially at night, when they made a grand display, looking like meteors as they flew up and then dropped into the city. After three weeks of this kind of work the Mexicans surrendered.

Mr. Clark went on with the army and participated in the battles of Cerro Gordo, Contreras, Cherubusco, Molino del Rey, Chapultepec, and the street fight in the City of Mexico. At the entrance of the gate of the city the American troops lay down at night to await daylight to resume operations. The men were very hungry, and many of them had nothing with which to appease it. Mr. Clark had a piece of coarse barley bread in his haversack, which he began to munch at as soon as they were settled for the night. Near him was Captain Van Horn, who, seeing the young soldier had something to eat, came close and asked for a piece, which was readily given, and the two sat there in the dark and consumed the barley bread together. The famous "Van Horn Wells," on the plains of Texas, were afterwards dug at his instigation, while on frontier duty in that desert and almost waterless country, and named for him.

Mr. Clark said that at the battle of Cerro Gordo many Mexican women, wives of the soldiers, were killed, greatly to the regret of the Americans, but it could not be helped. They would come in among the Mexican troops while under heavy fire.

The American army entered the City of Mexico on September 14, 1847. Mr. Clark helped to raise the Stars and Stripes over the palace.

At the battle of Contreras Mr. Clark said he saw a young soldier fall as if struck a dead shot, and when the battle was over he and several others went to see about him. He was dead, and no mark of a wound was on his person. Blood was coming from his mouth, nose, and ears. It was supposed that a large cannon ball came so near his head that he died from concussion.

In this battle Mr. Clark gave many wounded Mexicans water. Their cries and appeals to the American soldiers was touching as they writhed on the ground with shattered legs and arms from grapeshot, cannon ball, musket ball, saber and bayonet wounds, calling in their native tongue "Water, water," and when the cooling fluid was placed to the parched lips they called down the blessings of the Virgin and all of the saints upon the heads of the strangers from the north whose language they could not understand, but whose deed of kindness they could, exclaiming "Amigo! Amigo!" (Friend! friend!)

At the battle of Chapultepec, while charging down an aqueduct the command was halted. While bullets were whistling in every direction and cannon balls raking their position, Mr. Clark noticed a young man drop into a sitting position behind a pepper tree to avoid the shots, laughing as he did so, but had hardly got down before a cannon ball cut a hole through the tree just above his head. He vacated the position quickly, but still laughing.

At the close of the war Mr. Clark was discharged from the service at San Elizario, twenty-five miles below El Paso. Some of the officers signed a paper and gave it to Mr. Clark, stating that Amasa Clark had distinguished himself for bravery and good conduct at Vera Cruz, Cerro Gordo, Chapultepec, Molino del Rey, Contreras, and the City of Mexico. This was signed by Major Henry, commanding the post, Lieutenants McFersen and Whistler, and Orderly Sergeant Davidson.

After being discharged from the service, Mr. Clark came to San Antonio, and from there went to the Fredericksburg crossing on the Guadalupe, and soon after came from that place to the present site of the town of Bandera, in 1852. At that time there were but three families there, and all in camp making shingles. They were Judge Saner, now of Boerne, Kendall County, and the families of Milstead and Odum. The latter was afterwards sent to the Legislature. At the time of which we write the county was not organized, but attached to Bexar County. Game of all kinds was in abundance, plenty of wild bees and honey, and the streams full of fish. At that time the Delaware Indians lived on the Guadalupe River, north of the Medina, where Mr. Clark settled, about twenty miles. He camped and hunted with them a great deal, as they were a friendly tribe and remained so. One night he camped where Kerrville is now, with an Indian named Jim. He loaned Jim a horse to go on a hunt with him, and when the hunt was over sold the horse to another Indian and took his pay in bear grease and honey. This commodity he carried to San Antonio and sold for cash.

Among other settlers who came later on was one named Richard Davis. He went eight miles up the river, above the present Bandera, and camped with his family. His occupation was making shingles. Early one morning Mr. Clark started up there, but had not proceeded more than a mile and a half when he met Davis bringing the dead body of one of his little girls to the settlement. She had been killed by Indians. The circumstance was this: Three of his daughters—Amanda, the one killed, and Susan and Lucy—went to the spring after water, and while there Lucy saw three Indians rise out of the grass close by, and at once screamed out "Indians!" and ran, followed by the other two girls. The Indians shot arrows at them and hit Amanda, who ran about eighty yards and then fell dead on a large flat rock. She was shot through the heart. Mr. Davis and a man named Kit Stanford followed the Indians on foot, but did not catch them.

In 1856 Mr. Clark made one of the most remarkable escapes from death almost ever recorded. Himself, Dr. Thompson, and a Polander named Kendall went with two wagons to San Antonio and on their return trip camped on the road five or six miles from town. It was dark, raining, and cold, and they went to sleep around their fire. Robbers had followed them, as was supposed, from San Antonio, and coming upon them while asleep knocked all three in the head and robbed them and pillaged the wagons of what things they wanted or could conveniently carry off. Dr. Thompson was killed where he lay, but Mr. Clark came to his senses just before daylight and knew that he had been hurt. He was hot and feverish and wanted water, but on making an attempt to rise fell back and became unconscious again. The moon had risen and was shining brightly, the rain clouds having drifted away, when he first came to himself, but the second time the sun was up. He crawled to Dr. Thompson and shook him, but discovered that he was dead. All had scrambled away from the fire more or less when hit, and it seemed that the doctor had struggled with them some before receiving the finishing blow. His head was beaten into a pulp.

Mr. Clark had three wounds on his head, and Kendall was also badly hurt about the head. Clark crawled to him and tried to get him up to help hitch the oxen to the wagons, but he was not able. Clark was dizzy and hardly able to crawl about on the ground, but realized that something must be done. With slow and painful efforts he managed to unhobble two yoke of the oxen and hitch one yoke to each wagon. He now helped Kendall to get in one wagon in a position that he could drive, and himself drove the other and succeeded in getting to Milstead's house, near San Antonio. The alarm was raised and a party repaired to the scene of the tragedy. An old, rusty scopet barrel was lying in camp, covered with blood—the weapon which did the work. Mr. Clark left a trail of blood wherever he went while getting the oxen and hitching them to the wagons. His pockets were both turned wrong side out. Very little money was taken, as the men had purchased supplies in town, and most if not all of these were taken from the wagons and carried off. The body of Thompson was taken up and carried to San Antonio and buried.

There were a great many desperadoes and robbers around San Antonio in those days, and many people were killed. The two most noted of these characters of the desperado type was Bob Augustine and Bill Hart. A vigilance committee was organized to handle this kind of men, and they came into collision with Hart and had a desperate battle with him. He was killed, but he also killed Phil Stroupe, the city marshal. Hart had eighteen wounds on his body when he finally fell in the streets of San Antonio and expired. Augustine made his escape. Mr. Clark and Kendall remained under treatment until able to return home, but Kendall never entirely recovered and died two years after. The sunken places in Mr. Clark's head still show where the fearful licks were struck with the gun barrel forty-three years ago.

In 1861 Tax Assessor Murry, of Bandera County, was killed by Indians. He had started over to Sabinal Canyon to take assessments. An account of this is given elsewhere.

Captain Mitchell was also chased by Indians and shot with an arrow while out riding in his buggy near Bandera. The Indians kept the settlers nearly broken up in horse stock.

The place where Mr. Clark now lives, four miles southwest from Bandera, was first settled by a man named Hardin. In 1868 his son, about 15 years of age, went out one cold morning bee hunting, and was killed by the Indians. Failing to come in, parties went in search of him, and finally the body was found by O. B. Miles. The youth had made a good fight, judging from the signs around, and his gun and pistol were both empty. If he killed any the balance had carried them off. The body was naked, cold, and stiff when found, and Mr. Miles sat it astride behind his saddle, supporting it with one hand and guiding his horse with the other, until arriving at the home of the stricken parents. Mr. Clark was present when the remains were brought in.

It will be remembered by readers of the history of the Mexican war that some of the American troops deserted near the Rio Grande in Mexico. Some of these were troops that were stationed along the border before the war. Most of these were either killed or captured and shot afterwards. Some were whipped in the American camp. Mr. Clark said he was present when they were whipped and some hung. General Twiggs superintended the flogging and hanging. He made a Mexican do the whipping, and told him if he did not lay it on hard he would have it put on him. The Mexican put in good licks. Colonel Riley was first whipped. He was a burly, stout fellow. The Mexicans gave him his title after he deserted to them. These fellows, Mr. Clark says, fought desperately at Cherubusco, and shot some Mexicans who ran up a white flag. They lay thick around the cannon where they stood. Those that were only whipped and turned loose were those who deserted before war was actually declared. Sixteen of the others were hanged.

Mr. Clark is now engaged in the fruit and nursery business at his place, and has been very successful, especially with apples and pears. He was determined several years ago to show the people that Bandera County was a fruit country. His only regret is that he did not commence sooner. In 1898 at the Center Point fair on the Guadalupe, in Kerr County, he took seven premiums on fruit. He draws a pension of $8 per month for services in the Mexican war, and is justly proud of his record made there. Many more old settlers of Bandera County deserve mention for the part they took in undergoing the hardships of frontier life—watching for, trailing, and scouting after Indians. One of these especially is Mr. George Hay, who lives at Bandera. He did as much scouting and trailing and bringing back stolen property retaken from the Indians almost as any man in Bandera County, but was in no regular Indian battle. Then there was Valentine, Laxons, Mansfield, and many others. All had to take their chances of being scalped by Indians, and they did not know at what hour that event might take place.

KILLED AN INDIAN.

1873.

Taking into consideration the many years that Texas had a frontier infested by hostile Indians and the many combats the rangers and settlers had with them, comparatively few men engaged in these fights killed an Indian that he was certain of. Of course there were personal incidents during these years, and Indians were killed under circumstances where there was no doubt as to who was the slayer of the redskin. For instance, Nick Haby killed one at night while guarding his horses; Xavier Wanz killed one and brought his body home on a horse; Henry Hartman killed one while they had him rounded up alone in a thicket; John Bowles killed three one night at one fire with a shotgun; Big Foot Wallace killed several. But these are exceptional cases, and there were many more like them, it is true. On the other hand, however, where two or more are engaged in an Indian fight they are all shooting generally, and likely four or five at one Indian, who may be exposing himself plainly or performing some daring act. If this particular Indian is killed likely every man who fired at him will claim the honor.

Among those, however, who did kill an Indian that he got, and no one to dispute his claim, is Mr. Edward Tschirhart, who lives in Castroville, Medina County. The circumstance was this: In 1873 he and Joe Tschirhart, Nic. Tschirhart, Louis Tschirhart, and Louis Ahr were freighting from San Antonio to Fort McKavett. On the 5th day of July, 1873, they went into camp near the fort for the night. About midnight they were attacked by a band of Indians, who charged on horseback and commenced firing among the mules, stampeding them badly and killing one horse. At this time Joe Tschirhart, brother to Edward, was on guard and commenced firing with his Winchester at the Indians, and the camp was soon aroused. Edward Tschirhart, who had spread his blanket down near his wagon and was asleep, waked as soon as the firing began and sprang up, seized his Winchester, and ran around the end of his wagon to get a view in the moonlight, as the shooting and yelling of Indians was all on the opposite side of his wagon. As soon as he did this he saw an Indian very near him on a horse, and leaning low towards him to avoid the bullets which Joe was sending in his direction. The Indian had his face turned the other way and did not see Edward as he raised his gun to fire, and who took a fair aim by moonlight at his left side. The Comanche was greatly surprised when this gun fired so near him, and went over to the other side of his horse quickly, and in this position guided him rapidly away and was soon lost to sight. By this time all the men were shooting and the Indians were beaten off. Edward ran around the mules and succeeded in getting them all back to the wagons, and none were lost. At daylight the trail of the wounded Indian was found where he bled as he hung to his horse and galloped away. Two hundred yards from the wagons his body was found, where, when life was extinct, he had slipped to the ground. The ball struck him in the left arm, and going through the body came out where the neck joins the body. No one was firing at this time but Joe, and none of his balls could have taken the course the one did which killed the Indian from the position he occupied. There was no doubt that Edward killed him. He was evidently a chief, and this was one reason the fight terminated so quickly. They supposed he was killed, no doubt, by not hearing anything from him, but could not find the body, or they would have carried it away. The dead Indian had a shield, bow and arrows, six-shooter, and a knife, all of which were taken by his slayer. The bow and shield were sold for $35. The Indian also had three white scalps—a woman's and two children's. The latter were very small. There was also around the dead chief's neck a necklace made of the finger nails of white people strung on a buckskin string.

The teamsters got back all right to San Antonio without having any more trouble with the Indians.

F. L. HICKS.

Came to Texas in 1855.

Fabian L. Hicks was born on the 16th day of April, 1828, in Forrestville, North Carolina, and came to Texas early in 1855. After crossing the Texas line he pushed on towards the west and stopped at San Antonio. Soon after arriving here he learned of an expedition that was on foot to cross the Rio Grande into Mexico for the purpose of chastising the Indians who were depredating upon the Texas settlers and then retreating into Mexico when pursued. Mr. Hicks at once became enthused, and joining the expedition spent a considerable amount in helping to fit out and equip himself and others. The main instigator and leader in this move was Capt. James H. Calahan, an old Indian fighter and one of the survivors of the massacre of Fannin's men at Goliad. Among other leaders were Captains Henry and Benton.

When everything was ready the command set out and crossed the Rio Grande with something more than a hundred men, and went out in the direction where the Indians were supposed to be located. In the meantime, however, the Indians had been informed of this move on the part of the Texans and sent out a force to meet them, assisted by several hundred Mexicans, making a total force of over 600. This force drew up in front of the Texans between Piedras Negras and San Fernando. Captain Calahan ordered his men to charge them, which they at once did, but were met by a severe fire from the opposing force, who then broke their ranks to let them through. Mr. Hicks carried a double-barreled shotgun, well loaded with buckshot, which he held in readiness, determined not to shoot until he went to pass through them, so that he could be certain of execution. As they went through he threw his gun on a Mexican and fired one barrel at a few yards distance, but he squatted and the whole charge went over his head. He then turned and aimed the other barrel at an Indian on the left, and this fellow got the full benefit of the other load and fell in a heap on the ground. After getting through the line of Mexicans and Indians the Texans took up a position in a ravine and continued the battle. They had some men killed and some wounded as they charged, and among the latter was young Eustis Benton, who was shot in the head and fell from his horse. He was the son of Capt. Nat. Benton, who was also wounded, but had made his way to the ravine. Captain Benton was very solicitous about his son, and Mr. Hicks, Hughes Tom and Wesley Harris volunteered to go back and get him. It was a perilous undertaking, for the bullets were flying thick and the wounded boy lay in open ground. The three men made the run from the ravine on foot, and seizing young Benton bore him quickly back while the bullets kicked up the dust all round them.

The Texans remained in the ravine until night and then made their way to Piedras Negras, opposite Eagle Pass, leaving their dead in the hands of the enemy. This place (Piedras Negras) they burned, and then crossed the river back to the Texas side and soon made their way back to San Antonio.

Mr. Hicks now came up into Bandera County, looking at the country, and finally located there and went into the stock business and was very successful. Here he also married. While looking about over the country he one day went through the Bandera pass, at the north end of which he found the skeleton of an Indian which had been dug up by some one. Beads and other things were scattered promiscuously about. Mr. Hicks dismounted, and tying his horse proceeded to gather up the remains of the fallen brave and put them back in the hole they came out of, covering them up and putting two rocks across the place. These remains were those of an Indian chief who was killed in a battle here by the Texas rangers under Jack Hays in the early 40's.

Mr. Hicks was on many scouts after Indians. On one occasion he and others pursued a band to the head of the Medina, and came so close upon them, the trail being very fresh, Mr. Hicks proposed a halt while he reconnoitered. Going down into the bed of a creek where there was water, the Indian sign there was so fresh that Hicks knew they must be in the immediate vicinity. They had watered their horses there and the water was still muddy. In fact it seemed they had run away from the water as if they had detected the presence of the white men. Mr. Hicks now went down the creek a little further and then turned back, as the Indian trail had left the creek, and went among rocks where he could not see it. After getting nearly back to where the Indians had watered their horses he discovered an Indian sitting on his horse on the bluff, not more than thirty yards away, looking and listening. Hicks took a quick but steady aim at his side and fired. At the crack of the rifle the Indian uttered a loud squall and went tearing down into a ravine on his horse, and Mr. Hicks could hear him making a noise down there like a buzzard or something of that sort, as you might say, a kind of squawking noise. Hicks quickly reloaded his gun and went back to where he left his horse and the other men. They now went to look for the wounded Indian and the others, but nothing could be seen of them. Blood was found on the trail where the Indian ran his horse after Hicks shot him, but down in the ravine he had got with companions and they carried him away, the trail continuing towards the divide in a very rough country. Hicks wanted to follow on after, but the other men refused to go, saying the Indians knew of their presence now, and would be certain to ambush them somewhere. They now turned back to Bandera. One of the party had been shot by an Indian with an arrow only a short time before, right in the town of Bandera, just at dark. On the way back they met a squad of soldiers from Camp Verde, on trail of the Indians. They went on and found the Indian dead on the trail after they passed the place where he was shot by Hicks. Mr. Hicks also rendered good service aiding the sheriffs of Bandera in ridding the country of horse-thieves, robbers, etc. He died at his ranch above Bandera on the 2d day of January, 1899. He left a large family, all well provided for. Several of them had families and ranches of their own. Among these were Fabian, who married Miss Lucy Barrow. Gleamer married Miss Garrison; Cleophas married Miss Moody. One daughter married George Fee, owner and publisher of the Bandera Enterprise. Mrs. Hicks and the young children still reside on the ranch.

CALAHAN'S EXPEDITION.

1855.

In 1855 the Indians made a daring raid upon the settlers east of San Antonio and penetrated as far as the Cibolo along and in the western edge of Guadalupe County. Among those killed by them was Doc McGee, son of a Methodist preacher.

Not long after this raid, and in consequence of which, Capt. James Calahan determined to cross the Rio Grande, and if possible chastise the Indians. Mexico had long been a place of refuge for raiding bands of Indians who were hostile to the Texans. This movement of Calahan was sanctioned by Gov. E. M. Pease, who instructed him to cross the Rio Grande if necessary in pursuit of hostile Indians. Volunteers were now called for, and as soon as Calahan's company was full he advanced as far west as the Leona River, 100 miles from San Antonio. Here he learned that the Indians were continually depredating upon the settlers in this country and then retreating into Mexico when pursued. He now determined to cross into Mexico, and sent back to Seguin and San Antonio for more men. About thirty men at once left Seguin under the command of Capt. Nat Benton and a like number from San Antonio under Captain Henry, all being under the command of Calahan, whom they joined on the Leona, about seventy-five miles from the Rio Grande.

Captain Calahan left part of his men to protect the settlers on the extreme border, which reduced his individual company to sixty men. The three companies now set out and reached the Rio Grande on the evening of the 27th of September, 1855. Here, at the mouth of the Las Moras Creek, they remained for several days waiting for the river to fall, which was considerably swollen on account of recent heavy rains above. Besides the three captains in the expedition there were Eustis Benton (son of Captain Benton), Henry King, Hughes Tom, Ben Patton, John W. Sansom, Fabian L. Hicks, James McCormick, Hal. Holland, Willis Jones, Wesley Harris, Wall, Clopton, Bassham, Smith, Gregor, and of course many others.

On the 30th, the river still being very high and no chance to cross at that point, the command left camp about one hour by sun, and traveling all night at dawn found themselves near the town of Eagle Pass. Here the men were secreted in a cove between two mountains, and the captains went to the river to see if there was any chance to cross in boats.

The captains returned at 3 o'clock and reported the Mexicans unwilling to furnish boats for the men to cross. Captain Henry then proposed to take twenty-five men and secure the boats, while the others would march down the river to an old crossing three miles below. The men then separated to meet at the old crossing. Captain Henry and his party made their way to the boat landing, and the men were concealed behind a bank. The captain was to signal a boat as if wanting to cross, and when it landed was to place his handkerchief over his hat, which was to be the signal for the men to come from their ambush and take possession of it. Accordingly the captain made the signal and two boats put off from the opposite side and landed near Captain Henry, the signal was given to the men, who instantly made a rush for the boats and sprang into them. The Mexicans were then ordered to row rapidly down the river. This they at first refused to do, but being mildly persuaded by a cocked revolver they went to work with a will, and soon the perspiration was rolling from their brows and mingling with the muddy waters of the Rio Grande.

In a short time the boats arrived at the old crossing, just as the command rode up. It was now about dusk. That night men enough to protect the landing were crossed to the opposite side. The next day all crossed over except fifteen men, who were left to guard the pack mules.

This reduced the command to 110 men. At daylight on the following morning, the 3d of October, they set out for the town of San Fernando, distant about thirty miles. At noon, while the men were resting, a Mexican came to them with the information that the Mexicans were in force ahead of them, and would oppose their further progress. Calahan did not anticipate having to fight the Mexicans, but as he had come thus far he determined to proceed and fight anything which came in his way until he got a chance at the Indians, if he could find them.

After leaving this place and proceeding about five miles the command was fired on at long range from a dense thicket, and the Texans advanced rapidly towards it. They halted in front of it and were again fired on by Mexicans and Indians, who showed themselves. One of Calahan's men returned the fire and broke the leg of an officer's horse, and another shot wounded the rider, and they all retreated back into the thicket. In a short time, however, more than one hundred mounted Mexicans and Indians emerged from the brush and formed opposite the Texans for a fight. Calahan, believing there were more of them in the thicket, ordered his men to fall back hastily, as if terror-stricken, so as to bring the whole force upon him if there were any more concealed. This had the desired effect, and instantly 750 Mexicans and Indians swarmed out of the thickets with loud and continuous yelling, thinking the white men would be an easy prey. In this, however, they were badly mistaken. Calahan instantly halted his men and formed them into line of battle. The Mexicans and Indians then formed in front of the Texans until they reached the end of their line, and then lapped around them, almost surrounding their position. Calahan now rode down his line and gave the men a short talk, telling them their only chance was to make a desperate fight, and at the word of command to charge the enemy's line. Captain Calahan now placed himself in front at the head of his column and cried out with a loud voice, "Now, boys, remember the bloody son of McGee, and charge!" With an answering yell to this command the men charged, and in a few moments collided with the enemy and a desperate fight ensued. Pistols, rifles, and shotguns rang out on every side, mingled with the yell of the Texans, the warwhoop of the Indians, and loud imprecations of the Mexicans. The enemy were completely broken in front, and the Texans went through them and advanced about 300 yards to a deep ravine, and there took a strong position and awaited the enemy to act. In the charge through the Mexicans and Indians, Willis Jones, Hal. Holland, Clopton, and Smith were killed, and Eustis Benton, Henry King, Ben Patton, Captain Benton and a man named Gregor were wounded. Willis Jones was the son of Hon. W. E. Jones; Hal. Holland was from San Marcos; Clopton lived up on the Guadalupe, and Smith was from San Antonio. Captain Benton was wounded in the arm, Henry King in the shoulder, Eustis Benton in the head, Ben Patten in the neck, and Gregor in the breast.

While the Texans were dismounting and forming in the ravine and leading their horses into it they were fired on by about 200 infantry who were concealed in a thicket within gunshot of the ravine, and who had not as yet shown themselves. Here the Texans sustained a heavy fire until night, but without serious damage, as they were well protected by the banks of the ravine. The bodies of the dead fell into the hands of the enemy. Wesley Harris, of Seguin, assisted by some others, saved the body of young Benton, who had fallen from his horse and was lying in an exposed position. The ball had struck him over the left eye and remained somewhere in the head. A man named Wall, called by the men "True" Wall, killed the Mexican who wounded Captain Benton. After dark the firing ceased and the enemy drew off in the direction of San Fernando. The Texans then emerged from the ravine, and mounting their horses took the road to Piedras Negras.

Having arrived at this place, the inhabitants made some hostile demonstrations, and the Texans took a position under the banks of the river some 200 yards below the town.

An officer of the American garrison at Eagle Pass (on the Texas side opposite Piedras Negras) came down and called across the river, and asked if they needed any help in crossing. Being answered in the affirmative, he said they should have it, and returning to the fort ran up the Stars and Stripes and pointed six cannon towards Piedras Negras, so as to cover the rear of the Texans while crossing the river. The wounded were soon sent across with part of the force, and went into camp on the Texas side. In the meantime the Mexicans in the town became alarmed and commenced leaving, and soon the road to San Fernando was lined with men, women and children. Some of the Texans pursued them and took the guns from those who were armed.

Calahan now took possession of town and fortified himself in a large stone building, as he had heard rumors of a large force coming to attack him. He had two cannons brought into the building which he found in the town, and pointed them through some of the ground-floor windows. The men found plenty of chickens, eggs, pigeons, and pigs in the town to subsist on.

On Saturday morning, the 7th, Calahan thought it best to cross the river, and at once commenced crossing the horses, and by 3 o'clock had two-thirds of them across. At this time operations were suddenly suspended by a large force of Mexicans, said to be about 1200. The Texans had all left the stone house and were under the river banks, near the boats, when the Mexicans arrived.

The three captains had no idea of surrendering to this formidable force, but at once made ready to fight, although they only had eighty-five men on that side of the river. The Mexicans divided their force, sending a large party below the Texans, and the balance formed in front of them, about 360 yards off. The Texans at once opened fire on them with two small cannon which they had brought with them from town, which threw them into confusion, and they failed to charge, as they were expected every minute to do. Night soon came on and the Texans determined to burn the town and then cross the river. A heavy fire was now opened on the Mexicans by most of the men, while the balance of the men ran through the town and fired everything that would burn. Hughes Tom, from Seguin, applied the first torch. Many of the houses, being covered with grass and low, could be fired almost as fast as a man could gallop a horse. It was like setting a prairie of dry grass on fire. It caught quick and made a terrific blaze. About 7 o'clock, or a little after dark, Calahan ordered the men into the boats. The country for miles around the mountains and Rio Grande was lit up almost as bright as day by the burning town when the Texans embarked and pulled for the other shore. When about half way across, the small ropes which held the boat to the large one broke, and the men and boat went down the river about half a mile before they could land on the Texas side, which they finally did by aid of some oars which were found in the large boat. They now joined the other men at the camp above, where most of the horses and the wounded men were.

Eustis Benton lay three days from the time he was hit before he showed any signs of life. The only way they could tell that he was breathing was by holding a soft, downy feather close to his lips. On the third day he suddenly opened his eyes as one waking from sleep, and seeing men standing around him asked for his gun. He thought the battle was still going on. He remembered the ball striking him in the face, and then all was a blank until he came to himself on the Texas side of the river three days after. The ball was never extracted from his head, but he recovered with the loss of the left eye, behind which the ball was supposed to be. He was a captain in the Confederate army during the war, and married and settled in Arkansas when it was over. His father, Capt. Nat Benton, commanded a regiment during the Civil war, and lost an arm at the battle of Blair's Landing, in Louisiana.

MRS. C. A. WITT.

Came to Texas in 1852.

Among the first settlers on the Guadalupe River above the present town of Comfort was Mrs. C. A. Witt, wife of Rev. J. M. Witt, Baptist minister. Mrs. Witt was the daughter of Thomas Denton, and was born in Kentucky in 1849. She was also a granddaughter of Daniel Boone, of Kentucky pioneer fame. Her father was a soldier in the war of 1812, and died at Merry Oaks, Barren County, Kentucky. Her grandfather, David Denton, was a soldier under Washington, and passed through many of the stirring incidents of the Revolutionary war. When he died the following sketch of his career as a soldier was published:

"Departed this life at the Merry Oaks, at his residence in Barren County, Kentucky, on the 18th day of May, 1838, David Denton, Sr., aged 84 years. He served his country as a private soldier five years and eight months during the Revolutionary war. He was one of the heroic little band that crossed the Delaware in December, 1776, with Washington, and was in the battle of Trenton. He was again with his beloved commander in the battles of Princeton, Brandywine, and Germantown. He was with Wayne at the storming of Stony Point, and was one of the advance guard and with the first that entered the fort. He was at the siege of Yorktown and capture of Cornwallis and his army, and shortly after peace was made immigrated to the West and took part in most of the Indian wars that attended the first settlement of Kentucky, and in a close fight with an Indian was wounded with a tomahawk, that rendered him an invalid for life. He lived and died an honest man, beloved by all who knew him professing an unshaken confidence in his Redeemer, and died in hope of a blessed immortality. He was buried with the honors of war."

The above glowing tribute to the memory of an honest man, a faithful soldier, and model Christian gentleman, is nicely framed and hangs in a conspicuous place in the home of Mrs. Witt. There is nothing to show who is or was the publisher. It is in large, plain print, and has been well kept during all of these years by members of the Denton family. At the top of the frame just above the head lines of the memorial are the letters I. H. S., but Mrs. Witt does not know their significance.

She says her grandfather went with Daniel Boone to Kentucky and was in the terrible battle with Indians at Boone's fort, and it was there he received the wound from the tomahawk. Her grandmother, Mrs. Denton, was present at this fight, and molded bullets for Boone's men. For two years she could not go to the spring or to milk cows with safety unless Grandpa Denton was along with his gun for her protection. Mrs. Witt does not mean that her grandfather came with Boone to Kentucky his first trip when he discovered and explored the country, but with immigrants he brought to settle the country after the War of the Revolution was over.

Mrs. Witt came to Texas with her mother in 1852, in the spring, and in the fall of the same year settled at the mouth of Cherry Creek, where it empties into the Guadalupe River, four miles below the present town of Center Point. They were the outside settlers, and their nearest neighbors below were Schleador and Weadenfield, two Germans who lived about where Comfort now is. The first two years of their frontier life were spent in quiet, no Indians coming to molest them, as they had no stock and nothing to induce them to make a raid in this isolated place. Her mother had five children—two boys (Joseph and David) and three girls. The oldest boy was 12 years of age. One of her uncles, E. A. McFadin, came to Texas and settled and lived with them. Mrs. Denton also had two negro men, so if the Indians came they calculated to make a good fight with them. Mr. McFadin in after years commanded a ranging company, and Mrs. Denton's boys served as rangers when they grew up and in the Confederate army when the Civil war broke out. Joseph was the older and David the younger. The latter was killed by Mexicans on the Rio Grande. After the country began to settle up and stock to be brought in the Indians began to depredate upon them.

On one occasion they ran the children from the cowpen. David had gone across the creek after the cows, and seeing a steer running, kept a close lookout and soon saw the Indians, and at once ran back and told the girls at the cowpen to run, and they all escaped to the house. The men then armed themselves and went to fight the Indians. They got out of the way, but returned in the night and stole a quarter of beef out of the yard. The beef had been cut up and spread out on a scaffold. Some of the Indians decoyed the dogs off while others went into the yard and got the beef. In doing this they passed within fifteen steps of where De Witt Burney and Captain McFadin were lying asleep in a wagon. They dropped some of the beef in the yard as they were carrying it out. The Indians often came at night and roamed through the field, eating watermelons and roasting ears. They would also pull up potato vines, hunting sweet potatoes, until hardly any vines were left in the patch.

In 1859 the Indians came close to the house in order to get a gentle horse to drive off a bunch on. Captain McFadin and a negro man went to save the horse, and the negro saw something he thought was an Indian and fired at it with a load of buckshot and crippled him. The horses were now carried close to the house and guarded until daylight. As soon as it was light enough to see objects distinctly they repaired to the spot where the negro had fired at the Indian, and there found his shield and other things and plenty of blood. That day two boys coming from Bandera saw nine Indians. One of them was considerably in the rear with a blanket around him, and traveling very slowly, and was evidently the one wounded by Mrs. Denton's negro man.

The old log cabin is still standing where the mother first settled. The two negro men cut and hewed the logs and built the house. There was a fine spring close by at that time, but it is dry now. Just below the spring there is a very large cypress tree, which is a sight to people who have not been used to seeing large timber. Rev. J. M. Witt at one time measured it and found that five feet from the ground it measured thirty-three feet in circumference and would hold this girth thirty feet. It would measure forty feet at the base. Thirty feet from the ground there is a hackberry tree about eight inches in diameter growing out of a fork of this big cypress, probably the largest in western Texas. Rev. Witt settled here in 1867, and the same year married Miss Denton. He has a fine farm and ranch, and lives one mile west of the old Denton home. He accompanied the writer to look at the large tree in 1898, and says many people come to look at it.

JOE WILTON.

Killed by Indians, 1877.

Among the frontiersmen who have figured in Indian history on the Hondo, Black Creek, and other points near Devine, in Medina County, is Mr. Bee Tilley. While not participating in many Indian battles, Mr. Tilley was an actor in connection with one of those distressing frontier tragedies in which the bloody hand of the savage has brought mourning and wailing to the many hearthstones along the border and caused a settled gloom to come over the lives of fathers, mothers, brothers, sisters, and husbands, as all of these different relationships have met the rude shock of the savage and been made to mourn during the advance of the pioneers in settling up this vast State of Texas.

On the 22d day of April, 1877, a young man named Joe Wilton, 18 years of age, started from the ranch of Mr. Dan Patterson, who lived about one mile east from the present town of Devine, to go to a store on the Hondo kept by a man named Segenus, at the Eagle Pass crossing of the river. This place was west of the Patterson ranch, and the young man started there in the morning. His mother was a widow, and her boy not coming back at the proper time, she became uneasy and search was instituted.

On this day religious services were being held at the house of Rev. C. B. Hukill, who was assisted by Rev. Burkitt. Mr. Bee Tilley, who was one of the searchers for the absent Joe Wilton, went to the meeting, thinking likely the boy had gone there, but nothing had been seen of him. It was now nearly night. Rev. Hukill, who had not been on the frontier long, now told Bee that their horses had been carried off that day by men who had tin pans on their arms. "Indians," said Tilley. What they took to be tin pans on their arms where shields. Tilley was now almost certain that the Indians had killed young Wilton, and set out in the night to the ranch of Lon Moore, who lived on the Hondo below the crossing, to see if Joe had been there. On the way Bee saw the horse of the unfortunate Wilton (who had been killed), but did not recognize him in the uncertain light.

The horse was wounded and standing still. Coming to the ranch of Moore and waking him, he could get no news of the missing youth, but as yet no one had gone to the store. From Lon Moore's place Tilley, in company with Rufus Ketchum, went back to Patterson's, arriving there about daybreak, but still no tidings. A crowd of ten or twelve men now gathered to make a thorough search and to fight the Indians if they came in contact with them. There was no doubt now about Indians being in the country. Of those who gathered were Bee Tilley, Cull. Moore, Napoleon Harr, Charles Harr, Frank Jackson, Hay Moore, John Tilley, and Rube Ketchum. This party struck the trail of the Indians near Hondo and followed it to the head of Black Creek, ten miles distant. Here they halted and held a consultation. The Indian trail seemed to be leaving the country, and they now had some hopes that the boy was still alive. Rufe Ketchum and John Tilley were now sent across the country to the store, to see if he had been there, but he had not. Some of the men went back down the country, and the others followed later. When near Black Creek they heard a man hallooing and went to him. This man was Napoleon Harr, and he had found Wilton's horse, which was badly wounded and died soon after. The men now commenced with renewed energy to find the body. They soon found the trail of the Indians, who had made a turn beyond Black Creek and came down the country, and near here had met Wilton and began to chase him. The men soon found where this chase commenced and followed fast. Wilton had run a trail, and the tracks of the Indians' horses were on both sides of it. About 500 yards from here Hay Moore, who was in the lead, said, "Here he is." The body was lying under a liveoak tree with some white chaparral bushes around it. The boy had run in here after leaving his wounded horse, and was there killed, stripped, and mutilated. He had one bullet hole in the lower part of the neck between the shoulders, high up. One arrow in the left nipple went through the body, and the spike pushed the skin out on the opposite side. This arrow was in so deep that it was hard to extract it, so Charley Harr held the body down while Bee Tilley pulled it out. Besides these wounds there was a lance wound through the right breast, and another gunshot wound in the head and one in the hip. This last wound was evidently inflicted when the Indians first met the boy and before he turned to run, as it was in front. The men now left Charles Harr and Cull. Moore with the body and the balance went back to the settlement to carry the news. Bee Tilley went back with a wagon and brought the body in, and it was buried one mile east of Devine, not far from where the International road now runs. A tombstone now marks the spot, with name, date of death, and cause inscribed upon it.

XAVIER WANZ.

Came to Texas in 1845.

Mr. Xavier Wanz (pronounced Sevier Vance) was born in Strassburg, Alsace, in 1844, and came to Texas with his parents as part of Castro's colony in 1845. They landed at Port Lavaca and then came on out to Castroville. Mr. Vance of course does not remember anything of these times, being only one year old. His parents left Castroville and came fifteen miles further west and settled at a place called Vanderburg, four miles northwest from the present village and settlement of New Fountain. Vanderburg was near the old "Wall road," as it was called, an which marked the route of retreat of Wall's army after his defeat by General Caldwell at the battle of Salado in 1842. At the time of this settlement Mr. Vance says the route could be easily traced, and that the fight on the Hondo between the rear guard of the Mexican army and the rangers under Jack Hays took place two and a half miles west from the Vanderburg settlement and on the east bank of the Hondo. Mr. Vance there found some sabers, broken guns, dishes, and other things when a boy. When the writer passed the site of Old Vanderburg, on the way to see Mr. Vance, he discovered an old rock building nearly hidden by mesquite brush, and the old "Wall road" was 300 yards north of this. The rock house was built by Louis White, an American. When the settlement was made here the creek then called Lucky, but now Verde, was a bold, running stream, and derived its name from the many evergreens that grew along its bank and always gave it a verdant appearance.

This settlement began prosperously, but all at once a strange thing happened, which caused Vanderburg to be abandoned and the houses which they had so carefully and substantially built to go to decay. This was the sudden drying up of Verde Creek. It broke out again, however, four miles below, and most of the people moved there and started another village and called it New Fountain, suggested by the new flow of water. A few remained at the old town and hauled water. They were the Vance family, the two Decker brothers—Joe and Charley—and Louis

White. The latter stayed here until the breaking out of the Civil war, and being a Union man, went to Mexico and remained there until it was over, and then came back and finally died at Castroville. The Vance family remained a long time here, and hauled water from where Mr. Joe Decker now lives, and the elder Vance died here. The country around was open then, and the stockmen were in the habit of climbing to the top of White's stone house to look for their stock on the open prairies around. When Sevier was 14 years of age he had his first Indian scare, and a good one, as he expressed it. On that occasion he went out to hunt mustangs, armed with a six-shooter, and there being plenty of deer, fired five of his loads at them. He saw no Indians that day, however, but came back with an almost empty pistol and failed to reload it. At about 4 o'clock a. m. the Indians came. The dogs first discovered them and commenced barking, and the bells on the horses began to rattle lively. Vance did not think it was Indians, and went out in his night clothing and followed the bell, thinking it was mustangs among his horses. Going four of five hundred yards he discovered mounted men driving them, and some of them with guns on their shoulders. The Indians detected him by his white night garments, and wheeling their horses came towards him. Realizing now that it was Indians he turned and fled, his white figure vanishing before them like a specter of the night, carrying the pistol with the one load in his hand. On the way he came upon one horse the Indians failed to get, and tried to catch and mount him, but being unable to do so, ran on past his own house to that of Joe Decker to arouse him. He was pursued, and Mrs. Vance, who was on the lookout, said three Indians passed the house. These turned back and got the horse which the boy had failed to catch, and went on after their companions. Joe Decker got his gun and he and Vance went in pursuit, the latter still carrying the pistol in his hand, and in the excitement had forgotten as yet to load it. In about one mile and a half they came so close to the Indians they could be heard talking by the boys. Decker proposed to go back, as the Indians were too many and would kill them as soon as it was light enough. So they went back. Next morning Vance, Decker, and a Frenchman named Bushman again followed the Indians. Vance, being the youngest, carried the provisions. The trail was soon lost in the rough country, and they scattered to hunt it. Vance got lost from his companions and had to come back home. His horse was very tired, and he tried to get another to go back that night to McCoy's ranch on the Hondo, as he knew the other two men would have to go there to get something to eat if they did not come home, but failed to get the horse and had to remain. Decker and the Frenchman had found the trail of the Indians and followed it until nearly night without anything to eat, and then abandoned it and went to McCoy's to get provisions. This ranch was in Hondo Canyon, twenty miles from where Vance got lost from his party. The Indians camped a mile from where they quit the trail, but left in the night, and before day appeared at McCoy's ranch and killed some cattle and then left, carrying off some of his and Bandy's horses. Next day a scout was made up and attempted to follow the trail but lost it, and came back to the ranch to await until morning again. The trail was found next day and the Indians caught on the West prong of the Hondo in a dense cedarbrake, so thick they had to walk and lead their horses. When the white men came upon them firing commenced at once on both sides, but the Indians ran and left all of the horses. None of the settlers were hurt, and only one Indian wounded, and he got away, but the horses were all rounded up and brought back.

In 1867 Sevier Vance, Joe Decker, and his brother Charley started in the early part of the week with their wagons and ox teams and a saddle horse apiece to cut grass to cover houses, as they could get no shingles. They located their camp on the Hondo prairie and went to work, the distance from home being six miles. On Saturday morning, having their loads completed, they prepared to return home. The Deckers were to load the wagons, while Vance rounded up the oxen. It was about 10 o'clock when he got to camp with them, and as the water was out he and Charley Decker took the three horses and one keg and went after some, which was some distance off. When about half a mile from camp Vance noticed horses moving in the timber beyond the prairie and just coming out of the hills. Looking close it was discovered that mounted men were with them, and all about a mile distant. Vance said it was Indians, and they had better go back and inform Joe, as he was the oldest. When informed of the presence of the Indians he said it was not prudent to follow them, as they might be in large force and against three of them. Vance thought there were but few Indians, and proposed to follow them. This was agreed to, and the pursuit commenced. When the Indians were again sighted they were crossing a flat and just beginning to ascend a ridge, still driving the horses. They were now nearly within gunshot, and six of them in number. They discovered the white men and attempted to mount fresh horses, two of which turned back, followed by two Indians with lariats trying to rope them. Failing in this they went back, and all went into the brush on a small ridge. Vance had a Mississippi rifle and six-shooter, Joe Decker had a Mississippi rifle, and Charley a Spencer carbine. Vance was in the lead as they advanced, and the Indians fired at him with bullets and commenced yelling and charging, but he sat upon his horse, not being hit, and aimed his rifle. The Indians were all coming on foot, but fell to the ground to avoid the shot, and he held his fire, not being able to see them good, and the Indians arose and yelled and charged again. The fearless white man would not run, and again aimed at them, but they dodged and scattered back to their horses and mounted. All this transpired very quickly, and at this time Charley Decker came up by the side of Vance with his Spencer, having seven shots in it, and was told by Vance to cut down on them, as he had plenty of loads. The Indians lay over on the sides of their horses with only one leg exposed. Charley now fired and shot one of them through the leg, and two left their horses and took to the brush. The balance went on after the loose horses and Vance followed them. Joe Decker, who was in the rear and in a position to see clearly, discovered an Indian on horseback behind a thicket opposite Vance. He shouted to the latter, "Look out! There is an Indian behind the thicket." Vance now turned his horse and rode around to the lower side of the thicket; the Indian did the same on the opposite side, but neither saw the other until they met at the end of the thicket. The white man raised his gun quickly, but the Indian was also quick, and wheeled his horse into the brush behind some large bushes about fifty yards away. He leaned forward on his horse as he went, and thought he was hid, and partially straightened up. Vance had his gun on him trying to get a bead as he went, not wanting to waste a shot with a muzzle-loader, but now saw part of the Indian plainly, and taking aim fired. At the crack of the gun the Indian's horse jumped out of sight, and Vance could not tell if he hit the Indian or not, but thought he did. Determined to find out where he went, Vance rode out there to hunt him, keeping his revolver ready for instant use, and soon found him dead under his horse's neck. The Indian was on his hands and knees with his face to the ground, and his long hair spread out over the grass. He was a fearful-looking sight, and Mr. Vance said it almost frightened him when he rode up on him, but seeing he was dead, got down beside him. He was lying on a rope which was around the horse's neck, and had on a pair of leggings and a white man's coat. He also had a dressed buffalo yearling skin with the hair on tied around his waist, which with his own mop of hair gave him a very bulky appearance. He had shot the Indian square through the body, breaking his back. He now took the buffalo skin, bow and quiver of arrows and bow case and tied them to his own saddle; also the Indian's knife, which had no handle, but a buckskin string closely wrapped around the hand-hold. Mounting, he again pursued the Indians to try and recover the horses, which he soon succeeded in doing, as they had abandoned them and gone. The Indian that Vance killed had evidently stopped behind the thicket to kill him as he came through in pursuit. He returned to the dead body of the Indian with seventeen head of horses, and found the other two men there. They could not tell where Vance had gone, but finding the Indian he had killed, remained by the body.

After getting back to camp they coupled two wagons together so one man could drive two, and Vance drove the captured horses, and they got home before night. When they told about the fight and killing the Indian, some said they did not believe an Indian had been killed, and that he lost the things Vance had while running. This irritated the men, and on the following morning Vance and Charley Decker took one of the Indian horses, and going back to the spot loaded the Indian on him and brought him to the settlement, so that all the people who wanted to could look at him, and to prove their assertion. The Indian had brass rings in his ears as big as silver dollars. Vance scalped him, and then dragged his body about a mile and covered it up with rocks. The horse off which the Indian was killed belonged to Billy Harper, son of Judge George Harper and brother to Robert A. Harper. The latter still lives on the Hondo, has passed through many stirring scenes on the frontier, and is known to his many friends as "Uncle Bob."

Shortly after this raid the Indians made another one and stole some of Judge Harper's horses, some from Rev. William Fly, and some from negroes who lived in the Harper settlement. They had formerly belonged to the Harpers, and still lived in the country as freedmen. Next morning after the raid Mr. Fly came over to see Mr. Vance to notify him, and get up a scout to follow the Indians. Vance said "All right, we will get men enough." The party who gathered to go in pursuit were Sevier Vance, Rolly Harper, Charles Decker, and six negroes. The trail led towards Sabinal Canyon, and after entering it turned up Little Creek, and then went back towards the Sabinal River, passed through a pecan grove back of John Ware's field, stopped awhile on the river, and then went on towards the Frio Canyon. They crossed below the settlement and went in the direction of Camp Wood, on the Nueces. One place was found where they stopped and killed a mare and took some of the meat along with them, and here some of the negroes began to think they had gone far enough, and wanted to turn back, but Vance saw something on a hill standing still and could not tell what it was, whether an Indian or Spanish dagger, so the balance of the party were told to remain where they were, and he would go on foot up the mountain and see what it was. Decker followed, and then Rolly Harper, leaving the negroes in the valley, and they came on up the mountain, too. When arrived at the summit they were in the midst of an Indian camp, but the Indians were gone. There was their fire and cooked meat upon it. It was evident that they were just preparing to eat when one of them raised up to take a look and discovered Vance and his party. Forty yards away was a bluff, and in the valley beyond were the horses, except those ridden away by the Indians and a few taken along. Rolly Harper went back to bring up the negroes, and Vance and Decker took the trail of the Indians. In about a mile five head of horses were discovered near a thicket, and when all the crowd got together Vance said, "We will have a fight, now," and led the advance, the negroes riding close together in a bunch. Vance noticed this, and said, "Scatter out, there; the Indians will fire into you directly and kill three or four in a pile." They rode up to the horses, but no Indians were there. The horses were tired, worn out, and standing still. The Indians had left them when they saw their pursuers still following. By night all of the horses, eighteen in number, were collected and carried back to the settlement. This was in sight of Camp Wood.

In 1872 the Indians made another raid on the Hondo. They first struck the ranch of Widow Dean below and came on up, and early in the morning appeared in the Vance settlement. The families of Vance and Decker lived on the west side of Verde Creek, and Frank Vogel, Gotlieb Britsch, Louis Mumme, Charles Martin, Tampkes, Hallers, and others on the east side. The Indians first struck the Vogel place. The horses on this ranch had been kept stabled during the night, but had been turned out about daylight to graze, and Vogel had started to the field to work. He saw the Indians riding around the field, and at once turned back in a hurry, but before he could get his gun and return, the Indians had his horses and gone with them. Charles Martin ran over to Vance and Charles Decker, and told them about the Indians. They at once got their guns and pistols and went to the rescue of their horses back of the field, several hundred yards from the house. They soon found Decker's horse, and heard the bell of Vance's in the bed of the creek. The latter told his companion to wait for him until he could secure his horse, and then they would go back to the house and carry them to a place of safety. Both of them, however, ran down to where they heard the bell, but the horse was gone and the bell had quit rattling. The Indians had got the horse and taken the bell off. In this raid there were thirty-four Indians, as was seen afterwards, but were now divided. One party came up on the east side of the creek, and the others on the west. Those on the east got Vance's horse. The two men now followed the Indians to get the horses back if possible. They ran half a mile north, but not seeing them turned east some distance and still not seeing anything, turned back towards home again. While going up a brushy hill they saw the Indians, fourteen in number, not more than 125 yards away. Decker wanted to fire at once, but Vance said, "No; wait till they come closer." By this time the Indians had discovered them, and the two men arose from the squatting position they were in and commenced firing. They had Winchesters and plenty of cartridges. The first shot Vance fired hit an Indian, a large fellow off to one side on a horse. He did not fall, but leaned over to avoid another shot, and made off. The other Indians yelled and returned the fire, and the white men continued to shoot and yell and curse the Indians at the top of their voices. This fight and loud cursing and yelling was heard all over the settlement. The Indians finally retreated and the two fearless settlers pursued them on foot, when they separated, some going east and some west. Vance and Decker followed those who took the west course. Decker soon gave out and dropped behind, but his companion went on and caught up with one Indian who had stopped and roped a fresh horse. He was down putting a bridle on him, and had the bit in his mouth and the headstall over one ear, when Vance opened fire on him. The Indian retreated on foot and was pursued and fired at rapidly, jumping high and yelling at every crack of the Winchester. Vance had run so far and fast and was breathing so hard he could not hold on him, but ran and fired at the Indian for 200 yards, until he joined the balance. Decker was now hallooing, to Vance to wait for him, as he had given out and could not catch up with him. The Indian who had been pursued so closely mounted behind another, and several of them now fired at the bold, aggressive white man, who stood his ground and waited for his tired companion to come to him. Some of the Indians who were in this crowd had Decker's horse. He had left him and come with Vance on foot to help him retake his horse. The Indians soon retreated, and waved two red shawls as they went off. Three or four of them hung back and still continued to shoot at Vance and also at Decker, who had just caught up. It was some time before Vance could get his breath back to normal. The Indians seemed to be badly rattled by the pluck of the white men and rapid fire of the Winchesters. They finally all ran away, carrying the loose horses along with them. They raised a dust as they went down into the Hondo valley that looked like smoke on a burning prairie.

The two white men now went back to where the fight commenced, and found fourteen head of mules and horses which the Indians had left in their flight and fright. Three mules stood saddled and packed with horsemeat. They had killed this horse the night before near the Dean ranch. On the horses were also blankets and canteens. On the way back home with the horses the two men met Joe Decker, who had heard the fight and was coming to help them.

This was the best fight that two men ever made with Indians in this country. By their rapid fire and loud cursing they had practically put to flight thirty-four Indians and captured fourteen head of animals from them. It was only equaled by Henry Hartmann in his desperate battle alone. The Indians evidently thought that all the men in the settlement were after them. In the lot of recaptured stock there were three mules that did not belong in this settlement, but had been ridden in by the Indians. The scouts from the Hondo were in hearing of the fight, but they were on the way to the Widow Dean's ranch to strike the trail there, and were not aware that the Indians were in that direction, and that it was a fight they heard. It was a long ways off, and they could only hear the shots, and not those very distinctly. They got on the trail and came on up towards the Vance settlement, and then went on into the mountains. Vance raised a scout and came on behind the Hondo men. The Verde scout went nine miles in a northwest direction and found nine dead horses which the Indians had killed. They were not all together, but scattered along the trail. Seven miles further on they found a gray horse that was not hurt himself, but was sprinkled with blood on the shoulders. An Indian was either shot on this horse or else a wounded one had been carried on him until the animal gave out. Six miles further on, while going over a mountain, a bunch of men and horses were discovered. They were thought to be the Indians, but proved to be the Hondo scouts under the command of Isaac King. They yelled at the Verde men to see who they were. They all got together, numbering thirty-one men, and kept on in the pursuit. Some wanted to turn back, but Vance was not willing, and said he would trail as long as he could see. Two miles from here was Perry Wilson's ranch, where were young Wilson and a negro (some say a Mexican.) The Indians attacked them, but both made their escape, Wilson on horseback and the negro on foot in the brush. The Indians looked for him but could not find him, and this delay caused the white men to overtake them before night. Near this ranch the Indians killed eighteen head of cattle and horses (two of the latter), and cut out their tongues, hearts, and loins. While at this the scouts came upon them. The Indians were badly scattered, but at the approach of the white men collected to give them battle. They, however, dodged the issue and continued their retreat. As they went over an open country thirty-four were counted. Vance, Chris. Schumaker, Billy Johnson, and a Mexican named Casuse followed at a run, and the other men came on, being scattered for a mile back. Some stopped at the dead cattle and got knives and ropes. The Indians ran two miles, crossed the Hondo, went on to a mountain, and commenced firing on the advance of the settlers. By this time the horse ridden by Vance had failed, and he dismounted and went on foot. He had on a pair of leggings, and getting tired of these, stopped to unfasten them, and the Indians fired a volley at the time, hit the ground all around him, and knocked dirt in his face. The Mexican now came up and the Indians fired at him. He dodged and dropped when the puffs of smoke were seen, and was not hit, although the dirt and rocks were knocked up all around him. The Indians cursed him and said, in Spanish, "There, I liked to got you that time." He then took shelter behind rocks, and Johnson, Schumaker and others opened fire on the Indians from cover also. Vance also commenced firing, and twenty-five shots in all were fired. Vance now went back to where he had left his horse and waited for the other men to come, who were approaching as fast as they could, attracted and guided by the firing. It was nearly night when they came, and would not then go up the mountain, as darkness would come on before they could accomplish anything.

Vance saw a horse half way up the mountain, saddled, and a hackamore on his head and nose, and said, "Boys, let's go up and get him." He had seen the Indian jump off the horse and leave him, and was not afraid it was a trap. Vance set out up the mountain to secure the deserted animal, and Schumaker followed him. When they reached the horse Vance wanted to go on up and see where the Indians were. They went on up, and others of the crowd below came on up also to be in the battle, if it was a fight. The Indians were gone and had left four horses and two saddles. The latter were lying on the ground.

Vance thinks most of the Indians went on at first and only left a few to fire at them. They secured the horses, and all went back to Wilson's ranch that night. Wilson's son, who had escaped and raised the alarm, caused the Sabinal and Seco men to come out and strike the trail after the first party had abandoned it. They found where the Indians had camped that night after the fight, and saw beds of cedar and bloody rags lying about where they had been trying to do something with the wounded. The rags were twisted like ropes where they had tried to stop up the bullet holes with them. Mr. August Rothe was with this party, and told the writer about the bloody rags, etc. This was in what is the present pasture of Mr. F. A. Hicks. This was the last big raid by Indians in this part of the country.

Mr. Vance was very energetic after Indians, and vindictive against them. In 1870 they killed his aged mother. At this time the mind of the old lady was somewhat impaired and she would take trips alone in the woods, which caused the members of the family to be uneasy about her. On this fatal day she failed to return at night from a ramble, and Mr. Vance commenced a search in the night and fired guns, but no response came. Next morning a diligent search was made by many settlers and continued all day, but night came again and no tidings came of the missing lady. Large fires were built in the woods in various places, so if still alive they might attract her, but none of this proved availing. This was kept up three days, until finally the body was found by George Byers, three miles from home. She had been killed by Indians and the body was in the channel of Verde Creek between two rocks, where it had been thrown, evidently by the Indians after they had murdered her.

In this same year Capt. H. J. Richarz raised a company of rangers, of which Mr. Vance was lieutenant. His commission was dated September 10, 1870. He was very active as a ranger, and recaptured many head of stolen stock and returned them to their owners. He was on a scout with twenty-three men when part of Captain Richarz's company had their desperate battle with Indians near Carrizo, and says if he had been there with his men they would have given the Indians a good whipping. When the Indians killed Riff and Captain Richarz's son (two rangers), Lieutenant Vance followed them, but could not overtake them. He had just arrived at camp from a seven days' hard scout when news of the death of the boys came, and although the men and horses were tired, they went that night to where the men were killed, and at daybreak took the trail and followed it to the

Nueces. Captain Kelso had a company at this time at Camp Wood in Nueces Canyon. The captain was gone, and the Indians passed out near his camp. The horses ridden by Vance and his men gave out and lay down with them on their backs. Failing to get fresh horses at the post, the rangers went on with their tired horses until night, and next morning the lieutenant took six men and continued the pursuit on foot, but was compelled to return unsuccessful. Part of the dead rangers' clothing was found on the trail. Riff had a violin which he was carrying to camp from D'Hanis. The Indians split this in small pieces and scattered it along the trail. Vance says the murdered boys were good shots and had Winchesters and six-shooters, but thinks both were badly wounded at the first fire of the Indians, who were in ambush. They had been home on furlough and were returning to camp on the Leona, below Uvalde, and were killed on the Blanco between the Sabinal and Frio.

Mr. Vance has a nice ranch, plenty of water and grass, and also a fine farm. His place is five miles northwest from New Fountain. Four miles west is the place where he fought the Indians and killed one. Two miles from the house is where he and Charles Decker fought them. Half a mile away in his pasture is where the Indians killed his mother.

Mrs. Vance, who was a Martin, was raised here, and remembers hearing the guns and the cursing when her future husband and Decker were fighting the Indians. Her brother was a ranger, and was in the Carrizo fight. Mr. Vance has up to this time been fifty-four years in Medina County, and has never moved out of it.

J. B. WERNETTE.

Came to Texas in 1845.

Among those who braved the dangers of the western wilds at an early day, when the Comanche, Lipan, and Kickapoo Indians roamed at will over the vast domain then unsettled which lay between the San Antonio River and the Rio Grande was Mr. J. B. Wernette, now of Castroville. He was born in Upper Alsace, in 1835, and came to Texas under Henry Castro in 1845. The ship in which he sailed was the Robinson, the largest ship then afloat. The start was made from Antwerp, and they landed at New Orleans in fifty-one days from the time of setting sail. From this place he took shipping on a steamer for Galveston, Texas. The number of immigrants who came over in the Robinson was 360. On the way from New Orleans to Galveston Joseph Wernette, 6 years old, brother to J, B., was lost. The little fellow was playing on the deck and fell overboard. The captain stopped the ship and search was made, but the body of the unfortunate young immigrant could not be found. At Galveston, the immigrants who intended to go west took passage on a sail ship bound for Port Lavaca. Before arriving at that place the ship ran on a sandbar and remained fast. The captain ordered all the passengers to leave the front end of the vessel and concentrate at the rear, so that the front would lift and get clear of the bar. This was done and they got off as the captain had anticipated, and proceeded on their way. From Port Lavaca many of the people who were bound for the colony of Castro went on in carts, but the Wernette family went in wagons with their household goods, except the elder Wernette and three brothers. They came on foot and carried guns.

One night while traveling in a trail after they had arrived upon the frontier, not far from the San Antonio River, they discovered the faint glimmer of a fire far out in the mesquite brush. The elder Wernette told his companions to remain where they were and he would go to the fire and see who were there. On approaching the spot he saw twelve men all asleep around the fire, and Mr. Wernette stood close to them and observed them with great interest and curiosity, as he had never seen such people before. They were dark-skinned and had long, black hair. Mr. Wernette now retraced his steps to his companions and told them of the strange people he had seen asleep around the fire, and said that he came away without disturbing them. Just think of it! This newly arrived colonist, just from the crowded cities and country of Europe, standing in the midst of twelve sleeping Comanches on the frontier of Texas, far from the habitation of any civilized man, and curiously gazing upon their swarthy faces by the light of their flickering campfire. He did a fine thing not to disturb them. Next evening about sunset the four pedestrians discovered a smoke ahead of them on a hill, and Mr. Wernette again went forward to reconnoiter. They likely by this time had talked matters over and had to some extent realized that there was danger in such a wild country as this, and their scout advanced with more caution. Going through the brush, he arrived near enough to make discoveries without being seen himself. He saw a man beside a small fire broiling a piece of meat on a stick, and as his face was white, boldly advanced in view. The quick eye of the man discovered him, and jerking up his rifle he presented it at him, and said sharply, "Que viva." Mr. Wernette did not know what this word meant, but supposed from the man's action it was a challenge, and answered quickly, "Friend." The gun was lowered and the man said in English, "Come on." They soon came together and found they could understand each other, and had a talk. This man was one of Jack Hays' rangers, who was carrying a dispatch, and the place was on Calaveras Creek, eighteen miles from San Antonio. He saw the man many times afterwards, and they were always good friends. His name was John Lamon, and he afterwards died at Castroville.

The party arrived finally and safely at Castroville and settled there. Mr. J. B. Wernette says he never saw as many deer and wild horses as were in the country at that time. He says it is no use to say thousands—there were millions of them; more game than in any country God created. The settlers soon commenced to build rude picket houses. Some of the Indians pretended to be friendly and often came to the settlement, bringing wild turkeys and deer horns for sale. They would not bring small turkeys, but all large gobblers that would weigh fifteen pounds when dressed, and sold them for ten cents each, and deer horns the same. They got along all right with the Indians until the American settlers came from the east. One party of these, five in number, with their families camped near town. They had five wagons and some good horses and mares. The grass was waist-high near town, and the men made a corral of their wagons and put all of their best horses inside and hobbled the balance out. The first or second night the Indians came and got all of the horses which were on the outside and carried them off. Next morning Mr. Wernette, then a boy 11 years of age, went down to the camp of the Americans to play with some of their little boys whom he had got acquainted with, and saw the men trailing the Indians to find which way they had gone off with the horses. Many cut hobbles were seen lying about on the grass, and at that time Mr. Wernette did not know what all this meant. After getting the direction of the trail located, the Americans went back to their wagons and commenced making preparations to follow the red thieves and try to recover their stock. The young German boy saw them putting pones of corn bread in wallets, which was the first of this kind of bread he had ever seen. They had long rifles, and pouches and powder horns across their shoulders, and belts around their waists containing pistols, and long heavy knives in scabbards, and blankets rolled up and tied behind their saddles. This was all new and strange to Mr. Wernette. When all was ready the men mounted, and telling their wives good-by and to take care of themselves, they would be back some time, started off towards the west. Their names were George Hammer, George Allen, two Arnold brothers, and Dick Thompson. Their trip was not of long duration. They returned on the following day, bringing their stolen horses, four Indian scalps, with bows, shields, blankets, etc. The Indians were found in camp at the Quihi Lake, ten miles west from Castroville, and were not aware of the presence of the white men until they heard their rifles in their very midst. They were panic-stricken at the sudden and unexpected assault, and made but little show to fight, scattering wildly into the brush. These settlers who made such quick work with them had fought Indians on the Colorado and Brazos, and understood the business.

The Germans had never up to this time fought the Indians. In fact, they did not know how to trail them, and had no horses for them to steal. From this time on, however, they had to learn to trail and to fight them, and many became good Indian fighters, as the history of Castro's colonies will show. The Indians walked the streets of Castroville no more. Mr. Wernette says it would have been a good thing for them if all the Indians had been killed in the fight, for those who escaped told the news of the battle at Quihi Lake, and Castro's colony had to suffer for it. The Americans left and settled near where Lytle is now, and then some of them moved on further west. Every light moon now the Indians would come, and when horses were brought to the settlement the Indians would get them, and the Germans would have nothing to follow them on. One night the men of Castroville, during a light moon, said they would lay for the Indians. So twenty of them took their guns and went out of town near the foot of the hills and stood guard, walking back and forth like regular sentinels. Mr. Wernette's father went out with the old men, and he stayed with his mother. They had one little pony, and he was chained to a hackberry tree in the yard. The house was not finished, and had slats nailed across the windows several inches apart. Along in the night Mrs. Wernette through this window saw an Indian trying to get the pony, and said to her son, "Come here; the Indian will get the pony." The boy said, "No; let the Indian get him," and covering up his head lay still. The mother now reached between the slats across the window and tried to catch the Indian by the hair, and he ran away and let the horse alone. The old men came in about daylight, and thought sure they had saved the horses this time; but every one in town was gone except Mr. Wernette's, that was chained to the tree. The Indians saw the men on guard in the moonlight and went around them.

The first of Castro's colonists killed by Indians were F. H. Gullett, Vincient Chan, Joe Chan, and a young man named Bassalle. They went up the Medina about seven miles to start a farm and ranch, and the Indians killed all of them the first night. Mr. Nic. Haby found the bodies while turkey-hunting. He saw a camp, and thinking it was Indians, he crawled up to it and found the bodies all stripped and their guns taken away. One of the men, Vincient Chan, had fought them and broken one lance. He was found twenty steps from the fire. His entrails were out, and he had walked on them while fighting the Indians. Gullett had been pinned to the ground by a lance, but whirled over when it entered his body and broke it. He was the oldest man in the party. He has a son of the same given name now living at Lockhart. The piece of the broken lance was still in Gullett's body. The men were careless. They had made their camp in a thick place in a flat at the foot of a hill, but had made their fire against a dead tree, which during the night had burned up to the top and could be seen some distance off, and revealed the location of their camp to a band of Indians that was passing. The men were evidently all asleep and an easy prey. Their guns were stacked around another tree several yards from where they lay, but the Indians did not see them and did the work with lances without firing a shot. This was just before Christmas, 1847.

Before this time Castro took part of his colonists and went on a prospecting tour to Quihi Lake to arrange about putting a colony there and laying off a town. One day at the lake a man named Peter Frigger strayed off and the Indians captured him, and that night made him lie down by a fire, as he did not look like he wished to get away, but that night Peter commenced sliding on his stomach, and when about twenty feet away jumped up and ran and made his escape. Next day a searching party found him coming back.

Mr. Wernette knew Capt. Jack Hays well, and says he was the best Indian fighter in the West, and had the best set of men and as brave a lot as he ever saw. He also knew Big Foot Wallace, and says the Indians were afraid of him and would run when they saw him in command of a fight.

One night after the Civil war, while Mr. Wernette was living in the upper part of town, he carried his horse Bill across the river and belled and hobbled him. Late in the night he heard the bell rattling loud and fast, and said to his wife, "The Indians are after old Bill." Next morning he told his stepson if he would go and get old Bill he would give him a nice present. The boy skipped out and went quickly, but soon came back with the bell and hobbles, saying that was all he could find of him. That night the Indians got all of the horses on the east side of the river, but delayed so long in rounding up and getting them together that by daylight they had only proceeded with them as far as the head of Colevro Creek. John Green, a brave man and good Indian fighter, raised six men, and taking a near cut came upon them at the Verde pass and at once charged them. Green was ahead of his men and first encountered the Indians, but soon scattered them with his revolvers, but was himself severely wounded. The other men soon came up and all the horses were retaken and brought back, and Mr. Wernette got old Bill again. Green afterwards belonged to a company of minute men, and was first lieutenant. On one occasion he wanted to take a night scout and ordered the men to saddle up, but while saddling his horse, was shot and killed by a Mexican who belonged to the company, who then ran and made his escape into Mexico. What the trouble was about the writer has not been able to learn.

About 1847 a company of rangers was stationed on the Medina above town, about where the Haby settlement now is, and on one occasion the captain gave permission for seven of the men to go up the river above where the old Morman camp now is, to hunt bear. The rangers camped near the river, and unsaddling their horses left one man in charge, and the balance scattered in the mountains to hunt. A band of Indians saw the ranger camp, and came down out of the hills and attacked it. The guard ran off and took shelter behind a tree and aimed his gun, but would not fire on account of the Indians being so numerous. They got all the horses, but did not attack the position of the lone ranger, who stayed behind his tree a distance off and watched them. The hunters in the mountains heard the noise in camp and came back, but all of their horses and the Indians were gone. They had to walk back to camp, carrying their saddles part of the way, and then hiding them. The captain was very mad when they returned and told their tale of woe, and said it was a disgrace to the ranger service, and at once took nearly all of the company and followed the Indians.

He had a friendly Indian for a guide named Bill Chism, and the captain said to him, "Now, follow the trail; we want to catch them." Bill said, "Follow me; me catch." The trail was long and tedious to follow, over hills, rocks, and gullies, clear to the head of the San Saba River. But here they came upon the Indians in a village. The attack was made on horseback with great fury, the rangers bursting in upon the astonished Indians like a clap of thunder from a clear sky. As they went in the captain told them not to shoot the squaws, and many of these passed out close to the rangers, running between the charging horses. The bucks were headed off in every direction and many of them killed. They were completely rattled, and hurt but few of the rangers and killed none. One hundred head of horses were captured, but of those lost by the rangers on the Medina none could be found. The others were brought back to camp and there sold to the highest bidder, as no owners could be found for them. The people from Castroville went up to the ranger camp and bought many cheap horses, some for $3 or $4, and so the country was stocked with horses again.

The people in Castroville were not aware that the rangers had gone on this expedition, and two young fellows from town went up there one day. Two rangers had been left in camp, and becoming lonesome built a large bonfire of old boxes and barrels, which made a great blaze. When the two young men from town came in sight of this large fire they ran back and told that the Indians had killed all of the rangers and burned up their camp. There was great excitement in Castroville, and Castro told all the people to come to his place and fort up. Wagons were driven across the streets on both sides of the house and a close barricade made, as they fully expected to have the Indians to fight. One man would not fort up with the balance, but taking his wife got into a canoe and stayed on the river all night. Another who lived above town sent his wife and children in, but would not come himself, saying he would stay up there and let the Indians get him first. He had been a drummer in the army in Europe, and taking an old brass kettle beat on it all night. The people in town from where they were forted up could plainly hear the old kettle, and with but short intervals it continued its lonesome rattle through the night. Next morning a scout was sent up the river, who went to the ranger camp and there found the two young rangers in perfect ignorance of the great tumult they had caused. A swift runner went back to town with the information of the false alarm, and the people scattered back to their various abodes.

Mr. Wernette says that in 1856 he was at the Bandera pass and saw a great many bones there, mostly those of horses. At the north end of the pass, where the grass had recently burned off and exposed them, they were very thick. These bones were those of horses killed there by the rangers in Jack Hays' great battle with the Comanches about 1843.

JUDGE JAMES M. HUNTER.

Came to Texas in 1861.

Judge James M. Hunter, who at this writing lives at Rock Springs and is the county judge of Edwards County, is an old-time Texan, and has many interesting reminiscences of early days along the border.

Judge Hunter was born in Buncombe County, North Carolina, in 1829. The wife of Gov. Bob Taylor, of Tennessee, was his niece, being a daughter of his sister, Mrs. Baird, of North Carolina. He came to Texas in 1851 and first stopped at Fredericksburg, where he had a brother living, John Hunter, who kept supplies and traded with the Indians, who at that time were friendly. In the fall of 1852 he went to Seguin, in Guadalupe County, and put up the first billiard table that was ever there. In connection with the billiard table he also had a saloon, but not liking that business, sold out in the following spring.

At this time Maj. Robert Neighbors was a member of the Legislature, and was employed by the agent of the Peters Colony Company to take charge of a surveying party to locate lands for the company. These lands embraced the country along the Clear fork and tributaries of the Main Brazos and Wichita country. Major Neighbors employed Judge Hunter to raise a company as guards to the surveying party, for at this time the Indians were hostile again. The number of men to be raised was eighteen, and several of the Seguin men volunteered to go. Among these were William M. Rust, William Tom, Frank Biler, and Bud Grinage. They now went to Austin to complete the expedition. Before leaving Seguin Major Calvert presented Mr. Hunter with a pair of pistols that once belonged to his son-in-law Jack Hays, and which he had used in the Mexican war. The surveyors employed were W. M. Rust, from Seguin; Joe Bledsoe, John Hubbard, and a man named Smith, from Austin. Dr. Baker was physician and surgeon for the outfit, and he and others repaired direct to Fort Belknap on the Main Brazos. The surveyors drove their first stake on Pecan Bayou, and took up a connecting line from there to Belknap. This line was run by Rust and others. The party experienced no trouble with the Indians except a stampede of horses one night, but Hunter and Bledsoe got them back and none were lost. It was a very enjoyable trip. Game of all kinds was in abundance and plenty of fish in the streams. When the work was completed the expedition returned to Austin and disbanded, arriving there the last of November, 1853. The Legislature was in session, and H. E. McCulloch, of Seguin, was a member, and he and Hunter put up at the same hotel.

From Austin Judge Hunter went to San Antonio and was employed by George Giddings, brother to D. C. Giddings, to carry the mail from San Antonio to Santa Fe as conductor. Giddings was a contractor for mail lines, and one trip a month was all that could be made. Big Foot Wallace and Tom Rife had carried it the year before. This was in 1854. Judge Hunter stayed two years in this service, and during that time had three fights with Indians. The first fight took place at Howard's wells, known then as the springs. This vast country then was without an inhabitant from Joe Ney's ranch on the Seco, in the present limits of Medina County, clear on through a distance of 700 miles or more. When the stage arrived at Howard's wells, thirty-six miles from the Pecos, a halt was made to water the stock, and it was then the Indians made the attack, firing on them from the hills close by. There were eight white men in all, including the passengers and regular stage guards. The Indians numbered about twenty, and had three guns and the balance bows. The white men had Yaugers and rifles, and killed several of the Indians when they charged, but they were carried back into the hills and the Indians would come and charge again, but finally got enough of it and drew off. They were Mountain Apaches. The white men suffered no loss except having one mule killed, as they were protected by the stage and some ambulances that were along.

The next fight was between "Dead Man's hole" and Van Horn's well. This was an outbound trip, and the men along, besides the guards and driver, were Captain Skillman and three or four men with ambulances. They nooned together at "Dead Man's hole," and then Skillman and his party went on, but said they would stop at Eagle Springs and wait for the stage, as that was a dangerous place. After the party had separated and Skillman was out of sight, Hunter and his men saw fifty Apaches on the prairie bearing down upon them, and there were but thirteen of the white men. One of these was Dr. Giddings, brother of the contractor. The teams were now whipped up to a lively gait, but the Indians came faster on their ponies, and ran quartering across the prairie to intercept them, and when about 200 yards off Hunter said, "Stop, boys; we have got to fight these fellows. Side line the mules." The Indians also halted, and the chief said "Amigos." Judge Hunter said to Louis Dickens, who could speak Spanish, to tell that fellow if they were friends to stay where they were; that he was as close as they wanted him to get. The Indians now consulted awhile and all galloped off, but made a circle and came around in the road ahead of them and displayed a soldier's jacket on a spear, and also held up a letter to view, and then dropped it in the road. A week before this they had killed a military express messenger between Fort Davis and Fort Clark, and the jacket was his.

After the Indians dropped the letter they galloped off on the road taken by Skillman and his party, and Hunter was satisfied they knew he was ahead and were going to overtake him, so he pushed on with all speed with his men to the Limpia mountains to help him. The letter which the Indians dropped in the road was an official one directed to Washington by the quartermaster, which they had obtained from the dead body of the messenger. The Indians caught Skillman in camp shoeing mules, and were trying to get the drop on him by playing "amigos," but Skillman told them to get away and not come close, especially when he saw Hunter and his party coming. The Apaches were determined to have a scrape, and before Hunter could get there the fight commenced. The Indians made a complete circle around Skillman's ambulances, but he had brave men with him, and the rapid puffs of smoke that came from the vehicles proved to Hunter that they were making a game fight of it, and he and his men renewed their exertions to reach them, whipping their teams into a gallop and shouting words of encouragement. It was a most dangerous looking circle to attempt to pass through, but they went in firing right and left at the yelling Apaches, who also fired on them, but without effect, overshooting them with the scopets which most of them carried. The combined forces now beat the Indians off, and about sundown they left, having five killed besides quite a number wounded. The stage and ambulances caught most of the bullets and arrows, and some of the horses and mules were hit. The two parties camped on the battleground that night and continued their journey next morning without any further trouble from the Indians. The next fight took place at the head of Devil's River. The Indians attacked the camp at night and tried to stampede the mules, but were beaten off, and no damage was done to either side. On these trips Judge Hunter avoided as many fights as possible, seldom camping at the regular watering places. Many people were killed along this route, travelers and immigrants, as the numerous graves indicated. There were five at Eagle Springs. The only stage man killed on these trips, said Judge Hunter, was one of the stage guards of Big Foot Wallace. In 1856 the judge quit this mail service and went with Pellum and Garrison to New Mexico to run parallel and meridian lines to base townships and subdivisions, and was one year in this business.

In 1858 he went with Col. Earl Van Dorn on his Wichita expedition as contractor and sutler, but was not in the famous Indian battle that was fought on that occasion, but was coming back on Van Dorn's trail. The Indians were badly defeated and suffered great loss, but Colonel Van Dorn himself was badly wounded and had to be brought back on a litter. Ex-Gov. Sul Ross, then a young man, was in the battle, and was also wounded. Many more of the whites were wounded and some killed. Judge Hunter was at a place called Radzminski when Colonel Van Dorn was brought in, and says it was a wonder he did not die, as the case of medicine and surgical instruments was lost during the fight. The mule which carried them and the steward in charge both disappeared when the battle commenced, and were not heard of again. They had to send to Fort Arbuckle, in the Indian Territory, for medicine and instruments, the distance being forty miles. On this expedition they saw a lot of abandoned wagons and carts which had been left by Col. John S. Ford in one of his Indian campaigns.

During the Civil war Judge Hunter served as first lieutenant in the company of Capt. Henry Davis on the frontier and afterwards commanded the company, receiving the commission of captain from Gov. Francis Lubbock. While in command of the company he was in two fights with the Indians, the first at the head of the Pedernales and James rivers. The forces were exactly even—eleven rangers and eleven Indians. The trail was started on the Llano River and followed to where the fight took place. Six of the Indians were killed and the balance scattered. A ranger named John Benson was wounded with an arrow in the hip. The spike curled up in the bone like a fishhook, and the doctor had to cut it out. Besides the ranger, one horse was wounded. This was in February, 1863. The Indians were trying to get into a horse country. They only had two poor ponies, and were resting when the rangers came upon them. They stood their ground until the chief was killed, then became confused and ran, but would rally and fight when overtaken, and would run again when the rangers stopped to load their guns. The Indians were all young-looking fellows, and would have all been killed if the powder of the rangers had been good, but it was wretchedly bad. It was what they called in those days homemade powder, or Confederate powder, made in the south. The majority of the rangers were from the Guadalupe Valley, and were a fine set of men. The next fight was on House Mountain, but with no results, the Indians running and getting away. Before the Civil war was over this frontier regiment was sent to the Confederate army and left the frontier exposed. Judge Hunter then received a commission as major from Governor Murrah to serve in the frontier district from Burnet County to the mouth of the Rio Grande. He organized his district effectually for frontier protection, and remained in this until the close of the war.

In 1870 he again served as a ranger captain; had no fights with the Indians but many chases. This wound up his service in the military line. In 1876 he was a member of the Legislature, the district he was sent from being composed of ten counties, to wit, Mason, Gillespie, Kendall, Kerr, Medina, Uvalde, Menard, Edwards, Bandera, and Kimble. Edwards and Kimble at this time were unorganized. He was at one time county judge of Mason County, and also served that county as surveyor. When his present term is out (1898) he will have served Edwards County ten years as county judge.

During Judge Hunter's eventful career on the Texas frontier he has been associated with the following distinguished men: Gens. John B. Hood, Robert E. Lee, Fitzhugh Lee, E. Kirby Smith, Oakes, and Thomas. Robert E. Lee was a captain, Fitzhugh Lee was a second lieutenant, Oakes was a lieutenant, and all held some rank at the frontier posts. Fitzhugh Lee, he says, had a most exciting adventure in a fight with Indians on the Clear fork of the Brazos, in which he killed an Indian chief in a desperate and long-contested hand-to-hand fight.

When the writer saw Judge Hunter in 1898 he seemed to be in perfect health, and was a fine specimen of physical manhood. May he now rest in peace from his labors.

ED. ENGLISH.

Native Texan. Born in 1852.

Mr. Edward English, son of Capt. Levi English, was born in De Witt County, Texas, on the 28th day of April, 1852. His mother was Matilda Burleson, cousin to Gen. Edward Burleson, and for whom the subject of our sketch was named. She was also a cousin to Joe Hornsby, of the early settlers of that name, who lived on the Colorado and figured conspicuously in the frontier history of Texas. Joe Hornsby, it will be remembered, was with Josiah Wilbarger when he was scalped by the Indians, and was the last man to leave him. Mrs. English was a sister to "Buffalo" John Burleson.

Ed. English moved to the Leona River, in Frio County, with his parents when a small boy.

In 1860 the Indians came into that settlement on a raid and killed Leonard Eastwood and a man named Sanders, and wounded a third, John Spears. On that morning the three men ate breakfast at Eastwood's ranch and then separated. Sanders went up the river, and met the Indians, and was killed by them. The other two men went down the river on some business, and on their return met the same party of Indians, who attacked them and killed Eastwood. They gave Spears a hard chase and succeeded in wounding him in the back with an arrow, but he made his escape and ran to the ranch of Capt. Levi English. Young Ed. was there, and saw the arrow sticking in his back as he came up. The people all forted up at the house of Captain English for two weeks and then abandoned the country, most of them going to Atascosa County. The English family only remained away about six months, and then went back to the Leona. Many others came, and in 1865 quite a number of settlers were there. In the above named year the Indians made a raid and were pursued by Captain English at the head of a band of settlers and a desperate battle was fought with them, in which Bud English, oldest brother of Ed, was killed and his father wounded. A full account is given of this fight elsewhere. In this same year, in the fall, Captain English moved to Carrizo Springs.

In July of 1866 Ed., who was attending to the horse stock, took his little brother Joel out with him to hunt for horses on the range. They rounded up all of the horses but two, which were not found, and they continued the search for them until near sunset, and then turned up a creek to go home, and Ed. shot a deer. From here they crossed the creek and went out through a flat on the opposite side, traveling towards the west. Joel stopped at the creek to water his horse, and Ed. went on about 100 yards with his hat pulled down in front, as the setting sun was shining in his face. At this time he heard the sound of horses' feet in front of him, and looking up saw seven Indians about 150 yards distant, likely attracted in that direction by the report of his gun. They commenced to yell and charged him, coming in the shape of the letter V. Ed. wheeled his horse to go back, and as he did so an Indian fired at him with a six-shooter and wounded the horse in the hip. The Indian continued to fire, and the next shot went through the hindtree of the saddle and wounded Ed. in the hip. The whole band now closed around him, and he fired at the one nearest him on the right with a Ballard rifle and killed his horse, the ball breaking his neck, but the shell hung in the rifle, and it was thus rendered useless. The Indian after his horse fell, who was the same one who had fired the other two shots from the revolver, fired again. This shot cut the wristband from one of Ed.'s shirt sleeves, wounded him in the wrist, and knocked the gun out of his hand, which fell to the ground. All of the Indians now closed around, thinking the young settler had no more arms. He had a six-shooter, however, and began to draw that, when an Indian made a thrust at him with a lance. The pistol scabbard was one of the old-fashioned kind, with a flap that came down over the pistol stock. The lance of the Indian struck this pistol flap and went through it, but Ed. succeeded in getting the pistol out and shot the Indian dead from his horse. The ball went through his head, and he fell in a heap on the ground. The other Indians all ran to this one, and Ed. got clear and started for the ranch. Joel had made an attempt to get to his brother, but was cut off by an Indian, and was still circling around trying to get to Ed. The Indians now left the dead one and came in pursuit again, cutting off Joel, who had made another run to get to his brother. He had no arms of any kind. Ed., however, went to his rescue, and the Indians gave

ED. ENGLISH.

back when they saw the revolver in his hand. While it takes a long time to write these things, it all occurred in a few minutes. When Ed. opened the way for his brother to come to him he let his horse out towards the ranch again, but the Indians again cut Joel off. They made no attempt to kill him, but seemed to want to capture him. Edward again went to his rescue and drove the Indians back with his revolver. He now shouted to Joel to run his horse close in beside him and make him do his best. He did so, and the two brothers ran side by side with the Indians in pursuit. In crossing a muddy flat four of the Indians caught up with them. Ed. had to watch his horse to keep him from falling, and while doing this running through the boggy flat an Indian shot him in the back with an arrow, which struck under the shoulder blade. He turned on the Indians now and fired at them with his pistol, but failed to hit one as he knew of. Wheeling, he again ran towards home, the Indians in pursuit for a mile or more, and when in 300 yards of the house, the Indians turned back, Ed. firing twice more during this last run. Captain English pulled the arrow out of his son and did all that he could for him, but he came near bleeding to death, and had to stay in bed thirty days. This was one of the remarkable escapes so often recorded in frontier history. If young English had not remained cool and kept his head, as the saying is, during all this fearful ordeal through which he was passing, it would have ended like hundreds of others along the border, and he would have lost his scalp and his little brother been carried into captivity, if not slain. No pursuit of the Indians was made, as no other settlers lived there.

The next raid the Indians made was in 1870, about 200 of them. They first struck the ranch of Charley Vivian, fifteen miles above, and killed a Mexican there and captured a Mexican boy. They came down the main road, then to the ranch of Dave Adams. Before they arrived there, however, they came in contact with five cowboys, namely, William Bell, Joe Tumlinson, Si Hay, John Smith, and a Mexican. The boys were not able to make headway against such a band of Indians and retreated before them, and in the pursuit the Mexican was killed. Adams had his horses in the pen and was out there with them when the Indians made their appearance. They came around the pen and Adams left it and tried to gain the brush, but was cut off by the Indians, and took a position behind a mesquite tree to make a fight. His only weapon was a Ballard rifle, and the first shot he fired the shell hung, which left him at the mercy of the savages, and they soon killed him. This was evident from the fact that his gun was found a few days after on the battleground where the rangers fought them, with a shell fast in the barrel.

The Indians still kept their course to within one-half mile of Carrizo Springs. Nine men went to meet them when informed of their approach and fought them, some of whom were as follows: William Pickens, Rube Bell, Caldwell Roberts, Si Hay, and Joe Tumlinson. The names of the others can not be recalled. The Indians drove these back. The men from the upper ranch followed them, and going around beat them to the ranch. At the time the Indians were killing Adams a wagonload of people drove upon the scene, going to Carrizo. They were Jack McCurly (cousin to Ed. English), Jake Burleson, Pat McCurly, Pleas. English (brother to Ed.), Mrs. Matilda English (mother of Ed.). They turned the wagon and ran away from the Indians, and only two followed them, the balance being at this time engaged with the cowboys and Dave Adams. Jack McCurly was on horseback, and rode in the rear of the wagon and fought the Indians, telling those in the wagon to throw everything out that was heavy, so that the team could make better time. The two Indians were kept back by Jack, and they had no chance to shoot at the occupants. The people at the main ranch at the springs stayed together that night and stood guard. Next morning twenty-five men got together, led by "Buffalo" John Burleson, and pursued the Indians below Fort Ewell, eighty miles below the springs.

Ed. English and his father and two or three Mexicans went out and recovered the bodies of Adams and the Mexican that was killed and brought them in. They turned the body of the dead Mexican over to the Mexicans at the main ranch, and Ed. and his father took the remains of Adams to his own house and buried him in the yard. Captain English made the coffin, and while he was doing so Ed. dug the grave, and these two buried him. He was shot in many places with arrows and bullets. One of his fingers was shot off.

On the third day a squad of rangers came from Uvalde, under the command of Dr. Woodbridge, on the trail of the Indians who had committed depredations on Turkey Creek, in Uvalde County, on their way down. Among these rangers were Tom Blakeney, Doc Quebum, Billy Cox, John Whitney, and others, about thirteen in all. They were armed with Winchesters, and Dr. Woodbridge said, "Now, we want to find an Indian." Captain English said, "If you will stay with me three days I will show them to you." They then went out to the main pass and waited for the Indians, to catch them on their return from below. Each day a man was sent east and one west to see if the trail had passed up. About the third day Captain English, Doc. Quebum, and a boy went west and two east. These two saw the Indians coming, and returned and reported the same to the doctor, and he took what men there were in camp and went to meet them. When Captain English and his men came back to camp it was abandoned, and they followed on the trail of the rangers and came to where there had been a battle, several dead horses being there, and one dead ranger. They now took the trail of the Indians, thinking the rangers were still after them. In two miles they were overtaken, and twenty-five Indians came back to fight them, the chief and his warriors circling the white men and shooting at them, but Captain English told his boys not to shoot until they thought they could hit something. The Indians had shields and rode low on their horses, moving rapidly, and were hard to hit. Quebum finally shot at the chief and cut the string which fastened the shield to his arm, and it fell to the ground, and after they passed he ran and got it and waved it at the other Indians, and yelled as much like the chief as he could. The shield had a woman's scalp attached to it, the hair of which was very black.

The Indians now quit the fight and moved on again, followed by Captain English and his men, still thinking the rangers were ahead. The Indians camped at dark, and English rode so close to their camp that he was discovered and chased by fifteen of them, but made his escape and then came on back. It was when he first came onto the ground where the rangers fought them that he found the gun of Dave Adams with the shell hung in it.

Two rangers came to the springs and reported the main battle, and said all of the rangers were killed. They left, it seems, before it was over. Another account of the fight will be seen elsewhere.

Ed. English saw Dr. Woodbridge when he came to the springs after the fight. His hat was gone and he was riding behind Tom Blakeney, and his neck was badly swollen. During the fight an Indian knocked him off his horse with a bow and came near breaking his neck. Captain English furnished two horses to assist the rangers in getting back to their camp.

About 1872 the Indians came again, thirty-five in number, to the springs. Ed. English at this time had 1000 head of sheep and a herd of cattle. He was delivering the cattle to a shipper, and had sent the shepherd out with the sheep. Ed. went out while engaged in delivering the cattle without his gun, and heard shouting and yelling, and also fifteen shots fired. He ran back after his gun, and three men ran in and reported that his shepherd was killed. They were John Bell, Van Neill, and a Mexican. Ed. went to see about his shepherd and sheep, and found the Mexican herder killed and scalped. He brought him in and then went after the Indians, but could not overtake them. This time the pursuit was by United States troops under the command of Major Perry.

In 1874 the Indians came again and killed and captured all of Captain English's horses, about thirty head, and then came on down to within a mile of the springs. Ed. had a stock camp a mile from the route they were coming, and had forty head of horses there. A Mexican ran to the main ranch house and reported that he saw the Indians going in the direction of Ed's camp, and he at once mounted his horse and started over there, and heard shooting before arriving. On coming upon the scene he found his Mexican horse herder shot through with a bullet. Ed. asked what was the matter. "Oh, bad luck," said he; "lost all the horses. Look out, the Indians will kill you." On being asked where the Indians were, he said, "Right behind the brush there, cutting hobbles off the horses." English went around where he could see them, and counted twenty, but not being able to do anything, he withdrew, and next day with a party followed them to the Rio Grande, but they crossed over, and the men had to return without having an opportunity to fight them. The wounded Mexican died and was buried the following day.

In 1876, while Ed. was out on a cow-hunt with two white boys and two Mexicans, driving a bunch of cattle, he saw about forty Indians. One of the white boys and one of the Mexicans ran, but

Ed. told one of the others to hold his horse and he would shoot at them one time, anyhow. Before the boy could get around to hold the horse the Indians charged them, coming in a V shape. English fired one shot, and he and the boys retreated to a large thicket and entered. The Indians followed and fired 100 shots or more, but stopped at the thicket, and Ed. and his party went on through the brush and made their escape back home. This was his last scrape with Indians. He now lives in Kinney County.

HENRY HARTMAN.

Came to Texas in 1860.

In the summer of 1897, while the writer was traveling in the interest of the Galveston News in Medina County, he attended a picnic given by the thrifty German settlers around Quihi and New Fountain. Arriving on the ground in company with Judge M. Charobiny, quite a crowd had already collected in a beautiful pecan grove near the Verde Creek. The affair being under the auspices of the German Methodist church, nothing but temperance drinks were sold, such as soda water, etc. An abundance of everything good to eat that the country afforded was on hand and free to all. Speeches were made after dinner, and many old timers were present, and these more especially were the kind the writer was looking for. A small, quiet-looking man, who limped as he moved along, was pointed out as one who could give an interesting sketch of his life on the border. This man was Henry Hartman, and the writer was assured, if he could be prevailed on to tell the cause of his crippled condition, that every word would be facts and of more than passing interest.

Upon this the writer sought an interview, but at first was refused, saying it would not be of interest to other people, and to hunt up older settlers, who had a large experience to tell. At the request of his friends he finally consented to tell what he knew.

In giving this true account of one of the most desperate encounters with Indians, one such as but few of our most noted and famous Indian fighters have passed through, it will be clearly demonstrated what a brave and cool man can do under the most trying circumstances, and live to tell the tale.

Mr. Hartman came from the principality of Schaumburg Lipe to New Fountain in 1860. Coming at this rather late date was one reason he thought his experience would not be of as much interest as the older settlers who came with Castro's colony and helped to subdue the wilderness.

The trip across the ocean was made in the sailing vessel Wesser. Many storms were encountered, and at times it seemed that all was lost. The ship landed at Galveston, and Mr. Hartman came on out to the Castro settlements and first stopped at New Fountain. He stayed here several years and then drove stock to Kansas, but still New Fountain was his home for six years, when he moved to the upper Guadalupe, twenty miles above Kerrville, and there for some time engaged in hunting with two companions. This was in a dangerous locality, and they saw Indians several times. One man named Chris. Wachter lived above Kerrville, and on one occasion went to town, leaving his wife, brother-in-law, mother-in-law, and a negro man at the ranch. The white man and the negro next morning after Wachter left went half a mile from the house to make shingles, leaving the women alone. At this time a band of Indians were on a mountain, evidently watching the house, and when they saw the negro and white man leave made a descent on the ranch. One of them was standing in the door before their presence was discovered. Mrs. Wachter was young and stout, and as soon as she saw the savage she ran at him and knocked him backward out of the door and ran away, but did not escape the flight of arrows which followed, two wounding her in the back. She still continued her flight, however, and instead of going to the men who who were making shingles near by, ran to a mill one and a half miles away, where Hartman and others were at work, and was well nigh exhausted on arriving there. Mrs. Huepner was the only woman about the mill, and she pulled the arrows out of the stricken woman. Mr. Hartman and others repaired hastily to the scene of the raid, and on arriving at the house found it burned down and the body of the old lady in it. They now searched for the trail of the Indians, and went to the shingle camp and informed the men there what had happened. They had not even discovered the smoke of the burning house. The mountains were high all round, and the Indians could see from their summit all that was going on in the valley below without being seen themselves, and could easily escape when followed, so this band was not found by the trailers. The bones of the unfortunate woman were taken from the ashes and buried. She was evidently killed by the Indians before they fired the house. Mrs. Wachter recovered from the arrow wounds, and was still living in 1897.

Mr. Hartman came back to New Fountain and engaged in handling stock, and it was while in pursuit of this calling that he experienced one of the most thrilling chapters in his life's history. On the 11th day of June, 1873, he, in company with Louis Harting, Fred Folk, Charles Martin, and a negro named Johnson, went up on Verde Creek, fifteen miles from New Fountain, to gather a bunch of beeves. All were well armed except the negro, having three Winchesters in the crowd. The men, as they hunted the cattle, became careless. They had seen no signs of Indians, but had discovered men a long distance off, but paid no attention to them. They had rounded up some cattle, and Hartman saw some more at a distance, and leaving Charles Martin, a young fellow, with the loose horses which were brought along for a change, the balance went on with the cattle, so if those in the distance were theirs they could round them into the herd. While going to these cattle five or six men were seen in the distance, and Hartman said they were Quihi men looking for their oxen, and as before paid no more attention to them, and in fact was not expecting any Indians. After getting to the cattle another bunch was seen half a mile away on a hill, and Hartman, taking the negro with him, went off at a gallop to round up this bunch, leaving the other men holding the cattle already gathered. After going about 600 yards, and while passing a thicket, still in a gallop, they were fired on from ambush with firearms, ten shots or more being aimed at them. Hartman's horse was hit by a bullet just behind the saddle, breaking his back. The stricken animal gave three jumps and fell, turning on his side, and catching Hartman's left leg under him. The negro's horse was also hit, but he ran about 300 yards and then fell. The negro left him and went to the brush, but the horse regained his feet and ran again, but again fell, and died half a mile away. The Indians, seeing the white man's horse dead and lying on him, thought sure they had him, and came yelling around him, thirteen in number, and all shooting at close range with guns and six-shooters, but in their wild excitement failed to give him a wound, but knocked the dirt all over him. Some were firing pistols at not more than ten paces. Some men under these circumstances would have been powerless through fear to have done anything, and would have fallen an easy prey, but not so Henry Hartman. His Winchester was in the scabbard on the horn of the saddle, and this by a powerful effort he reached and drew out. The Indians, seeing their paleface foe was not dead, despite the fusilade and great dust they had raised, but on the contrary seemed very much alive and self-possessed, and with a dreaded Winchester now in his hands, beat a hasty retreat back to the thicket to reload. There were twelve on foot and one mounted.

All of this happened very quickly. Although Hartman had his gun in his hand and the Indians had retreated, he was still pinioned to the ground by his dead horse. He knew that as soon as the Indians reloaded their guns and pistols they would fire at him from cover and he would have no chance at them, so he began to make desperate efforts to release his leg, and succeeded after many trials in quick succession. After getting free from his horse he ran to a sumach thicket, and the Indians commenced shooting at him again. Crouching low on the ground, watching with gun ready to shoot, he waited for further developments on the part of the Indians, and while so doing saw the negro Johnson crawling in a thicket, and about the same time heard a battle open back at the cattle. Another band had attacked them besides those who were after Hartman.

The place in which the hard-pressed man had taken refuge did not afford any security except to partly hide his body from view. None of the bushes would turn a bullet, and they were cutting the twigs all around him, and finally one knocked his hat from his head. He saw the Indian that did this. He had crawled up behind some bushes and could see Hartman, and fired at him with a revolver. As he exposed himself to take another shot Hartman fired at his face, but went a little too high, wounding him in the top of the head, and knocking a white man's hat off he had on. The Indian quickly left this position and crawled away. During all of this time Hartman was watching in front the direction from which the shots were coming, but the Indians resorted to a trick to get the white man. They sent one of their number to crawl around through the bushes and take him in the rear, and shoot him unawares while he was looking for danger in front. This would likely have been successful, but the wily savage was like some hunters who, having slipped upon a deer, begin to breathe hard just as they are about to shoot. Hartman heard him breathing close behind him as he was raising up over the bushes and about to fire. Quickly turning he fired, and the Indian did the same, but his ball hit the ground almost under the white man, while the Comanche got a Winchester ball through the heart and fell forward on his face, his pistol falling almost on Hartman. The Indians still continued to fire, the balls cutting through the sumach bushes here and there.

Hartman was now determined to leave his place and go to a dense thicket which he could see, but which was beyond the Indians, and he would have to run the gauntlet to get there. He dared not fire much, as he only had six cartridges in the magazine of his Winchester at first, and two of these had been fired. He had a full box in his saddle pockets, but they were under his dead horse. With him, to think was to act, and soon as he made up his mind to leave the place he ran out and boldly charged the Indians with gun presented, and they scattered back towards their thicket and let him pass, but repeatedly fired at him. It was in this run that he got the wound that made him a cripple for life. The Indians behind fired after he passed them, and a ball struck him in the bottom of the foot, coming out in front and tearing the instep all to pieces. The force of the ball knocked him down, and the Indians, thinking they had him this time, came yelling and shooting around him once more. In this, however, they were again mistaken. Their invincible foe regained his feet and faced them with leveled Winchester, and they again scattered back to the thicket. The one on horseback came very close and Hartman intended to kill him, but as the Indian quickly threw himself over on the horse he would not risk a shot, but turned and managed to get into the thicket. Here he lay, with his gun ever ready to shoot, until the sun went down, but the Indians did not assault his position. This was a liveoak thicket with many big saplings in it, and afforded good protection. His foot bled a great deal, and soon after getting to cover he had to cut off his boot on account of its rapid swelling. He now also discovered that he had another wound in the leg, but not so severe. By the time night came he was very thirsty, but could not walk a step. As the hours passed on his thirst became so intense he determined to make an effort to reach water. Taking off his leggings, he cut one of the legs into strips and wrapped them tightly around the wounded foot, drawing the broken bones together as best he could, hoping by thus bracing them he would be able to walk. This, however, failed; as soon as he attempted to bear any weight to step the foot would give way and he would fall. The only chance was to crawl. The Hondo River he knew could not be far, and he determined to make an attempt to get there. His battleground was between the Verde Creek and Hondo.' All night long he crept and crawled, carrying his gun along with him. Of course he had to make many halts to rest, as he became exhausted from thirst and painful locomotion. When daylight came and he could get his bearings, he found that he had only succeeded in getting about 400 yards from the starting point, and that in the opposite direction from the water. A shower of rain came during the night, which to some extent relieved his thirst and the high fever which had set in. He would lick the water from the bushes as he crawled. Nothing more was seen or heard of the Indians.

After daylight he crawled out of the brush onto a hill where he could have a view of the country, but kept in some bushes on the top of it, so that he could see without being seen.

The Indians failed to find the negro, but stripped both dead horses. They also defeated the men who were with the cattle, and got all the loose horses. The companions of Hartman had no chance to aid him, although they saw his horse fall with him. A band of nine Indians attacked them about the same time, and they had to give way. This made twenty-two Indians in all of this raiding party.

The negro made his way to the settlement that night and reported that Hartman was killed, and that the Indians had carried him off on a horse. From his place of concealment he saw the Indians place the one Hartman killed on the horse that was in the party and go off, and he thought it was Hartman, not having seen him when he ran from that place.

The other men also reported him killed, and his friends sent out an ambulance to bring in the body and picked out a place to bury him. Guided by the negro, they found the dead horses and the bloody ground where he killed the Indian, but thought it was Hartman's blood, and that, as Johnson said, the Indians had carried him off. They now drove around looking for the body. About two hours after Hartman got on the hill he heard the rattle of the vehicle, and crawling out of the bushes he stood on one foot, leaning on his gun so that they could see him. They were very much surprised to find him alive, and soon had him as comfortably situated in the hack as circumstances would permit, and started back to the settlement. They had found the hat which Hartman had shot from the Indian's head, and it had a bullet hole through it. A party had come up in the night to hunt for the supposed dead body of Hartman, and passed so near him that he saw and heard them, but supposed it was the Indians, and remained quiet. This party was still out, but soon came upon the scene, and all went back together. There was great rejoicing among the people when the hack arrived. The wound in the leg was not severe and soon healed, but the foot was in a bad condition for many months, and will always make him a cripple.

Mr. Hartman was a ranger under Captain Richarz, and missed being in the terrible battle near Carrizo by being on a scout up the Nueces when it was fought.

J. M. ADAMS.

Came to Texas in 1849.

Among those who came to Texas at an early day when the country was wild and full of hostile Indians, none made a better record as brave men and Indian fighters than the Adams brothers, Cood, William, Henry, Dave, and James M., the subject of this sketch. Henry was killed by Indians at the Chalk bluff in Nueces Canyon in February, 1861. Henry Robinson, another noted Indian fighter, was with him at the time and was also killed. Dave was killed in 1870 near Carrizo Creek, also by Indians.

James M. Adams came to San Antonio in 1849. On the way out when he and his party came to the Guadalupe River, opposite New Braunfels, in Comal County, it was found to be badly swollen by recent rains, and a halt was made for it to run down sufficient to be forded without danger. During the time of waiting quite a crowd of travelers collected on the east bank of the river, among whom was Asa J. L. Sowell (father of the writer) and Calvin S. Turner (uncle of the writer), two of Capt. Henry E. McCulloch's rangers who came up from Seguin. The rangers sat on their horses a short time after riding up and surveyed the situation, and then expressed their intention of trying to cross. Some one expressed an opinion that it was not safe, and advised a longer tarry. Turner says, "I do not suppose it would drown a fellow," and they went into it. When the main current was reached the horse ridden by Sowell went down, and he was compelled to abandon him and swim back to the place of starting. The people on shore became greatly excited when they beheld the desperate efforts the ranger was making to gain the shore. He finally succeeded, and to the great surprise of the onlookers brought his gun out with him, which was one cause of his laborious efforts. Turner came back when he discovered his companion could not make it, and tried to swim his horse to his assistance, but seeing it was not needed he turned his attention to the horse, which had landed some distance below, and was trying to get up a bank. The horse was rescued, and nothing was lost except a pair of saddlebags. After waiting a short time the two rangers made another attempt to cross, and were this time successful. The others went over later.

In 1852 Mr. Adams went on a prospecting tour in company with two men named Daley and J. Snyder. A negro named Tom, who belonged to Snyder, was also of the party. The object of this expedition was to look at the country and prospect for gold and silver in the valley of the Rio Grande near Donna Anna, on West River, in New Mexico. It is surprising any of them lived to get back and tell the tale. They went into the very heart of the stronghold of the Mountain Apaches, who at that time were very hostile and vindictive towards white men. One day at noon they camped in the prairie near the head of a long draw that wended its way to the Rio Grande. The head of this draw was depressed several feet, and made what we might call a sinkhole. Having had no trouble as yet with Indians, they were not much concerned about them. All of a sudden, however, soon after stopping they discovered a band of 150 Apaches riding over a swell in the prairie towards them. They soon commenced yelling and charging. The four men saw no hope, but being well armed, determined to give them the best battle they could. They retreated towards the draw, firing as they went, and had the satisfaction of seeing several of the redskins fall from their horses. During this retreat the Indians were firing at them and Snyder was badly wounded, having his thigh broken by a ball. When he fell, the negro Tom lifted him up and carried him on his shoulders into the sinkhole. Here the men made preparations to stand a siege, provided the Apaches did not storm their position at once and overpower them. Snyder could still use his gun, and so accurate was the aim of the white men that an Indian would fall at almost every fire. They now began to widen the distance between them and the draw. They shot both arrows and bullets, but could do no execution, as the white men were entirely hid except when they would go to shoot, and then only the top of the head and eyes could be seen. The Indians yelled a great deal and made some weak charges, always wheeling their horses before getting very near the fatal sinkhole, and make a circle back.

The Indians finally settled down to a regular siege and concluded to starve them out, keeping in plain view during the day and howling and yelling around them at night. Four days passed, and the situation was unchanged. The men were starving for food and perishing with thirst. Snyder was nearly dead for the want of medical aid, and one and all now gave up all hope of ever getting out alive. The bloodthirsty Apaches still yelled and whooped and watched for the palefaces to come out.

Night had come again, and with it some hope. It had become cloudy, a slow, drizzling rain set in, and it was intensely dark. They must not miss this chance to escape. The Indians were still on the alert, but a man could not be seen twelve inches from his eyes. It was thought escape could be made down the draw by moving away in perfect silence and keeping in touch with each other. But what about the wounded man? He could not walk one step. Nigger Tom solved the problem. He was a powerful man physically, 6 feet 6 inches in height, 35 years of age, weighed 240 pounds, and proposed to carry his master. The horses and pack animals had all fallen into the hands of the Indians at the commencement of the fight. Everything now being agreed upon and arranged, Tom tenderly shouldered his master, who dared not groan, no matter how excruciating the pain. Adams and Daly took the four rifles and went in front, ready to shoot at a moment's warning, and all moved silently off into the black night.

Our readers must bear in mind that this draw was not a narrow gully, and that the Indians could place themselves in it and bar their progress. On the contrary it was wide and covered with grass, and was simply the depression between the swells of the prairie, and in daylight would afford no protection except the place the men had just vacated, where the sinkholes were. It was a desperate undertaking, but this was the last chance for their lives, and they moved on, hardly daring to breathe. No doubt the Indians had warriors posted at various places, but they were quiet. Not a sound was heard, nothing could be seen, and the Indians knew that a sound from them might bring the deadly rifle ball from out the darkness. An hour passed away, and they began to breathe more freely. No sound had been heard, and it was several miles back to the dreadful battleground. The white men now moved faster, keeping as best they could in the darkness towards the Rio Grande. The misty rain had to some extent alleviated their burning thirst and made them stronger. When daylight came, which they dreaded to see, it was thirty miles back to where they had left the Indians. The devoted Tom bore up bravely through this terrible ordeal, but was now well night exhausted, although frequent short halts had been made through the night. One thing which buoyed them up when morning came was the fact that the Rio Grande was near. They managed to cross this, and in eight days more they arrived at the copper mines in Old Mexico. This last traveling was not forced; they took their time and shot game by the way. From here they finally made their way back to their various homes, when Snyder recovered. Tom remained true to his master even in Mexico, and saw him safely back home. He was given his freedom, and never wanted for anything as long as a member of the Snyder family was around.

In 1854 Capt. Henry Skillman, who had a contract to run a stage from San Antonio to Santa Fe, employed Mr. Adams, among others, as stage guard. This was dangerous employment, as the line ran through the Comanche country in Texas and the Apache in New Mexico. The first serious trouble they had with Indians was at Howard's Wells on a return trip. There was a rich Philadelphian's outfit along, making seven vehicles, including the stage, and thirteen men, including the driver, guards, and passengers. The man from Philadelphia was named Henderson, and he had $300,000 in the hacks. Louis Oge was the conductor and driver this trip on the stage. While halted at the wells, seventy-five hostile Indians put in an appearance, and Oge made quick preparations for defense by running the hacks and stage in a circle and making breastworks of them and the mules and horses. The Indians charged at long range, but before they came close enough to do any damage Oge was ready for them, and the battle commenced. The Indians were so badly hit by the first fire from the inclosure that they fought shy and circled the wagons many times, yelling and shooting under their horses as they ran. This was kept up four hours, and then they withdrew with considerable loss. On account of their protection among the vehicles the white men suffered no loss, but there was sad havoc among the mules and horses, five of which were killed and many wounded. During the four years this line was run men were killed nearly every trip. When Skillman gave up his contract Mr. Adams went with a contractor named Butterfield and often met the Apaches again, but had no more serious conflicts with them.

At this time Mr. Adams said Big Foot Wallace ran a line from San Antonio to El Paso, and had a fight on Devil's River in which he had three men wounded. The Indians trapped them in the pass and shot from the bluffs.

In 1855 Mr. Adams was in an Indian fight at the head of the Nueces river. It was fought by citizens and soldiers, twenty-five men in all. It was a hotly contested field for a time, and seven of the white men were wounded. The Indians finally retreated, leaving forty of their number dead on the ground. The lieutenant who was in command was a West Pointer, but his name can not now be recalled.

In 1859 his brother, William C. Adams, led a company of men on an expedition into the mountains of the Nueces, and had a battle on the West prong. The Indians made a poor fight and lost nine of their number without inflicting any loss on the settlers, who numbered twelve, and the Indians many more.

Mr. Adams came from Llano to Medina City, in Bandera County, where the writer interviewed him in 1897. He said he was with Big Foot Wallace many times, and that he was a very intelligent and educated man. His brother, Sam Wallace, he says, was killed with Fannin at Goliad.

The last Indian fight Mr. Adams was in he went out with Lieutenant Johnson and some soldiers. They had stolen some horses from Adams and others. They found the Indians at the head of Paint Creek, not far from South Llano. There were but two Indians—a buck and a squaw—but the former made it very interesting for the soldiers. As soon as he saw the white men, and knew there was no chance to escape, he killed his squaw and then charged the crowd, and succeeded in wounding five of them before they could kill him. He knocked two soldiers off their horses with his bow.

Mr. Adams died near Medina City in the fall of 1899.

FRANK BUCKALEW CAPTURED BY INDIANS.

In about the year 1867 Frank Buckalew, son of Robert Buckalew and nephew of Berry Buckalew, Sr., who brought him to this country, was at work for Judge Davenport in Sabinal Canyon, above the forks of the river. His parents had died, and he and two sisters were all living at the same place on the Davenport ranch. At the time of which we write an ox had lost a bell, and Frank and a negro boy were sent to hunt it and instructed to search around the foot of a certain mountain, near a cedarbrake where the ox was wont to graze which had been so unfortunate as to lose his bell, and thereby get a boy into a world of trouble, as the saying is. The white and the black boy were unable to find the bell, but located something in a thicket which they could not make out the nature of, and kept getting nearer for a closer inspection. It had something red about it, and seemed to be in a heap on the ground among the bushes. Finally the white boy said he was going to throw his hat at it, and did so, but at the same time the inanimate looking lump on the ground began to materialize and expand, and that very suddenly, and developed into a powerful Indian, who sprang towards them with a whoop. The boys turned and fled, and terror lent speed to their legs and they gave the Indian a lively chase, but finally he struck Frank on the head with a bow and captured him, and the negro boy made his escape. The lad was now taken up the mountain by the Indian, who drove him along ahead of him, and when they arrived at the crest an old chief was discovered sitting on a rock, and the captive was conducted to him. The chief took a good look at him, and then addressed him in broken English with the inquiry if he was a German or an American, and at the same time vouchsafing the information that if he was a German his life would be spared, but if an American they would kill him. This was a severe test for a boy of his age, but he told the Indian he could not help it, that he was an American, and to do with him as he liked. This rather stumped the old chief, and he looked at him some moments in silence, and then gave orders for his clothes to be stripped off. This was at once obeyed, and the boy was ordered to go out on the brow of the mountain where he could see the house and call his sisters to come to him, as if in great distress. By this time several Indians had assembled, but they were afraid to make an attack upon the house, but no doubt would have done so had they known Judge Davenport was gone, who had ridden away after sending the boys to hunt the bell. Frank did as the Indian bid him and called his sisters, and they wanted to go to him, but they knew something was wrong, and were afraid to, and soon found out from the negro boy about the Indians. The Indians went west from here and stopped in the head of Nueces Canyon. They wanted more horses and were going down this valley on a raid, but did not want to carry their captive along for fear he would give them the dodge, or they would have a battle with the white men and lose him. They finally decided to leave him there alone, and to prevent his escape they placed him face down in a gully and tied his hands and feet together over his back and thus left him. They were gone a long time, and the hours were very tedious to the captive on account of his awkward and strained position and the thought of his captivity and no chance to help himself, as it was useless to pull at his cords, as he soon found out. The Indians were very successful, and came back before night with a bunch of horses, and untied the boy and made him help catch them. By this time he was very sore and stiff, and his body full of pear thorns and briers where they had driven him through them naked. After the horses were caught an Indian motioned to Frank with his hand. He thought the fellow wanted him to come up closer to him, and he did so, but was at once knocked down with a chunk of wood. The Indian wanted him to sit down by the motion he made, and adopted this forcible plan to make him understand it. From here the Indians went to the Pecos River, where was a large camp of them. They were Comanches, and soon a large body of Lipans came over from Mexico to fight them. A hard battle ensued, but the Comanches were the victors, and drove the Lipans back across the Rio Grande with a heavy loss. The Indians on this and other occasions discovered that their captive white boy was not a coward, and said when he grew up they were going to make a chief out of him, and commenced training him by dividing the Indian boys into two squads, placing him in command of one, and making them fight a sham battle with blunt arrows. During a charge and excitement of the fight young Buckalew shot a young Indian in the head too hard and came near killing him, and was badly scared in consequence, thinking now for certain the Indians would kill him, but on the contrary they applauded the act, and crowding around patted him on the back and cried "Bravo! Bravo!"

One one occasion a squaw picked him up, and laying him across her lap drew a sharp knife along his throat; but as he did not flinch she put him down again without injury. He thinks that if he had shown any fear she would have killed him.

During this long stay here in camp on the Pecos part of the employment of Frank was to make arrows after they had learned him how to construct them properly, and he soon became an expert at the business, as well as how to shoot them. He made trips with the Indians into Mexico to sell arrows and other trinkets, and on one of these occasions was seen by a Texas ranchman who lived on the Texas side of the river, and being satisfied he was a captive, hired a Mexican to ascertain the fact, and said if he could get him to the east side of the river and bring him to his ranch he would give him $150. The next time the boy was seen by the Mexican he asked him if he was not a prisoner from Texas and if he did not want to come home, and answering these questions in the affirmative, he was told to go back with the Indians, but to get two of the best horses there were in camp and come back into Mexico with them, and he would conduct him to a ranch across the river. Frank did this, and in a short time was back with the horses, and he and the Mexican set out and swam the Rio Grande, but had some difficulty in getting out on the other side on account of the steepness of the bank. The horses could find bottom to stand on, but could not climb out. They succeeded finally in getting over the difficulty by digging the bank down with butcher knives. They soon made their way to the ranch of the generous Texan, and he paid the Mexican for his services, but he was to conduct the boy home, which he did, and turned him over to Mr. William Davenport at Bandera, where he was joined by his sisters. On the way back one night was spent at the ranch of Judge Newman Patterson on the Sabinal, and the judge and other citizens of Uvalde County helped to pay the ransom. He looked very much like an Indian in their garb. His hair was also long and he was much sunburned. He was 12 years of age when captured, and they kept him eleven months. He still lives in Bandera County, and is a Methodist preacher. He is a cousin to Berry Buckalew, Jr.

BERRY C. BUCKALEW.

Berry Champion Buckalew was born on the 15th day of February, 1824, in Laurens County, Alabama, and came to Texas in the early 50's from Arkansas. He had four milk cows, and these he broke to the yoke and worked them in his wagon to Texas, and then traded for some young steers and milked his cows. In 1856 he went to the town of Bandera and then settled on Laxon's Creek, but soon after moved to Sabinal Canyon and lived at the Blue waterhole on a ranch of Judge James Booker Davenport, and kept some stock for him on shares. During this time he went back to Laxon's Creek, where his nephew was making shingles, and carried a load of them to San Antonio and sold them. With the proceeds of the sale of the shingles Mr. Buckalew bought supplies, and loading them into his wagon started back home, and on 26th of January, 1866, arrived at Cosgrove's ranch, on the Seco, at the foot of the mountains, and ate supper there about sundown. His team was very tired, and he borrowed a yoke of oxen from Cosgrove to pull his wagon on home. But a very curious thing happened. He was unable to hitch the oxen to the wagon, although they were perfectly gentle. They continually plunged and tried to get away, and were finally turned loose and Buckalew started on home, the distance being five or six miles. Before he started, however, Cosgrove told him he had better not go, as Indians were in the country and he had seen two of them. "No," said Buckalew, "I have been gone so long I am anxious to get home," and drove on. This was on Friday evening, and he left the ranch about dusk. On Saturday morning Mr. Cosgrove saw a horse across the creek in the flat, and sent a negro after him, thinking it was one of his, but when the boy came back he said the horse did not belong to the ranch. Cosgrove now went over to look at the horse himself, and found that he belonged to Buckalew—one he lead behind the wagon to drive up his oxen on every morning while camping on a trip. Mrs. Cosgrove now said, "I will bet you anything the Indians have killed Buckalew." Her husband thought not, and said she was too easily scared. On Sunday some cowmen ate dinner there, and Mrs. Cosgrove told them she believed Buckalew was killed. A man named Redmond Givens lived at Cosgrove's, and hearing all of this he went over on the Sabinal to the Davenport ranch and asked Mrs. Buckalew where her old man was. She answered that he had not yet returned home from his trip. Givens now told of the circumstance of his passing their ranch, and an alarm was at once raised. Givens went up the canyon to Waresville after men to help hunt, and got Ben Biggs, Joel Fenley, Wilson O'Bryant, and probably some others, and on returning they closely searched the road on both sides of it back towards Cosgrove's. The body was found one and a half miles from home, some distance from the road, down in a gully, as was also the wagon and team. One ox was dead, having been shot by the Indians, but the other three were still hitched to the wagon alive, but unable to get out of the ravine. Mr. Buckalew was lying on his back and a pile of rocks under his head, and three arrows in his body. It was evident he was walking beside his wagon when the attack was made upon him, and the Indians came up in his rear and shot one arrow in his back, and as he whirled around to confront them two more were sent into his breast. Probably then the team left the road and ran away, and he followed, trying to get some protection from the wagon, until it went into the ravine and the oxen stopped from inability to proceed any further, and here the Indians killed him, beating his head badly in doing so. The body was taken home by the men who found it, and washed and dressed in the Sabinal River.

Mr. Berry Buckalew, Jr., who now lives on Pipe Creek, in Bandera County, was 6 years old when his father was killed, and remembers well how he looked when laid out, and went up and kissed him. He thinks his father lived until just before the body was found, and that he placed the rocks under his head himself. His reason for this is, and a very good one, too, that the body was yet warm, although having been there two days and nights. It is likely the led horse broke loose when the team ran, and came back towards Cosgrove's.

After the killing of her husband, Mrs. Buckalew went back to Bandera, bought a lot in town, and sent her children to school. Here after a time (in 1868) she married James W. Siers, a veteran of the Mexican war, and then moved back to Laxon Creek. Their nearest neighbors were William Walker and Harvey Stanard, about one-fourth of a mile away. A widow lady named Moore lived with the family of Mr. Walker. On one occasion she started to visit Mrs. Curtis, who lived in Mono flat, just below where Medina City is now, and not far from Mr. Walker's place. Not more than half a mile of the distance had been made when the unfortunate woman met a band of nine Indians. The place was on top of a hill, and she turned and ran back from them and succeeded in getting within 200 yards of the house before she was killed. Mr. Siers heard the woman scream, and said to his stepson, Berry, "The Indians are killing some one," and all ran out of the house to look, and discovered the Indians going rapidly around a hill, all on foot. Young Buckalew seized his gun and ran in the direction of the noise of the woman when she was killed, but when he arrived on the ground Mr. Walker was already by the body. Mrs. Moore was lanced through the body, going in at the back, and she had fallen on her face and great quantities of blood had issued from the mouth.

Mr. Walker said if he had known what the situation was he might have been able to have saved her, but thought it was the children hallooing and playing when he heard her screams. He now told Berry Buckalew to go and tell Harvey Stanard, and he set out rapidly to do so, but soon met three Indians and aimed his gun at them, and they dodged back and ran away, and he was in doubt as to whether to empty his gun or not unless they charged him. Even if he killed one the others might get him with their arrows before he could reload or get away from them. He then went on to Stanard's, and he said the Indians passed his house in a fast run. A runner was now sent after Mr. F. A. Hicks, who, as soon as he heard the news, raised a squad of men and set out after the Indians and pursued them closely, but finally the trail was lost among the rocks in the mountains.

Mrs. Moore was buried in the Arnold graveyard, on Laxon Creek. Some time before the Indians came upon Mrs. Moore, Berry Buckalew saw the Indians running horses, but thought they were girls, on account of their long hair and being on foot. He was in the field piling cornstalks, and said to Mr. Siers, "What are the girls running the horses for?" He looked towards the hill where they were, and at once exclaimed, "Hell! those are Indians." The horses were rescued and the Indians went on, and the excitement was not over when they ran and killed Mrs. Moore. Some woman on the creek washing also saw the Indians on a hill looking at young Buckalew piling the stalks, and thought they were cowmen. They evidently had a notion of coming down into the field and trying to kill him.

Mrs. Buckalew, left a widow the second time, still survives and lives with her son Berry, on Pipe Creek.

LON MOORE.

Born in Texas in 1844.

Mr. Alonzo Moore, better known as Lon, was born in Prairie Lea, Caldwell County, Texas, in 1844. His father, Daniel Boone Moore, came there in 1843, and built the second house that was built there. The first one was built by Captain James H. Calahan, one of the survivors of Fannin's massacre, and who led an expedition into Mexico in 1855. The elder Moore helped to build Captain Calahan's house, and then built his own soon after. Daniel Boone Moore, father of Lon, was born in Kentucky, and was a cousin of the famous Daniel Boone, the first pioneer of the "dark and bloody ground," and for whom he was named. Lon Moore's mother was a Linscomb, and was a cousin of Col. James Bowie, who died with Travis and his heroes in the Alamo, so Lon has distinguished ancestors on both sides of the house. He has one brother named Haywood Travis and another Rezin Bowie, the latter named for a brother of Col. James Bowie. Cull is another brother and all are old time Texans and Indian fighters. Lon Moore is a plain, unassuming, western stockman, and no one in the West in better known than he and his erstwhile boon companion, "Seco" Smith. Many nights have these two spent around the campfire on the frontier, scouting for Indians and stockhunting. Daniel Boone Moore came to the Hondo with his family in 1852, and settled in Medina County ten miles south of Hondo City, the present county seat of Medina County, at what is now called the Lon Moore crossing on the Hondo River. The elder Moore was an old time Indian fighter, and died at Devine in 1892.

When Lon was 12 years of age the Indians made a raid down the Hondo Valley, and men were gathering to follow them. Lon, although so young, had the spirit of a frontiersman and Indian fighter, and mounting his horse with a long old rifle went with the crowd, ten in number, who soon got on the trail and followed it rapidly. Among the men were Big Foot Wallace, captain; Tom Hale, Manuel Wydick, Howard Bailey, Henry Adams, and Lon. The others can not not now be remembered. They overtook the Indians at the Presidio crossing of the Hondo. They had fifty head of horses, but abandoned them at sight of the white men and made a poor fight. They lost two killed and soon ran and scattered, and the settlers rounded up the horses and drove them back. Lon fired his rifle, but does not know if he hit an Indian or not.

In the early 60's the Indians made another extensive raid and killed many people and carried off a great deal of stock. Among those they killed on that raid was Pete Ketchum. Mark Harper and others were on the trail and found the body of Ketchum, but it was so badly disfigured about the face that no one recognized it but Mark Harper, and he at once said, "That is Pete Ketchum, and no mistake." The body was carried to the house of old man Daniel Moore, who was his father-in-law. The Indians were followed on down towards the Chicon, and the settlers were there joined by Big Foot Wallace, who was placed in command. These same Indians killed a young man named Long and scalped one of his sisters, thinking they had killed her, but she recovered and afterwards married "Seco" Smith. They also killed a negro, besides other white people, and gathered up many horses. Quite a lot of settlers, among whom was Lon, continued the pursuit under Wallace, overtook the Indians at the head of Seco, defeated them, and brought all of the horses back.

The Indians made a raid in the Hondo valley again during the Civil war and killed a boy named Hood, who lived at the Redus ranch. The settlers followed them into the mountains and were joined in Sabinal Canyon by a squad of rangers under command of Lieutenant Patton of Captain Montel's company. Lon Moore was with the rangers and belonged to the company. The Indians were found in camp in the mountains. There were fifteen of them and twenty of the rangers and settlers. The charge was made on them with loud shouts. The Indians strung their bows and tried to outyell the whites, but did not succeed, and soon ran, leaving four of their number dead on the ground, —the chief, one squaw, and two warriors. Lon ran close to one Indian and shot him with a pistol, breaking his leg, and he fell off a bluff. Moore leaped off after him, but made a narrow escape, as the wounded savage made a dangerous thrust at him with a lance, but the active young ranger sprang to one side and shot the Indian three times more, and killed him. He and others ran one Indian some distance and shot him repeatedly with pistols, but could not kill him. After the fight he told the men he had killed the chief, and showed them where he lay. Lon then tried to scalp him, but his knife was dull and he made slow progress. Some of the men told him it was not his knife but his heart that had failed him, but he finally got it off. The Indians had killed his brother-in-law, Pete Ketchum, and mutilated his face by cutting off his nose and skinning off the beard, and then, not being dead, dragged him through the prickly pears until life was extinct.

The men gathered up the spoils of the Indian camp, among which were twelve American saddles taken from men whom they had killed. Lon got a knife from the chief which had belonged to the boy Hood, whom they killed at the Redus ranch. It was brought back and given to the boy's mother. A party went back to this battleground some time after, who were not in the fight, to look at the dead Indians, and said the bodies of the Indians had been covered with brush. One lone Indian had returned and done this. It had rained since the fight, and all other tracks were obliterated but his, which had been made since the rain. Nearly all of the Indians who got away were wounded. There was so much shooting that Lon said he was as afraid of his own party as the Indians.

Lon Moore, Big Foot Wallace, and six other men had a running fight with Indians on the Seco, ten miles below D'Hanis, but they got into the bottom without much damage being done to them, but had to give up the horses they were driving off.

On one occasion the Indians captured a boy named Monier, on the Francisco, near the Moore ranch. The boy was with his stepfather Monier, and they tried to get to Moore's, but the Indians cut the boy off and captured him, and he was never heard of again by his people. He went by the name of his stepfather, but his right name is not remembered. The Indians were followed to the Llano, but were not overtaken.

On another occasion a band of Indians was followed by settlers from the Hondo to John Kennedy's ranch, and he was placed in command. The Indians were overtaken at the foot of the mountains at sundown and attacked, but escaped into a cedarbrake. These were the Indians that killed Wolf and Huffmann. Lon Moore was of this party, and says no Indian was killed, but they got the horses back, and two saddles, one bow, and arrows. The horses belonged to William Redus.

During the Civil war the Indians made a raid on the Hondo and killed Rube Smith, one mile west of his house, on Liveoak slough. Smith and Manuel Wydick were out on foot hunting horses and had separated, when a large body of Indians attacked Smith. Wydick from the top of a hill saw them running him, and heard his pistol shots, six in number, but could give him no aid against such odds, and ran in with the news. At this time Lon Moore and Nathan Davis were also out and had separated. Moore heard Smith shooting, but thought it was Davis firing at havilinas. A party went back after Wydick came, and soon found the body of Smith, which they carried home, and raised men to follow the Indians. The Indians numbered about thirty-five, and camped the first night on the Hondo and killed three beeves and partly cooked them. While on the trail the settlers found where a wounded Indian bled on a rock, and strips of Smith's clothing, which had been used for bandages and which had been thrown down, very bloody. Lon Moore afterwards went back to the spot where Smith was killed, under a persimmon tree, and cut his name and date of death on the tree. He also found eight spikes in the trees around the spot where he made his stand to fight them.

The Indians were overtaken at 12 o'clock on the day following the killing of the beeves. The men along were William Mullins, Nathan Davis, Lon Moore, Jerry Bailey, Manuel Wydick, Roe Watkins, Zed Watkins, Louis McCombs, Sam McCombs, Wesley McCombs, John Brown, and a schoolteacher named Bradford. The place was in a valley not far from the old Fort Ewell road, between San Miguel and Cescadara creeks. The Indians wheeled around when the white men charged, and the fight commenced. In this first onset the Indians were repulsed and some of their party wounded. The Indians being in large force, the settlers went back in the timber and dismounted to continue the fight there, and sent off two men, John Brown and Louis McCombs, to get the rangers to come and assist them, who were about twenty miles below. In this first charge Lon Moore's horse ran in among the Indians and was shot, and Moore slightly wounded in the arm with an arrow. He shot one Indian at close quarters with a pistol, and he slapped his hand to his breast where the ball struck him. The horse turned when hit and went back to the other men. The Indians retreated in among some rocks. The two men who went after the rangers slipped away without being seen, so the Indians would not pursue them.

When the white men came into view again the Indians discovered that two of them were missing, and yelled and charged, thinking these two had been killed. The fight lasted off and on all evening. The white men would charge and rout the Indians from the rocks, and then would have to retreat and load, and the Indians would charge and rout them. Many arrows stuck in the trees, and the settlers would pull these out and break them to keep the Indians from getting them in case they had to leave their position. During these charges and countercharges and retreats Nathan Davis was badly wounded with an arrow, which went through the right shoulder, the spike coming out on the opposite side. It was taken out by William Mullins. The horse ridden by Mullins was killed in his tracks with an arrow, which went in at the edge of the saddleskirts, and the spike came through on the opposite side. The horses ridden by Davis, Monroe Watkins, and Bradford were all wounded. At length, during a charge on the part of the Indians, their chief was killed by Mullins, which put an end to the fight. He fell close to the white men, and the Indians made one desperate attempt to recover his body, some of them even grabbing at his hair, but were beaten off. This was a strange fight. The Indians and white men swapped positions time and again, and the loose stolen horses were captured and recaptured as often as they changed. In this way Mullins mounted one of Rube Smith's horses, which the Indians had, when his was killed. During the fight, when both parties were keeping close under cover, Lon Moore and Roe Watkins went out to give the Indians a dare to draw them out, but were fired on without the Indians showing themselves. "Uncle Jerry" Bailey, the oldest man in the crowd, and very brave, would go in front twenty or thirty steps and watch for a chance to shoot, but one time would have been caught if it had not been for Lon Moore. The Indians charged, and the guns being empty, the men mounted to leave the timber and take shelter somewhere else until they could reload, but Uncle Jerry was slow to mount, having to run from his advanced position back to his horse, which, being frightened at the near approach and the loud yelling of the Indians, would not stand. Moore, seeing his critical condition, spurred his horse back and held the other until the the old man could mount, and when they wheeled to run some of the Indians were close upon them. The men when they left the timber would make a circle and dismount among the rocks which the Indians had just vacated, and there load their guns. The Indians finally left the battleground and went to a waterhole. One Indian died before they reached the water, and they hung his bow and shield on a limb and threw his body into the waterhole when they reached it. The Indians were followed to a point above Bandera by the rangers, and there they found where five Indians had been buried. Near the graves were two mules and a horse.

During the war, when Lon Moore was a member of Captain Montel's company of rangers, an expedition against the Indians on a large scale was gotten up. The intention was to invade the stronghold of the Comanches in the northwest. Thirty men were selected from each company on this part of the frontier, making 130 in all, and all under the command of Captain Montel. When the command arrived at a point high up on Devil's River some of the men wanted to come back. Montel stepped out and said, "All those who want to go on come and stand on my right." All of his own company came over and stood by him, and the other men turned back. Montel and his men now went on until they came to a place called the Black Hills, between the head of Devil's River and the Texas line. Here they saw many wigwams in a valley, and the captain said, "Now, all those who are willing to go down in there and fight them step to the right." All responded. "Now, boys," said Montel, "I see that I will have to say go back, you will not do it. I was in hopes you would say go back. There are too many for us."

The Indians had discovered the presence of the rangers and followed them back to the Colorado, and one night while they were camped ran a thousand or more buffalo through the edge of their camp. The intention was to run them square over the rangers, but they turned. Six pack mules and two saddle horses were cut off, and went with the buffaloes. The design of the Indians was to stampede all the horses and leave the rangers afoot. They followed the trail of the buffalos thirty miles to rescue their stock, but came upon an Indian trail that turned in on the buffalo trail, and knew they would get them, so turned back.

On this trip they subsisted on the return fifteen days on buffalo meat without bread. They were also without tobacco, and the first place they struck where they could get any was Fort Mason, and they had to pay $2.50 a plug for it in Confederate money.

Lon has been on fifty Indian scouts and in seven fights, most all of them under Big Foot Wallace.

THE COX FAMILY AS INDIAN FIGHTERS.

While traveling in the Dry Frio Canyon in 1897, seeking information of the frontier days, the writer was told by several parties of an interesting frontier incident which took place in the Nueces Canyon and that Mrs. Sirrilda Whistler was likely the only person that was accessible that could give an accurate and detailed account of the affair; she was in the battle, and although a small girl at the time had a good memory, etc. The writer sought an interview, and obtained in substance the following facts:

Mrs. Whistler was the daughter of Mr. Wiliam Cox, and was born in Fannin County in 1851, four miles from Bonham. In 1861 her father's family moved to Brackett, and in 1865 to the West prong of the Nueces River. No one lived there at the time, and the country was wild and lonely indeed. Of this new settlement, besides William Cox and family, was his son Henry and his family, and John Bingham and his family. They all lived in tents near each other, and two months passed away before any signs of Indians were seen. Henry Cox's tent was about fifty yards from his father's and John Bingham's a short distance on the other side, the old man being between the two. As is usual on the frontier during a long period of quiet and peace, the settlers became careless, and when the Indians did come were poorly prepared to receive them.

On the eventful morning in question Henry Cox was at his father's tent, and his family were at their own, fifty yards away. No close watch was being kept, and the Indians came over the hills and into the valley near the camps before any one discovered them. They were twenty-five in number, and all on foot. Mrs. Bingham was the first to see them, and exclaimed, "Lord, God! Look at the Indians!" At this time they were about 100 yards from the tent of the elder Cox. He heard the announcement of Indians by Mrs. Bingham, and at once seized his old flintlock rifle and went out to make a fight and defend his family as best he could. Another mistake, however, had been made by the old man. He had fired his gun at a turkey that morning, and had neglected to reload it. Standing, however, in full view of the approaching and now yelling savages, he began hastily to load, but was hit by an arrow in the knee before he could do so, and was badly wounded. Reaching down he pulled it out, but the spike remained in the bone. Henry now came to his father's assistance, but without his gun, it being in his tent. The old man coolly finished loading his gun, and together they charged. A shot from the old rifle wounded one Indian badly, and he ran into a mott of timber close by. At the first discovery of the Indians the elder Cox had shouted for all of them to concentrate at his tent. A little 4-year-old girl of Henry Cox made a run to get to her grandfather's tent, but was caught by the Indians, who were retreating from the old man and Henry, and going into the mott of timber. John Bingham and his wife attempted to reach the tent, and were both shot and wounded by bullets, or a bullet properly, as the same ball wounded both in the legs, but they succeeded in reaching their destination. The Indians now began to plunder the tent of Henry Cox, and got his gun. His wife before this time had made her escape with one of her children to the old man's tent, and it was while making this run the Indians got the little girl. One younger child was left sitting under a wagon. Our readers must remember that all of this transpired very quickly and under great excitement, Indians swarming all around, yelling, shooting, and bullets whizzing. Old man Cox had retreated back to his tent, but seeing Henry's little 2-year-old child under the wagon, made a run and rescued it. Bingham had no gun, the Indians had Henry's, and the old man had to fight the battle alone. The brave old man was equal to the occasion. He would ram another ball home as fast as he would fire, hitting an Indian every shot. He killed one just as he was coming out of Henry's tent with his arms full of things. The Indians certainly did not know the almost unarmed condition of the white men, as they could have made a charge en masse and overpowered them at once. They dreaded the ominous crack of the old rifle, and were soon all out of sight in the bottom, but still within rifle shot. The chief had a whistle, which he would sound when wanting his men to come closer. Old man Cox wanted to kill him, and watched his chance to do so, believing that his fall would put an end to the battle and the balance would take their departure. He had him located by the sound of his whistle. He was behind a tree in the brush, but very close to camp. His warriors seemed to be further back, and he wanted them to come up and charge. Finally he turned to give a blast and exposed part of his body. At that instant the rifle cracked from the tent, and he fell dead in his tracks. This shot also sealed the fate of the little captive girl. She was at once put to death in retaliation for the slain chief. She was killed with a lance, and her screams could be heard as the cruel blade entered her body.

It was about 10 o'clock when the chief was killed, and soon after the Indians took their departure in silence, keeping up the river in the timber, hid from view. Before this they were yelling and keeping a continual noise. When they went to leave the valley they came into view going up a mountain, and the white men watched them until they disappeared. The old man and his son now went into the mott where the Indians were, having fears for the safety of the child, but not seeing anything of her concluded the Indians had carried her off captive. They saw the trail where the chief had been dragged, and followed it until his body was found in a waterhole, which they pulled out and scalped, and then came back, but on the way found the dead body of the little girl. In the evening the sad burial took place, and the survivors made preparations for flight. During all of this time old man Cox was limping around with the spike still in his knee. The Indians had taken all their horses, and nothing was left but one yoke of oxen to convey these three families away. Next morning, however, the start was made for Brackett, the wounded and small children in the wagon and the balance on foot. After a great many hardships they succeeded in arriving at the fort. Three of the Indians shot in this battle died on the retreat, and were afterwards found.

At the time of this fight Mrs. Whistler was 14 years of age, and remembers of all the incidents distinctly. Her family has had a great deal of trouble on the frontier. She had one sister, brother-in-law, and their three children all killed by Indians near Brackett, and a brother 13 years old killed by them on the Eagle Pass road. He was alone at the time, and no particulars can be given. The others were moving in a wagon when assailed and massacred.

Mrs. Whistler has been married twice. Her first husband was Ben Maples. He was killed in a difficulty, and she married Mr.

Ross Whistler, her present husband. They live in Dry Frio Canyon, near her cousin, Capt. Joshua Cox.

Capt. Joshua Cox is a nephew of the old man William Cox, who made such a game and successful fight with the Indians. He is an old settler and Indian fighter himself. When the fight above described took place he was on Elm Creek, seven miles east of Fort Clark. They all come together from Fannin County, and he had his first experience with Indians on Elm Creek in 1864. While out on a horse-hunt nine Indians charged him and Nilus Cantrell. Seven of the Indians ran around a thicket and two charged straight towards them. At nine yards distant Cox and Cantrell both fired, and each hit his Indian. They wheeled, and the white men pursued them until they ran over a bank and disappeared. The other seven ran back the way they came as soon as the guns fired. One of the wounded Indians was shot through the body, which shot also broke his left arm. He took a shirt off which he had on, and tying it tightly around his body rode his horse six miles to a waterhole, and dismounting there tied his horse to a tree, and lay down by it and died. On the seventh day his body and the nearly starved horse were found. The horse belonged to William Pafford. The Indian had seven pairs of moccasins and a flintlock rifle. The head and shoulders of another Indian were found by the cowboys in the Anacatchi mountains, and this was supposed to be the other one shot on that occasion. His horse was also found, and had a short piece of rope around his neck. Cantrell shot the Indian who died at the waterhole.

In 1867 Mr. Cox had another fight with the Indians twenty-six miles from Uvalde, on the Nueces River. His father, Nathan Cox, Tom Bingham, Zood Pulliam, and himself had the fight. Pulliam and a Mexican were herding cattle when attacked by the Indians, and retreated to the ranch of Captain Cox, about one and a half miles away. During the retreat, however, the Mexican was overtaken and killed. When the reinforcements went back the Mexican was still alive, but lanced in seven places, and did not long survive. The Indians were overtaken while crossing the Nueces River. They had a number of horses, and were trying to cross them by pushing them backwards off a bluff into the water. Capt. Josh. Cox shot at two Indians close together, and one of them fell into the river, but swam across to the other side badly wounded, and it was supposed he died. The other men who were in the rear did not fire for fear of hitting Captain Cox, who was between them and the Indians. All were in a trail one behind the other when they came upon the Indians, who scattered when Cox fired and crossed the river rapidly. Only three head of the horses were recovered.

Another fight took place on the Chaparosa Creek, three miles from Pete Bowles' ranch. The men in this fight were Josh Cox, Archie Cox, Hugh Cox, Henry Cox, Irvin Cox, Dave Cook, and William Carter. The Indians, twenty-five in number, were in an open prairie and could be easily counted. There were twelve on horseback and thirteen on foot. The mounted ones were first seen and charged by the whites and fired on. Those on foot were concealed in the grass near by, and then they rose up and commenced yelling and shooting. The fight lasted nearly an hour, and in that time the Indians were beaten back a mile to the brush, and it ended there. The horse rode by Captain Cox was wounded. His first shot broke an Indian's thigh, who was riding a paint horse. He left the fight, and his broken leg could be seen flopping as he galloped off. Two Indians were killed on the ground. The last shot fired by Hugh Cox hit an Indian in the back, but he hung to his horse and was supposed to be lashed on. The white men were armed with Spencers, six-shooters, and Winchesters, some having one kind and some another, but mostly six-shooters. Irvin Cox had no arms of any kind, and there were only three guns in the crowd, and the men who had these did most of the shooting. The Indians avoided a close fight, and the revolvers were mostly saved for that. They ran repeatedly and shot wild. The white men fired many shots with the repeating guns and many Indians were hit. Out of the twelve on horseback only five were left in the last charge. Mexicans from Mexico said these were Kickapoos, and that more than half of them were killed and wounded. They crossed the Rio Grande and went into Mexico after the fight.

DESPERATE RUN FOR LIFE.

Some time during the Civil war occurred one of those desperate chances for life which frontiersmen sometimes have to take and pass through when coming in contact with Indians on the border. On the occasion of the circumstance mentioned above, Billy Allen and one of his cousins, whose given name was Ranse, the other not being remembered, went out horse-hunting from the Allen ranch on the Tehuacana Creek, in Frio County. They were young fellows, being not more than fifteen years of age. The horses which they were in search of had been gone for some time, but had been heard from as being on the Seco prairie, some distance from old man Allen's ranch. When the boys arrived at the place designated as where the horses were supposed to be, they rode out into the prairie and began their search. Off some distance in the prairie a lone grove of timber was seen, and near it grazed several horses. Thinking these to be the horses they were in search of, the boys rode towards them, not apprehending any danger. Neither had defensive arms of any kind, except, as you might say, those which nature had provided them with. When near the horses one of them threw up his head to look at them, and it was discovered that he had on a halter. Ranse at once exclaimed, "Billy, one of those horses has on a halter." "Indians!" exclaimed Allen; "we must run for it." The distance to the grove was about 100 yards, and rank grass grew all around it. The Indians, about a dozen in number, were lying down in the grass near the edge of the timber or small grove, holding their horses by ropes while they grazed. They all sprang to their feet when the horses first gave sign of the approach of something, and by this time the boys had wheeled their horses and were making off. The Indians all mounted and followed them. About 400 yards away was a hill which was bare on top, but had thick brush around the edges. Drowning men will catch at straws, someone has said, and towards this place the boys ran, hoping likely that here they could abandon their horses and conceal themselves. Even this slim chance, however, was not to be. An Indian on a fast sorrel horse ran around them and turned them back on the prairie again, and the whole gang closed in after them. For some time the Indians were distanced, but finally the one on the sorrel came close upon them. Up to this time no attempt to kill the boys had been made. The Indians perceived they had no arms, and wanted to capture them. Fearing, however, they would get to the brush, the foremost one drew a large pistol having a brass handle. This he waved three times around his head, yelling, then presented it and fired. The ball struck Ranse in the back and came out through the stomach. The stricken boy remained on his horse for some time, but when he began to show signs of weakness by swaying in the saddle, Allen took hold of him and held him on. A short distance further, and Ranse begged his cousin to turn him loose and save himself, saying he was killed and could not stay on his horse any longer. But still the gallant Billy held him. At every jump of the horse the dying boy swayed forward or back, to right or left, and then finally with a sudden plunge went to the ground, nearly pulling Allen from his horse, who made a desperate attempt to hold him. During this time the Indians had scattered to right and left, and the one with the pistol was riding in the rear. He had slowed up some, adjusted his rope, and now came close again, swinging it in the air to rope Allen. The boy watched him, and when the lasso was launched gave his horse a dexterous turn and avoided the loop. He was now near two other Indians, who were also twirling their ropes to give him a turn. He ran between the two, ducked his head low when they threw, and they missed. In this way for miles around and around in the prairie they ran. He was headed off in every direction, and had to run the gauntlet of ropes to get through them. This was kept up until the horses of both parties were run down. At this time, after making a most desperate run, with the last remaining strength of his horse Allen gained the chaparral which skirted the big prairie, for the first time since the chase commenced. The Indians entered after him, but they could no longer use their ropes, and Allen soon dodged them. His faithful horse was nearly dead, and soon lay down with him. The Indians could be heard passing around on both sides of him, but the chaparral and prickly pears were so thick they failed to see him. Allen remained here for some time, fearing to leave the spot, as he might be discovered, but finally with some urging induced his horse to get up, and slowly threaded the intricate openings in the brush and made his way back home, without seeing anything more of the Indians. When the saddle was taken from his horse the poor animal walked off a few yards, lay down, and soon died.

A party went back to the scene of the tragedy, but nothing was seen of Indians, and they secured the body of the slain boy and brought it in. He had been scalped and badly mutilated.

About this time Mr. Sam Pue had a terrible run from Indians, was wounded, but made his escape and recovered from his injuries.

ED. TAYLOR.

Came to Texas in 1857.

Thomas Edward Taylor was born in Wilcox County, Alabama, on the 12th day of March, 1831. Came to Texas from Mississippi in April, 1857, and the same year, in June, came to Uvalde County and settled on the Sabinal River, ten miles below the Eagle Pass road. Indians raided the country frequently, and Mr. Taylor scouted and trailed after them at intervals for seven years.

In 1862 he joined Captain Montel's company of rangers for frontier protection. They served a double purpose as Texas rangers and Confederate soldiers, being subject to the then existing Confederate government. Their camp was in Seco Canyon, at a place now known as Ranger Springs. In the summer news came to camp of an Indian raid below the mountains, which extended as far south as Atascosa County. The information was brought to the rangers by Demp. Fenley, then a boy, who had been sent on this errand by his father, John Fenley, who then lived in Sabinal Canyon. The Indians had turned back and were then heading in that direction, driving about sixty head of stolen horses. About a dozen men from camp, under the command of Lieut. Ben Patton, went in pursuit of them, among whom was Ed. Taylor, Pete Bowles, John Cook, Lon Moore, Dan Malone, Jack Davenport, and Harrison Daugherty, a citizen not in the service. In the meantime the Indians had passed up Sabinal Canyon to the head of Salt Marsh, and then took to the mountains, pursued by the settlers from below. The rangers and settlers got together in the mountains between Sabinal and Frio Rivers, and all followed the trail, which led a northwest course, and finally came in sight of the Indians encamped in the valley of a small creek. The men dismounted, and keeping under cover went up the creek to the camp, which was surrounded by a bluff except on the side next to the mountains, and the men had to climb this bluff before they could see the Indians. The latter were taken completely by surprise, and when the white men came upon them ran without attempting much resistance.

A great deal of firing was done by the settlers and rangers, and most of the Indians killed had more than one ball in them. Mr. Taylor ran after one and shot at him with a Mississippi rifle just as the Indian went over the bluff, and he fell to the bottom and was found there after the fight. After the Indians had been scattered and some killed, John Cook, Lon Moore, and Dan Malone all got after one Indian, who had a broken arm, and commenced shooting at him with revolvers. The chase led up a ravine towards the mountains, and soon all parties were out of sight and nearly out of hearing, but at frequent intervals shots could be heard in that direction. After some little time a great racket among the rocks and brush was heard, with shots interspersed. The boys had headed the Indian some distance up the ravine, and were bringing him back on the other side, and here a strange thing happened,—all at once the Indian disappeared and could not be found. He was shot in many places, and no doubt died. The stolen horses were collected and carried back. Three Indians were left dead on the ground and more were wounded, but hid in the brush and rocks and could not be found. Mr. Taylor and others came back to the battleground some days after, and the dead Indians were all covered up with brush. Some who escaped had come back and done this.

Mr. Taylor was made a Mason in 1863 in Hondo lodge, which was on the east bank of the Hondo River, about four miles east of the present Hondo City, county seat of Medina County. He now lives on the Leona River, in Uvalde County, not far below old Fort Inge.

Mr. Taylor is a man of sterling integrity and has many friends, and is known as "Uncle" Ed. Taylor.

JOHN LEAKEY.

Came to Texas in 1847.

Mr. John Leakey, who built the first house in Frio Canyon, and for whom the town of Leakey was named, which was the county seat of Edwards County until removed to Rock Springs, is one among the most noted characters of the pioneers of the Southwest, and was born in Warren County, Tennessee, in 1824. His grandfather was a soldier under Washington, and did good service in the cause of freedom in the long, bloody war of the Revolution. The subject of our sketch came to Texas in 1847 and first settled in Rusk County, but moved from there in the fall of 1853 and came to Uvalde County, stopping at the Dan Brewster place until the following year, and then settled on the Sabinal River below the mountains, where Henry Shane now lives. In 1855, which was a very dry year, he and Mr. Newman Patterson opened up an irrigating ditch, and while living here Mr. Leakey became involved in a difficulty in which he killed one man, wounded another, and was himself badly wounded.

One one occasion in 1856 Mr. Leakey and his wife went on a visit to Sabinal Canyon, and stopped one night at the house of Mr. Aaron Anglin. An old negro woman slept in a small house in the yard, and during the night waked Mrs. Anglin and told her Indians were around. Mr. Anglin was gone at the time, so Mr. Leakey was aroused and informed of the fact in regard to the presence of Indians, and he secured his pistol and walked out into the yard. Three Indians were concealed in the shadow of some trees near the house, and the dogs were barking at them. The barking of the dogs, and the peculiar actions of one that always tried to get into the house when Indians were about, was what excited the fears of the old negress in regard to them. Mr. Leakey could not tell where the Indians were until they began to shoot arrows at him, which struck the ground at his feet, however, and did no damage, the distance being too far. He now began to fire in the direction the arrows came from, and the Indians ran, pursued by Mr. Leakey, who continued to fire at them until his loads were exhausted and then returned to the house and stood guard the balance of the night. When daylight came he examined the ground, and found the trail of three Indians, two of whom were wounded, as the bloody trails indicated. We will say here that at this time Dr. Ben Thomas was in Mexico practicing medicine among the Mexicans and Indians, and one day two wounded Indians were brought to him for treatment, both shot in the hips. He told this when he came back to Texas, and it was supposed these were the ones who were wounded by Mr. Leakey that night. If this was so they were either Kickapoos or Lipans, for these two tribes lived in Mexico and the Comanches in Texas, on the great plains.

After a short search on the morning in question Mr. Leakey notified the settlers in the canyon, who were few at that time, and four of them volunteered to take the trail of the Indians. They wer Gid. Thompson, Sebe Barrymore, Silas Webster, and Henry Robinson, Mr. Leakey making five. They did not expect to find the Indians very soon, unless it was those Mr. Leakey had wounded. They took time to get ready, Mrs. Anglin fixing up some cooked provisions to last several days, which were put in a pillow slip. Their plan was to follow on the trail of the Indians on foot until they found them some night in camp, and then make an attack upon them. There were more of them than those three mentioned, but not so near the house. When the settlers took up the main trail it was found to lead in a southwest direction towards a high range of mountains two miles distant. Mr. Leakey had the provisions strapped across the back part of his neck and shoulders, but not a morsel of it was ever eaten by either of the party. At this time the Indians, about twenty-five in number, were in ambush on top of the mountains, awaiting the approach of the white men, whom they could plainly see following their trail in the valley below. For fear they would not come straight into the trap on account of losing the trail in the bushes and rocks on the sides of the mountain, the Indians cut down bushes at intervals so that it could be easily followed, but still the unsuspecting white men did not "smell a rat," as the old saying is. It was very tedious and exhausting climbing the mountain. There were steep ledges, slanting rocks, huge boulders, scrubby cedar, and tangled vines to surmount and tear through, so that when the five settlers arrived at the crest of the mountain they were hot, tired, wind-broken, and in no first-class condition to commence a battle. Henry Robinson was an old trailer, and in front when the ambush was reached, which was just on top of the mountain in a cedarbrake and short undergrowth of brush, with large rocks here and there. When the Indians began to raise up with bows in hand and arrows adjusted they were quite close and looked to be very numerous. Robinson, who had fought Indians before, saw at a glance that they were in a trap, and confronted by a largely superior force. Quickly aiming his rifle he fired and wheeled back, telling Mr. Leakey to do the same, who was the next man to him. Leakey had, however, sprang forward and was making a vain effort to fire his gun at the jumping, yelling, painted savages, who in a few moments were all around him shooting arrows. Thompson, Barrymore and Webster were in the rear a few yards, and all leveled their rifles and fired, called to Leakey to run, and then went back themselves. The gun which Leakey had was a new, borrowed rifle, and one he had never fired. It was double-triggered, and Mr. Leakey had been used to shooting a single-trigger gun. He had failed to spring the trigger, and therefore could not pull the hammer down. He had the muzzle almost at an Indian's breast and jerked at the trigger hard enough it seemed to break it out, but seeing it was useless, threw it down and pulled his pistol. He shot one Indian fairly in the ribs at only a few yards distance, and he fell. He now began to get in his work on the Indians and backed away from them, keeping them at bay, although repeatedly wounded. He could not go back the way he came and the way his companions went, for by this time the Indians had cut him off from that direction and were forcing him towards a steep and rugged cliff. His pistol finally refused to fire, and thinking he had exhausted his loads, he now for the first time turned his back to the Indians and plunged over the cliff, rolling and tumbling, catching here and there at bushes and rocks for 100 feet or more, and finally coming astride a tall, slender, cedar sapling, which bent with his weight, and he rode this down over a ledge and found a stopping place. He was now nearly dead with wounds and exhaustion, and lay down under a wild cherry tree. Presently he heard the Indians above him, evidently looking to see if they could discover him lodged anywhere. Thinking he would have to fight again, he examined his pistol, which he still held in his hand, and to his surprise found one chamber loaded. The reason of this was the fact that an arrow spike had struck between the cylinder and barrel, and the small point of the spike had broken off and was tightly fixed there so that the cylinder could not revolve to the next load. Mr. Leakey had snapped several times after the pistol failed to fire, not noticing in the terrific combat that the cylinder did not revolve when he drew the hammer back, and that it fell on an empty chamber each time he attempted to shoot. The Indians thought Leakey was dead, and two of them came down by an easier descent than that which the white man had taken, to scalp him. There was life enough in him yet, however, to make another fight, and getting to his feet he charged them, presenting the pistol. The two Indians no doubt thought the white man, as he was not dead, had had ample time to reload, and having had some experience only a few minutes before with what dexterity he could handle a six-shooter, beat a hasty retreat back the way they came, Leakey cursing them as they went. This cursing was the first intimation the other men had that Leakey was not killed. When Leakey got clear of the Indians one of them picked up the rifle which he had thrown away, and coming out on the cliff where he could see down the mountain, discovered the other white men in their retreat. Webster was ahead, Barrymore next, and Thompson in the rear. Robinson could not be seen, having stopped under cover to load his rifle. The Indian understood the gun, and springing the trigger, aimed at Thompson and fired. The ball passed just above his right ear wounding Barrymore in the hip, and they all soon halted, as the wounded man kept falling. Robinson now came to them and wanted to shoot the Indian, who was still in view, but the others objected, saying if he did the others would scalp Leakey. "He is not dead yet," said Robinson; "listen at him cursing the Indians." Those of the party who were not hurt went to Leakey, and Thompson gave him some water. They also pulled the arrows out of him and stopped the flow of blood as best they could, which came from the nine wounds which he now had on his body. Seven of these he received while facing the Indians at close quarters, and two after he began his retreat, one of which was in the head with an arrow, which carried his hat with it. One arrow went lengthwise of his arm while extending it to shoot. When Leakey threw down his gun and pulled the pistol Robinson was still near him, and an Indian was just in the act of shooting the latter with an arrow when Leakey shot him down. Mr. Leakey was carried back to the settlement, and was six weeks recovering from his wounds. The pursuit of these Indians and massacre of them by the settlers in the Leona River is given in the sketch of Mr. Thompson and others. The provisions carried by Leakey were completely saturated with his blood and could not be used.

In 1857 Mr. Leakey moved to Frio Canyon, and was the first settler there. He had been all over the country, explored it thoroughly, and picked upon a lovely spot in a pecan grove on the banks of the Frio River for his future home. He vowed he would live there in spite of the Indians, and his house is there to this day. He had many adventures with the Indians, however, and at times it seemed that he would be unable to sustain himself. But in a few years other settlers came in, and they helped to protect one another. Among those who came next were Kit Stanford, Thacker, Basham, Aldridge, Van Pelt, Dale, Frank Hilburn, Rain, Wall, and others.

On one occasion Basham and Aldridge were camped on the river making shingles, and the latter borrowed Mr. Leakey's gun to kill a deer. He killed one on the spot where the town of Leakey now is, and was about to proceed to skin it, but detected an Indian behind a tree watching him, and not knowing how many more might be around, beat a hasty retreat. A man named Carter, who lived with Leakey, went back with him, but no Indians were seen, and they brought the deer in. Signal smokes were seen on the mountains, and all the men went to look for the Indians but Mr. Leakey. He remained to protect the women and children. Mr. Wall saw some of the Indians and ran them three miles up the river, but did not get any of them. Lieutenant Wood had a fight with them in Nueces Canyon and succeeded in killing some of them, and they stopped raiding for some time.

In 1859 the Indians stole a large drove of horses in the lower part of the canyon, and the settlers began to rally to fight them. The soldiers at Fort Inge were also notified, and a squad of them came to help the settlers. Mr. Leakey and others, including Richard Ware, Clabe Davenport, and Courtney, struck the trail of the Indians on Blanco Creek, east of the Frio, and it led north. While starting the trail in the rough, mountainous country, Mr. Leakey fell down a rocky bluff, and was so badly hurt that he could hardly mount or ride his horse, and announced the fact that he was too badly bruised to proceed in the pursuit, and would return home. Others of the party said if he went back they would, too. Not wishing for the chase to be abandoned or the force weakened too much, Mr. Leakey went on. The trailing was one of the roughest imaginable, all the way through the mountains. Many crippled colts and horses were found along the way. The Indians were overtaken on the divide at the head of Sabinal and Frio rivers, in an open but rocky country. There were about twenty white men, and they outnumbered the Indians, but the latter were game and gave them a desperate fight. They had about eighty head of horses, and ran at first sight of the white men through a very rocky place, and the settlers flanked on both sides and some circled around them, and the Indians went into a burnt cedarbrake, and the fight commenced. Many shots were fired by the white men, and the Indians charged, fighting at close range. They were close observers, and would charge a white man and sometimes run him if his gun or pistol were empty. On one of these occasions Mr. Leakey saw an Indian closely pursuing Courtney, who had exhausted his shots. Although hardly able to ride he ran between them and cut the Indian off, and shot him six times with a revolver at close range, and he quit the fight, and went off about 200 yards and laid down under some young cedar trees. Leakey, while loading his pistol, watched him, and seeing young Clabe Davenport near, told him to go down there and shoot the Indian in the head. The young settler did so, but first advanced on the hidden warrior cautiously, knowing the danger if he was able to fight. Coming into view he fired, but said it was no use, as the Indian was about dead. This was quite a mixed up fight, and many personal combats took place, especially when the Indians were routed from the cedarbrake, where five of them were killed. One powerful Indian, who was called at that time Blackhawk by the settlers, was very brave, coming close to the white men and wounding some of them. During the fight Mr. Leakey came in contact with Blackhawk and shot him eight times, but failed to bring him to the ground. He was one of the few who escaped from the battleground, but no doubt perished. During the latter part of the fight, when the Indians were running, one fell in a gully, having both hips and left arm broken. Leakey was close behind on a splendid mare, and she jumped clear over him. When he passed the Indian held his bow with the right hand and pulled an arrow back with his teeth and shot at him, but missed, the arrow glancing along the rocks ahead of him. A sergeant who belonged to the soldier squad came along and finished the wounded Indian by a shot in the head with his carbine, and was promoted to a lieutenancy for this when it was reported to headquarters. Two white men and several horses were wounded in the fight. The stolen horses became badly scattered during the fight, but were nearly all collected and carried back to the settlement.

Mr. Leakey has been on many scouts after Indians. On one occasion he followed them to the head of the Nueces River, but citizens and soldiers came in ahead of Leakey and his party and fought a battle with them just before they arrived on the scene. They met some of the settlers, who had killed one Indian and recaptured a lot of stolen horses taken from a man named Ragsdale. They also rescued a negro boy who was a prisoner among them. Here a squad was raised to help Ragsdale to Fort Clark with his horses, and Leakey was put in command of it.

On one occasion a man named Hilburn was living with Mr. Leakey, and becoming tired of deer meat, went out to hunt some hogs belonging to Leakey, for the purpose of killing one. The hogs were wild, and Hilburn advanced cautiously while looking for them. The morning was foggy, and when the hogs were found an Indian was also discovered in a stooping position watching them, evidently waiting for a good opportunity to shoot one. Hilburn was a quick shot, always firing when the gun came to his shoulder, and on this occasion at once fired and broke the Indian's back. He went back from here and told the news, and two men went back to where the Indian lay, and he was still alive. They talked to him in Spanish, and he said he was a Kickapoo. When he died these two men buried him, not far from the present town of Leakey.

In 1861 Mr. Leakey went with a wagon to haul cedar poles which he had previously cut in a brake. When he arrived, before commencing work he placed his gun against a fallen tree, and his three dogs lay down near it, but on the opposite side of the log. In driving about gathering up his load Mr. Leakey lost sight of the spot where his gun was, but had two revolvers buckled around him. At this time a band of Indians was coming down a deep gorge near by, and one of the gang acting as spy and scout was on the high ground, but traveling parallel with the others. He discovered Mr. Leakey's gun, but did not see the dogs, and while in the act, as was supposed by his tracks, of taking the rifle, the three dogs sprang over the log and seized him. The Indian ran and plunged off the bluff into the gorge, carrying the dogs along also, who still held on to him, and followed the other Indians, and the dogs still kept after him. Mr. Leakey heard the scuffle, and thinking the dogs had a bear, ran to his gun, snatched it up, and followed. By this time dogs and Indian had gone over the bluff, and still thinking it was a bear, Leakey followed, a bend in the gorge hiding them from view. The other Indians wounded the dogs, and they came back. The truth now dawned upon Leakey, and looking about him he discovered the gorge full of Indian tracks, and retreating back climbed out of the gorge and got his team and went home. The dogs were able to follow, and all got in safely.

The writer, while collecting these reminiscences, spent a night with Mr. Leakey in Frio Canyon. When asked how many wounds he had on his person, he laughed and said, "You will have to strip me and count." The old man had thirteen prominent wounds on his body, besides bruises and scratches, but the writer took his word without counting. These wounds are all in front from his knees to the top of his head, made with bullets, arrows, knives, etc. The worst one is on the front of the head, several inches in length, and is plainly visible through his scattered gray locks, and this was one inflicted by the breech of a shotgun.

Mr. Leakey has been a member of the church, and firmly believes in the religion of Jesus Christ, and is a Mason of long standing. No man ever left his door in distress when it was in his power to aid him.

C. G. JARVIS.

Came to Texas in 1865.

Among the settlers of Frio Canyon who deserve notice is Mr. Charles G. Jarvis, not so much on his record as an Indian fighter, although he has seen some of that, but as one of Lee's veterans who gallantly and unflinchingly followed the Stars and Bars on many hotly contested fields, and shed his blood in defense of the "lost cause." The war has been over for a long time, but still we read with interest the deeds of valor performed by our devoted Southern boys, and the old soldiers who followed the Stars and Stripes will many of them join us in giving them praise for their dashing courage and devotion to the cause which to them was right and just.

Mr. Jarvis was born in Algiers, La., in December, 1843, and in 1852 moved to Missouri and settled in St. Francis County. When the Civil war broke out he joined the State guards, commanded by Colonel Schanebel. These were disbanded in six months, and he then entered the Confederate army under Gen. Sterling Price. Mr. Jarvis participated in his first battle at Oak Hills, or Wilson Creek, as some call it. Then in regular order came the battles of Springfield, Elkhorn, Farmington, Iuka, Corinth, Grand Gulf, Port Gibson, Baker's Creek (called by the Federals Champion Hills), Big Black, and siege of Vicksburg. In all of these battles Mr. Jarvis did his duty as a brave soldier, as will be attested by his old comrades who may chance to see this sketch. Charles Jarvis is a man who does not like to make a display in regard to the part he took in these various engagements, and is too modest to recount any of his own deeds of personal valor, but pays glowing tribute to comrades who fought by his side. On the 18th of May he was twice wounded at Vicksburg, receiving one ball in the left arm and one in the right shoulder. In twenty days he reported for duty. After the surrender of Vicksburg he was paroled, and then exchanged in September, 1863. He was in the Georgia campaign, and took part in the battles of New Hope Church, Latimore, and Kenesaw Mountain. The latter was one of the bloodiest of the war, considering the time and numbers engaged. The Federal troops attempted to storm the position of the Confederates on Kenesaw Mountain, but met with a most crushing defeat and a perfect slaughter of men, and without doing much damage to the Confederates. Mr. Jarvis said he saw the blood running down the hill in small rivulets from one ledge to another. The Federals deserve great credit for their bravery on this occasion, coming as they did to the works and attempting to get over them while suffering such great loss of men. Colonel Blood of the Union forces fell near the works, and his dead body fell into the hands of the Southern troops when his men retreated. Mr. Jarvis says he was a fine-looking man, and they buried him with the honors of war, showing their appreciation for the chivalry and almost matchless courage he displayed on that occasion.

The next battles Mr. Jarvis engaged in were Vining's Station, Peach Tree Creek, and siege of Atlanta. He and five others crossed the Chattahoochie River and captured a sergeant, six men and thirteen mules, all within long range rifle shot of the Federal cavalry headquarters. The cavalry came out and pursued them, and they placed their prisoners on the mules. They put two on one mule, and one of them was an Irishman. He began to complain at their rapid gait, and said he could not ride the bloody mule, he bounced so, and began to hump up as if about to fall. Jarvis reached him with his gun, gave him a punch, and told him to straighten up there. "All right, be Jasus," said the Irishman, and at once rode erect.

The Confederates fell back to Lovejoy and an armistice of ten days was agreed upon. From there Mr. Jarvis followed Hood up into Tennessee, and fought in the battles of Big Shanty, Ackworth, and Altoona. In the last named he was wounded in the right thigh, and when his command retreated he followed the army, badly hurt as he was, rather than be captured. A comrade named Johnny Cockery stayed with him to help him along. In the retreat Jarvis pulled off his pants, as they irritated the wound, and all at once discovered some women and children by the roadside watching the soldiers pass. He told his companion to stay between him and the women and to go slow and keep step with him, so that he would not be exposed. His comrade was full of fun, and at the critical moment walked fast and left the wounded man limping along with nothing on but his shirt. When he recovered from this wound he went into the secret service until the final surrender. Among those who were with him in this service were J. M. Bond, a Methodist minister, now living in Granger, Williamson County, and John L. Carlisle, living in Italy, Ellis County.

At the close of the war Mr. Jarvis came to Texas and helped Peck Johnson put up a herd of cattle in Brown County, and started with them to California. He stopped, however, at Las Cruces, N. M., and went to Denver, Col. From there he went to Durango, Mex., and drove a herd of horses; then to El Paso, Texas.

In 1870 Mr. Jarvis had charge of a train belonging to Ward B. Blanchard. At Fort Quitman the Indians made a raid and captured sixteen head of mules belonging to the train. He applied to Maj. A. P. Morrow, who was in command of the fort, for troops to follow the Indians, but the major said, "No use; impossible to catch them." He then asked for horses to follow them on, but this was also refused. Jarvis went back to camp and studied over the situation some time, and finally concluded he must have the mules back, as he could not move his train without them. There was nothing but a few wagon mules in camp, but he mounted himself and four teamsters on these and commenced the pursuit. The route was long and rough, through gorges and over mountains, but so tenacious and energetic was the chase that sixty miles were covered that day, and when night came on they were in sight of the campfire of the redskin marauders. Jarvis got the camp well located, which was in a gorge with bluffs around, and then rested, waiting until daylight to make the attack. The Indians had killed a mule and sat up late that night eating and singing, which could be plainly heard by Jarvis and his men. The light of their campfire above the bluff could be seen. They thought they were safe for the night. Just as day began to break, Jarvis took his men to the bluff and looked over. Only one Indian was up, and he was sitting down on the opposite side of the fire. The others were lying down and away from the fire, and could not be seen. At this time one of the men, some of whom were Mexicans, cocked a Spencer carbine, which made a loud click on the cold, frosty air. The quick ear of the Indian caught the ominous sound, and he looked up towards the top of the bluff and started to rise. No time was now to be lost, and the order to fire was given. One gun went off in the air, sending the bullet towards the stars. One struck the fire in front of the Indian, and the other three went through his body, killing him instantly. The other Indians made their escape, as it was still dark, especially in the gorge. Jarvis collected his mules, and without further incident got back and moved his train.

In 1873 he married Miss Mattie Watkins, of Guadalupe County, Rev. C. Shapard performing the ceremony. He came to Frio Canyon in 1886, and is now engaged in farming and stockraising. He belongs to the Methodist church, and was made a Mason at Frio Town in 1884, made a royal arch in Uvalde, July 3, 1890, and is now worthy master of Leakey lodge No. 622.

CAPT. JOHN H. ROGERS.

Native Texan. Born in 1863.

Capt. John Harris Rogers was born in Guadalupe County, Texas, on the 19th day of October, 1863. His father was Pleasant William Miles Rogers, son of Isaac and Mahala Rogers. His mother was Mary Harris, daughter of John and Laura Harris, all old settlers of Guadalupe County. The father of Captain Rogers was a Confederate soldier during the Civil war, and participated in some hard-fought battles in the Louisiana campaign. In one of these the Confederates got the worst of it, and the boys who carried the "bonny blue flag" were forced to retreat. Mr. Rogers came very near being captured on account of his horse falling into a ditch which he attempted to leap, and was unable to extricate himself. The Federal cavalry was close upon him, but at this critical moment he was rescued and carried safely off the field by his brother-in-law, Lieut. John Wesley Harris, who gave the unfortunate young soldier a mount behind him.

While Captain Rogers is not an old man, he has made a reputation as a brave and gallant Texas ranger surpassed by but few, and deserves a place in the history of southwest Texas. On the 5th day of September, 1882, he joined Company B of the rangers, commanded by Capt. S. A. McMurry. There was no lieutenant of this company, and John McNally was sergeant. Afterwards McNally was made a lieutenant, as was also Sam Platt, of Austin.

Just before young Rogers joined the rangers they had a fight with train robbers at Ranger Station on the Southern Pacific road, wounded one and captured all but one of the balance, as it was supposed.

Captain Rogers remained with this company fifteen months, and then came home in December, 1883, and spent the holidays.

He enlisted again in the following spring in the company of Capt. Joe Sheely, at Cotulla, La Salle County. William Scott was lieutenant and W. T. Morris sergeant. The latter is now sheriff of Karnes County. In 1885 Captain Sheely severed his connection with the company and Lieutenant Scott was made captain. Sergeant Morris married a Miss Harper, of Yorktown, and also resigned, and J. A. Brooks was made sergeant. The company left Cotulla and established a camp in the Nueces Canyon. In the fall of 1885 the command went to Mitchell County, and in the following year went after fence-cutters in Brown County. Captain Scott was in command, and the outlaws were surprised in camp. The captain was in front, and commenced firing as soon as he perceived them. The rangers all followed suit, and when the smoke cleared up two fence-cutters were seen lying dead on the ground. This was the first battle of young Rogers.

From Mitchell County a detachment of the rangers were ordered to Sabine County to arrest a gang of murderers and outlaws who had defied the civil authorities, and in fact the whole country. These desperate men were old man Conner and his three sons—Fred, William, and John. They were splendid shots, and lived almost like Indians in the dense pine forest which nearly covered that part of the country. When the rangers arrived in the vicinity of the Conners they were to meet a man at a certain designated place after dark, who was to pilot them to the camp of the outlaws. He had been with the Conners often, and in fact had been placed in this work by the rangers on a previous trip, when they had failed to locate their men. He was a citizen of this locality, and had bought out the Conners, and they were now living in a camp in the dense pine woods, covered with underbrush. Two other citizens were with the rangers— Judge Polly, from Hemphill, and W. W. Wethered, from the town of Milam. The rangers rode around in the vicinity of the camp in the early part of the night, and their trail was discovered by the Conners while they were out fire-hunting with a torch. Apprehending the significance of this trail, they at once repaired to their camp and prepared for defense. They took off the bell from a pack horse so that its rattling would not betray their position, and awaited developments. On this night the citizen spy had hunted with the Conners, but finally excused himself and said he would go home, but instead came to the rangers, who were a mile or more away. The Conners discovered the trail of the rangers by their torchlight after he left. The spy intended to be guided to some extent by the bell on the pack horse in piloting the rangers through the dark woods to the stronghold of the outlaws. He carried them, as he thought, to within two or three hundred yards of their camp, and then went back a short distance, not wanting to be seen by the Conners. Captain Scott had told the man before this to slip down the gully on which the camp was situated and take observations, but not hearing the bell, he was afraid he had missed the place. This was a new camp, and he had only been there in the night time. While he was gone on this reconnoitering expedition he thought he heard one of the Conners cough, and so reported. Captain Scott now told him not to leave the place, as he might be needed for a guide after the fight, and dismounted his men, who tied their horses to the trees. The party was now divided. Two rangers and two citizens were sent to the left, and the captain and five rangers went to the right. As the latter were the men who fought the battle, we will follow them and give their names, which were, besides the captain, Sergeant Brooks, Frank Carmichael, J. H. Moore, John H. Rogers, and William Treadwell. The intention of the captain was to find the camp between the two parties, but to remain near enough to each other so that when firing commenced they would not shoot by accident any of their own men. The right and left separated too far, and both parties passed the camp without discovering it. Captain Scott and his party finally came to a gully, and Sergeant Brooks said if this was the one they were camped in it was no use to cross, but to turn back and keep up on this side. This was done, and all moved cautiously along. It was now nearly day. The time was the last day of March, 1886. Just at daybreak John Rogers saw the outlines of a man in a squatting position, and called the attention of Sergeant Brooks to the fact, but at this time the man raised up and the rangers covered him with their Winchesters. He backed ten steps to a tree and stopped. Rogers called to him and asked if he was one of their own men. Without replying he raised his gun to fire, and was instantly killed by three shots from Scott, Rogers, and Brooks. One ball went through his head and two through the body. All struck about the same time, and he dropped instantly in his tracks. This was Bill Conner, second youngest. Simultaneously with these shots came a volley from ambush fired at the rangers, which wounded John Rogers in the side, spinning him around, and killed James H

Moore, of Center Point, Kerr County, Texas, who was shot through the heart, dying instantly. Captain Scott now received a wound and fell, shot through the lungs. Another volley came quick, and young Rogers was wounded the second time, and he fell to the ground. He had his gun in position to fire, and the ball struck his left arm and went through the muscle between the main artery and the bone, cutting the nerve. Sergeant Brooks now advanced on the hidden marksmen and continued to shoot in their direction, but was soon shot through both hands. He had his gun up to fire, and a ball glanced on the under side of his gun barrel, shot three fingers from his left hand, and lodged in the right. Unable now to work the lever of his Winchester, he sank to the ground to avoid other shots, and crawled back to Rogers on his knees and elbows. Then, with bloody and shattered hand, he drew his pistol, gave words of encouragement to the boys, and renewed the battle with his unseen foes. The bullets were now flying thick and striking the ground around the wounded men. Rogers was paralyzed in the left side and arm, but had use of the right, and with this worked the lever of his gun, holding the barrel between his knees, and fired repeatedly from where he lay on the ground. The Conners finally retreated, and the firing ceased. Captain Scott was lying to the right of Rogers, and the latter made an attempt to reach him, but was unable. The other two rangers who had not been hit and had sprang to cover during the fearful fusilade, now came forward, and Carmichael placed a coat under the head of Captain Scott and elevated him so that he could breathe better, as in the position he was lying he was strangling with blood. He lay there now, and gave orders as to what should be done coolly and calmly. One man was to be sent to Hemphill, the nearest point, for doctors to give immediate attention, and Private Crowder was to go to San Augustine, forty miles away, after the best surgeon there. Crowder had been left at the house of one of the relatives of the Conners, with orders to arrest anyone who came there, and a citizen carried him the message from his captain. A doctor soon arrived on the scene and dressed the wounds of the stricken men, the shot fingers of Sergeant Brooks having to be amputated. The ball was cut out of Captain Scott; it had lodged below the shoulder blade on the left side. A daybook saved the life of John Rogers. The ball would have gone directly through his body had it not first come in contact with the book. It went through the book, however, but deflected and passed out through the left hip. It will be noticed that all of the men who received wounds were struck on the left side, and it would appear that the Conners were aiming for the heart. This, however, might not have been the case. Men shooting from behind a tree generally aim from the right side of it, and the first part of the man's body he sees at whom he is about to fire is the left side, and in quick, hot work he fires his piece as soon as he covers that part of the body. The trees behind which the Conners stood were thickly peppered with balls, showing with what true aim the rangers sent their shots in the direction from which came those of their foes, who were completely hidden from view during the battle.

The next day after the fight, April 1st, the wounded men were removed to Hemphill, nine miles away. Captain Scott was carried on a litter, and Rogers and Brooks in a wagon. They suffered a great deal on the way. The brave and gallant young Moore, who lost his life in this battle with the outlaws, was carried to Hemphill and buried before the wounded rangers reached there. His was the most largely attended funeral ever known there. Many ladies came and dropped bouquets in the grave of the dead hero. The citizens were all kind and sympathetic, and came to see the rangers in great numbers. The wounded were all kept in one house, and many ladies came every day with flowers and nourishment. The relatives of Moore at Center Point were notified of his death, and Capt. Frank Moore, sheriff of Kerr County, his uncle, came at once. He carried the horse, saddle, and pistol of the gallant boy back home. The horse, a fine sorrel pacer, was kept in the Moore family until he died. When Captain Scott recovered he married Miss Georgia Lynch, of Waelder, Gonzales County, Texas.

When young Rogers so far recovered as to be able to travel he obtained leave of absence, and came to see his mother at Kingsbury, Guadalupe County, his father having died when he was very young. When this leave expired he went back to his company, which had been continuously hunting the Conners ever since the fight, but being unable to find them, the rangers came back west to San Angelo, Tom Green County. Sergeant Brooks was now captain of the company, and John Rogers was made sergeant.

While at San Angelo, Sergeant Rogers and a deputy from Mitchell County followed a couple of horse-thieves and accidentally met them in the road, rather to the surprise of both parties. One of them raised his gun to fire, but Rogers was too quick for him, getting in the first shot, wounding him in the arm, and he dropped his gun. The sergeant then jumped down and caught his horse by the bridle. The deputy had his man covered, also, but turned his head when Rogers fired, and he succeeded in getting his pistol out, but in his haste let it fall, and both were captured and put in jail in San Angelo.

From Tom Green County the rangers moved to Rio Grande City and stayed there two years, and then in 1890 came back to Cotulla. In the fall of 1892 Catarina Garcia raised his revolt, and Sergeant Rogers went out with five men to locate him and his band, who numbered 165. In one of his deserted camps papers were found which disclosed forty names of men and officers. Sergeant Rogers went twice to Laredo and begged for help, and finally a squad of soldiers came under the command of Captain Hardie. This officer was a fine man, and was very popular among the rangers. It will be remembered that Garcia was not making war against the Texans, but was organizing his force in Texas for the invasion of Mexico in the hopeless and useless endeavor of overturning the Diaz government. The rangers and soldiers in conjunction broke up his band in Texas, and many of them were captured. Garcia himself was not taken, but made his escape to Cuba and joined the army of Maceo, the Cuban patriot, and lost his life in battle with the Spaniards.

On the 10th of October, 1892, Sergeant Rogers, having obtained leave of absence, married Miss Hattie Burwell, at Cotulla. Soon after this important event in the life of the gallant ranger the company was sent to Realitos, Duval County. Sergeant Rogers was commissioned captain of the company by Gov. James Hogg on the 1st day of January, 1893. Tupper Harris, of Kingsbury, Guadalupe County, was elected first sergeant. The company was stationed at Alice. Curran Rogers, brother of the captain, belonged to the company, having joined soon after the Conner fight.

The company remained at Alice five years, and then came back in June, 1898, to Cotulla, relieving Captain Brooks, the gallant sergeant in the Conner battle, who had been placed in command of a company, and his command went to Alice.

In September Sergeant Harris resigned, and H. G. Dubose was elected to fill the vacancy.

On the 18th of March, 1899, Captain Rogers received an order from General Scurry to repair to Laredo with a detachment of his men to assist State Health Officer Blunt in enforcing quarantine regulations, there being a great epidemic of smallpox at that place. Mexican citizens of Laredo who had the disease objected to being moved from their homes to the pesthouse or hospital which had been provided for those afflicted. When Captain Rogers arrived at Laredo he quartered himself and men at the Hamilton Hotel. On the 19th he took A. Y. Old ("Augy") and repaired to the scene of moving the patients. The Mexicans had a clash with the city officials, in which several shots were fired on both sides, and hundreds of them now swarmed together on the streets, yelling and hissing. Captain Rogers, having but few men, wired Governor Sayers to use his influence with the war department to call out troops from Fort McIntosh if found necessary. Operations were now suspended until the morning of the 20th. In the meantime General Scurry wired Sergeant Dubose at Cotulla, to proceed with all of the men there to the assistance of Captain Rogers at Laredo. He arrived on the 20th with rangers W. A. Old, W. L. Wright, Creed Taylor, and James Moore (cousin of the James Moore killed in the Conner fight). The ranger companies at this time had been cut down to not more than a dozen men each. Sergeant Dubose reported to Captain Rogers at the Hamilton House, and he and his men were quartered there. Just before starting the pest wagons, information came that at a certain house in East Laredo arms and ammunition were being concealed for the purpose of resisting the officials of the quarantine when the removal of patients commenced. Captain Rogers at once repaired to the place designated, in company with the sheriff and three Mexican officers. One house was searched, nothing found, and no resistance offered. Here A. Y. Old and special ranger Thomas Raglin joined Captain Rogers. The party now proceeded to the house of Agapeta Herrera, and presenting a search warrant, told their business. He then called the sheriff to one side and had a talk with him. Two brothers of Agapita were present, and they commenced pacing back and forth across the yard in a very nervous manner, and at the same time closely watching the rangers. The sheriff finally grabbed Agapita and beckoned to the Mexican deputies. The Mexican in this talk with the sheriff had refused submission to have his house searched. The two brothers now ran into the house, seized their Winchesters, and ran through a gate which was between the street and their yard. Captain Rogers fired on them, and the Mexicans jumped behind a wall, and Agapita got loose from the sheriff and obtained possession of his Winchester. The captain was watching the two Mexicans behind the wall, and did not see Agapita when he secured his gun. The first he noticed of him he was aiming his gun at the captain, and had crossed the street in the rear, and Captain Rogers wheeled and fired at him, wounding him in the breast. Shooting at this time was general, the other two rangers having opened fire. Their hats were covered with lime from the whitewashed walls of the house against which they stood, the balls striking over their heads. About the time that Captain Rogers fired his second shot he was badly wounded in the right shoulder by a shot from Agapita, and another ball also cut his thumb. Augy Old now fired two shots in quick succession at Agapita, hitting him both times in the head, and he fell dead in his tracks. During this time the sheriff and Mexican deputies had left the yard and gone into another street. The ball that struck Captain Rogers broke the bone just below the shoulder joint, rendering his right hand powerless. The left arm had been disabled in the Conner fight and was not strong, and thus left powerless he withdrew and went down the street towards the Hamilton House, where he could get medical assistance, as he was bleeding profusely. The other two rangers held their own with the Mexicans, but finally withdrew. Captain Rogers, becoming very weak, hailed a hack before reaching his destination, and was taken in and conveyed to the hotel. Before reaching there he met City Marshal Joe Bartlow, who asked what was the trouble, and was informed of the fight. Sergeant Dubose and the other rangers were also met coming in a run with Winchesters. They had been 'phoned by Dr. Blunt that a fight was in progress. Although bleeding and suffering, Captain Rogers ordered the hack to stop, and gave orders to his men what to do. He told Dubose that now was the time to call out the soldiers, as they had permission to use them, and to wait and get them; to be prudent, take matters in hand, and do the best he could. At the hotel the wounded captain was met by Frank Earnest and other friends, and assisted to his room, where Dr. McKnight attended him. In about twenty minutes news came that fighting was going on again in town. The rangers under Sergeant Dubose, becoming impatient, repaired to the scene of the late fight, and there found about fifty armed Mexicans assembled around the dead body of Agapita. They opened fire on the rangers when they appeared, and a general fusilade commenced. At the first fire from the rangers the Mexicans scattered quickly and promiscuously to cover behind fences, etc. The rangers, although only a corporal's guard, as you might say, also went to cover and held their own, and quite a battle ensued. One Mexican repeatedly fired a Winchester from cover, and for some time the rangers could not locate him. Creed Taylor, the youngest ranger in the party, had a slide magazine shotgun, and changing his position he obtained a view of the Mexican, as he to some extent uncovered himself to fire, and gave him a load of buckshot, which turned him over. There was more sign on this Mexican after the fight than any that could be heard of that was hit. There was no chance to find out how many were killed or hit. Five had the assistance of doctors afterwards. Sergeant Dubose received one ball through the pants leg, and Special Ranger O. N. Wright was badly bruised by a spent ball in the groin. After the fight the rangers repaired to the hotel and informed their captain what they had done, and was told to go on with the work of removing patients. This was done without any more resistance.

On the 21st Captain Rogers was removed to the Santa Rosa hospital, San Antonio, and placed under the treatment of Dr. Graves. Dr. Wilcox, of Laredo, came as far as Devine with him, and then returned. Dr. Graves told the captain he could save his arm, but would likely have to make it shorter, and that evening at 5 o'clock he operated upon it, cutting out one inch and a half of bone. The captain had to lie in one position six weeks, but when able to sit up, was carried to his mother's house, who lived in San Antonio. In three weeks more he went back to his command at Cotulla, and is there now in command of Company E, doing business at the same old stand, and has up to date (January 3, 1900) served the State as a ranger nearly eighteen years.

Captain Rogers is related to Col. Nat Benton, who lost an arm at the battle of Blair's Landing, in Louisiana, during the Civil war. Colonel Benton and his young son Eustis were in the Calahan expedition in 1855, and were both wounded in the battle of San Fernando, in Mexico,—the son severely in the head. Eustis was a captain in the Confederate army, and faithfully followed the Stars and Bars.

JUDGE M. F. LOWE.

Judge Marcellus French Lowe, the subject of this sketch, was born in Atascosa County, Texas, west from Pleasanton, the county seat, on Padillo Creek. The date of his birth was March 28, 1855, and he was the first white child born in Atascosa County.

From this place he moved with his parents to McMullin County and settled on the bank of the Frio River, nine miles below the old Laredo road. His father, James Lowe, Sr., was a stockman, and had many experiences with Indians—trailing, fighting them, etc. He had extensive cattle interests in the Southwest, and established several branch ranches, one of which was on the Nueces River, about thirty-five miles from his place of residence, and known as the San Jose ranch. It was in charge of an old Mexican, called a "remudada"—one in charge of horses, or a "remuda."

In 1871 the elder Lowe sent his son Marcellus, then 14 years of age, and one of his negro hands, a boy of the same age, named Sam Heritage, to the San Jose ranch after a herd of about eighty head of horses. They were to carry these horses to Alligator Lake,—where they were to meet Moses McLean, a negro in the employ of Mr. Lowe on one of his ranches. Moses had written or sent word to Mr. Lowe that he was in need of the horses, and would be at the lake on a certain day, and would there receive them if he would have them sent down there. Young Lowe and the negro boy arrived at the ranch late in the evening. The ranch house was nothing but a small picket affair, and stood on rising ground overlooking a mesquite flat, across a small draw or ravine, with rising ground beyond towards the east. About sundown a man named Stringfield drove up in an ox wagon, having with him his wife and three children—two boys and a girl, the latter being the eldest. They camped for the night near the yard fence. They were coming from Preata, or Black Creek, and going to Alligator Lake. Early next morning the old Mexican went out and brought up the horses which were sent for, and young Lowe, who was acquainted with the Stringfield family, went out and asked them to come into the house for breakfast. They said no, they had some, and would go on. At this time the old man had the oxen hitched to the wagon and was about starting. Marcellus went back into the house, and in a minute or so the Mexican remudada ran into the yard on a pony, exclaiming, "Indios! Indios!" At this time rapid shots were heard east, in the direction taken by Stringfield. He had crossed the little creek and was on the rising ground beyond about 200 yards, when young Lowe ran to the door to look. The sun was just rising and the wagon was in plain view, surrounded by a large band of mounted Indians, who were shooting towards the wagon with guns and arrows. Mr. Stringfield could be seen fighting them and trying to defend his family, who were all getting out of the wagon and screaming. One of the little boys was riding a horse and attempted to escape on him, but two mounted Indians ran around him, one on each side, and one of them lifted the boy from his horse and placed him behind on the animal he was riding. The little fellow tried hard to pull loose from the painted savage, but was unable to do so. Young Lowe could plainly hear the screams of Mrs. Stringfield, and also calling on him for help, saying, "Oh, for God's sake, Marcellus, come and help us." This was repeated several times, but the boy was totally unarmed, and it would only have amounted to the useless sacrifice of his own life to have responded to the appeal. Judge Lowe says he will never forget this heartrending appeal to him for help in this fearful ordeal, and the tone of the poor woman's voice as it floated out on the early morning breeze has never been erased from his mind. After all was over at the wagon the Indians faced towards the house, as if to make an attack upon it. The old Mexican at once commenced strategy. He had in the house, besides himself and wife, young Lowe, and the negro boy and another Mexican. One Mexican had run away from the place and hid himself in the Nueces River near by, only keeping his head out of the water. He carried a six-shooter with him, and this only left one revolver at the ranch, and was all the firearms at hand. The old remudada, however, determined to make a display of strength. He put a crowbar in the hands of Lowe, gave an old saber to the negro boy, a stick to the Mexican, and himself took the revolver, and marching his crowd out in plain view of the Indians, waved it and dared them to the combat. The rays of the rising sun glinted on the crowbar and saber, and gave the impression that all were armed with firearms. The Indians, however, divided into two parties and approached the house. The old Mexican retired with his force inside again before they arrived near enough to discover his deception, and barred the door. He then, when they came in hearing of his voice, began to give orders in a loud voice in the Spanish language, so the Indians could understand him: "You stand here and shoot, and you there; one stand there and fire; you stand at the door and shoot," etc. The Indians understood, halted, consulted a short time, and then retired, dreading the fire from a foe under cover. They rounded up the eighty head of horses and went away with them.

About this time Lowe heard a little girl crying at the gate, and went to her. It was one of Stringfield's, and she had managed to make her escape to the house, although lanced in several places. Her first thought was about her father and mother, and she asked young Lowe to go back with her to them, as they were killed by the Indians. She was taken into the house and her wounds dressed by the Mexican woman. When there were no longer any Indians in sight, Lowe and others went to the wagon. Stringfield was dead, lying full length, shot both with arrows and bullets. His wife was also dead, killed with arrows. They had left the wagon in a vain endeavor to get to the ravine which ran near the house, but were killed in the mesquites, eighty yards from the wagon. The man was lying with his head west and feet east; the wife with head north and feet south. Her head was close to the middle of the husband's body, the two making a **T**. The two boys were carried off. The bodies of the unfortunate slain were buried where found. The little girl said the Indians broke her father's arm at the first fire, and that he could not shoot good. No doubt his shots were ineffectual.

These same Indians had first made a raid on Moses at Alligator Lake and got all of his horses except two. At noon he arrived at the scene of the tragedy and found all of his horses in a bend of the river, where they had escaped while the Indians were engaged in the battle with Stringfield. The elder Lowe and others followed the Indians, but could not overtake them, but found a small skeleton on the trail, which was supposed to be that of the youngest Stringfield boy. The little girl recovered.

Judge Lowe now lives at Pearsall, county seat of Frio County, and is district judge of the Thirty-sixth Judicial District. He was educated at Bingham's College, in North Carolina, and after returning to Texas was a member of the Nineteenth Legislature. He is very popular, and has many friends in the Southwest.

CAPTAIN ALONZO REESE.

Came to Texas in 1852.

Captain Reese was born in McNairy County, Tennessee, on the 6th day of September, 1837, and came to Texas in January, 1852. His father died in 1842, and he came to Texas with his mother and two older brothers, Sidney and Adolphus. They first settled in De Witt County, on the Guadalupe River, near Clinton. Not having good health in the lower country, the Reese family concluded to move further west in the mountain country. Accordingly Sidney and Adolphus came out and explored the Medina Valley, and liking the country bought land on Bandera Creek, not far from the present town of the same name, and now county seat of Bandera County. They returned home, and the family came out to the new home in 1854. There were but few settlers then where Bandera is now. Among these were P. D. Saner, R. H. and De Witt Burney, — Milstead, — Odum, and Malcolm Gillis. Charles De Montel had a sawmill where Bandera is now, and had quite a lot of hands with him making shingles from the cypress timber which was at that time abundant and of fine quality.

There was one settler on the Helotes, eighteen miles from San Antonio, named Forrester. The Lipan Indians pretended to be friendly, and one day a band of them came to the house of Forrester and came inside of the dwelling. The settler apprehended no danger from them, and when they took notice of his rifle in the rack and wanted to look at it, he handed it to them. No sooner had the treacherous rascals became possessed of the gun than they turned it upon Forrester and shot him dead on the floor. A general massacre of the family then commenced, and only Mrs. Forrester escaped and made her way to San Antonio with the news. The Indians after leaving the place came up the Medina valley and passed out near where the Reese family lived. At this time the Fourth United States cavalry was stationed at San Antonio, and at once came out to the scene of the tragedy and took the trail of the Indians. The Reeses saw the soldiers as they passed by on the trail. This was their first alarm of Indians. Being new comers, they knew nothing about Indian depredations, and were resting in fancied security. The Indians passed out two and a half miles north of Montel's mill.

At this time there lived in the Guadalupe valley,. eighteen miles north, near where Center Point now is, Mr. Rufus Brown, an old Texan and brother to John Henry Brown, the historian. A short time after this Lipan raid Mr. Brown came over to the Reese place and warned them of the danger they were in at their present location, and advised them to move over into the Guadalupe valley, near him. This advice was at once acted upon, and the change made. At this time the Reese boys were all young and unmarried. The Burneys also came over, and all grouped together at Brown's ranch for protection.

Soon after this a lot of Mormons came into the country, under the leadership of O. L. Wight. They were originally from Missouri, but before coming here had stayed awhile on the Pedernales River, southeast from Fredericksburg, in Gillespie County. When they came into the Guadalupe valley they stopped on Verde Creek and put up a sawmill for Dr. J. C. Ridley for the purpose of sawing up the cypress timber there. This mill was in about seventy-five yards of the present residence of W. E. Pafford. A settler named George Nichols put up the Pafford house. After the mill was finished the Mormons left and settled at Bandera, but soon moved from there and stopped at a place that still goes by the name of "Mormon Camp," below Bandera.

The Indians made raids on the settlers every light moon, and they were always expected at that time.

About 1855 Governor Pease authorized the raising of minute companies for frontier protection. These companies were to be raised among the settlers themselves and officered by some of their own number. They were to draw pay for the time they were in actual service, scouting or pursuing Indians. In 1855, at the instigation of some of the settlers, for better protection in the Guadalupe valley, a company of infantry was sent out and went into camp on the spot where Camp Verde now is. Seeing the inefficiency of such a force on the frontier, they were recalled in 1856, and Captain Palmer was sent out with a company of cavalry. He built Camp Verde, and it became a permanent station.

The Indians continued to raid on the settlers, and such was

their atrocious deeds of murder, robbery, and carrying off white people—men, women, and children—into captivity, that only the most daring pioneers remained in the country.

In 1861 the State government of Texas authorized the raising of a regiment of men for frontier protection, to be stationed at intervals on the outskirts of the settlements from the Rio Grande to Red River. Scouts were to be kept out all the time and range back and forth between stations, so as to detect any trail of Indians coming out or going into the settlements. This was a good plan, and resulted well. This was kept up until 1862, and then this force was turned over to the Confederate government, but by a reorganization, in which most of the old rangers re-enlisted, was retained on the frontier until 1864.

Mr. Alonzo Reese belonged to one of these companies. commanded by Capt. James M. Hunter, and was lieutenant of the company. On one occasion Captain Hunter sent Lieutenant Reese with ten men on an extensive scout. On James River, a tributary of the Llano, an Indian trail was found and closely followed to the head of the Pedernales River. Here they came upon the Indians, eleven in number, all on foot except two, and they were badly mounted on poor, shabby ponies. Among the men present besides the lieutenant was his brother, Adolphus Reese, J. W. Benson, Jake Banta, and McCann. The Indians, seeing they could not very well make their escape from a mounted force, halted and prepared for a fight. When the charge was made by the rangers, some of the Indians fired at them with revolvers and others with arrows. When the rangers commenced firing, some of the guns failed on account of a damp day and a very poor quality of Confederate powder. After firing a few rounds, however, the Indians turned and ran as the rangers came up close to them. In this fusilade they killed the horse ridden by Adolphus Reese. The rangers kept after the Indians, occasionally some one firing, and others making ineffectual attempts. Lieutenant Reese, coming near an Indian who was running and throwing his shield back and forth around his back and shoulders to ward off bullets, called to Jake Banta close by, who had a good gun and good powder, if he could not kill the Indian. Banta dismounted, so that his aim would be better, and brought him to the ground. Other Indians turned back to the fallen one and stood him on his feet, but as he was not able to go they let him loose again. He fell to the ground again, but as he did so he drew a knife and stabbed himself to the heart. The Indians scattered widely and the rangers scattered after them. Lieutenant Reese had a shotgun, and coming in range of one fired and brought him down. The Indian lay stunned for a few moments, but then began to get up and Reese's gun was empty. At this time Adolphus Reese came up with a loaded gun, and his brother said, "Look out, Dolf, that Indian will shoot you," as his brother started to go up to the Indian, who at this time was resting on his knees. Adolphus, thus warned, stopped, and aiming his rifle shot the Indian through the head and finished him. The Indians, by scattering and taking advantage of the ravines and thickets and the bad condition of the rangers' guns and ammunition, had only one more killed, but several wounded. The dead Indians were scalped and their shields, bows, and other things taken. Of the rangers, J. W. Benson was wounded in the thigh with an arrow, and McCann in the thumb. This terminated the scout and the rangers went back to camp. Lieutenant Reese was afterwards captain of the company, Captain Hunter being promoted to major.

All three of the Reese brother still live in the Guadalupe valley, have large families, and have prospered in stockraising and farming.

BATTLE BETWEEN RANGERS AND INDIANS.

1875.

In the latter part of the summer of the above named year Capt. Rufus Perry was in command of a company of rangers and stationed on the San Saba River. At times, however, when the grass became short in the vicinity of camp, a move was made to better range. On the occasion of which we write the San Saba camp had been abandoned and a new one established in Menard County. One morning while here Scott Cooly and another ranger went out to kill a beef for the use of the company, and while searching for one discovered a band of Indians going west. The camp of the rangers was in the opposite direction, and several miles distant. The two men, seeing the Indians were not disposed to run them, conceived the idea of trying to entice them in the direction of camp by charging towards them, firing their Winchesters, and then turning and running away as if afraid of them. The Indians failed to fall into this trap, and continued on their course. Cooly now told his companion to return to camp and inform Captain Perry of the situation, and he would follow the Indians and keep them in sight until a force could arrive sufficient to fight them. The country was broken, rolling prairie, and the Indians were easily kept in view. At this time Major Jones, who was in command of all the rangers on the frontier, was in the camp of Captain Perry with an escort of thirty-five men, making his tour of inspection and paying off the rangers. When the news of the Indians was brought to camp Major Jones and his men had their horses saddled and were about to take their departure, but mounted instead and set off to find the trail of the Indians. Perry's men followed as soon as they could get ready, under the command of Lieutenant Roberts. Captain Perry remained in camp. The combined force when all got together on the trail was sixty men, which greatly outnumbered the Indians. The latter, knowing they would be pursued, by the absence of one ranger and the other following, traveled fast. Twenty miles were thus passed over before they were sighted by the pursuers. By this time all of the horses except eight had given out or dropped so far behind they could not be seen by those in front. Those in front were all Perry's men, except one citizen of Menard County. None of the escort or any of the balance of Perry's men were in sight. Here at the end of this twenty-mile run the rangers first came up with their comrade, Cooly. He had never lost sight of the Indians during all of this time. Now, with him added, their force was nine and the Indians eleven. Among the rangers present were Lieutenant Roberts, Scott Cooly, Thurlow Weed, Charles Bartholomae, and the citizen. The balance of the names can not now be remembered. A charge was now made, and a run of two miles more brought them close to the retreating Comanches, who, seeing the diminished force and their own horses failing fast, halted, faced about, and prepared for battle. The rangers made no halt, but came up close and commenced firing with Winchesters, the lieutenant shouting, "Give it to them, boys." The Comanche chief charged the lieutenant and commenced firing at him with a Spencer carbine, and wounded his horse in the shoulder. Roberts also commenced shooting and killed the chief. The Indians had six-shooters, besides bows and a few guns. Their fire, however, was quick and ineffectual. Another Indian fell dead near the chief under the fire of the rangers, and the balance wheeled their horses and once more sought refuge in flight, firing back at the rangers with revolvers. One of the rangers was wounded in the breast during this fusilade with a pistol, and several saddles were hit. One by one the Indians fell on the prairie, and four horses were killed in the long chase. One Indian, when his horse fell dead under him, came back among the rangers making signs of surrender, and was captured. Only three Indians were now left, and they abandoned their played-out horses and continued their efforts to escape on foot. By this time the rangers were again scattered, and only four were around the captured Indian. One of these was left with the Comanche to keep other rangers who were following from killing him when they came up. During the short halt with the captive Indian, the three now on foot were making good time across the prairie, running faster than tired horses. The three rangers, however, spurred up their jaded steeds and again pursued them. Among these three rangers were Charley Bartholomae and Scott Cooly. Bartholomae was on a splendid horse and had fired many times, being always well up in front. Three miles were covered, and again the rangers were nearing the fleeing Indians, who, seeing their case was hopeless, stopped in some rocks and bushes and prepared again to give battle. When the rangers arrived they circled around the place and commenced to look for them. One was discovered and killed by a ranger the first fire. Another ranger rode so close to one he sprang from behind a rock at him, yelling loudly, and attempted to adjust an arrow to his bowstring, but his hand shook so from nervous excitement that he was unable to do it. The ranger fired quickly, but missed the Indian. Charley Bartholomae fired three shots at him in quick succession with his pistol, having exhausted his Winchester ammunition, but also failed to bring him down. The other ranger now fired with a Winchester and killed him. The third Indian could not be found. It was evident he had left the place before the rangers arrived and lay down somewhere in the tall grass on the prairie, and could not be seen. The long return trip was now made on very tired horses. The trailing and long running fight was twenty-nine miles. Ten of the eleven Indians were killed or captured —nine dead on the ground. Most of them were scalped. Scott Cooly took a strip out of one's back for the purpose of trying to make a quirt or something out of it, but when he hung it on a bush in the sun at camp it nearly all went to grease and dripped away. During the fight, as fast as the Indians would empty their revolvers, they would throw them away, and several of these were picked up. The captured Indian was taken to Austin by a squad of rangers, and when they saw the crowds of people come to look at him they conceived the idea of turning it to profit. They carried the Comanche to the operahouse, and there charged 25 cents admission fee for people to look at him. For one day they did a thriving business, but the adjutant-general heard of it, put a stop to the show, and took the Indian away from the rangers and had him sent down to the penitentiary, where he finally died.

Charley Bartholomae was born in Guadalupe County, but now resides in San Antonio.

FROM A PHOTO TAKEN AT REAL'S RANCH, KERR COUNTY.

DISASTROUS BATTLE WITH INDIANS IN KERR COUNTY.

1857.

In 1857 the Comanche Indians made a raid into Kerr County in the vicinity of Kerrville, and then went back up the Guadalupe River valley. A party of seven young men mounted their horses and set out in pursuit of them. Their names were as follows: William Kelso, Spence Goss, Jack Herridge, Tom Wherry, Dan Murff, Tom McAdams, and Newt. Price. All but Kelso were inexperienced in Indian warfare. He had been a ranger and should have been more cautious, and the terrible disaster which followed might have been averted. They trailed the Indians to a point twenty-five miles above Kerrville, and then stopped to cut a bee tree. At this time the Indians were on a bluff near the river, and watched the white men until they left the place where the honey was found and went into camp. This was ascertained afterwards by finding the place where the Indians had congregated on the bluff, and then following the trail to the spot where the unfortunate young men had made their camp for the night. Their camp was in a thicket, and their horses were staked in the open glades around. The night was cold and a bright fire was kept burning for some time, plainly indicating to the Indians the exact location of the camp. The guns of the party were stacked around a tree several yards from the fire. About daybreak Tom Wherry and Dan Murff arose and rekindled the fire, and then taking their guns went out to hunt a deer The balance of the men also got up and stood or sat around the fire. At this time the Indians had crept close upon them, and before the white men were aware of their presence had secured their guns and made the attack upon them. Some of the men had revolvers, and these defended themselves as best they could. Kelso shot an Indian down, and he fell near the fire. The Indians made such a furious onslaught, and the settlers were so badly shot up at once, that they soon scattered into the brush, each man trying to save himself. When Murff and Wherry heard the firing at camp, and knowing its significance ran back to help their comrades, Murff ran almost among the Indians, and stopping in an open place discharged his gun at them. Almost at the same instant he received a ball in the breast and fell dead on the spot. This shot was from some of the settlers' own guns. Wherry was shot in the breast with an arrow, and after firing his gun escaped into the brush. Spence Goss was sitting down by the fire with his feet drawn up close to his body, facing towards them, and an Indian fired at him with a short Mexican gun called a scopet, carrying a large ball and three buckshot. The charge struck him in the right leg below the knee, broke the bone, and went on out through the thigh. With a powerful effort he dragged himself away into a thicket and lay down. Kelso was shot crosswise through the small of the back with an arrow, but jerked it out, and shooting an Indian down he made his escape into the brush. Tom McAdams was shot in the neck through the windpipe with an arrow, but managed to get away. Newt. Price was standing with his back to the Indians, and was hit in the shoulders with a load of buckshot from one of their own guns. He also made his escape into a thicket. Jack Herridge was sitting by the fire with his shoes off, warming his feet, and only having a small, single-barreled pistol called a derringer, sprang away in flight without being hit. He was the first man to reach the settlement, but his feet were so bruised and lacerated by rocks that before they healed the bottom of his feet came off. The Indians got all of the horses except those of Murff and Wherry. When they started on the deer hunt they turned their horses loose to graze until they got back. They took fright during the battle, ran away, and made their way back to Kerrville. Some time after the fight, when the Indians were gone, Kelso, Wherry, and McAdams got together and started for home on foot, but they made but slow progress. Kelso could scarcely walk, and McAdams was constantly sick and vomiting, caused from swallowing blood from the wound in his neck. Wherry was also badly wounded; the arrow made such a deep wound in his breast, that as he breathed the air would escape through the aperture with a whistling noise. They were several days getting to Kerrville. Goss and Price both escaped into the same thicket, but were not aware of each other's presence. Both were weak from loss of blood and fainted, or, as they expressed it, went to sleep and lay there for several hours. When Goss came to himself again he called for his companions, and was answered by Price near by. These two now got together and went about a mile, Goss dragging one leg after him. Here they found a small cave and spent the night in it. Next morning Price proposed, as he was able to walk, to try and make his way to the settlement and send relief to Goss. He started, but never reached there. He died ten miles from where he had left his companion. In the meantime searching parties were out hunting for Goss and Price, not expecting to find either alive. Goss remained at his cave eighteen days, vainly hoping as each sun ran its course and went down in the west, that before another setting sun help would come. Of course he knew not that his unfortunate companion lay dead ten miles away, where he had sank exhausted to rise no more. No one else knew where he was, and the searching parties had gone round and round his position. During the day he would crawl around in the dense thickets and eat grapes and haws and lie in the cave at night. A small spring branch near by furnished him with water. He had his pistol, but would not shoot anything for fear of attracting a band of Indians. After remaining in this condition for the length of time mentioned above, Goss gave up all hopes of any one coming to him and started towards the settlement, using a forked stick to aid him in getting alone. After traveling several days in this way he was found one day sitting down leaning against a tree by Judge Patton, who was out on a bear hunt. Patton helped him to get to the camp of a man named Miller, eight miles above Kerrville. In the meantime a party of searchers had found the trail of Goss, and could easily follow it by the holes he made in the ground with his stick. They found him at Miller's camp, and from thence conveyed him to the house of his brother-in-law, Joshua D. Brown. Mr. Brown was the founder of Kerrville, which was named after James Kerr, relative of the Browns. Murff was buried where he fell, in a shallow grave, but well covered up with rocks. Shortly after, however, a runaway negro came along, disinterred the remains, stripped the body, and appropriated the clothing to his own use. The negro then placed the body back, but wolves dragged it out again. Hunters found it and brought the skeleton to Kerrville and buried it in the cemetery there. Hunters also found the skeleton or bones of Price two years after, and his boots, with bones in them, were brought to town. Also a daybook and 25 cents in money in a purse, and from these the remains were identified.

When Kelso drew the arrow from his wound during the fight and threw it down he failed to notice in the excitement of the time that the spike failed to come with the shaft. For twenty years the wound would not heal, until by a surgical operation the iron arrow head was discovered and removed, and the wound then healed.

Mr. Daniel Adolphus Reese, who gave the writer the particulars of this most sad frontier episode, was living near Kerrville at the time, and helped to search for Goss and Price. He came to Texas in 1852 from the western district of Tennessee. He first settled in Dimmit County, and came to Bandera in 1854, and he built the first house there out of poles to put corn in. People had no houses at first, but lived in camps. He moved from there into the Guadalupe valley. In 1856 Kerr County organished, and Mr. Reese was elected county clerk and helped to lay off the town of Kerrville, which was the county seat. In 1863 he belonged to a ranging company commanded by Captain Hunter, and was in an Indian fight on the head of the Pedernales River, in which three Indians were killed, some of the rangers were wounded, and Mr. Reese had his horse killed. His brother, Alonzo Reese, was in command of the scout. Adolphus was commissary and quartermaster sergeant, and only came on this scout for recreation. His proper place was in camp.

Mr. Reese also gives the following Kerr County history:

In 1859 there lived, five miles above Kerrville, a settler named Roland Nichols. One evening he went out about a mile from home to kill a turkey. When he failed to come back at night the family became alarmed and neighbors were notified. Mr. Reese responded, but nothing could be done until morning. In company with others the trail of Mr. Nichols was then followed up a draw to a point about a mile from the house. Here it turned abruptly in another direction, and the plain trail of numerous Indian tracks on both sides of it told the tale of the missing man. Nearly a mile from here his body was found beside a tree. He had halted here and got the tree between him and the Indians, and the tracks showed he had circled around it repeatedly while they were trying to kill him. The bark was raked from the tree all around where he had held to it with both hands in a vain endeavor to keep the trunk between him and his foes. He had one arrow in the breast, and one arrow and one bullet wound in the body. The bullet and arrow had first struck the left arm about half way between the elbow and shoulder, and then penetrated the body not more than a half inch apart. Going back to the spot where the Indian sign was first discovered, it was evident that here was where the unfortunate settler received the arrow in the breast from ambush. The prints of his knees were in the sandy soil where he had come down either to fire his rifle or from the shock of the wound. If from the latter, he dropped his gun without firing, but recovered and ran to the spot where his body was found. His gun was discovered after a search, covered up in the sand, where the Indians had left it, and it was still loaded.

In 1860 Mr. Samuel Lane lived two miles above Comfort, on the Guadalupe River. In the fall of that year he started on horseback up the river to visit a man named John Conner, who lived near where Center Point is now, above the mill on the north side of the river. The property is now owned by some of the Moore family. Mr. Lane was not armed, and was riding along eating pecans when the Indians rushed upon him from a thicket near the road and shot one arrow into his breast. He now left the road and ran his horse towards a pecan mott several hundred yards away. Before reaching this place the Indians shot several arrows into his back, and forced him from his horse and dispatched him. When he failed to come home on the next day the family became uneasy and sent a runner up to Conner's to see if he was there. Finding no trace of him, the messenger went on to Kerrville and made known the facts there. District court was in session, with Judge Stribbling on the bench, but court was adjourned, and judge, jury, and lawyers went to search for the missing man. Mr. Adolph Reese was one of the searching party, and says they did not find him until the following day, making the third since he was killed. In one hand he had a turkey wing gripped, which he was carrying to Mrs. Conner. In the other hand were pieces of the pecans and hulls, and pecan kernels between his teeth. Mr. Reese and his brother-in-law, Judge Starkey, Foster Cocke, De Witt Burney, and several others took the trail of the Indians, which led a west course through the mountains over a very rough country. They came to one place where the Indians had camped, killed a cow, and eaten her. While riding around in the camp Judge Starkey let his gun go off accidentally, and killed Foster Cocke's horse. Further on the Indians went down such a steep, rocky mountain, they had lanced their horses to make them go down, as was evident from the amount of blood along the way. The white men could not get their horses to go down, so had to leave them with a guard and continue the pursuit on foot. In Hondo Canyon they found the dead body of a Frenchman whom the Indians had killed. The pursuit was kept up to Sabinal Canyon and then abandoned. They would have caught the Indians at the place where they went down the steep bluff if night had not been at hand. The blood from the horses was fresh, not having as yet congealed on the rocks. No doubt they saw the trailers coming, and this was why they forced their horses down such an unreasonable place. Here, however, they entered a cedarbrake, and dark coming on, all trailing had to cease until the morning, and this gave the Indians a long start again.

ROSS KENNEDY.

Mr. Ross Kennedy was born in Monaghan County, Ireland, December 12, 1827, and set sail from Belfast for America when a young man, and arrived at New York about 1850. He came over on the ship Rainbow, commanded by a Yankee captain named Hope. The time consumed in the voyage was twenty-one days and was uneventful, except one fire aboard ship, which originated between decks, but did no material damage. Young Kennedy displayed a decided inclination for the sea and life of a sailor, which attracted the notice of Captain Hope, and he volunteered the advice to the young man that he had better put such notions out of his head; that sailors had a hard life, and that dogs on his place at home were treated better than they.

From New York Mr. Kennedy drifted to Texas and brought up on the Rio Grande, coming up the gulf on the ship John Stroud. Near Powder Horn she was thrown on her beam ends in a squall, but was soon righted without damage. In 1851 he went to Eagle Pass and obtained work from the government, going to Fort Clark and helping to build the garrison there. From Fort Clark he went to Powder Horn and acted as receiving clerk there for the government, and then in the capacity of wagon master of a government train, and finally was put in charge of the United States sutler store on the Pecos. From there he came back to Fort Clark and again served as wagon master, seeing many Indians on these trips, but was not attacked by them. At this time there was a treaty made between Mexico and Texas, by which the latter was to keep Texas Indians out of Mexico, and one one occasion Mr. Kennedy was placed in charge of a band who had passes but had overstepped their bounds, and were being carried back to where they had obtained their passes. On the route a terrible storm was encountered one night, and all of the Indians made their escape. During these years Mr. Kennedy also rode a pony express from Fort Inge to Eagle Pass. On one trip he fell in with Capt. Henry E. McCulloch and a small squad of his rangers and rode some distance with them. During the time a large buck sprang up near the road and went off at a rapid run. One of the rangers wheeled his horse around, and raising his rifle quickly fired and brought the deer down dead in his tracks. It was such a good shot it was remarked about, and McCulloch asked the ranger if he was in the habit of doing that. He had belonged to another company and only recently joined that of McCulloch, and in reply told him to ask his former captain.

While on this line Mr. Kennedy also had charge of a line up to Fort Clark, and put a man to ride that named Henderson, who on one occasion dismounted at noon, pulled off his saddle so that his horse could cool off and rest, and was about to proceed to make a cup of coffee for himself, when he discovered a band of Indians swooping down on him from the prairie. Hastily throwing his saddle back onto his horse, he vaulted into it from the ground without fastening the girth, and in that manner ran a desperate race with the Indians, the girth popping the horse underneath, which rather aided in accelerating his movements, and arrived safely at the fort.

In after years when Mr. Kennedy was leading parties after Indians, and men slow in saddling and mounting, he would say "Boys, you can't saddle and mount a horse as quick as Henderson."

In 1856 Mr. Kennedy moved to Uvalde County and settled where he is now living, six miles east of Sabinal station, on a tributary of the Sabinal River called Ranchero Creek, but sometimes called Comanche Creek by the old settlers. At this time the Indians were not troublesome to a great extent, and the settlers considered themselves as in no danger of their lives. The first man killed after Mr. Kennedy moved into the country was Louis Thompson, in Frio Canyon. He was a young man lately from Alabama, and had been married but a short time. He had started to Uvalde with a wagon, but stopped on the way to gather pecans, when a band of Indians came upon him, cut him off from the wagon where his gun was, and killed and scalped him. This band of Indians before this killed a man named White in Hondo Canyon, near where the main wagon road is now, thirty-five miles west of San Antonio. He was riding a wild horse when the Indians came upon him, and fell an easy prey and was soon killed and scalped. We stated above that Thompson was killed first, but if the same band of Indians did both murders White was the first victim, as the Indians were going west when they killed Thompson, and the Hondo is east of the Frio.

In 1859, the day before John Davenport was killed by Indians, Mr. Kennedy was out with his wagon after a load of wood, and his brother-in-law, Mr. Ebenezer Rankin, was out on horseback hunting for a bunch of horses which he wished to drive to the ranch of Mr. Kennedy, where he was staying at the time. Before the latter finished loading the wagon Mr. Rankin dashed up excitedly and said, "Did you see those fellows running me?" Mr. Kennedy said "No. Who were they?" "Indians, I think," said Mr. Rankin. The two men now awaited developments a few minutes, but as no one put in an appearance Kennedy finished loading his wood and went home, while Rankin went on, finding the horses, and drove them in.

This band of Indians was evidently the same or part of those who made themselves felt so sadly in the settlement on the following day, which was October 28th, the date of the killing of John Bowles and John Davenport. On this day Mr. Kennedy went to a store on the east bank of Sabinal River, where was also a stage stand on the main road from San Antonio to the Rio Grande country. The Southern Pacific Railroad crosses there now, and the store stood about where the section house now is, one mile west of the present Sabinal station. When Mr. Kennedy left the store to return home Mr. John Davenport was coming down the hill into the channel of the river on the west side. He stopped a short time at the store and then kept on the road towards his home, which was also on Ranchero Creek above Mr. Kennedy's place. The latter was riding a young horse that he was breaking, and the animal showed signs of uneasiness at one place near some thickets. Mr. Kennedy also saw buzzards at this place, and was inclined once to ride by the place to see if anything was dead there, but changed his notion and went on home. If he had done so, riding as he was a young, awkward horse, he would no doubt have been the victim instead of Mr. Davenport, for it was from here that the band of Indians made their onset upon Mr. Davenport when he came along on a slow, stubborn mule. The Indians had meat or something that attracted the buzzards. One reason, it is supposed, why they failed to come out and give Mr. Kennedy a chase was the fact that he was mounted on a horse, and they feared he would escape and give the alarm of their presence in the settlement. They had already killed John Bowles, and his mutilated remains were at this time lying in the prickly pears and chaparral six miles to the south, near Pilot Knob. When Mr. Kennedy arrived at home he went on without dismounting and caught another horse near by, which he saddled and mounted and came on back to the house, turning the young horse loose where he made the remount. By the time he arrived back at the house again Mr. Louis Lee was there with the news that Mr. John Davenport had been killed and scalped by the Indians.

Mr. Lee lived with the Davenports and did blacksmith work for them. Mr. Kennedy now went in a gallop to Mr. Davenport's ranch, but when he arrived there his brother John and others had repaired to the scene of the killing, which was not more than one mile and a half from where Mr. Kennedy last saw Mr. Davenport riding down the hill at the river. A man named Rooney came along with a train and saw the dead body, and came on to the Davenport ranch, which was near the road, and he or one of his Mexican drivers reported the fact to Mrs. Davenport, who was not aware of who it was, but at once had grave fears that it was her husband, and Mr. Lee at once set out to investigate and soon discovered the sad fact. Mr. Kennedy remained at the ranch until his brother John and others brought in the body, and he helped to wash and dress it. It was nude and very bloody. John Kennedy went with the party that followed the Indians and fought a battle with them on the edge of the plains, in which Lieutenant Hazen and others were badly wounded, and he and Judge McCormick went to Fort Clark, a distance of eighty miles, to procure surgical aid for the lieutenant.

In the meantime the alarm had been raised in regard to John Bowles. It was certain he had been killed by Indians, but his body could not be found. Mr. Ross Kennedy helped the searchers seven days, but the body was not found for three weeks. Pete Bowles, son of the slain man, continued to hunt, and one day while standing on Pilot Knob saw a buzzard light down about half a mile to the south, and repairing to the spot, there found the remains of his father, reduced to a skeleton. He had been out hunting his horse about one mile east from the Patterson settlement, from which place he started, and was ambushed and killed near some prickly pears and chaparral bushes. A stone now marks the spot.

In 1860 the Indians made another raid and killed old man Schreiver near D'Hanis, and then come on up to the ranch of Mr. Kennedy early in the morning. At this time a young Mexican about 18 years of age, who was in the employ of Mr. Kennedy, was out about 500 yards from the house in a southwest course hunting horses, and was attacked by the Indians and shot with an arrow. He ran and fell within 300 yards of the house. Mr. Kennedy was in the cowpen, and heard the Indians yelling. It was a still morning, and he said he never heard Indians make as much noise as that bunch did. Stock was stampeding all over the flat, bells rattling, and the Indians all yelling. Mr. Rankin was also out hunting horses. The Indians first tried to cut him off from the ranch, and it was then they ran upon the young Mexican. Mr. Kennedy ran from the cowpen and secured his gun, and by that time Mr. Rankin had arrived. The former expressed his belief that the Indians were killing his Mexican and he would go to his assistance, but Mr. Rankin told him it was no use, as he watched him run until he fell, and was satisfied he was already dead. Mr. Kennedy, however, went on, and Mr. Rankin went with him. The Mexican was found on his face, dead, and with the arrow in his hand which he had pulled out as he ran. The body was carried to the house, and Mr. Kennedy and Mr. Rankin at once began to alarm the settlers and organized a pursuit of the Indians.

Now comes in an incident showing the courage and endurance of some of the woman of the southwest frontier. Mrs. Kennedy was left alone at the ranch with the dead Mexican at her own request, urging her husband to leave her and follow the Indians until he caught and chastised them. Among those who gathered and took up the trail of the hostiles were Doc (Louis) Lee, Jack Davenport, L. C. (Clabe) Davenport, Emory Givins, Ross Kennedy, John Kennedy, and Ambrose Crane. On the west side of the Sabinal River this party were joined by William Knox, a man named Glass, and another man whose name is not now remembered, and all kept on in the pursuit of the Indians, but in about six miles the trail became badly scattered and was hard to locate satisfactorily. This was caused from the fact that here the Indians had come upon Huffman and Wolf, two cow-hunters, and a running, scattered fight had taken place for a mile or more across the prairie east towards the river, and finally the bodies of the slain men were found, as was also one dead Indian and his horse standing near, and the shirt which had been taken from the back of the slain Mexican at Kennedy's ranch. The trail was plain from here and was followed rapidly, Ross Kennedy being elected captain and directing the pursuit, and Ambrose Crane was trailer. Twenty miles further on, at the mouth of Blanco Canyon, Crane stopped and pointed to the Indians' horses in a glade between a cedar brake and ravine, and Kennedy motioned for his men to dismount and tie their horses, intending to slip around the Indians and cut them off from the cedar brake. Knox objected to this, and the men who came with him decided with him that it was best to charge at once on horseback, although it was not right for him to hold out against the majority, who had already dismounted and tied their horses at a signal from their rightful captain, Ross Kennedy. Rather than not have a concert of action, however, Kennedy and his men mounted and the charge was made, but a failure to do any good except to capture the horses of the Indians was the consequence. The Indians saw them coming and at once disappeared into the brakes, and none were killed. Quite a lot of horses, bows, shields, and arrows were taken. The Indians were cooking a yearling which they had killed. Huffman's mule, with his pistol on the pommel of the saddle, was taken, but Wolf's horse was not seen. The recaptured horses were driven back that night, and Mrs. Kennedy relieved of her lonely vigil with the slain Mexican. Next day a party went back and buried the bodies of Huffman and Wolf.

In 1861, while the brother-in-law of Captain Richarz was herding sheep three miles from D'Hanis, on the Seco, he was attacked and killed by Indians. The trail was taken up by men from below, and they came by the ranch of Mr. Kennedy and got him, Henry Adams, and others to help in the chase. The Indians had killed Dave, the brother of Henry Adams, and he was ready to go on every scout after them. Capt. Joe Ney commanded this scout. The trail led northwest and passed the Tom Wall settlement on the Frio, and then led up East prong towards the divide. At camping time the trailers were above the main springs in the dry draws, and the only chance for water was at

some dripping bluffs, where it would take some time to catch
enough for a man to drink, and the horses had no chance for any
at all, thirsty as they were. There was just about enough water
here for bees, and they were numerous, sucking at the banks.
Mr. Kennedy was not satisfied to stay here, so he took a scout
farther up and found a little pool with sufficient water for the
men, but still not enough for horses. He reported this fact to
Captain Ney, and it was agreed to move up to it. The horses
were hobbled so they could graze some, but guards were placed
to keep them out of the little pool of water through the night,
but were to let them have what was left in the morning. There
were twenty-five men in the party, and it required a good deal of
water for them. During the night horses were heard plunging
into water further up the draw, and an investigation disclosed
the fact that it was the Frio waterhole, about one mile from
where they first stopped at the dripping bluffs that evening. Mr.
Kennedy had often been at the Frio waterhole, but had never
approached it from that direction and was not familiar with the
draw below the pool, which was almost out on the divide, and the
last water in that direction for many miles. Daylight disclosed
the fact that the Indians had stopped here, cooked meat, and
roasted soto heads. The trail now went out onto the divide and
led towards the West prong of the Llano. Near the head of
this stream they came in sight of the Indians and a general
charge was made, but this was abruptly stopped by running onto
the bank of a creek which was full of drift and tree tops from
overflows, and the horses could not cross it, although there was
but little or no water in the channel. With some difficulty a
crossing was found, but by this time the Indians had discovered
them and made their escape. All of the horses were captured
except what they rode off in their flight, and they took time to
pick the best ones and got away fast. They could be seen running in the distance, and finally disappeared in a cedar brake.
The men now came on back and made a dry camp for two hours.
Mr. Kennedy's horse was crippled in the charge in trying to cross
the jammed-up little creek, and he had to mount one of the horses
captured from the Indians. The head of the crippled horse was
tied up so that he could not eat, and when night came he was
placed in front on the back track and true to his animal instinct

he was not at fault, and before day led the men back to the Frio waterhole, where man and beast enjoyed its cool waters after spending one day and nearly a night crossing the dry rocky divide. The Indians were driving one heifer along which they intended to eat, and the white men killed it for food, but the meat was not good on account of the poor animal having been lanced several times, and the flesh had become feverish from the wounds. Nothing occurred of interest back to the settlement. During the pursuit Mr. Kennedy often went on elevated places to take a view, and finally Henry Adams commenced following suit, and while on one hill motioned for Ross Kennedy to come up there. He had found an old-time cart wheel of the Mexican make, having mesquite hub, and all of a very heavy and clumsy makeup of not more than three or four parts to the wheel. The hub was buried in the ground, with the rim resting on the surface. When and under what circumstances the old wheel was left on this mountain of course no one present could tell, but it was surmised it was abandoned here by some of the early Spanish explorers and prospectors who at various and sundry times went all over the country long before the advent of the Anglo-Saxon. The nature of mesquite is like that of cedar and will hardly rot.

In 1858 the Indians carried off a large drove of horses belonging to Dr. Isbel, whose ranch was on Frio, at the foot of the mountains. Men were collected to follow them, and Ross Kennedy, James Davenport, and Emory Givins went from their settlement and joined the other men further up the country. The trail led through the mountains up the Blanco towards the divide. On a rock in the mountains the men found where the Indians had made a picture of Dr. Isbel with paint. There were a few soldiers along from Fort Inge, and after the divide was reached one of these saw the Indians half a mile away. Mr. Kennedy now changed rifles with John Leakey at his request, as the latter had a sore or bruise, likely from falling in the rocks, under his left arm, and his rifle being very heavy, he could not hold it well; the other was lighter. When the Indians saw the white men they changed horses quickly and tried to make their escape, and also to draw the fire of our men at long range, which they did. Their intention was to get to a large cedarbrake in the distance, as the country around them was open, but they finally stopped, as they saw the white men were well mounted and would run among them. They dismounted in some scattered burnt cedar and the fight commenced. After the first shot from the rifle which Mr. Kennedy carried he found himself in a difficulty. The ammunition for his gun would not fit Mr. Leakey's, and he was unable to reload. By this time the Indians were among the white men, and many close personal combats took place, in which two men were wounded and several horses, including the one ridden by Mr. Kennedy. John Leakey's horse was also wounded, and died from it some time after the fight. One arrow came near wounding Mr. Kennedy in the throat, just grazing the skin under the chin. He finally made his way to Leakey, who had a revolver and was fighting an Indian at close range, but took time to exchange guns again. Most of the men dismounted and took trees on the Indians. Mr. Kennedy got down beside a burnt forked cedar stump, and laying his gun in the fork watched an Indian who had a short gun and was behind a log, trying to get a bead on Mr. Kennedy. Finally he fired, and his ball knocked up so much gravel and with such force into Mr. Kennedy's face that it cut the blood out, and he had the appearance of being badly wounded. He then fired and killed the Indian. They finally retreated, leaving two dead on the ground and another in the chase, and others badly shot. Some of the loose horses were killed and others badly scattered, but most of them were gathered and driven back to the settlement. There were about thirty men in all, but Mr. Kennedy at this late day can only remember the following: Henry Robinson, captain; James Davenport, Emory Givins, John Leakey, John Daugherty (afterwards sheriff of Uvalde County), — Courtney, Lease, Barrow, Isbel, and Tom Wall. When the party arrived at the Isbel ranch, badly worn out and hungry, a bountiful meal was prepared for them, and while eating, the most of them were telling what part they took in the battle and of the Indians that they were certain had fallen by their hand. Mrs. Isbel was greatly interested in all this, and noticing that Mr. Kennedy was eating and saying nothing, turned to him and said, "Mr. Kennedy, didn't you kill any Indians?" "No, madam," he said; "from the number these other men have killed there were not enough to go round, and none left for me to kill."

On one occasion a raiding party of Indians was followed far

to the northwest, Mr. Kennedy in command. They passed around the heads of all the rivers, and finally the leader told the men they were losing ground; that the trail was actually getting old ahead of them. The men had to ride the same horses all of the time and camp at night, while the Indians were changing horses and traveling at night; so the expedition was declared off, and they turned back. They were also out of provisions, and all of the watered country had been passed. One man killed an antelope, and although it was old and tough it was eaten. Among the men were James Davenport, Clabe Davenport, Emory Givens, and others.

In 1861 the Indians made a big raid and went all over the country and far below the mountains. They killed a number of people and secured many horses. The settlers from below followed them under Big Foot Wallace, and Mr. Kennedy got the news, gathered a few men, and met the others between his ranch and D'Hanis, making twenty-five or thirty in all. The trail led up Big Seco, and was followed fast on account of the large drove of horses. The Indians left a spy behind, and he was discovered by Lewis McCombs and others on a mountain in the valley. The Indians had laid an ambush for the white men at the head of the canyon, and they stopped in the valley, rested their horses, and ate dinner in plain view of this ambuscade; but the Indians kept well concealed and watched them from the mountain side in the rocks and bushes. When the men again took up the trail and commenced the ascent of the mountains the advance was fired on and pushed back to the men below. The Indians used shotguns and pistols which had been taken from slain settlers, and all that saved the advance from annihilation was the fact that the Indians overshot them. Wm. Davenport was wounded, also several horses, and all went back to the foot of the mountain and made a stand. Captain Wallace told the men to lie down under a rock ledge and shoot as opportunity offered. The Indians could not see them without coming very close, and finally commenced detaching large rocks from the mountain side and rolling them down among the men. They came crashing through at a fearful rate, and some narrow escapes were made. One struck the breech of Big Foot Wallace's gun and came near breaking it. Mr. Kennedy soon tired of this kind of warfare, and called for volunteers of those who had long-range guns to ascend the hill in their rear so they could see the Indians and open fire on them. John Kennedy, Louis Oge, and John Vinton responded. They all had Enfield or minie rifles, and as soon as they arrived at a point where they could get a good view, opened on the Comanches, who at once commenced retreating further up the mountain, carrying their dead with them. They were not aware the white men could reach them so far, and several fell before they could get out of range. One was made to move at a distance of five or six hundred yards; he was sitting on a mule on top of a mountain watching the battle. As soon as the fight was over the settlers went over into Sabinal Canyon and spent the night, and next day went after the Indians again and got ahead of them on the divide, but by the impatience of one man who fired too soon, or let his gun go off accidentally, the ambush which had been laid by Captain Wallace was discovered and the Indians scattered, but a large number of horses were retaken and carried back. Of the men along Mr. Kennedy can remember, besides the captain, Lewis McCombs, Louis Oge, John Kennedy, John Vinton, Judge Davenport, William Davenport, Fount Tinsley, Chris. Kelley, Malcolm Van Pelt, Frank Hilburn, and a man named Hill.

In 1866 the Indians made a raid into Uvalde County and killed a man named John Sanders, who lived on the east bank of the Frio near the main road. His sons were out near the Nueces River hunting mustangs, and the old man started to their camp with a wagon to carry provisions to them. While en route the Indians came upon him and killed him. He was bald-headed but had a beard eighteen inches in length, and the Indians scalped his face and part of his neck to get it. They then came upon another man named Eastwood, and roped him and dragged him to death.

In 1873 Mr. Kennedy drove a herd of cattle out to Comanche Creek, a few miles above Fort Stockton, and left a Mexican to attend to them, but the cattle drifted towards the Pecos River. Another cattleman named Frank Rooney had stock on the same range, and he also had a Mexican in his employ to look after stock, and when the cattle drifted both Mexicans went in company to the Pecos to look after them, and both were killed by the Indians and thrown into the Pecos River. After some time had expired and the Mexicans failed to return, another party was dispatched to see what had become of them, and their bodies were found lodged against the Pecos pontoon bridge, where they had floated from above. Both of the bodies were in such a state of decomposition one could not be told from the other, except that one had a quirt on his left wrist. Mr. Kennedy said this one was his Mexican, as he was left-handed and always carried his quirt in that way. George Frasier, William Morris, and others went to hunt for the Indians, but could not find them. Morris was in charge of Mr. Kennedy's cattle, and the Mexican was working under him. The Indians took the horses and equipments of the dead Mexicans, even their clothing, and nothing was left on either one of the bodies except the quirt above mentioned.

The wife of Mr. Kennedy was Miss Jane Rankin, who also came from Ireland with some of her people when very small, and landed at New York. She still survives, and has passed through all the dangers and trying scenes of frontier life bravely, and did her part well. One one occasion she cooked breakfast for twenty-two men who came to her house hungry while trailing Indians. Mr. Kennedy says that such things as have been narrated in this sketch were common occurrences for twenty years, being repeated at almost every full moon. He had two sons, George A. and Ross R., and seven girls—Margery K., Jane, Mary E., Rosalie, Clara, Vine V., and Minnie Maud. His sons-in-law are Louis Peters, James Durham, Len Heard, Tom Adams, and C. W. Giffin. Young Ross married Miss Allie Kelso, of Uvalde; Rosalie, now Mrs. Heard, first married Mr. Chas. Barnard, who died in Sabinal; Vine V. married Dave Malone, now deceased, and she and her two children are living with her parents at the old home on Ranchero Creek. Miss Maud, the youngest, is single.

THE FORTY IMMIGRANTS FROM DARMSTADT.

In regard to this immigration scheme we find the following in the San Antonio Express under date of February 27, 1900:

[The following account, taken from the Texas Historical Quarterly, represents the substance of an interview with Mr. Reinhardt, of Arneckeville, De Witt County, who is one of the first settlers in this community. The visionary undertaking here described has become famous among German-Americans in this State on account of the connection with it of Hon. Gustave Schleicher, Dr. Herff, and many other prominent men.—Rudolph Kleberg, Jr.]

This colony owed its origin to the efforts of Prince Solms-Braunfels, Baron von Meusebach, and H. Spies, each successively holding the office of general agent of the Adelsverein.

The Adelsverein, or Union of Princes, was a corporation composed of a number of counts and dukes belonging to the lesser German nobility, and having for its object "the colonization and promoting of German immigration to Texas on a large scale."

The colony was organized in 1846 in Darmstadt. It was named in honor of Bettina v. Armin, a German writer, but was better known as the Darmstaedter Kolonie, while its members were generally called the Vierziger (men of the forties.)

Prince Solms had been in Texas as early as 1814, and his accounts, as well as those of Spies in writing and speeches, caused a sensation among the students of the universities of Giessen and Heidelberg. Solms also made a speech to the students of the industrial school (Gewerbeschule) in Darmstadt, where I was studying, and his extravagant descriptions made the students mad. He remarked that there was no demand in the old country for all the professional men whom the universities were turning out, and that they must find a new and developing country where their services would be in demand. He glowingly described Texas as a land of milk and honey, of perennial flowers, of chrystal streams, rich and fruitful beyond measure, where roamed myriads of deer and buffalo, where the primeval forest abounded in wild fowl of every kind. And what he said was true. It is a glorious land, and I am glad I came here.

PRINCE SOLMS-BRAUNFELS.

It was in this way that Gustave Schleicher, a graduate of the University of Giessen, and already an engineer on the Meinecker road, and Wundt, a student of law, were won for the enterprise. A communistic society was organized, of which friendship, freedom, and equality were the watchwords. It had no regular scheme of government so far as I know. In fact, being communistic, the association would not brook the tyranny of a ruler. But the guiding spirits were by common consent Messrs. Wagner, Herff, Schleicher, and Schenk. Being the youngest of the whole company—I was only 18—I was of course rarely consulted. The general director of the industrial school had purchased my freedom from my father with the understanding that I should botanize in Texas. I was well satisfied as first, and Herff and Schleicher treated me like a son.

In February, 1847, we left for Hamburg and remained there for several weeks until our ship had discharged her cargo. In April we sailed. Our party consisted of about forty men, of whom I remember the following:

Herff, physician.
Schulz, physician.
Schleicher, engineer.
Lerch, architect.
Zoeller, architect.
Freidrich, lawyer.
Wundt, lawyer.
Fuchs, lawyer.
Schleunig, lawyer.
Amelung, lawyer.
Hesse, lawyer.
Wagner, lawyer.
Herrman, forester.
Schenck, forester.
Kuegler, forester.
Voght, forester.
Louis, forester.
Strauss, mechanic.
Flach, mechanic.
Schunk, carpenter.
Neff, carpenter.

Neff, butcher.
Deichert, blacksmith.
Hahn, lieutenant of artillery.
Kappelhoff, ship carpenter.
Michel, brewer.
Ottmer, miller.
Bub, hotel keeper.
Mertins, student of theology.
Backofen, maker of musical instruments.
Lundheimer, naturalist.
Mueller, agriculturist.
Rockan, American who joined in Victoria.

There was no one in our party who could speak English except the cook, who had been in America several times. Dr. Herff had learned the language from books, and could manage to make himself understood.

We had a good voyage, with no incidents of general interest. We landed at Galveston, July 17, 1847. Dr. Herff and Spies, who had sailed ahead of our party, here met us and we were quartered in the William Tell Hotel, kept by a Swiss, and the only inn there at that time. A grand reception awaited us, and being a jolly company, we found no difficulty in showing our appreciation.

As the schooner which was to carry us to Indianola was undergoing repairs, we waited several weeks. When the ship was at last in condition to sail she was pressed into service as a transport by the United States government, the war with Mexico being then in progress. We finally succeeded in getting another ship, but when we were ready to sail the captain was on a "spree." In spite of this, however, we started off, yet before we were far out the ship struck a sandbar and some planks flew out from behind. The captain began to lower the boat on the pretext of going ashore and securing aid, but before he could carry out his purpose Dr. Herff, with drawn pistol, informed him that if it came to drowning the captain would be compelled to stay and perish with us. Here Kappelhoff, who was a ship carpenter, took charge of the vessel, and by keeping close to shore we reached Indianola after five days.

Here twenty-four ox wagons had been waiting for us three weeks, since Meusebach, the general agent of the Adelsverein, had seen to everything. In addition he there bought two wagons with six yokes of oxen each, and two mule teams of eight mules each, for we had an immense amount of baggage. In addition to what we had brought from home and had purchased at Darmstadt we had laid in a big supply at Hamburg and Galveston. We had supplies of every kind imaginable—for instance, complete machinery for a mill, a number of barrels of whisky, and a great many dogs, of which Moro was the largest, being three feet high. We came prepared to conquer the world.

In Indianola $10,000 in American gold was paid to us, as a premium for settling Fisher's grant, by Consul Lee. After a journey of four weeks our train reached New Braunfels in August. Our trip was comparatively uneventful. We camped on the prairie, and sang and drank, and enjoyed ourselves the whole way, as only the German student knows how to do. We lived like the gods on Olympus, and our favorite song on this tour was

"Ein freies Leben fuehren wir,
Ein Leben voller Wonne," etc.

In New Braunfels Schenk and I fell sick with typhoid, while Deichert had the misfortune of being thrown from a horse and breaking his leg. Thus we were unable to move for nearly five weeks, but the whole company waited for us, having no thought of leaving the sick. In New Braunfels on the Verein Shegel (Union Hill) a treaty was made between Meusebach, Spies, and von Koll, representing the colony, and the Comanches, by which the Indians agreed to vacate to our party the tract lying between the Llano and San Saba, and known as Fisher's grant. The Indians were here represented by their chief Santana (also written Santa Anna) and two others, accompanied by Baron v. Kriewitz, Santana's squaws, and his doctor.

Kriewitz had been among the Comanches several months as commercial agent of the colonists at New Braunfels and Fredericksburg, according to the wish of the savages themselves. But the Indians did not trust him, looking upon him as a spy, and it is said that his life was thrice saved by Santana's daughter. Kriewitz at the making of the treaty was dressed like an Indian, but at last one of our party recognized him and gazed intently at him. Hereupon Kriewitz touched him under the table with his foot. Kriewitz was then handed a piece of paper and pencil, and wrote back that he was Kriewitz, but that he could not hold open communication with them now; that on the journey back to the Indian camp he would try to get away. He went back with the savages as far as Comanche Springs, and escaped and lay hid in New Braunfels three days while the Indians came to look for him. They came to our own room, and there I saw Santana for the first time. But as far as the treaty went they kept that to the letter, and later they visited our settlement, as they had stated at the time of the treaty. We were also faithful to the compact.

After the sick had recovered we set out for Fredericksburg, stopping a few days at Comanche Spring, later Meusebach's farm. Kriewitz was our guide, and as he rode ahead of us one could not have told him from an Indian. Having again spent several days in Fredericksburg, we set out for our tract, Kriewitz again being our guide. Of course we had to move slowly, and when we arrived at the Llano we hunted a ford for three days. The best one finally proved to be but a few yards from our camp, where we had to lift the wagons four feet on a rock in the bottom of the river by the aid of windlasses, and this work took us from morning until night.

The Llano then was a beautiful stream, clear as crystal, and known in our party as the "silver Llano." One could see the bottom at the deepest places. The whole country was covered with mesquite grass as high as the knee, and abounded in buffalo and deer.

On the other side we came to a big liveoak, and here camped. Putting our wagons in a circle, we constructed a big tent in the center, planted our cannon, and put out a guard. Feeling perfectly secure in our fortified camp, we celebrated that night until 3 o'clock. A bowl of punch was prepared and we sang our favorite songs, while those who could performed on musical instruments, of which we had a whole chest. We gave "Lebe Hoch, United States! Lebe Hoch, Texas!" for we were all good patriots. This was in the early part of September, 1847.

We built a large structure of forks and cross beams, which we covered with reed grass. It was forty feet long and twenty-two feet high. Afterwards we constructed an adobe house, covered with shingles. A large pecan tree supplied us with 10,000 of these. In this house was a fireplace twelve feet broad and built of rock. On the roof Strauss put an artistic weather vane. Here we celebrated the Christmas of 1847, and again had a glorious time.

As I have said, the Indians kept their agreement to the letter. In November, 1847, they visited us, as they had promised. At the time I was herding cows, several miles from our camp, when two Indians rode up. From their signs I supposed they wanted something to eat, and I handed them some bread out of the pouch I carried. Evidently not trusting me, they made signs that I should eat first. The fact was that a great number of Waco Indians had been treacherously poisoned by a band of cowboys. It was a dastardly deed, and the Waco's thereafter became the most hostile of the tribes, as before they had been the most amicable. Well, the end of my interview was, they took everything I had and galloped off. They were hardly out of sight when I saw a big crowd of savages riding up, and as they drew nearer I recognized the chief Santana. Upon my asking him if he were not the chief, he seemed greatly surprised that I should know him.

The Indians camped only a short distance from us. During the night a number of our utensils were stolen by the squaws, but the next day the men returned them. For everything we gave them we were paid back threefold. As they stayed some time, we became well acquainted. Whenever we came into their camp they would spread out their deer skins, bring out morrals full of the biggest pecans I ever saw, and tell us to help ourselves. They even tried to learn German from us, in spite of the difficulty they found in pronouncing some of the words.

Several Mormons arrived in the early spring to settle, but did not carry out their intention. Shortly afterward Bickel, who had made himself notorious in Fredericksburg, came with some of his followers and began a settlement, known as the Bickeliner. The leader, however, soon disappeared. He had two wives, who constantly quarreled. Next came the Castellaners, who founded the settlement of Castell, which still exists. Their families came in March, 1848.

In the summer of 1848 our colony of "Bettina" went to

pieces like a bubble. As I have said, it was a communistic society, and accordingly had no real government. Since everybody was to work if he pleased, the result was that less and less work was done as time progressed. Most of the professional men wanted to do the directing and ordering, while the mechanics and laborers were to carry out their plans. Of course the latter failed to see the justice of this ruling, and so no one did anything. We had made a field and raised 200 bushels of corn—our whole year's crop. According to our contract with the Adelsverein, this company was to furnish us with supplies for the first year, but the next we were to shift for ourselves. As it was, we still had a plentiful supply of everything, yet that was bound to end some time, and there was absolutely no prospect of our ever providing for ourselves. I began to see this plainly. Having made arrangements with some teamsters who had brought us some goods, I started for Fredericksburg. Before I got there eight others were on their way thither, and thus our colony went to the four winds. Bub was killed on the road by Indians.

I went to Mayersville, De Witt County, Texas, and in that neighborhood I have lived ever since. When after forty-eight years I met Dr. Herff in San Antonio, we found, as far as both of us could determine, ten of our company were still living.

THE OLD CHURCH AT FREDERICKSBURG.

This old church, a true cut of which is shown, was built in 1847, and was nonsectarian. Any and all people of whatsoever faith in religious belief were welcome to worship there, and the laying of the cornerstone was observed as a great gala day by all the people who had commenced this settlement at Fredericksburg, far out on the Texas frontier, and one of the curious and unique features of the occasion was the presence of a large band of Comanche Indians, who helped to celebrate the occasion. A treaty had been made with them by Baron von Meusebach a short time before, and he was called the savior of Fredericksburg, for no doubt but for this timely treaty the place would have been destroyed and the people slain and driven away. When the town built up and the streets were laid out in order it was found that the old church was in the middle of

OLD CHURCH AT FREDERICKSBURG.

the main street, and four years ago, in 1896, it was decided to remove it. A photo was taken of it, and with another jubilee it was removed, but this time without the presence of the Comanches. Where were they? The bones of the most of them lie scattered along the Texas border, where they met death at the hands of soldiers, citizens, and Texas rangers, for they soon broke their treaty.

J. D. FENLEY.

Came to Texas in 1853.

Mr. Joel D. Fenley was one of the early settlers of Sabinal Canyon, and deserves a place in history among the pioneers of southwest Texas. While not having the opportunity of participating in the bloody battles with savages as others had done, it was no fault of his. He was ever ready to mount his horse and go in pursuit of raiding bands of Indians, or go and help to bring in and bury his unfortunate neighbors who met death at their hands. It was his misfortune or good fortune to always fail to get into a close fight with the numerous bands whom he trailed many long and tedious miles over the mountains and through tangled brakes and gorges.

Mr. Fenley was born in Fairfield district, South Carolina, in 1828, and came to Texas and to this region in 1853. His ancestors served as scouts in the Revolutionary war. When Mr. Fenley came to this valley but few settlers had preceded him. Of these was Capt. William Ware, whose daughter he married in 1854, and Gideon Thompson. Indians were numerous and very hostile, and he soon learned to watch and trail and guard against their frequent inroads. One Sunday morning in 1858, as Mr. Fenley was mounting his horse to go to church, a rapid rider came from up the West, or Anglin, prong of the river, bringing the news of an Indian raid in their settlement ten miles above. Mr. Fenley called to his wife, telling her to fix up the cold victuals on hand, while he got his gun and ammunition, mounted again, and set out rapidly with the messenger to the scene of the raid. Other settlers rallied to the call, and when they arrived at the upper settlement and all came together there were present Robert H. Kinchaloe, Jack Kelley, Chris Kelley, James Davenport, Gid Thompson, Green Snow, and likely a few others. The Indians had passed the ranch of Aaron Anglin and gone across the mountains towards the Frio. This was an old route of the Indians going and coming from one canyon to the other. This old trail is still to be seen, and is called by the mountaineers "the old Indian trail."

After the settlers had gotten through the pass and come to the valley of the Frio, near the river, they discovered a crowd of dismounted men in an open prairie near the river. From this distanse, nearly half a mile, they were unable to determine if they were Indians or white men, but as they were directly on the trail which the party was following, it was decided they were Indians and they charged them. Great confusion was noticed among the other crowd, and they commenced to mount their horses. As fast as a man would vault into the saddle he would run towards the river, until all were strung out in that direction west except two, and they ran back through the prairie at a most terrific speed up the river north. The Sabinal men were coming in a charge from the east. One red-headed fellow attempted to mount, but his girth broke and his saddle fell off. Leaving his horse, he followed the crowd on foot, and arrived there almost as soon as they did. His red hair looked like a flying meteor as he sailed through the open flat close on the heels of the horses. These Frio men, however, were not so badly frightened as to run clear away. They were going to cover to fight a battle, and dismounted in the timber along the river. When the Sabinal men came over the slope of the river bank into view, from every cypress tree along the margin of the stream protruded a human head and long rifle. Of course this close inspection revealed the identity of each party, and the Frio men with much laughter came from cover and all got together. The two men who had run off up the river had stopped on a hill to take observations, and seeing the mixing of the two bands came back also. In the wild charge of the men from the Sabinal they failed to notice the cause of the dismounted men in the prairie. Out where the Frio men ran from stood a wagon, and beside it lay a dead man. They had seen the wagon, it is true, but passed below it, not knowing the situation. The slain man was named Thompson, and he had been killed a few hours before by the Indians whom Mr. Fenley and his party were trailing. Mr. Thompson was on his way to the lower settlement and had a yoke of oxen to his wagon, and was crossing the open ground as the Indians came into it from towards Sabinal Canyon. From the sign of the circling horse tracks they had surrounded him, and he had no chance for his life. As is usual with the victims of the fierce Comanches, he was horribly mutilated and his yoke of oxen gone. A man named Kit Stanford was to have gone with him, but was delayed in starting and came on afterwards on horseback and discovered the dead body soon after the killing. Mr. Stanford then galloped back and gave the alarm. The upper Frio men assembled, and had just arrived upon the scene and dismounted when charged by the Sabinal trailers. This occurred just about where the Patterson irrigating ditch now leaves the river, and about one mile and a half from the present Rio Frio postoffice, and five miles below Leakey, the former county seat of Edwards County before it was moved to Rock Springs, at the head of the Nueces River. Some of the men now carried the body of Mr. Thompson back to his bereaved family, and the others went on in pursuit of the Indians. From here the trail led northwest across brushy and rock mountains until near the head of the West prong of the Nueces, when the hostile camp was located in a cedarbrake. They had stopped, killed Thompson's oxen, and were cooking the meat. The white men would have surprised the Indians had it not been that at the time they were advancing cautiously upon the camp they met the Indian's horses being driven out to graze, and those in charge gave the alarm by loud yelling when they saw the white men, and the others scattered into the brush. Only one squaw and a captive white boy were seen when the camp was charged, and they both ran and were soon hid in the thick brakes. The boy could have been easily killed, as he was very close to them, and some said they believed he was an Indian, but when he looked towards them his face was too white for a redskin. This boy had been seen several times by white men in Indian battles, but he always ran and they could never get hold of him. He was finally killed—mistaken for an Indian—an account of which is in the sketch of Richard Ware. Who he was no one knew. On his present occasion thirty-two head of horses were captured, all of which belonged to settlers, and they were returned to their owners.

When Berry Buckaloo was killed on Seco, Mr. Fenley went with others and helped bring in the body. They washed it in the Sabinal River where the wagon road now crosses going to the station. Many arrow spikes were in the body, which were all carefully extracted before burying it.

When Mrs. Kinchaloe, his sister-in-law, was so badly wounded, he helped to bring her away, and she stayed at his house part of the time while recovering from the fearful wounds inflicted by the Indian lances.

On another occasion Mr. Fenley and others followed the Indians from Sabinal Canyon to the Nueces and located their camp, but they discovered the white men and left. They had killed a mare and were eating her. Demp. Fenley, in scouting around, discovered thirty wigwams which they had left, and had the scouts known it they were in a trap and in great danger of being all killed between bluffs in a gorge, but it seemed the Indians did not take advantage of it. They were winding about in these hills for some time and the Indians were watching them. Another scout came back afterwards and found painted on a rock at this place the pictures of the nine men who were looking for them. On another rock was painted two hands turned back to back, indicating to other Indians who were expected to come there that nine white men had been there, and that they had gone one way and the Indians another. On another occasion Mr. Fenley followed the Indians west to Nueces Canyon and was joined there by the noted Indian fighter Edward Westfall, who was then the only settler in Nueces Canyon. They abandoned the trail too soon, as was afterwards learned. Had they gone over one more mountain they would have found them. Westfall said that on this occasion the Indians had 600 head of horses.

Mr. Fenley kept his horses in a strong pen built of split logs, with the gate close to the gallery of the house, but almost worn out with constant watching, and getting careless, one night the Indians got them. His brother-in-law, Mr. R. H. Kinchaloe, came to his house that day riding a very good horse which he had just paid $80 for. He liked the animal very much, and was bragging on him. He spent the night with Mr. Fenley, and this horse was taken also.

Mrs. E. A. Fenley, wife of Mr. Joel Fenley, was born in Montgomery County, Texas, in 1841, and came to Sabinal Canyon in 1852 with her father, Capt. William Ware, one of the famous twenty-two captains who led their men to victory on the plains of San Jacinto. Mrs. Fenley was one of the first white children that ever saw this beautiful valley, and of course has been familiar with all of the attending horrors of a border life.

On one occasion, after she was married and living down on Onion Creek, her brother Richard Ware, who lived there also, was digging a ditch, and one day was surrounded by a band of Indians. Drawing his pistol, he commenced firing and backing towards the house. He succeeded in hitting two of them and keeping them off. Mrs. Fenley heard the firing and yelling of the Indians, and running into the house told Mr. Fenley the Indians was after her brother, and to go and help him. Mr. Fenley seized his shotgun and pistol and started to him, but Mr. John Ware told him to come back and get on his horse. He did so, but thinks this delay kept him from killing an Indian, for if he had kept on at the time he would have met four of them face to face in a trail. As it was, while he was getting his horse the Indians were getting other horses near by, and Mrs. Fenley was standing looking at them. The wife of Richard Ware, when she heard the firing of his pistol, got his gun and started to him with it. John Ware also went. Mr. Fenley tried to stop Mrs. Ware from going, but she went and got to her husband with the gun, but he had already whipped the Indians.

It was here Mrs. Fenley lived when her sister, Mrs. Kinchaloe, had her noted battle with the Indians and Mrs. Bowlin was killed. That morning one of the children was sick with sore throat or diphtheria, and Mr. Fenley was going after Mrs. Binnion, who was the only doctor in the country. When passing the house of John Ware, where Rev. John L. Harper was preaching, Mr. Ben Biggs galloped up and told the news of the killing of Mrs. Bowlin and the wounding of Mrs. Kinchaloe. He galloped back, hitched up his wagon, and came with all haste, the distance being ten miles. When Mrs. Kinchaloe saw her sister, Mrs. Fenley, she said: "I wanted to die before you all came, but now since I have seen you again I want to live."

Mrs. Fenley still lives in the canyon, honored and respected by all who know her as a model Christian lady. Mr. Fenley died in 1899.

DEATH OF CAPT. PHILIP DIMMITT.

1841.

When the American pioneers began to settle in southwest Texas they not only had the Indian tribes to contend with, but also freebooting bands of Mexicans who often crossed the Rio Grande and killed and carried off the property of the Texans and sometimes the settlers themselves, and confined them in loathsome dungeons in Mexico, where sometimes they spent years before being liberated.

In the year 1841 Capt. Philip Dimmitt, long distinguished as a pioneer and gallant defender of Texas, became their victim. He was engaged with some workmen on the 4th of July in erecting a mercantile establishment on Corpus Christi bay, about fifteen miles below the present town of Corpus Christi (then known as the rancho of Aubry and Kinney), when the place was visited by Captain Sanchez, aid-de-camp to General Ampudia, with a party of fifteen cavalry, who took Captain Dimmitt and his men prisoners, and after plundering the establishment conducted them to Matamoros. From this point they were taken, with others, to Monterey and delivered over to General Arista. By his order they were ironed and started to the interior under a guard commanded by Captain Chaffind. That officer was a humane man, and had the irons taken off after the first day's march. On the third day they arrived at Saltillo. Here their anticipations of a long imprisonment and horrid treatment were such that they resolved to attempt their escape. They proposed to procure a quantity of mescal (a Mexican liquor), well drugged with morphine, and give it to the guards, and while they were affected by it to make their escape. Two physicians who were among the prisoners were charged with this part of the programme. After being supplied with this mixture, they arrived at the place where they were quartered for the night. In the night, after the guard had been well supplied with the liquor from water gourds, the signal was given to make the attempt to escape. By some means, however, the morphine proved inefficient, and the mescal alone had only served to keep the guards more wideawake and to stimulate their courage. There were nineteen of the Texans, and a few of them had guns that they had succeeded in picking up as occasion offered, and they succeeded in getting out of their quarters, although the guards were more than a hundred. They succeeded in getting off some distance before daylight came, and a messenger came to them from Captain Chaffind, stating that if they returned they would be forgiven; if not, he would have Captain Dimmitt shot, who had been confined separate from his men, and therefore not able to escape with them. The captain heard of this threat, and knowing Mexican treachery generally, and that it would be carried into execution and likely all of the others shot if they returned, determined to end it all and relieve his men by taking his own life. He had morphine about his person, and at once took a large dose of it. He then wrote a letter to his wife in San Antonio, made disposition of his property, and lay down on his blanket to die. A few prisoners were in confinement with him, and these he requested to convey his letter and manner of death, if they ever returned, and tell the Texans to throw the mantle of charity over his act. "I do not fear death," he said, "but dread the idea of ending my life in a loathsome dungeon. Tell them I prefer a Roman's death to the ignominy of perpetual imprisonment, and that my last wish is for my country's welfare." Soon after he sank into a sleep from which he never awoke.

Thus died Capt. Philip Dimmitt, a noble spirit, who virtually died for his men, and by whose hands the first Lone Star banner of Texas was unfurled to the breeze on the height of La Bahia (Goliad). The other prisoners, when they learned of their captain's death, continued their flight and reached Texas.

One of these murdering bands of robbers was met by Capt. Jack Hays and about twenty-five of his rangers. A battle ensued, in which the Mexicans were defeated with loss and driven to the Rio Grande. None of the rangers were hit, as the robbers fired as they ran. This took place ten miles below Laredo, and the Mexicans were commanded by Capt. Ignacio Garcia. Six of the party were killed and twenty-five captured.

Captain Dimmitt owned property in San Antonio and also

in Seguin. He had four sons—Texas, Alamo, Napoleon, and James. One daughter was named Josephine, who married Mr. William Medlin of Seguin. He died there some years ago and left his widow and two sons, William and Philip. William died, but Philip and his mother still reside there.

TRAILING INDIANS.

Mr. G. P. Hodges, an old settler of Uvalde County, and who was raised in the west, furnishes the facts for this detailed account of Indian trailing by the settlers. He says that in those days, especially during light moons, if a gun was fired at night the near neighbors were up and listening. The presence of Indians was made known by firing guns, blowing horns, or yelling. Runners on swift horses would go day and night to alarm the isolated settlers of a raid, and men would gather to fight them. In 1871 the Indians made a raid, coming east from the Nueces and Frio country towards the Hondo. When they got to the Frio Canyon they stole horses from Mr. J. F. Patterson, and the recollection of Mr. Hodges is that they killed a boy there who was working for Mr. Patterson, taking care of his cow ponies. Coming on east, the Indians struck the Hondo at the ranch of widow Dean, and about dusk shot at Joe Dean, who was standing by the yard gate talking to his brother-in-law, Jesse Campbell. The latter, seeing the Indian near by, drew a pistol and fired at him as he began to retreat, and wounded him. He jumped high and dropped his bow. Other Indians were now seen, and several shots were fired at them by Dean and Campbell. That night they sent runners up and down the Hondo to alarm the settlers. At that time Mr. Hodges was very young and lived on the Hondo with his uncle, Judge Harper. He joined the men, nine in all, that went from their settlement.

The party had agreed to meet at Joel Fenley's place, who lived where Hondo City now is. They were to collect and get there as soon as possible next morning, so as to strike the trail early. They arrived without breakfast, which Mr. Fenley furnished them, and also provisions to take on the trip. The men in this party were Isaac H. King, Jesse Campbell, Joe Dean, William Johnson, Hardy Cocke, Phil. Hodges, one Mexican, and two negroes. When they made the start from Mr. Fenley's, Isaac King was elected captain. The objective point now was Mrs. Dean's ranch, so as to be certain to get on the trail. It was taken up here and was very tedious to follow, as the Indians had scattered in gathering up stock. About seven miles from the Dean place a halt had been made by the Indians to dress the wound of the one shot by Campbell. This had been done in the night, soon after the Indian was wounded, and blood was seen here on the ground, where they had worked with him.

The men kept on, and arriving at the Verde Creek found there had been a terrible scattering among the Indians, and evidently they had trouble there. It was afterwards ascertained that Sevier Vance and Joe Decker had fought them there early in the morning. King's party got the trail together again and kept on, and about noon turned in towards the Hondo river and came to it at Barnes bluff. This place takes its name from an old miser who used to live there in a cave and kept his money in a hollow tree in the river channel. During an overflow the tree washed away, but after the water subsided Barnes found his tree lodged in a drift, and got his money again.

During this halt at the bluff Vance come up with a party on the trail and all went together. Late in the evening, while on rising ground, Elam's and Wilson's ranch on Ward's Creek could be seen, and that many men and horses were there and badly scattered. At first it was supposed to be Wilson's outfit, until the distant men began to collect at sight of the settlers and make off.

At this time the trailers were scattered for half a mile. Joe Dean, Bill Johnson, and Phil. Hodges were ahead, and the first to see them. They intended to wait until their captain and other men came up, but seeing the Indians commence to run, put spurs to their horses and followed them, at the same time waving their hats for those in the rear to come on. They ran about five miles, and by this time most of the horses ridden by the white men had given out. Finally, when the Indians went to the top of a mountain, but few were in front, but they at once commenced the ascent and crowded the Indians so close they turned back on them and a lively fusilade commenced. There were but six men in this fight on the side of the mountain, and about thirty-five Indians. There was a continual pattering of bullets around them, but they held the ground until reinforcements came up and fourteen men then charged to the top of the mountain. It was expected when they arrived at the summit that a hard fight would take place, as the Indians had the advantage of position and numbers, but when they saw the whites reinforced and coming to them, they retreated to the other side of the mountain and continued their flight. The settlers now returned to Wilson's ranch to see what discoveries they could make there. They knew that young Tom Wilson and a Mexican were on the ranch, and expected to find them killed. They could not be found about the place, and were supposed to be dead somewhere. It was afterwards learned that they saw the Indians coming in time to make their escape. Tom Wilson's horse was hitched near by, saddled, and he sprang on him, gun in hand, and waved it at them to let them know he was armed, and galloped away towards a thicket, where he dismounted and tied his horse, then pushed back in the brush and lay down and watched, but they did not follow him. The Mexican also ran away on foot and hid himself in a thicket. They heard the men fighting the Indians on the mountain, but supposed it was the latter killing cattle. Wilson lay in the thicket until night, and then came out and silently went away, leaving his horse, as he would make too much noise on the rocks. It was twenty-five miles to Judge Harper's ranch, and to that place the young settler walked in the darkness and reported the Mexican killed, as he thought it was impossible for him to escape, the Indians were so near when discovered.

The Mexican walked to old D'Hanis and reported there that Wilson was killed. They both kept so close in the brush they were not aware that the settlers were at the ranch, although only a few hundred yards away. The Mexican went out at the back door as the Indians were coming up in front and making a play at Wilson, and escaped unobserved. A party returned to the ranch a few days after and found Wilson's horse still tied where he left him. These were an unusually cruel set of Indians to stock. They killed eighteen head of cattle and only cut out the loin steak of each, and every horse they had to leave they killed. If a horse gave out they would throw a lance into him and leave him thus to die. Quite a lot of things were captured, such as lariats and leggings, and also the saddle and clothing of the boy they killed on the Frio.

JUDGE HENRY MANEY.

Came to Texas in 1851.

Judge Henry Maney, who at this writing lives at Pearsall, Frio County, is an old-time Texan, and has passed through many stirring scenes. He was born in 1829, in Rutherford County, Tennessee, seven miles from Murfreesboro. He was a son of Maj. Henry Maney, and came to Texas and to Seguin, Guadalupe County, in 1851, arriving there on the 16th day of April, and was living there when the Indians made their last raid east of San Antonio, which terminated on the Cibolo, without penetrating far into Guadalupe County. In 1852 Judge Maney married Miss Mary Malinda Erskine, daughter of Maj. Michael Erskine, one of the most prominent families of Guadalupe County. He went back to Tennessee in 1853, and returned in the following spring. At this time Major Erskine was on the eve of starting overland to California with a drove of beeves, and requested his son-in-law to make the trip with him. This was agreed to, and the start was made.

The country west of San Antonio at that time was all frontier and infested by hostile Indians, and it required a strong escort to pass safely through. The escort obtained consisted of thirty-five men, and was commanded by Capt. James H. Calahan, who was employed by Major Erskine for a consideration of $1500 for the trip.

Only twelve men of this guard were under pay, the balance working their way to California.

The expedition started from San Antonio on the 25th day of April, 1854. The cattle consisted of something more than 1000 head of beeves, half of which were purchased from Tom O'Conner on the coast, and had never been inside of a pen except to be branded.

Nothing of interest occurred until reaching the Hondo River, forty miles west of San Antonio. Here, while in camp, a terrible storm came up at 1 o'clock in the morning, with a great deal of rain. The keen claps of thunder startled the cattle, and they broke away in a violent stampede, and when daylight came not a hoof could be seen except one, and he had a broken shoulder, and that was all that kept him there. He was killed for beef. A week was spent here collecting the scattered cattle, and all but 40 head were recovered. These made their way back to Guadalupe county.

During the trip a halt was made every Sunday to rest. The cattle stampeded many times and gave a great deal of trouble until the open prairie country was reached, and nothing of interest transpired until they arrived at the head of Limpia Creek and made camp in the canyon, on the spot where Fort Davis was afterwards built.

A halt was made here two nights and one day. On the second night the Indians found the herder asleep and cut off three head of work oxen and made an attempt on the main herd, but failed. They carried away the three oxen. The next morning their trail was taken up and pursuit commenced. The trailer was a young Mexican, twenty years old, who led Captain Calahan and eleven men. The trail led to a deep chasm in the mountains, ten miles from camp, and here the Indians had slaughtered the oxen, and were having a feast when Calahan and his men came upon them. A charge was at once made and the battle commenced. The Indians were in large force and met the onset with a countercharge, and fired many shots with firearms and with arrows. Calahan was an old Indian fighter, and one of the survivors of Fannin's massacre. Seeing, however, that he was not able to stand against the Indians with a small force, he ordered a retreat, but carried the horses of the Indians with him for some distance in a desperate attempt to get clear of the canyon with them. Seeing the Indians were about to cut them off by making a detour through the hills, he dropped all but two mules and ten horses, which he succeeded in getting into camp. One of the party, named Mann, had his clothing pierced with an arrow, which was the only casualty among the white men, and as they could not hold the ground, they were unable to tell what damage they inflicted on the other side. These Indians were Muscalara Apaches.

From this place to the Rio Grande, a distance of ninety miles, there was no water for the cattle, but they had water enough along with them for the horses and men to make out on, so that they would not suffer to any great extent.

After leaving the tableland at the head of Limpia Creek it took four days and nights, lacking four hours, to reach a canyon six miles from the Rio Grande. This was a good place to hold the cattle, as they had begun to smell the water and were hard to control. Four head became violently insane and escaped to the mountains. The beeves were now cut off into detachments of sixty head and driven to the water, and one was lost on arriving there. He swam the river and went into Mexico.

By 8 o'clock in the morning all the cattle, mules, and horses were watered. There were 100 head of the latter. All came quietly out and lay down after quenching their thirst, and were very tame on account of being so full of water. Skittish beeves heretofore would allow themselves to be touched; in fact, were not able to run away.

From there the cattle were carried up the river to Fort Thorn. Major Richardson, in command there, cautioned Mr. Erskine about the Apache Indians, who could not be relied on, although a treaty had been made with them, and advised him to keep them out of camp. They went on from here and crossed the Mimbres River and came to a point about fifteen miles east of the village of Santa Cruz, and there went into camp. Here they found a letter torn up and scattered in the grass. The fragments were collected and put together so it could be read, and it proved to be a letter from Dunlap warning them to be on their guard against Indians, stating that the day before, while their party were at dinner at this place, the Indians came down upon them and cut off 120 head of cattle from their herd, besides forty head of mules and horses, and killed his brother-in-law and partner, Houston, while he was attempting to recover them. Erskine's party now looked around and discovered the grave of Houston. Dunlap and Houston had started through with a herd some time before, and knew that Erskine was behind them.

Major Erskine and his party now went on to Santa Cruz village and found Dunlap in camp on the river of the same name, below town, in company with John James of San Antonio, who was also with beeves for the California market. They remained several days here to recruit stock. The other outfits also remained. There was another dry stretch ahead of forty-five miles from the town of Tucson to the Gila River. While waiting here Captain Calahan went among all the herds and called for volunteers to follow the trail of the Indians who got off with the stock of Dunlap and Houston. Eighteen men responded, of whom were J. Box Roberts, Ig. Johnson, John Lewis, J. H. French, and Henry Maney, all from Guadalupe County. From other places was a sergeant of the regular army whose time of enlistment had expired, and who had joined the cowmen to make a trip to California. Also from Guadalupe County was J. Mann and a Mexican called "Teck." In addition to these men who were willing to go was a lieutenant from the Mexican garrison with twenty-five men, who acted as guides.

As the sun was going down the party set out up the Santa Cruz River, traveling that way three hours, and then turned to the right at an angle of 45 degrees and moved steadily on. After the turn of the night, about 1 o'clock, an alarm of Indians was raised in front and a charge was ordered. The enemy fled across the plain, and after half an hour's chase it was discovered that the supposed Apaches were a bunch of mustangs.

Calahan now ordered the men to dismount and rest, but just as they were about to stretch their weary limbs on the grass the sharp crack of a rifle was heard in the rear, and the cry of "Indians! Indians!" was again raised. Every man was again soon mounted and on the alert for a fight, and a cautious reconnoissance was made around the spot from which the sound of the rifle seemed to have come. Instead of Indians in the grass, however, greatly to their surprise they found old Teck down on the ground beside his horse, drunk, where he had fallen during the charge on the mustangs. He became intoxicated during the long night ride on mescal, which he got from one of the Mexican soldiers. Old Teck, not being able to mount after he fell off, and fearing to be left, fired his gun to bring his crowd back. Calahan was a man of high temper, and roundly cursed the old Mexican, and told him if he did not return to camp he would kill him. Teck went back as soon as he was able to ride. A three hours rest, and then again in the saddle, following the lead of the Mexican soldiers. They knew the country so well and the general route of the Indians when going out, that they saved time by this night ride, even if they could see no trail. They knew it would be found in some of the valleys when daylight came, or likely discover the Indians from the summit of some lofty mountain. When daylight came they found themselves in a postoak-timbered valley, with a ridge on the right and high mountains on the left. At 11 o'clock that day one of the men killed a cub bear, but large enough for all to have meat for dinner.

After leaving the noon camp a short distance, the spies returned and reported Indians beyond the ridge to the right in the San Pedro River valley, which the men were now rapidly approaching. As it drew nearer the river the ridge began to decline into a valley. The Indians were coming into the San Pedro valley, and toward the end of the ridge which terminated in the valley. The spies discovered the Indians when several miles away, and Callahan's men slowed up so as to give them time to approach the end of the ridge, for there was where the captain wished to fight them. The Indians had not as yet discovered the Texans and Mexicans. Spies were still kept ahead, and in about half an hour returned again and reported the Indians going into camp on the San Pedro, and near the end of the long ridge which was between the Indians and the pursuers, and distant from the command not more than 150 yards. The order was now given by Callahan to dismount, tighten girths, fix guns, etc. Command to mount was then given. Calahan moved to one side, but in front, pulled off his hat, put spurs to his horse, and said "Charge!" During this time the Indians were not aware of the near proximity of an enemy. The men of Calahan were hid behind the end of the aforesaid ridge in the timber. They went into the Indians at full speed around the point, and took them completely by surprise, but a hand-to-hand fight at once commenced. About ten of the Indians had not dismounted, and these at once fled from the fight and crossed the San Pedro. They were not again seen except in the distance, after the battle was over. The Indians who had dismounted and partly unpacked their horses had no chance to remount, and the only thing for them to do was to fight or die. Those who were left to fight the battle alone were about twenty, and they yelled defiantly and sent flights of arrows. Only one Indian had a gun and with this he shot a Mexican soldier dead from his horse, firing over his shoulder as he turned to run. The ball struck the soldier between the eyes. The lieutenant who was in command of the Mexicans was a slender, delicate man of the Castilian type, and fought only with a saber, with which he killed one Indian, and cut and hacked others badly. The man French, who was mounted on a mule in the charge, came in contact with an Indian, and his animal stopping suddenly, the girth broke, and French was precipitated violently over his head to the ground, breaking his shotgun off at the breech above the guard, leaving the lock and triggers intact. Near him an Indian was attempting to mount a horse on the opposite side from French, who raised his broken gun and fired over the horse, killing the Indian. There was just enough of the rear of his gun left to draw back the hammer and pull the trigger. About the time that French fell the men all dismounted and turned their horses loose, as the Indians commenced retreating towards the bank of the river. They rolled on the ground like hoops, discharging an arrow each time as they went over. They went over the bank onto the second ledge, and went on rolling through the high grass and still shooting arrows. The men advanced on foot to the bank of the river, which was not more than a creek in size, and fired at the Indians when they could see them. During this time the sergeant who had joined the expedition at Fort Thorn received an arrow in the left shoulder, and several others were hit about their clothing. One horse belonging to Major Erskine was wounded by an arrow. The sergeant was standing close to Henry Maney when the arrow struck him, and he said "Oh!" quick and loud. Maney looked and saw the arrow sticking above the collarbone. It had gone through a heavy overcoat and cape and remained transfixed in the body, where it remained until the fight was over, he not being able to withdraw it. Near the bank of the creek on the opposite side and in front of the men, grew thick bushes, in which some of the Indians hid themselves and in the crevices of the bank. One Indian climbed to the top of the bank and was shot in the head by a man named Walters, and fell with his brains running out. Henry Maney was the first man to cross the creek where the Indians did, and saw two on one horse making off. He gave chase after them, as he had again mounted his horse for the purpose of crossing. He ran about 200 yards and came close enough to shoot and was about to do so when called by a Mexican who belonged to the command named Pedro, who said "Stop! Stop! My Indian, my Indian!" He was accompanied by two Mexican soldiers with lances. Maney stopped and gave place to them. In the chase which now ensued one Indian was shot by Pedro and fell from the horse, and the other was wounded and soon overtaken. One of the Mexicans on a roan horse threw a lariat over him which settled around his arms, and wheeling his horse quick, jerked him to the ground and set off at almost full speed, the wretched Apache bounding along on the ground. The other Mexican soldier followed with a lance and threw it into him every time he hit the ground, until he was dead, and then dismounted and scalped him. Mr. Maney could plainly hear the rasping sound of the lance each time it entered his body.

Judge Maney could now hear no more firing, and went back to the other men. Captain Calahan said he believed some of the Indians were hid in the bushes, and called for volunteers to beat up the brush and kill them. Several went, among whom was Ig. Johnson of Seguin, who was killed at the battle of Manassas during the Civil war. French and Lewis also went, Calahan leading. The latter finally crossed the creek himself and left the boys to hunt in the brush. Going down the river, he looked into a crevice where water had been during an overflow, and found two Indians in there. One charged him with a lance and was shot and killed. Then the other came out. Calahan attempted to shoot him with a pistol, but it failed to fire, and the Indian came at him with a lance, when the captain had to call for help. Maney was in forty steps of him and raised his gun to fire. He was in the act of touching the trigger, and could barely hold his fire, when the wounded sergeant raised up in front of the muzzle of the gun, and he had to desist. The sergeant was lying down in the grass, and not knowing that Maney was about to shoot, raised up to look at Calahan when he called for help. The captain snapped twice with his pistol, knocked the lance aside with it as it was about to enter his bowels, and then jumped into the river. Maney, who had dismounted, again sprang on his horse and dashed to the opposite side of the stream. While this was taking place, the other men were killing Indians whom they had found in the brush. Maney thought the Indian was going out at the gap or horseway up the bluff and watched for him there, but instead he walked slowly toward the ford and seemed perfectly devoid of fear from the bullets that clipped around him, fired from across the river, and one from Maney's gun, who was in thirty steps of him. The brave finally sank down and died. This ended the fight, Henry Maney firing the last shot. The dead

Indians were all scalped, mostly by the Mexicans, who did it for the reward offered for them by the Mexican government. Twenty-one dead Indians were counted on the ground. In the beginning of the fight a Mexican boy 15 years old, who had been captured four years before, fell down and cried out with a loud voice in Spanish, "I am a Mexican! I am a Mexican!" and continued to do so as long as the guns were popping around him. Sixty-five head of cattle, ten horses, and two mules were gathered up by order of the captain, who also ordered an immediate return to camp, as they were in the heart of the Apache country. It was now 3 o'clock in the evening. They arrived at Santa Cruz next morning at 9 o'clock, forty-five miles, bearing the dead body of the Mexican soldier tied across the horse. His family was there, and they, with many others, gathered around and set up a wailing cry by the women and groans by the men. The parents of the captive boy lived at Tucson, and he was carried there by the Mexicans. The balance of the trip from there on was uneventful, and the return to Seguin was made by Maney and Calahan by way of New Orleans from San Francisco.

Judge Maney was by profession a lawyer, and practiced in Tennessee before coming to Texas. When the Civil war broke out he served the Confederacy in the company of Wm. P. Hardeman, Riley's regiment, Sibley's brigade, in the Arizona expedition, and took part in the battle of Val Verde, where he received a severe wound in the left leg. There were six in his mess, and three of them were wounded. He stood and witnessed the charge of the lancers commanded by Captain Scarbrough. Lieutenant Long led the charge with forty men, and Judge Maney could plainly see the Federal troops when they raised their guns and fired at them. Twenty saddles were emptied by the discharge and ten of the lancers died on the field. The charge was a failure and the survivors came back in disorder.

Col. Tom Ochiltree was in this battle, and before this came off the boys thought he was a coward. They thought the "Red-headed Ranger," as they called him, had no pluck, but after they saw his red head flaming like a meteor on the battlefield, as he dashed from point to point carrying dispatches, or urging his foam-covered horse where the battle raged hottest and bullets flew thickest in the deadly onset of charging lines, they changed their opinion. When the Confederate troops retreated, although they had gained the victory here but were not able to hold the country, their wounded fell into the hands of the Federals, but were paroled.

Judge Maney was paroled by the famous Kit Carson, who was in command of the men who had charge of the prisoners. One company was cut off and captured at the battle of Glorieta, after the Val Verde fight. After the wounded recovered sufficiently, fifty men were started back home together, Judge Maney being elected captain. All came near being drowned while crossing the Rio Grande on a raft. They had to stay here four days and eat mustang meat, but finally arrived at Seguin on the 15th day of August.

Mrs. Maney came to Texas in 1840, and has also witnessed many exciting scenes. She was in sight of the burning of Linville by the Indians, and saw the vast host of painted savages as they started back to the mountains, and saw them pursue and kill Dr. Bell on the prairie.

CAPTURED AN INDIAN.

1876.

Mr. James A. Hudspeth of Kerrville tells the following interesting incident of border life.

In December, 1876, his cousin, Joseph B. Hudspeth, lived in Hondo Canyon, eighteen miles west of Bandera, having moved to that place several years before. One night in the above named year and month, in the early part of the night before the family had retired, Mr. Hudspeth was sitting by the fire, and was attracted by the furious barking of a young dog that he had. On going out in the bright moonlight to learn the cause, he discovered what he thought to be a blanket lying on the ground a short distance from the house. Thinking the children had left it there, he advanced to the spot and stooped to pick it up, but to his surprise the blanket got up and attempted to get away, and seizing it in his arms a struggle commenced, and he knew he had an Indian. He now called to his wife to come and bring the gun. She did so and made an attempt to shoot the Indian, placing the muzzle of the gun against his head and pulling hard on the trigger, but it would not fire, although the hammer had been drawn back, or cocked, to use a more common expression. The reason of this was the fact that it was a double-triggered gun, and Mrs. Hudspeth had failed to spring the trigger. Mr. Hudspeth now told her to desist, as he could hold him, and at once carried him in the house to the light, and saw that it was an Indian boy about 13 years of age, but wiry and strong. He was nearly naked, only having a leather clout about his waist and the old blanket. He was guarded all night, and next day carried to Bandera and placed in the house of Mr. James Hudspeth. The young Indian could neither speak Spanish nor English, and was kept here several days without being able to get any information out of him. About this time a squad of Texas rangers came along. Their guide could speak Spanish, besides several Indian dialects, and came in to see what he could make out of him. After trying him on several, he finally addressed him in the language or dialect of the Tuscalaro Indians. This he understood, and at once commenced conversing, saying he was of that tribe, and had been a captive among the Comanches since he was six years of age. He had been on a raid with them and had become lost, and was trying to steal a horse from Mr. Hudspeth to get out of the country on. Only a few days before this time the Indians had killed Jack Phillips six miles west of Mr Hudspeth's house, and it was supposed this was the band he was with, although the young Indian said nothing about this killing. Now the rangers were after this band of Indians, and crowded them so close that several of their horses gave out and were left on the trail, and it was supposed it was at this time the boy was left, but before the killing of Phillips. The horses of the rangers gave out also, and they turned back at Wallace Creek.

After a few days the young Tuscalaro was turned over to a Mexican named Polly Rodrigues, who was also guide and trailer for soldiers, rangers, or citizens in their pursuit of Indians. He stayed with Rodrigues about two years, and then left the country on one of his horses—borrowed, stolen, or bought, I can not say which. In about the same length of time, however, he returned again and lived with him. He seemed to have no inclination to leave again, and is in the country somewhere yet. Mr. James Hudspeth has been in Kerrville about four years, and saw him there once since. He was glad to see Mr. Hudspeth, and shook hands with him, as he always did when meeting him. Mr. Hudspeth gave him clothes while at his house in Bandera, and the Indian had never forgotten it.

Mr. James Hudspeth came to Texas in 1864 from Arkansas and settled in San Saba County in November of 1865. This was then the frontier, and he was on many scouts and trails after Indians, but never got into a battle with them. He settled on Wallace Creek, and in 1869 was still living there and teaching a country school. One evening he had just arrived at home from the schoolhouse, and had unsaddled and hobbled out his horse, when he saw Wiley Williams, one of the neighbors who lived about 300 yards above, running toward him with a gun in his hand, and when within speaking distance, he exclaimed: "I've salivated one of them." "Salivated one of what?" said Mr. Hudspeth. "An Indian," said Williams; "I have killed an Indian, and I want you to go with me to get him." "All right," said Hudspeth, "but you go first and get William Harkey, and

I will saddle my horse and be ready when you return to accompany you." Harkey lived down the creek three or four hundred yards. While the horse was being saddled, Mrs. Hudspeth, who was out looking around, suddenly exclaimed: "Come here, Mr. Hudspeth, and look. I see a lot of Indians, and they are putting another one on a horse." He did not come in time to see them, as he was hurriedly saddling his horse. When Harkey and Williams came the three proceeded to the spot where the latter said he had shot the Indian. The circumstances, he said, were this: He noticed some cattle on a hill with heads up looking at something, and thinking it was a wolf, got his gun and slipped up there to get a shot at it. While so doing he discovered the Indian in a crouching position watching the horse that Mr. Hudspeth had just hobbled out. Williams laid his gun against a mesquite tree and took aim. He could see the Indian's shield pressed against his left side, but fastened to his left arm, as they always carry them. He aimed above the shield and fired. The Indian at once sprang to his feet, but fell again and lay there. When they came to the spot the Indian was gone, but plenty of blood was found. The balance of the band was near by and carried him off, and this was what Mrs. Hudspeth had witnessed. Some dogs had come with the men, and they at once took the trail of the Indians, followed by the three settlers. Two miles up the creek they came to a cedarbrake which the trail entered and the dogs and men followed. The dogs, however, soon came back with their hair up, and scared. Mr. Hudspeth, who was in the lead, stopped and said: "Boys, if we go in there we will be killed; they can see us and we can not see them." It was now dusk. Williams said if anyone would follow he would go on in. Harkey said he would go, but Mr. Hudspeth turned his horse around and said, "All those that want to go in there and get killed, can do so; I am going back," and with that rode off and the other two followed. Next morning they returned and made a thorough search, but could not find the dead Indian, but found his shield covered with blood, and his bow and quiver of arrows. The bullet had struck the shield high up and went through it. It was braced against his body, was the reason of this. When used in battle with the arm bent in front, the shield hangs loose on the elbow and gives to a ball, and it will glance off.

Three weeks after this, six miles from here, a man while riding in the hills found the body of an Indian where it had been placed under some rocks, directed to the spot by buzzards.

After this Mr. Hudspeth lived on the San Saba River, four miles above the town of San Saba, and one night discovered an Indian by moonlight in a stooping position coming down the fence for the purpose of getting a horse which was inside the inclosure near the fence, and also near the house. Now, before this time Mr. Hudspeth had traded for a Spencer carbine, which was a repeating gun, the cartridges being in the breech, and which had to be thrown into the barrel by a lever. His first thought was, "Now I will kill an Indian," and cocked his piece, without throwing in the cartridge, having been used to a muzzle-loader, and at the moment had forgotten. He intended to let him come to a certain panel in the fence and then cut him nearly in two if he could. He had time to take careful aim, as the Indian was coming slow, slipping along half bent, and of course the gun snapped, and the Indian vanished like a vision of the night, but pursued into a thicket by the dog. The dog soon came back, however, with hair the wrong way, and taking a position in the yard, barked the balance of the night. The Indians (for more were around) finally got to mocking him. Mr. Hudspeth watched the most of the night, but would occasionally drop off to sleep, and Mrs. Hudspeth would keep him roused up. He told her there was no danger of them approaching the house any more that night, knowing they were discovered. Next morning Indian tracks were thick all around.

On one occasion Mr. Hudspeth came very near getting into an Indian fight. He and Harkey and Williams and a man named Henderson and his son got on an Indian trail and finally divided, Hudspeth and Harkey going one way, and the balance of the party the other. Williams and his party found the Indians, ten in number, and fought the battle. They were compelled to retire, and the elder Henderson was badly wounded with a bullet.

DR. J. C. NOWLIN.

Came to Texas in 1855.

Dr. James Crispin Nowlin was born in Caldwell County, Kentucky, April 16, 1817. In 1821 he went with his parents to the western district of Tennessee, but came to Texas from Mississippi, by way of Missouri and Kansas, in 1855. Dr. Nowlin was a slaveholder, but not liking the situation in Kansas, came on to Texas and first settled in Gonzales County, and in 1856 moved to Kerr County and settled near the present town of Center Point. Those who were living in the settlement at this time were the Reese family, Dr. Ridley and family, Joshua Brown and family, and De Witt Burney. Tom Saner was the outside settler up the river above Kerrville. At the settlement of Kerrville there was nothing but a few cabins and camps. George Phillips and Dr. Scott and family lived at the mouth of Silver Creek and Mrs. Denton lived at the mouth of Cherry, below the present town of Center Point, and was the first settler in this part of the country. A Mr. Long and George Nichols lived on Verde Creek, and Nichols had a sawmill there. A company of United States cavalry was stationed at Camp Verde, commanded by Captain Parmer. Henry Moore, a single man, nephew of Dr. Nowlin, came with him to this country.

About February 12, 1857, the Comanche Indians made a raid through the settlement and stole quite a lot of horses, getting seven from the doctor and two from Henry Moore. Captain Parmer of the regulars was notified of the raid, and at once sent fourteen men to get after the hostiles. The captain also sent two horses to mount Dr. Nowlin and Henry Moore, who were anxious to go on the chase. He also sent Polly Rodrigues, a Mexican guide and trailer, who knew all the country and was an experienced Indian fighter. One of the horses stolen by the Indians was taken from near the chimney where he was tied for safety. When the soldiers and guide came from Camp Verde the start was made and the trail taken up at the crossing of the Guadalupe, one mile from Dr. Nowlin's house. Here the Indians had tied ropes to the trees around in a circle so as to catch horses and mount them.

This place is now in the pasture of Alonzo Reese. The Indians went a northwest course and confined themselves to the roughest country they could find, and killed and ate two horses on the way. For seven days the pursuers followed the trail until they came to the head of South Concho.

About 4 o'clock in the evening of the seventh day the doctor and the guide were ahead, both trailing and separated about eighty yards, when the doctor discovered the Indians. They were in camp, but saddling their horses to leave. At a call from Dr. Nowlin the guide came to him, and they charged. By this time the Indians had discovered them and met the charge in fine style and the border battle commenced. Dr. Nowlin fired the first shot from a shotgun at an Indian who was coming towards him, yelling and throwing up his shield in front of him. The Comanche jumped high at the fire of the gun but did not fall, although badly hit. The guide now made a rush for the horses, telling the doctor to keep firing while he secured them. He tried the other barrel of the gun, but it failed to fire. By this time all of the men had dashed up and were firing rapidly. Dr. Nowlin now dismounted, but the guide yelled to him not to leave his horse, as the Indians would charge and get him. This he had no intention of doing, but stood by his side and tried to pick powder into the tube of the barrel of his gun that failed to fire. While doing this an Indian fired at him with a flintlock musket loaded with slugs, one of which struck his horse in the neck near the throatlatch of the bridle, and he fell dead in his tracks.

Dr. Nowlin noticed when his horse fell that he had also been struck by an arrow. The Indian who killed the horse began to reload again in a hurry, but put his ball down first, and when he tried another fire at the doctor it flashed in the pan. Dr. Nowlin at the same time was playing on the Indian with a six-shooter, and soon moved him further off. Three of the Indians were very brave, and charged within twenty-five yards of the main body of the white men. A good deal of firing was done on both sides, the Indians yelling and jumping from side to side as they fought, and trying all the time to scare the white men's horses. A Mexican named Jim Tafoyia charged an Indian and ran him about 100 yards, snapping his six-shooter at him repeatedly, putting the muzzle of the pistol against the Indian's side, but it failed to fire. The Comanche, seeing he had a chance for life, pulled an arrow as he ran and quickly shot it over his left shoulder, and would have killed the Mexican if it had not been for an overcoat which was rolled up tightly and lay across the saddle in front of him. The arrow went through this, cutting thirty-two holes in the folds, and slightly wounding Jim. This stopped him, and the Indian got away. When the Indians quit the fight they went quickly and soon disappeared, leaving none dead on the ground. No doubt some received mortal wounds and ran away to die, or were assisted away by the others, which they always do if they can make a stand-off and have time. Badly wounded Indians leave a battle at once as soon as hit, and sometimes will travel for miles before lying down.

After the battle was over a badly wounded man named Martin was brought to Dr. Nowlin to receive medical aid. He was a soldier from Camp Verde, and was wounded with a bullet. The ball had passed through the left lung, and blood was running from his mouth, and he was vomiting blood. This fact puzzled the doctor, blood coming from a man's stomach, and the wound in the lung. The doctor could do but very little to relieve him. Fort McKavett was the nearest point where shelter and better attention could be given the wounded man, and it was decided to take him there. He lived to make the trip of thirty miles or more, but died the same night of arrival. Dr. Nowlin was still curious to know the cause of Martin vomiting blood, and after the man died he and the post surgeon made an examination of the body and found that the upper part of the stomach had also been cut by the ball, which let blood into it from the perforated lung. Now the next thing was, how did the same ball do both with the man in an upright position? The cause was finally figured out. During the pursuit of the Indians at one time the men suffered very much for water, and when they found some this man, as Dr. Nowlin expressed it, "drank like a cow," and his stomach was so powerfully distended that it came up under the lung, and the ball passed through the upper part of it. They were then close upon the Indians, and the fight commenced a few minutes after.

Dr. Nowlin says he never saw but five Indians in this fight. There might have been more, as it was brushy in places. He heard men tell at Fort McKavett that there were twenty Indians, and that five were killed. The spoils were five horses, two mules, and five buffalo skins. The horses and mules were all they had, and the doctor did not believe these were the Indians they were on the trail of, from the fact that none of the stock belonged in the Guadalupe valley. He thinks this band was coming from another direction and happened to stop for a rest near the trail of the others. No search was made at the time to ascertain.

Henry Moore displayed great bravery during the fight, although suffering from consumption, which finally killed him.

In 1859 Dr. Nowlin moved his stock to Kendall County and settled on Curry's Creek.

In October, 1868, the Indians made a raid on Curry's Creek, first showing themselves at Mr. Ammond's, on the Guadalupe River, ten miles from Nowlin's ranch, killing some stock and carrying off others. This was about the 28th of October. On the same night a runner was sent to the doctor's neighborhood, informing the people there that Indians were in the country. On the following day a company of rangers, commanded by Captain John W. Sansom, hunted all day for the Indians, and in the evening found where they had crossed Curry's Creek. The people were then notified that the Indians were in their settlement, and guards were put out at the different ranches. At this time Dr. Nowlin had two young men hired, named Francis Keiser and Charley Williams, and put them on guard at his horselot at night. He had gathered up his best horse stock and put some of them in a small pasture near by and locked others in stables. In the early part of the night it was evident Indians were around on account of the commotion among the horses in the pasture. The Indians were in there after them, and had made gaps in the fence and were trying to drive them out, but the horses would run by these places. The two boys on guard at the lot got in a corn-crib with their guns and thought best to remain quiet and await developments, but as the night wore on they fell asleep.

About 2 o'clock in the morning, the Indians failing to get the horses out of the pasture, two of them came to the lot to see what chance there was of getting some there. They took down the fence to the field lot and orchard, so they could get out easy if discovered. About this time a dog on the place discovered the presence of Indians, and set up a furious barking which awakened little Kate Nowlin, and she began to cry. At this time the two young men were fast asleep at their post in the crib. The doctor waked up and told his little daughter not to cry, as the dogs would not hurt her, and to go to sleep again. But all at once the stillness of the night was broken by "Bang! bang!" in the direction of the corncrib. Dr. Nowlin sprang clear into the middle of the floor, and seizing his gun ran out without dressing and shouted, "What's up, boys?" "We have killed an Indian," came a voice from the crib. On coming to the spot an Indian was discovered down on his hands and knees, but not dead. Not wishing to shoot him again, the doctor picked up a hoe-handle and struck him a powerful blow on the side of the head, and he fell over. He repeated the blows until he was dead, exclaiming with each lick, "We will show him up! We will show him up!" The barking of the dog had awakened the boys, and looking out through a crack they saw the two Indians by the moonlight. One was in plain view near a fodder stack, and the other was behind the fence with only the top of his head visible. At this Indian behind the fence Keiser said he would shoot, and Williams was to shoot the other. The ball from Keiser's gun struck the Indian at whom he aimed in the top of the head and he fell; but Williams was a little slower to fire and his Indian started to run and he missed him. He made his escape, followed by the dog, who ran him several hundred yards. The dead Indian had on a polecat-skin cap, and his companion one just like it, which he lost in his run from the dog. The Indians had no weapons, they having been left in their camp on a hill, which was afterwards found.

The doctor now sent his son to notify the people that the Indians had been to his ranch, and to "look out." They had divided and scattered all over the country, being at the ranches of Sansom, Calahan, Reese, and Judge Jones on the same night, and two at each place, and succeeded in getting off with some stock. Calahan had a fine horse tied to the gallery post which he was watching, but went to sleep and the Indians got him. He also had two fine mules close by, but they failed to get these on account of the approach of Dr. Nowlin's son, who came at full gallop to give the alarm.

The camp of the Indians was found less than a mile from the doctor's and the same distance from Wesley Calahan's. On a rock near by were twenty marks, and one of them crossed out. Also one bow and quiver of arrows were found by the doctor.

These no doubt belonged to the dead Indian and had been left, thinking he might have escaped and would need them.

In 1870 Dr. Nowlin was appointed surgeon to a company of rangers commanded by Capt. John W. Sansom and stationed at Camp Verde. In the spring of 1871 the company was ordered to Fort Griffin, on the Clear fork of the Brazos, and soon after arriving there went on a long scout to the head of the Big Wichita River. The Tonkaway chief, Castile, was along, as was also one of his warriors named Bill. This fellow was a good scout and trailer, and kept ahead of the company all of the time. One evening the rangers stopped to pick mulberries, and while engaged in this Tonkaway Bill came back and reported that two Comanches were coming just over the hill. The rangers at once mounted, and on coming to the crest of the rising ground or small hill saw the Indians and gave chase. After running one and a half miles and turning down another hill one of the Indians was dismounted by his girth breaking, and was soon killed. The other one ran across the prairie nearly two miles before he was overtaken. Many shots were fired at him without effect, and he was nearing the timber when his horse was killed by William Causten. The Indian was brave, and charged the rangers, making the arrows fly, but was soon killed and scalped, and left on the prairie where he fought his last battle with his paleface foes. Dr. Nowlin turned him over and saw three bullet holes in him. He also had an old wound in the leg, which caused it to draw, and was shorter than the other. The only damage among the rangers was one with a sprained wrist, caused by his horse falling with him. This the doctor soon set right.

In 1872 and part of 1873 Dr. Nowlin was in command of a minute company. In 1876 he was appointed physician and surgeon for Capt. Neal Caldwell's company of rangers. On one scout during this time at the head of South Llano the rangers got word that the Indians had captured some horses from a party of buffalo hunters, and at once went in pursuit of them. On Saturday they struck the Indian trail at the "buffalo pond," and filling all of the canteens, pushed on after them. A camp was made that night on the plains, and all the water used up. No more could be found, and they were compelled to quit the trail and travel down one of the draws of Devil's River in search of some. On Sunday night they made another dry camp and tied up all the horses. The trailer, Alexander Merritt, walked a good deal, and having drank up all of his water the first day, was now suffering intense thirst. Captain Caldwell had a little water, and Dr. Nowlin told him to give it to Merritt. The trailer was called and the water offered to him, but he would not accept of it, because the other boys had none. All the next day the men suffered so much that they crossed a large Indian trail and paid no attention to it. All eyes were scanning the country in search of water. On the next day they found plenty of water, a large spring coming out from under a mountain. The doctor said, "Boys, drink light, and do not let your horses have much." Some did not hear this order, and going to a pool below the spring, drank so much it made them sick. The command stayed here one day and a half, and then the men did not want to go back the way they came, but seeing a black cloud up that way thought it might rain and furnish water, and were finally prevailed on to start. William Layton was on the left flank as spy, but had to head so many ravines that he became lost and was unable to find the command. The rangers were uneasy about Layton, for fear he would perish for water. The lost ranger, however, found water and filled his canteen, and camped alone when night came. Next morning, not knowing which way to take among such a network of ravines and hills, he gave his horse the bridle, and the instinct of the animal carried him directly to the trail of the rangers. He had to spend another night alone, however, as the command was some distance ahead, but on the next day overhauled them.

In 1876 Dr. Nowlin belonged to Capt. Henry Moore's company of rangers, and was stationed at the head of Bear Creek, fifteen miles from the present Junction City, in Kimble County. On the day before Christmas of the above named year, in the morning, the Indians made a raid into the settlement where Junction is now and killed a boy half a mile west of town, and two miles further killed a man on North Llano. The people were afraid to leave the settlement to notify the rangers until late in the day, but finally one man ventured out and arrived at the ranger camp about an hour by sun. The rangers at once got out and crowded the Indians so close they were compelled to abandon some of the stolen stock, which stood on the trail covered with sweat when the men came upon them.

It was hard trailing through the cedarbrakes and over rocks, and finally the horses played out and the pursuit had to be abandoned. The rangers turned back at Wallace Creek (named for Big Foot Wallace, who owned a tract of land there), one of the tributaries of the Medina River. This was the band of Indians that killed Jack Phillips between the Hondo and Sabinal, ten miles or more south from where their trail was abandoned.

In 1869 the Indians made a raid, and one of them was killed at Judge Jones' ranch. The Blanco men followed the Indians and kept in sight of them all day, and when night came crossed the divide and notified the settlers on Curry's Creek of the raid. Pink Jones and a Mexican named Serelda went out at night and took a stand at the corner of the field fence to watch for the Indians, and finally saw two coming towards them. They let them came close, and both fired. Just at the moment, however, the Indians discovered them and turned. Jones missed his, but the one which the Mexican fired at was badly wounded, leaving a trail of blood for some distance. He lost his scalping-knife, which was picked up on the trail. Some time afterward the skeleton of an Indian was found in the hills with a belt and empty knife scabbard around the waist. The knife picked up on the trail of the wounded Indian just fit the scabbard, and no doubt this was him.

Dr. Nowlin has lost stock altogether while living on the frontier valued at $13,000, and never recovered but one animal back from them. The doctor was an active, stirring man, however, and always had plenty. He died at his home at Center Point, Texas, on the 8th day of December, 1898, in the eighty-second year of his age.

JACK HARDY CAPTURED BY INDIANS.

Negro boy. Born in Kerr County.

When the great State of Texas was being settled by white men who were continually pushing to the front along the border from nearly every State in the Union, there were those who brought their negro slaves with them, and some of these had thrilling experiences with Indians. They were killed, scalped and carried into captivity the same as white men, and had to meet all the dangers of frontier life as well as their masters, and often fought bravely around the frontier cabin in defense of white women and children.

Among others of these slaves and ex-slaves who have been carried into captivity, and who have a tale to tell, is Jack Hardy, who now lives in the Guadalupe valley near Center Point.

While the writer was on the hunt for frontier history in the Guadalupe valley country, several of the prominent citizens there told me of Jack Hardy, and would like for me to get a history of his captivity among the Indians, and also said that they would vouch for the truth of his statements, and that no colored man stood higher in their estimation than he.

Jack Hardy was born on the Guadalupe River, in Kerr County, half a mile above the town of Center Point, forty-two years ago, and belonged to Dr. John Ridley.

After the Civil war, when all the slaves were free, Jack lived near Comfort, below Center Point. On one occasion, when he was about 12 or 13 years of age, he was sent to mill with a turn of corn, and it was then the Indians got him. He was in sight of home on his return, and saw the Indians when some distance, and could then have made his escape, but thought they were white men, as some of them had on hats. He paid no more attention to them, but jogged along the road, not apprehending any danger, until four of them came up behind him. While some laid hold upon him others jumped down and caught his horse by the bridle and threw his sack of meal to the ground, and said something he could not understand. Up to this time he had never seen Indians, and still did not know who they were. He noticed they were curious-looking men, but to keep on the good side of them he removed his hat and spoke to them as politely as he could, but as they did not return his salutation he supposed they did not like niggers much. He soon discovered they had long hair, carried bows and shields, and the truth dawned upon him that they were Indians, from descriptions he had heard of them from old settlers and Indian fighters. He cast one glance towards home and could see some of his people in the yard, but it was too far off for them to detect what was transpiring. The young negro, when he realized that he was a prisoner and would have to go with the Indians, adopted a wise course, and that was to be obedient and not get scared at anything they might do to him. He noticed that there were fifteen of them, and that they were tall, fine-looking men except two, and they were very low in stature and very ugly. His first initiation to captivity among Comanches was a severe whipping with a liveoak stick, the scars of which are still to be seen on Jack's head. They now gave him bow and arrows, and made signs that if the white men came upon them he must help fight. They also had guns and pistols, and one of them could talk English. Jack thinks he was a white man, as he would not talk to him much.

This was on Saturday, at 1 o'clock, and the captive had nothing to eat until Sunday at 3. The Indians took a westerly course through the hills below the mouth of Verde Creek, leaving Center Point, or the settlement there, about three miles to the right north. On a tributary of the Verde now inclosed by the pasture of Messrs. McElroy and Vaughan, and in charge and run by Mr. James Crotty, they came upon the cabin of Ed. Terry, due south from the present town of Center Point, about two and a half miles. Mr. Terry was a short distance from the house, sitting down riving boards from cypress blocks which he had brought from the Verde Creek, one mile north of his place. As he had his head down he did not see the Indians when they approached, and one of them stopped his horse and aimed a gun at him. Jack sat on a horse near by and with bated breath watched the whole proceeding, but dared give no warning note to the doomed man. When the gun fired Terry sprang to his feet, ran about forty yards, and fell. Another Indian now went to him and lanced him, and he soon expired. By this time the other members of the family were screaming and running away from the house, pursued by others of the Indians, who killed two of the children and captured a little girl about 8 years old. Mrs. Terry made her escape, and as she sprang over the yard fence she threw her baby boy Joe into high weeds, and the Indians failed to discover it. They shot many times at her, but she sprang into a deep gully near by and eluded them. When she reached the settlement and the alarm was given, a small party of settlers repaired to the scene of the killing and buried the slain man and his children, and also rescued the little boy, who was crawling about in the grass and weeds not far from the spot where he was thrown.

The Indians from the cabin went towards the Bandera pass and ascended a high mountain to the left of it and there halted awhile. While here they placed Jack on a rock, and pulling off his hat jerked his head back and put a sharp knife to his throat, as if about to cut it. The negro was badly scared but showed no outward sign, and even leaned his head back further so as to give them a better chance to cut it good. The Indians now laughed, and turning him loose, said "Bravo! Bravo!" They now pulled a lot of wool out of his head, and holding it up, let the wind blow it away as they sifted it through their fingers. At this they also laughed very much. From here they went down the mountain and took the Bandera road, and after dark went through the town two and two abreast, and crosed the Medina River a little above. They now came back on their trail and captured a sorrel horse in the edge of town. They had killed a cow somewhere, and when they finally stopped to rest they ate her paunch. They had one horse along that would pitch every time an Indian got on him, and one morning they put a rope on this horse with a loop over his nose as they were about to start, and sat the little Terry girl astride him. Jack thought sure the vicious horse would kill the poor child, but strange to say he went along perfectly docile. An Indian now tried him, and he pitched all over an acre of ground.

When the Indians would camp at night Jack thought sure the white men would catch them by morning, but no pursuers came, and in this way they traveled through the mountains and crossed Hondo, Seco, and Sabinal canyons, the latter just below where Utopia is now. When they came to the Blanco, still further west, they made another halt on top of a mountain, and three of them took Jack and went down into the valley after water. While doing this they saw a white man coming up the valley towards them. The three Indians howled like wolves when they saw him, and all of the other Indians came to them. One Indian was left with the captives, and fourteen of them ambushed the white man, who came along all unconscious of the trap laid for him. The Indians all had guns and pistols, and raised up and commenced firing at him at not more than thirty steps distant. The white man turned quickly and made a terrible plunge through the brush, pulling his Winchester as he did so and firing one shot, but was then seen to fall from the left side, and then both horse and rider were lost to sight. The Indians yelled fiercely and went in pursuit, and soon came back leading his horse with blood on the saddle, and one of them had his hat, which was a brown plush. Well, thought Jack, one more white man dead. He soon found out, however, that they did not get him. They failed to show up his scalp or gun. The scabbard was hanging to the horn of the saddle. The Indians would point to the blood on the saddle and gloat over that. They fired fourteen shots with guns and pistols, and Jack says if they had used their bows they would have got him, for he had seen them shoot deer and never miss. They handled firearms awkwardly.

The writer expects to get a full account of this remarkable escape from Indians, but will say here that the man was Chris. Kelley, who lived on Sabinal, and that he was not wounded, and got home all right. The blood on the saddle was from deer hams he was carrying.

The weather had now turned very cold, for it was in December, and commenced to sleet and snow. The little girl's bare legs were about to freeze as she rode across the bleak mountains behind one of the Indians. They made her a pair of moccasins which came above her knees, and she fared some better. That night when the Indians camped it was very cold and sleet was falling rapidly, but despite all this they tied Jack down as usual flat of his back, legs stretched one way and arms the other, to stakes in the ground, with his upturned face exposed to the bitter blast. He had his hat on, and by working his head back and forth managed to bring it over his face and held it there with his teeth to keep the wind from blowing it back, and by that means kept the sleet out of his face and to some extent alleviated his sufferings.

During this cold spell the Indians killed a steer, and ate all of it up from 2 o'clock one day until 2 the next. They ate all the time while in camp. The rascals did not seem to fear pursuit. They carried water in cow paunches, and it was as cold as ice. When Jack went to take a drink he took but little on account of it being so cold, and the Indians, noticing this, made him drink a quart without stopping. He said it nearly killed him, and he felt like his head was going to come off.

One of the Indians made a hair rope, one end of which he gave to Jack and he took the other, and made signs for him to pull hard. He wanted to let loose his end and give Jack a fall, but the boy turned loose his end and let the Indian fall after giving one strong pull. He was very mad, and Jack had to keep out of his way to keep from getting hit. One of the Indians made a girth, and Jack was lying on his stomach watching him, and when the Indian got through he pulled out a six-shooter, put the muzzle of it in the negro's mouth at a full cock, and then placed his finger on the trigger. Still retaining his presence of mind, Jack opened his mouth wider so the Indian could push it further if he wanted to, and they all laughed as he drew it out, and said, "Mucho bravo!" The Indians were very mean, and tried to annoy their captives as much as possible. They made them throw rocks at each other, but Jack would miss the little girl every time on purpose.

After the weather moderated the Indians came on over into Frio Canyon and robbed a cow camp, and then crossed the Frio and went on to a high mountain overlooking the settlement on the Patterson ditch farm. Some of the Indians had stopped in the valley to catch some horses, and four of them who had the captives stopped on the mountain to wait for them, and here Jack made his escape. He was about fifty yards behind, and all at once concluded to make his escape. He jumped down and pulled off his bow and quiver and laid them on the ground so he could run well, but at this time an Indian looked around and ordered him back on his horse. The negro made signs to him that he was fixing his blanket, and the Indian looked down the valley to see where the others were. About this time they were just getting on top of the mountain, and the Indians saw some houses up the valley and had their eyes on them. Jack now ran down the mountain through the brush, and when the Indians looked around again he was gone; they were not aware which way he went, and could not find him. The little girl saw him when he started, but said nothing. Down near the foot of the mountain he hid under a bluff, and he thought sure he heard the Indians coming after him and gave up all hope, but when he looked around it was an old muley cow coming under where he was to lick. He was nearly starved, and broke icicles from the rocks and ate them, and then coming on down into the valley he went to an old house which he could see in the distance. When near the place he saw a man riding near him and carrying a Winchester, and being afraid of him, he began to whistle so as to attract his attention without coming up to him too suddenly. At the sound of his voice the man turned his head quickly and Jack cried out "Good evening, sir."

The white man said, "Who are you?"

"I am a little nigger boy, sir, and just got away from a bunch of Indians that had me," said Jack.

"The h—l you say," said the man with the gun. "I thought there were Indians over there, the way them d—d horses were cavorting around."

This man was John Dickson. He was a kind-hearted man, and took the half-frozen, half-starved negro to his house and gave him warm clothes and plenty to eat, and getting all the information he could in regard to the Indians, mounted his horse and alarmed the settlers.

How the Frio men gathered and pursued the Indians, fought a battle with them in Dry Frio Canyon, and rescued the little girl, will be found in the sketch of John Patterson.

Jack finally drifted back to the Guadalupe Valley, hiring himself for a time to James McLemore on the Hondo.

CAMP VERDE.

Established in 1855.

This old, historic frontier post, around which cluster so many reminiscences of ante-bellum days, is situated in Kerr County, on the Verde Creek, twelve miles south of Kerrville, two miles north of the famous Bandera pass, and six miles west of Center Point, on the Guadalupe River.

This post was established by an act of Congress in 1855, for frontier protection and for a camel post. In 1856 forty camels arrived, with twelve Armenian drivers and their families. A sketch had been made of an eastern caravansary in Asia Minor, and it was reproduced at Camp Verde in every minute particular. It was built in a rectangular shape except the north wall, which made an angle, the distance from each corner to this angle being 150 feet. This wall was sixteen feet high and made of concrete and timber, called "pise" work. The timber came from Pensacola, Fla., and it cost the government $125 per thousand to get it here. The south walls were not so high, and in front was an open court, in which was a well with the old-style Egyptian sweep. This project of using camels on the Texas frontier was an idea which originated with Jefferson Davis. He thought that camels could cross the desert country with more ease and quicker than horses and go longer without water, which would greatly facilitate carrying dispatches and following Indians. This was all true enough. The camel could cross these desert stretches better than a horse if it had all been desert sand, but Camp Verde was situated too far east, and was in a mountainous, rocky country, over which the camel with his soft, spongy feet, only suited to sand, could make but little headway. The tough Spanish pony could beat him. Later it might have succeeded, when the line of posts was extended out to the great plains, but the project at Camp Verde was a failure.

Capt. I. N. Palmer was the first commander at this post, and he rose to the rank of general in the United States army during the Civil war. Major Bowman next occupied the position, and died here. Lieutenant Wheaton, afterwards a general, also commanded here. Gen. Robert E. Lee and Gen. Albert Sidney Johnston were also at this post, and it was from here that General Johnston started on his expedition across the plains to operate against the Mormons in 1857. The Johnston fork of the Guadalupe was named after him.

The post was surrendered to the Confederates in 1861, and occupied by them until 1865, when the United States government again took possession of it. The camels being a failure as far as following Indians was concerned, they were sold in 1868 to Bethel Coopwood. Up to that time they had increased to 125. The price Coopwood paid for them was $12 and $14 around. Part of the breeding stock was then sold to a man here in Texas, who raised them for a circus, and the remainder was bought by a Californian (that is, of the breeding stock), who raised them for their hair value. The strong camels were sent to Mexico to be used by a transportation company, a scheme of Mr. Coopwood's, but it failed. They were left some time in Mexico, and their feed bill ran up to $800, when they were sold to cover it. They were redeemed by the Vance brothers, and brought back to the United States and placed with a bunch in California.

Some of the camels escaped, and their offspring are now wild on the plains of Texas, New Mexico, and Arizona. They are occasionally seen by cowboys, and some few have been run down and wrongfully shot by them. Some few escaped from Camp Verde and went into the mountains here, and a good price was paid to have them brought back in case anyone found them. At that time they had not become wild, and could be easily managed when found. A German boy living near Castroville caught one and carried it to San Antonio, and the authorities paid him a good price for it.

During the cholera score of 1892 General Wheaton, who was in command of the department of Texas, sent some officers to Camp Verde, who took an option lease on the property for a year, with a privilege of longer time, so they could absolutely have a quarantine camp by closing roads and stopping all travel to this place. This arrangement was made with the Commissioners Court through Mr. J. A. Bonnell, who then owned the Camp Verde property. He purchased it in 1875. It is now owned by his son, W. H. Bonnell. After the purchase of the property by the elder Bonnell, one day while the hands were at work the skeleton of a camel was turned up by a plow. An old negro man in the settlement said he knew how it came there, but at first would not tell his tale until he was assured that nothing would be done with him for any wrongdoing on his part. He said soon after the war he, in company with several other negroes, one night went out on a chicken-stealing expedition, and along towards day sat down in an open glade to rest. A dense fog had arisen, and objects could not be distinctly seen at more than a few feet distant. Directly a hideous object came out of the brush towards them, and they were all greatly frightened, thinking it was the devil. At first they all prayed, thinking it was no use to run. When the poor old camel, however, for such it was, came and poked his cold nose in some of their faces, and they realized what this nocturnal visitor was, their courage came back, and being armed with pistols, all commenced shooting and soon killed the old camel. The washings from the hills soon covered the remains and there he found a grave—the last of his race. He had come back from the hills near the old caravansary, where he had spent so many days.

Part of the old caravansary was still standing when the writer was there in 1898. The timber was all taken out and carried to San Antonio and sold, leaving the wall unsupported, and most of it had fallen down.

The present owner of the property, Mr. W. H. Bonnell, has a large establishment and keeps a public house. He has many summer and winter boarders. The latter come from the far North to escape the long winters there, and others come from the South and interior of Texas to escape the heat of summer. The place is beautiful, warm in winter and cool in summer, with plenty of game near in the hills.

REV. A. L. JAMES.

Rev. Andrew Larkin James was born in Comanche County, on Restly's Creek, near the Erath County line, March 4, 1860. This place was a cow-ranch fort, where the people assembled in times of Indian raids, and as all lived in one settlement near together, they could take refuge on short notice when the alarm of Indians in the country was heard. Of the families in and near the fort were those at Croos' mill, Braggett's ranch, Galbreth's ranch, Barbee's ranch, Monroe Whitesides, Ratliff's ranch, Enoch James, father of our subject, and William M. Stone, his grandfather. These two were partners in business under the firm name of Stone & James. In this same year, 1860, several members of the Braggett family were killed by Indians, including men and women. Most of the people after this assembled at the "cow ranch fort," which was eighteen miles east of the present town of Comanche, which at that time was not in existence. Old Cora was the county seat, twenty-two miles southeast, and Restly's Creek was twelve miles north of this place. At the commencement of the Civil war the Indians were more hostile than usual, and Enoch James, with many others, moved to the town of Comanche, which was just starting. Some of the families moved east and left the frontier. The Indians raided around Comanche constantly, killing people and carrying off stock, and even coming into the town on moonlight nights and carrying off stock. During these raids the James family had an old, gentle hack horse which was carried off three times, but on each occasion. he would give out in a half day's travel and they would turn him loose, and the faithful old animal would come back home.

It was among such scenes and incidents as these that young James was raised until he was about 12 years of age, when he became a participant in one of those bloody chapters of frontier history. At this time, about 1872, two young men employed as teamsters by James & Stone, who had a store in Comanche, started to San Saba with two wagons and mule teams loaded with wheat and corn. The young men were George Wallace and Frank Brown, and a young man named Bush. Grissum, who was out for his health, was with them. One of the teams consisted

REV. A. L. JAMES.

of six mules and the other four, the former having the wheat. It was fifty miles to San Saba. The boys traveled half the distance the first day, and just before sundown drove out of the road to make their camp for the night. Before they commenced to unharness the mules a man named John Roach rode up on a pony just from San Saba, and said he would camp with them. Of course this was agreeable, and he unsaddled his pony and turned him loose to graze. The Indians had made no raids for some time, and the fear of them was about over in that country. At this time, however, there were about thirty Indians in a ravine near by, watching the movements of the three young men. They had evidently discovered the wagons coming and ambushed them, thinking they would pass near, and even let Roach pass so as not to give the alarm to the drivers too soon, for fear they would make their escape. When, however, Roach met them and turned his horse loose they perceived the white men were going to camp, and came out of the ravine and advanced towards them, thinking no doubt to make easy work with the four white men. About this time Brown, who was a new comer in the country, asked Roach if he was not afraid of Indians, to travel alone in that way, and his reply was that he had not lost any Indians and was not hunting for any. . At this moment Grissum discovered the Indians, and said to Roach, "Whether you are hunting for them or not, you will be apt to find them, for here they come now." Brown knew nothing about Indians, but was brave, and said, "Boys, we will have to sell out the best we can," and took the shotgun out of the wagon, the only weapon they had. Roach had a five-shooter, and was also a fearless man. The Indians came yelling and were soon close upon them, shooting both bullets and arrows. Brown was wounded twice with bullets, once in the face and once in the arm, but he stood his ground and told the other men to cut the mules out of the wagon and each of them would mount one and try to make their escape, and let the loose mules follow them. In doing this several mules escaped and ran to the Indians, as did also the pony of Roach, but Brown held on to one and aimed his gun at the Indians. The chief was in front, finely dressed, and had his shield up in front and advancing, having dismounted from his horse. Brown now aimed under the shield and fired the last load from the shotgun, and, as he expressed it, hit the Indian in the flank and inflicted a mortal wound. The chief caught hold of a sapling to keep from falling, and jumping up and down uttered a peculiar noise, and many of the other Indians crowded about him. Brown says, "Now, boys, is your chance to get away." During the firing George Wallace was shot in the arm, and Grissum had a ball to pass through his coat under the arm. The mule which Brown had held on to during all of this confusion of yelling Indians, firing, and plunging mules, was a wheeler, and had on a saddle, which he succeeded in getting into and started off, as did all the others except Roach. The mule which he mounted was wounded and threw him, and he himself had an arrow shot through his body. Brown turned back to stay with him, but the wounded man begged him to leave and save himself while he could, as he himself was killed and no assistance could be rendered. The brave friend now reluctantly turned and galloped away after his companions. The Indians did not follow, but at once came all around Roach and commenced a desperate battle with him. He had not as yet fired a load from his pistol, reserving it for just such a hand-to-hand struggle as was now inaugurated, and succeeded in keeping them at bay, and again mounted his wounded mule and dashed away, and succeeded in getting clear of them. In a four-mile run the mule fell dead in his tracks from the wound which he had received, and Roach succeeded in dragging himself half a mile further and then sank down exhausted. He was unable to extract the arrow, as it was through the body, the spike protruding on the opposite side from the shaft, and here he had to remain in the most excruciating agony for many long hours. Out of the five shots in his pistol during his desperate battle he killed four Indians. The men who escaped up the road back towards Comanche arrived there just before day with the news, and a party was at once raised and went back to the wagons. Frank Brown, not being familiar with the dress of Indians, supposed the one he shot was a woman, on account of the long hair parted in the middle and the loose, gaudy dress with many fixtures and beads, and told the men who went back if they found a dead Indian woman there full of buckshot, it was him who killed her. He also said he hated to do it, but she was in front and coming at them with a shield before her, and that he aimed under it and fired. The party expected to find the dead and mangled body of Roach. They were unable to do so, but discovered many bloody signs of the desperate battle. A short distance off a grave was found, with a dead horse near it, with a rope around his neck and the other end in the covered grave. This was a rather peculiar circumstance, and when the grave was opened the dead body of the chief was found in a sitting position and holding the other end of the rope in his hand. He was taken out and examined, and twelve buckshot holes were found in his body around the waist. He had on a breastplate made of several pieces of ivory or bone, crossed and lapped in such a way that a bullet would not penetrate it. His arm shield, which he held in front of him, was found with him, and it had five scalps of women attached to it, one of which was that of a red-haired woman. John Roach was found the same day, nearly perished for water, by one of the negro cowhands of Captain Cunningham. He was brought in, and the arrow taken out of him and the wound dressed by Dr. Montgomery. Strange to say he recovered, as did also all the balance of the wounded men. The graves of the four Indians Roach killed were also found.

Twenty-three men now gathered from Comanche and South Leon to follow the Indians, all under the command of Capt. James Cunningham. Among the number were four or five of the captain's sons, all good Indian fighters. After the men had left Comanche, several boys of that place from 12 to 14 years of age were determined to go on this chase, and made up a crowd of their own. They were Andrew James, the subject of our sketch, then not quite 12 years of age, Freeman Clark, Joel and George Cunningham, and a young fellow named Neighbors. They were delayed in getting off on account of one of them having no saddle, and it was some trouble to find one they could get. They also had to rustle for firearms. Young James got a shotgun and the others got old cap and ball six-shooters, or as some called them, "snap and ball." They now set off rapidly on the trail of the others, but had their ardor somewhat dampened when they did catch up by the old fellows trying to drive them back. They begged and even cried to be allowed to go. Captain Cunningham, who was an old Indian fighter, said, "We had better drive you back now than to have to bring you back dead. Boys are like young hound pups, hard to manage, and will run off after every rabbit that jumps up." This is certainly the first instance on record where young Texas lads cried for an opportunity to fight Indians. The two Cunningham boys went back, but James, Clark, and Neighbors followed on in spite of all. The latter was the eldest of the three. The trail of the Indians led into the Salt Creek mountains, in Brown County, and Captain Cunningham and his men camped near them when night came and used the utmost caution, so that their presence was not discovered. A complete surprise was the result early on the following morning, so much so that some of the Indians had not yet arisen when the onset was made, led by Aaron Cunningham, one of the sons of the captain. The Indians had no time to mount horses, and scattered on foot in various directions, fighting as they went. Three Indians ran off to one side in company, and were charged by the kids who had cried to come. Freeman Clark was on the best horse and took the lead, closely followed by Andrew James, while Neighbors came in the rear. Clark soon caught up with his Indian and aimed his old pistol at his breast, and it snapped. The Indian also had a pistol, and passing under the neck of Clark's horse, shot the unfortunate boy dead from his saddle. In the meantime the other two Indians had sprang behind trees and opened on the other boys, one with a pistol and the other with arrows, and killed both of their horses and wounded young James twice, one bullet and one arrow wound. But the lad who cried to fight Indians did not lose his head in this terrible dilemma, but fired both barrels of his shotgun at an Indian who had left his tree and was running and shooting back, and no doubt got in his work, for the Indian was killed. About this time, however, a reinforcement came to the boys. Larkin Stone, uncle of young James, seeing the terrible havoc that was being made of the young Indian fighters by the three experienced warriors, dashed in at full speed with a shotgun and two revolvers and commenced a rapid fusilade. He first killed the Indian who had just killed young Clark, and then the one behind the tree, picking him out nicely with a pistol shot as he partly exposed his body to shoot. This Indian had fired at Stone with a pistol just as he killed the Indian that shot young Clark, and struck the hilt of one of his pistols with such force that it bruised his side considerably. All three of these Indians were killed. In the meantime the fight, though badly scattered, was going on with the balance of the band, and it was an hour before the pursuit was ended. Nine more Indians were killed, making eleven in all. About twenty bows and shields were picked up, besides pistols and some Spencer carbines. When young James was examined it was found that he had one ball through the leg below the knee and one arrow above the knee, which had penetrated to the bone and was still fast in the wound, and was with difficulty withdrawn. He was placed on a blanket between two mules and slowly conveyed back home to his parents, where by good nursing he soon recovered. The funeral of young Freeman Clark was the largest that was ever seen in Comanche up to that time. He was a teamster for James & Stone, and was liked by all who knew him. Only one Indian raid was made after this in that part of the country.

Andrew James was converted in 1885, and has been in the ministry as a Baptist preacher since 1892. He now lives near Center Point, Kerr County, Texas, and is in the Southwest Missionary work in the Medina River Association.

He has an old rifle which belonged to his grandfather Stone, which has killed many Indians, the last one being in Comanche County. On that occasion Mr. Stone was out hunting in the Leon bottom, and discovered an Indian sitting on a log with a gun across his lap. The old man took aim at him and tumbled him off and then beat a retreat back, as he knew not how many more might be around. He returned with a party and found the dead Indian by the log.

CAPT. NEAL COLWELL.

Came to Texas in 1860.

Captain Colwell was born in Dade County, Missouri, in May, 1844. His father, Thomas Colwell, was a soldier under General Jackson in the war of 1812, and participated in the famous battle of New Orleans, fought on the 8th of January, 1815.

In 1850 Thomas Colwell immigrated to California, going the overland route across the plains. His was quite a large outfit, consisting of five wagons with five yoke of oxen in each, and one spring wagon and ambulance for the members of the family to ride in. Besides this, he carried extra horses for the vehicles and 100 head of Missouri cattle. In his pay also, as guards, were fifteen men under the command of Captain Stockton.

This was a long, tedious trip, and fraught with many dangers and hardships. Many Indians were met on the route, but most of them were friendly. Near Carson River, however, one night a hostile band made a raid and stole all of their horses and part of the cattle. Next morning the guards followed them on foot and succeeded in getting the cattle back, but not the horses, and they now had to work oxen to everything. Finally Mr. Colwell bought several head of horses from some friendly Indians and continued his journey, but was followed and overtaken by another band, who claimed the horses, saying they had been stolen from them by the ones who sold them. There was no other alternative but to give them up, and the Indians drove them back.

The subject of our sketch was then but 6 years of age, but distinctly remembers all of these things, and says one circumstance which made a most vivid impression on his mind was crossing the desert, which consumed two days and nights of travel. It was a sandy country with no water on the route, and was strewn with abandoned wagons and other possessions of those who had gone the trail previous. Feather beds had been ripped to save the cloth, and the feathers had been scattered promiscuously by the winds across the sandy wastes. He saw men chopping spokes out of wagon wheels for fuel, and yokes and chains were lying in front of abandoned wagons where they had been dropped and the given-out teams carried on to water and grass. These wagons were public property for anyone who was disposed to pick them up, as the owners never returned for them, not being worth a trip back in the deep sand to recover them. The elder Colwell exchanged wagons several times, finding some he liked better than his own among the hundreds that strewed the desert plain. Twelve miles from Grass valley an enterprising individual was found by the roadside selling grass and water, the latter at $1 per gallon. The Colwell family finally reached their destination, and Mr. Colwell went into the stock business. His cattle were the first Missouri stock to cross the plains, and some of them sold for $150 per head. None but Spanish stock had been here previously. Gold dust was the circulating medium in trade, and each dealer, in whatsoever business he was engaged, had his scales to weigh gold dust.

In 1852 the elder Colwell died, and in 1856 Mrs. Colwell went back with her family to Tennessee, her native State. Here young Neal Colwell attended the Black Grove and Newmarket schools until 1859, when his mother with her family came to Texas, and reached Kerr County in 1860.

In 1862, during the progress of the Civil war, young Colwell enlisted in the company of Captain Eugene B. Millet, Thirty-second Texas cavalry, the regiment commanded by Col. P. C. Wood. Their field of operation was in Louisiana, opposing the invading army under General Banks. He participated in all of the battles and skirmishes, thirty-two in number, with the exception of Mansfield, his last fight being at Yellow Bayou. During one of these battles, while the regiment was under fire and not replying to it, awaiting orders, one man became very nervous, and said there was no use talking, he could not stand it, and would have to move back. Sergt. John C. Douglas of Seguin told him to come and stand with him, and he would try and keep him up to the fighting point. He stood for a few minutes until a bucketful of canister shot tore up the ground in front of him, when he wilted again, and Douglas told him to go, and he went. Their horses were tied in the rear, and this man rode a swayback he called Rainbow. He was a humorous fellow, and telling afterwards of his flight from the battlefield, said that when he mounted he picked old Rainbow up with his spurs and shook him three times, and when he let him down he fairly flew, only hitting the road in high places. After the war Captain Colwell came back to Kerr County and engaged in farming and stockraising.

In 1875 a frontier battalion was organized to operate against the Indians, and he was appointed captain of Company F. Pat Dolan was first lieutenant, F. C. Nelson second, and there were seventy-five enlisted men. There were six companies in all, the whole being under the command of Maj. John B. Jones. Their station (Captain Colwell's men) was the headwaters of the Guadalupe River. Their scouting territory embraced the country from the mouth of the Pullium prong of the Nueces to the mouth of the South fork of the Llano, where Junction City now is. Much scouting was done, and with such energy that the Indians were kept in check without any fights, but came very near getting one band. On this occasion George Danner, William Baker, and Joe Moss were camped with a wagon four miles east of the Frio waterhole hunting game and wild honey. They had found a bee cave in a gorge and were robbing it, when they were attracted by the barking of a dog at their wagon on the hill. Climbing out to see what was the matter, they discovered a band of nine Indians, who had taken their wagon horses and were carrying them off, the dog following and barking at them. The distance to the Indians was about 600 yards, but Joe Moss had a buffalo gun, and taking a pop at them, he killed one of their horses. The Indians now killed the dog and rode on. At this time Baker was out on a hunt and riding their only remaining horse. When he returned and learned the situation he at once rode to the camp of Captain Colwell, nine miles distant, and informed him of the presence of the Indians. He set out at once to the scene with thirty men. The trail of the Indians was taken up at 5 o'clock and followed until night. It led south towards the head of the Sabinal River, and the trailing was tedious and slow, being in a timbered country abounding in high grass. The rangers camped on the divide at the head of the river, having no water, and were moving again as soon as the trail could be seen on the following morning. As they turned down into the head of the canyon a belled mare and colt were seen, and had they known the situation here they could have waited and caught the Indians, for the latter had only gone down in the valley to camp by water, and came back to the divide next morning, but not on their own trail of the previous evening. They crossed over into another valley and came out near enough to see the mare, which they captured, and killed the colt. While they were doing this Captain Colwell and his men were trailing them to where they camped and back on the divide, where the dead colt was found, and the mare gone. Part of this time only a ridge intervened between the Indians and the rangers. The trail now led down the divide between Cypress Creek and the Frio, which came in above the town of Leakey. Here on a high point the Indians stopped for noon, having a good view of the country for several miles, and evidently saw the rangers on their trail and hastily decamped, which fact was indicated by signs of cooked meat, etc. They intended raiding Frio Canyon that night, for as yet they only had one horse besides those they were riding. This one they had stolen from Sam Larrymore on the head of the Pedernales, and had been pushed out from there by citizens who were now on their trail behind the rangers, but went back when they learned that Captain Colwell was after them. At the noon camp of the Indians the captain left the pack mules with Sergt. W. G. Coston and five men to follow on, and he and the others pushed on as rapidly as the rough nature of the country would admit.

To give an idea of the difficulties which had to be surmounted in crossing these rocky mountains, the following incidents will be a fair sample: In many places the rangers had to lead their horses, and in one of these Captain Colwell was leading his by the rope with the bridle reins over the horn of the saddle, and coming to a four-foot ledge, the horses had to make a powerful spring to clear, and all succeeded but the captain's horse. When he made his spring the bridle reins tightened and pulled him backwards, and he fell in such a position with his feet up hill that he had to be turned over before he could get up. At a similar place, one of the pack mules with Sergeant Coston's party fell backwards and rolled to the foot of the hill with his pack.

The Indians were crowded so close that the water in the little branches which they crossed was still muddy when the rangers would cross. If there had been any open country they would have been caught, but all was brakes, mountains, and canyons.

Much blood was on the trail where the Indians had spurred their horses. On the West prong of the Frio two men were discovered some distance off in a little valley, and not knowing whether they were Indians or white men, and wanting to be sure to get them if the latter, Captain Colwell deployed his men and completely surrounded them. When the cordon was drawn close and they were caught in the circle, it was discovered that they were white men. The latter were greatly surprised to see armed men riding towards them from every direction, and at first were alarmed. They were busy cutting a bee tree, and did not notice the approach of the rangers until they were close upon them. They were also on the trail of the Indians, but had not noticed this fact, having come into the valley after the Indians crossed it. One of the men was named Ragsdale. The rangers made another dry camp. They had no provisions, but about 10 o'clock in the night Sergeant Coston caught up with the pack mules, and they got something to eat.

The Indians had the advantage of the night, when the trail could no longer be followed, and got another good start ahead. They were followed, however, until 3 o'clock on the following evening, when a heavy rain came up and obliterated all signs of the trail. Captain Colwell now went down the Nueces, hoping to find the trail again, but could not do so, and the pursuit was abandoned. The Indians were not heard of any more.

In December it became necessary to reduce the ranger force, and the company of Captain Colwell was cut down to forty men and the lieutenants thrown out. Afterwards Major Jones allowed one, and W. K. Jones, who is now county judge of Val Verde County, was appointed. He was brother to the ranger captain, Frank Jones, who was killed in Mexico. Soon after the company was reduced Captain Colwell was sent down into the Rio Grande counties with his men to stop the depredations of bandits. The territory to scout over was from Ringgold barracks to Brownsville. By vigilant work the outlaws were kept in check during the winter. The command was now ordered in to be disbanded, and Captain Colwell instructed to turn over State government property, mules, etc., but with the view of organizing a new company for further operations against Indians and lawless characters. The home of Captain Colwell was near Center Point, in Kerr County, and here he had the government mules and a man employed to look after them. They were turned out during the day and rounded up and penned again at night. On one occasion a mule failed to show up, having strayed, and that night the Indians made a raid through the valley and carried him off, and also a horse belonging to Monroe Surber. Captain Colwell followed the Indians far towards the west, over the rugged mountains, but failed to overhaul them, as they scattered and went various ways.

At this time Lon Spencer and a companion, whose name can not now be recalled, were out on the head draws of South Llano hunting game or mustangs, and saw two Indians coming towards them a long way off, and ambushed them. When they came within gunshot each selected his man to shoot at, and both fired. Spencer killed his Indian, but the other man missed, and one got away. Now, it happened that these two Indians had the mule and horse which were stolen at Center Point, and they were recovered. Spencer brought back the recaptured property, as also the scalp of the Indian and his rigging.

In 1876 another company was organized with Captain Colwell as commander. Their scouting territory was the same as before, and they did a great deal of it. On one scout of ten days, while returning, they came upon some cattlemen at Paint Rock, on South Llano, who were carrying a herd to Kansas. They informed the rangers that the Indians had made a raid on another cow outfit at Green Lake, six miles above, and captured eleven head of their horses. Captain Colwell at once repaired to the scene with his scouts and took the trail. Their only chance for carrying water was in canteens, and as the Indians had gone out through a dry country, the captain cautioned the men to be saving with the water. It was warm weather in April, and the water soon gave out. On the second day, at night, a dry camp was made in a draw, and the men were suffering very much with thirst. They looked bad—skin dry and lips swollen. During the night they were very restless, and moaning in their sleep. Some arose and scratched in the dry gravel of the draw, trying to find moisture. Aleck Merritt, the trailer, had walked a great deal in following the trail, and had long since used up all of his water, and was suffering more than the others, who had ridden their horses. Captain Colwell and Dr. Nowlin were lying on their blankets together, a little apart from the rest, and were commenting on the long distance Merritt had walked and trailed, and expressed an opinion that he was certainly more thirsty than the balance. The captain had preserved some water in his canteen for an extreme emergency if it came, but now called Merritt and made known to him the fact, and offered him some of the water and explained to him the reason. This unselfish and true Texas ranger refused it, because he thought it would look wrong in him to accept it when the other boys had none, and went back to his pallet and suffered on through the long night and until 9 o'clock the following day. When the water was found the men could not very well be restrained, and many of them drank until they were sick. Eighteen Indians had camped here the night before, as was indicated by the imprint of their bodies in the rank grass where they slept. Just below, in the same little valley, a like number had spent the night and held a bunch of horses there. It is likely well enough that the rangers did not come into contact with this band, numbering thirty-six to their twelve, in the famished and weakened condition they were in. The scout was held here two days.

George Beakley's horse had given out and was not able to keep on the trail of the Indians, and the captain did not want to leave him alone, so a return towards camp was made, Beakley riding a pack mule and slowly leading his jaded horse. The captain had flankers on both sides while on the move, and one of these, William Layton, became lost from the command. He was seen during the greater part of the day, but finally he was missed and the command halted. The captain got on an elevated place and searched for him with a spy glass, but could not discover him. He hated to leave the man, but it was useless to go back to hunt for him, as they could not even guess where to look. The grass was fired with the hope that the smoke might be seen by him and to some extent guide him, and the scouts moved on. The men would soon be out of water again, and it was twenty-five miles back to it. Provisions were left in a tree, so that if the lost ranger should strike their trail he could find it. Two nights passed before anything was seen or heard of him, and he was about given up as lost in fact, when on the third day he overtook them. He had crossed the trail of the rangers once and did not see it, and turned back when he discovered that he was going too low down the country. His horse took the trail when he came to where the grass was burned, and followed it as true as the needle to the pole. It was at the next water that the provisions were left in the tree, and by the time he reached that place they were very acceptable to the hungry ranger. Layton had not been in the service long. An old-time Texas ranger would not have gotten into such a scrape as that.

In the following December Captain Colwell was put in command of Company A, which acted as escort to Major Jones, and was almost constantly employed in going from one post to another, inspecting, paying off, etc.

In 1877 Major Jones, with Captain Colwell's command, Pat Dolan's, and Frank Moore's companies, were ordered to concentrate. Captain Dolan was in Nueces Canyon and Capt. Frank Moore was on the Llano, where Junction City is now. The purpose for assembling the rangers was to round up the whole country around the heads of the Nueces and Llanos, and arrest every man in it. This part of the country had become headquarters for all the desperadoes, outlaws, horse and cattle-thieves, and fugitives from justice in the whole Southwest and from the East, and the intention of apprehending every man was to be certain to get the right ones, as the rangers could not distinguish the guilty parties. Each man was examined, and he had to give a satisfactory account of himself before he was turned loose. Forty men out of this round-up proved to be the persons wanted, and they were carried to Junction City and there confined in shackles in a place called the "bull-pen." Junction City was just being laid off. There were only a few houses there—no jail or court house—although it was designated as the county seat of Kimble County. Judge Blackburn had arrived there to hold court, and the rangers remained to give protection in case any of the outlawry kind gave trouble. But these at the time were all in durance vile in the "bull-pen," and everything passed off smoothly during this first term of court in Kimble County. Court was held under a large liveoak tree, and to give color to this primitive court of justice in the wilderness, a swarm of wild bees were working in the tree under which were assembled judge and jury, lawyers and witnesses. The arrested men were all turned over to the civil authorities.

After this Captain Colwell went to Frio Town and operated in surrounding counties, capturing outlaws and desperate characters in that part of the country. During this service he and his scouts apprehended more than forty men and brought them to justice.

These last rangers were different from the first—the Indian-fighting rangers. Many of them were detectives from other States and different parts of this State. The first ones were of the cowboy style—good riders, trailers, and shots, wearing leggings, many of them, and buckskin. The last ones, however, did splendid work in their line, which was fraught with as much danger as fighting Indians. This service was continued by Captain Colwell until 1879.

Governor Roberts was in the executive chair during the last mentioned date, and Major Jones was made adjutant-general and Captain Colwell quartermaster of the frontier battalion. His business was to make tours of inspection, furnish rations, and recommend changes of men or companies from one place to another.

During this service information was received that lawless characters were operating south of Fort Davis, in the Chenati mountains, where there were no rangers. General Jones ordered Sergt. Ed. Seiker to take four men and one Mexican guide and repair to the scene. As these men figure in a fight with the outlaws in which one of them lost his life, their names will be given, as follows: Sam Henry, Tom Carson, L. B. Caruthers, — Bingham, and the Mexican, name not known. At Fort Davis Sergeant Seiker learned that the most daring of the desperadoes were four in number, one of whom was named Jesse Evans, from New Mexico. They would rob stores in daylight in Fort Davis and terrorize the citizens generally, and the latter had offered a reward of $500 for their capture.

The rangers learned through a negro named Louis, who occupied a neutral position between the two parties, that the outlaws' stronghold was in the Chenati mountains. He also told the latter that the rangers were after them. They believed the negro was wholly on their side, and that their position was not known. They also told him if only four rangers came to hunt for them he need not put himself to the trouble to inform them, but to keep them posted in regard to a larger force.

From the fort the rangers went south about eighty miles to

near the Rio Grande, on a little creek in the Chenati range, and there, while hunting for trails, discovered four men on horseback above them. As this corresponded to the number of men they were hunting, and in their range, they turned and started towards them. The outlaws, for such they were, turned and ran, and soon commenced firing at the rangers who were in pursuit. This settled their identity, and Sergeant Seiker and his men put their horses to the utmost speed to overhaul them, firing as they went. The chase lasted two miles, until the outlaws came to a mountain which was flat on top, but on the opposite side was a ledge of rock four feet in height which ran around the circle of the mountain. The fugitives went up the mountain, across its flat crest, down the ledge to near the base, and there dismounted, tied their horses, and came back up to the ledge and took a position behind it to fight the rangers. When Sergeant Seiker and his men arrived at the mountain and found out the position of the desperadoes, they went up to near the crest, dismounted, tied their horses, and advanced to assault their position on foot. The Mexican had stopped back with the pack mule. The rangers deployed as they went, but were soon fired on, and a desperate charge was made across the open ground, in which Bingham was killed. His comrades were charging straight ahead, firing rapidly with their Winchesters, and did not notice his fall. The bullets flew so thick along the rim of the ledge that it was death to an outlaw to get his face above it.

The leader, Jesse Evans, kept his head above, and was fired at by Sergeant Seiker, who was charging straight towards his position, but his first ball hit the rock in front of him too low. For an instant the outlaw ducked his head and then raised it again, but only to receive a ball between the eyes from the Winchester of the sergeant. The other three became rattled when he fell and ran around under the ledge, keeping their heads below, and almost ran against the muzzle of Tom Carson's gun, who had charged to the brink of the ledge and was looking over, with his gun cocked and finger on the trigger, trying to see them. Before he could fire, they begged for life, and began to throw down their arms. The other rangers congregated at this point, and Sergeant Seiker ordered them to hand up their guns and pistols and come out from under the ledge. This all happened in a very short time, and now for the first time it was discovered that Bingham was killed. The others then wanted to kill the prisoners, but were prevented by the sergeant. The sad duty of burying a dead comrade now consumed several hours, as they had nothing to dig with except bowie-knives. The horses of the outlaws were brought up, on which they were mounted, securely tied, and the rangers took their departure, leaving the dead desperado under the ledge where he fell. The trip back to Fort Davis was made without further incident, and the captives put in jail there.

To take into consideration the disadvantage under which the rangers had to charge across open ground upon a sheltered position of desperate men armed with the best repeating guns and the members nearly equal, and the rapidity with which they made themselves masters of the situation, this fight has but few equals in any warfare.

The jail at Fort Davis was of Mexican model, and was a regular dungeon. The main building was square and made of dobies, with rooms in the center and doors opening on the outside into the courtyard. The jail was in one corner of the building, and blasted out of the solid rock to a proper depth and then covered over the top by strong timbers securely fastened. The egress was by a trap door. No light was in there. Into this place in utter darkness the captured outlaws were placed.

At this time Captain Colwell had just arrived, having been sent down there by General Jones to ascertain if any more men were needed at that place. Finding the necessity, General Jones was informed of the fact, and Capt. Charles L. Neville and his men were sent. The rangers were quartered at the court and jail inclosure, and some of them stood guard there all the time. The citizens of this place and Fort Stockton greatly rejoiced at th changes which had been wrought, and had a great respect and admiration for the Texas rangers. Before this they were afraid to open their mouths in condemnation of the lawless acts which were constantly being committed in their midst. They were murdered by these desperadoes on the least provocation. The $500 reward which they had offered for the apprehension of the four leaders of this gang they cheerfully paid to the five rangers, or to the four survivors of the desperate battle. Of course such service as this was expected of rangers without any compensation except their monthly pay, and it was not for any reward that they ran the bandits down and killed and captured them, and they did not expect anything. They accepted the gift in the spirit in which it was given. The donation was from wealthy men—merchants and stockmen.

INCIDENT OF VICTORIA'S RAID.

After the incident above narrated Captain Colwell was ordered by General Jones to Ysleta to inspect the company of Capt. George W. Baylor. At that time Victoria, the famous Muscalera Apache chief, was in Old Mexico, south of the Rio Grande, with a strong band of desparate warrors. He had been fighting the United States troops in New Mexico, and getting the worst of it, had run down in there for safety. His presence there being a menace to citizens of Mexico, troops were sent up from Chihuahua by order of the Mexican government to attack him. Officers of the United States troops in Texas, believing that if he was driven out of Mexico he would cross the Rio Grande into Texas, had troops scattered through the mountains at all of the watering places to intercept him. Colonel Grierson was in command of these forces, with headquarters at Eagle Springs, forty-five miles east of Fort Quitman, on the Rio Grande. On the El Paso stage route a buckboard was run one day, and a jerky, or two-seated hack, the next. Captain Colwell went down from Fort Davis on the jerky. The captain only had on his revolver, but one of his men put a Winchester in the vehicle, saying he might see Indians on the route. A man named Baker was driver. Nothing of interest occurred on the trip down, and they arrived all right at Ysleta. Several days were spent here attending to business, and then the start was made on the return trip to Fort Davis. At Fort Quitman news was received that the Mexican forces had fought Victoria and his band, making a stand-off affair, and had gone back to Chihuahua, and also that after the fight Victoria had crossed the river and was now in Texas. Captain Colwell now knew that the trip back to Davis would be fraught with much danger. Besides him in the jerky was one negro soldier, a boy named Graham on his way to Fort Davis to act as hostler there, and the driver. The latter thought the Indians would attack them at Quitman Canyon, but if they passed that place all right they might get safely through. They expected to meet the buckboard at dusk at Eighteen-mile waterhole, where a short halt was to be made to get water. In the evening five men were seen on large horses, who at a distance had the appearance of United States soldiers on account of the horses. One came towards them a short distance and then went back. The captain now felt somewhat relieved, thinking the country was being well patrolled by the regular troops. About dusk the waterhole was reached, but Baker and his buckboard were not there. This caused some uneasiness, but Captain Colwell got out and said he would fill a vessel with water and they would continue their journey. I will here describe the peculiar team which worked to the vehicle. They were small mules, and had been trained to run all the time on the road, and when they were harnessed and turned loose from the hitching post they started off at once in a gallop, and could not be stopped quietly until they reached the next station, so when Captain Colwell alighted and was filling his canteen the driver had to let the mules run around in a circle until he was ready to mount again. One startling fact which the captain and his party were not aware of at the time, was that on this very day a battle had been fought with Victoria's band in a few hundred yards of this waterhole, in a little canyon just back of it, in which a squad of the Tenth cavalry had been routed with the loss of five or six men and horses, and they had retreated back to Eagle Springs. The dead horses were lying almost in view of the road, and the men in the valley back, who had been taken for soldiers, were the scouts of Victoria mounted on United States cavalry horses which they had captured. It had been agreed by the party in the hack, if the Indians came upon them, that the driver should give his gun to the boy Graham and let the team run in the road, and the balance to fight the Indians as they went, unless a mule was killed, and then to stand and fight to the best advantage, but with little hope of ever coming clear. If they had known what was ahead the situation at this time would have seemed more desperate. The non-appearance of Baker with the buckboard was ominous. After leaving the waterhole the mules in the jerky went at a lively rate for three miles, and then shied at something by the road. It was the buckboard with one mule dead, the other gone, and beside it lay two dead men—the driver

Baker and a passenger. They were evidently killed about sundown, as they should have been at the waterhole at the time the other vehicle was there. No doubt they ran and fought the Indians until one mule was killed, and then died beside the vehicle. Very little time was taken to look around here. The situation was appalling for the captain and his party. Indians were all over the country, battles being fought and men killed in various places. The driver was told to slow down his team. The captain sat with his Winchester in hand, admonished the men to keep cool, have their guns in readiness, and to keep close watch on both sides of the road; they were in for it, and must face the situation and get out of it the best they could. They arrived all right at Eagle Springs, and reported the killing of the two men in the buckboard. Baker was warned by the soldiers who had fought the battle near the waterhole not to start on his trip, and they told him he was certain to be killed there. For four days Victoria's band swarmed along this road, and finally crossed it at Van Horn's pass and went in the direction of Rattlesnake Springs. The troops, being informed of the route, went around them and laid an ambush at the springs. Here impatient, restless men spoiled all, as is the case on many occasions of ambuscades. Firing commenced too soon, and the Indians turned back and recrossed the Rio Grande at the same place where they did in coming over. Victoria was quite a general; he knew the Mexican troops were gone by this time, and the coast would be clear on that side.

In the following winter Captain Baylor came down from Ysleta with his men to investigate the killing of one man and the wounding of another in the Quitman pass. At the same time Captain Neville came down from Fort Davis with his men, and the two commands met at Eagle Springs. The combined forces now, after finding the trail of the Indians, which were Victoria and his band, again followed in rapid pursuit to the Guadalupe mountains, and here located the camp of the Indians by their smoke and surrounded them. A fight ensued, but the hostiles soon discovered that it was a considerable force of Texas rangers that was upon them, and began to scatter and break through the cordon and get away. Six were killed on the ground and many wounded. One wounded squaw was captured and brought back. Some of the United States officers paid the rangers a compliment when they returned by saying they had done more good in ten days than the United States troops had all summer. Victoria was finally killed and his band scattered.

Captain Colwell's service ended on the frontier in 1883, and he has since lived at the old home, near Center Point, Kerr County. He has had many offers of honorable positions, but has refused them all, one of which was the nomination to represent his district in the Legislature. He accepted some public work in the organization of the Center Point Fair Association, and served as its president four years. He married Miss C. E. Martin of San Marcos, sister of Judge W. W. Martin.

Mrs. Colwell witnessed a rare sight during the frontier days, which few women every had the opportunity of doing. On one occasion she accompanied the captain and his escort far out on the border, where he went to inspect some posts, and saw the rangers running and killing buffalo.

FRONTIER INCIDENTS.

The following incidents of frontier life were obtained from Mrs. Elizabeth Fessenden, who is familiar with all of the facts. She is the widow of Mr. Samuel Fessenden, an ex-ranger, old frontiersman, and Indian fighter, who came from Guadalupe County in 1862 and settled on the frontier. Prior to this, however, when a young single man, he had been all over the Texas frontier in the early 50's with a surveying party around the forts of Graham, Griffin, Belknap, and others, and had much experience with Indians. In 1859 he went south and married Miss Lizzie Tate, in Victoria County, and then came to Guadalupe, and from there to San Saba County and settled near Richland Springs, and soon after joined a company of rangers commanded by Capt. Riley Woods. This company scouted a great deal, and Mr. Fessenden was in many chases and fights with Indians.

In 1863 they followed a band of Indians and overtook them near the "Peg-leg" crossing of the San Saba. They were surprised in camp, but ran and dodged and hid so quickly that none of them were hit by the fire of the rangers except one. This fellow took refuge behind a tree and prepared to fight, and some of the rangers stopped to fight him. The Indians had no time to mount their horses, and all went off on foot. The white men scattered in pursuit, but soon came back to where the lone Indian had made his stand, and all commenced shooting at him, but took trees on him also, as no one wanted to be killed by a wounded Indian if it could be avoided. Many balls struck the tree behind which he stood, and he was hit many times, but continued to yell defiance and shoot an arrow at every man that exposed himself the least bit, and kept them dodging continually and keeping close behind their trees. Finally Jesse Poe said he was going to get out from behind his tree so that he could see the Indian good, and put in one good shot and finish him. But as soon as he left his place and exposed himself fair the Indian shot an arrow into his forehead, and he sprang back behind the tree again. Two other rangers, seeing he was wounded, went to him, and both had to pull at the arrow before it would come out. It had struck just above the eyes, firmly and fast in the skull, but the spike did not reach the brain. This was the last shot of the Comanche, for he was in a dying condition, and the rangers went to where he was and finished him.

Mr. Fessenden and another man were sent back to the settlement with Poe, and the others again went in pursuit of the Indians. The wounded man was brought to Mr. Fessenden's house, and the wound washed and dressed again. Mrs. Fessenden can remember how pale he looked, and said his head was badly swollen, and his eyes closed up when the bandage was removed. The party also had the scalp of the Indian with them.

In the same year another band of Indians was followed and overtaken where Brady City is now, in McCulloch County. It was in an open country, and the Indians saw the rangers coming at some distance, and a long chase commenced. Only two of them could be overtaken—a warrior and his squaw, both on the same horse. Many shots were fired, and finally the horse was killed and the warrior wounded; but he was able to get to a thicket and put up a game fight. The squaw went in with him and helped to fight the rangers, and they had to do some fine dodging to keep from being hit, but they fired continuously into the thicket, not being able to see the Indians, but located them by the arrows that came out. Finally the warrior was killed and the squaw ran out with hands up; no one fired at her, but took her prisoner. The man was supposed to be a chief from the fine rigging he had on, all of which was taken off and brought back. Mrs. Fessenden saw this rig, earrings, scalp, etc., of the slain brave. The captive squaw was sent to a reservation.

KILLING OF BEARDY HALL BY THE INDIANS.

In the spring of 1864 Mr. Hall lived in San Saba County, on Richland Creek, three miles from Mr. Fessenden's place. He had a good horse, which he never allowed to run on the range for fear the Indians would get him. Still he did not believe so many reports about Indians being in the country, when men were continually coming in and reporting "Indian sign." One morning, however, he met his fate. He had started to San Saba town, fifteen miles distant, and was riding his good horse. He also carried a six-shooter, but said he did not expect to find or see any Indians. He did not go the direct way, but took devious windings, and had proceeded about five miles when he was suddenly confronted by a band of Indians at a place called Round Mountain. He made a desperate attempt to get away, and was supposed to have fought the Indians as he ran. By some means, however, they went round him and cut him off in a circle of yelling Comanches, and they killed him in half a mile of Uncle Jimmy Wood's place. Some members of the family heard the Indians yelling and supposed it was coyotes, and even thought it strange that they would yelp at this time of day, as it was about 10 o'clock in the morning. These same Indians had stolen all of the best horses on Harvey Creek, and only a few men were on their trail, but they came upon the body before it was cold. One of these men was Pick Duncan and another one was named Hall, but no relation to the slain man. The Indians got his horse, pistol, and shoes, and also scalped him. A scout of rangers were out at that time, but did not strike the trail of the Indians as they were going in, but got after them as they came back. Mr. Fessenden was along, as this was the same company mentioned before. These rangers were home men, and took turn about scouting, half a dozen or more at a time, and when one scout returned another one took their places and went out, while those just returned went home until their turn came again. Mr. Fessenden had been at home, but took his turn with this second scout, which now found the trail. The Indians were overtaken near the head of the San Saba River and surprised in camp. A sharp running fight took place for some distance, in which three Indians were killed and all of the horses recaptured, including Mr. Hall's horse, as was also his hat, clothing, moral, and pipe.

THE HOUSE OF YOUNGBLOOD ATTACKED.

In 1864 Mr. Fessenden moved to Blanco County and settled on Hickory Creek. Three miles from him, on Grape Creek, lived the family of Youngblood. He had died, and a man named Sam De Buss was a hired hand on the place, but at the time of which we write he was away. Three of the children—a boy and two girls—were about a quarter of a mile from the house when the Indians came upon them. They soon killed the boy, but the girls ran swiftly towards the house, followed by the Indians, who kept shooting at them with arrows until both were wounded, but they succeeded in getting into the house, the mother holding the door open for them and screaming for them to "Run! run! run!" during the desperate race. There were two rifles in the house, and Mrs. Youngblood took up one of these and at once commenced a battle with the Indians. They succeeded in getting to the door, and were trying to force it open, when the brave woman killed one of them. After firing both guns the woman would pick up first one and then the other, and present it when they advanced, and the Indians would skip back around the corner. There were six of them when they came to the house, and when they left and were last seen only five were together, but what they did with the one who fell in the yard and they carried away could not be ascertained. Up to the time the Indians left the mother had no time to attend to her wounded children, but now pulled the arrows out of them. One was shot in the head and the other in the body. Both got well, but the one wounded in the head was ever after partially deranged. De Buss came back before night, and went out and brought the body of the little boy in. He was 10 years of age, and the girls were 8 and 6. After night De Buss came to the house of Mr. Fessenden and waked him up and told him the news, and they went to the camp of the rangers on Cypress Creek and aroused them. Mr. Fessenden's eyes were very sore, and as soon as daylight came he went back home, but on the way came very near falling into the hands of the Indians. He crossed their trail, but did not see it on account of his eyes, and was not aware of his danger at the time. The rangers saw the trail as they came on behind him, and it was so fresh that De Buss, who was with the rangers, declared his belief that the Indians had killed Fessenden, and a search was made for his body. Not being able to find it, the trail was taken up and the Indians overtaken. A fight commenced, but the Indians ran at the first fire and made their escape, with some wounded but none killed on the ground.

MRS. ALEXANDER KILLED BY INDIANS.

In the winter of 1867 there lived in Kerr County, eighteen miles above Kerrville, William Alexander and his wife. Also in the same house lived his son-in-law, Mr. Wachter, who had married his daughter, Nancy. At the time the Indians made the raid Wachter and Alexander were both away, having gone to Fredericksburg with shingles, leaving the two women alone. The first intimation they had of the presence of Indians was one standing in the door. Mrs. Wachter was a stout young woman, and at once ran at the Indian and knocked him out of the door with a smoothing iron which she had in her hand, and then ran on through the balance of the band who were in the yard, at the same time calling to her mother, who was in the back yard, to run. The Indians were shooting arrows at her, and as she turned to look back for her mother she fell over a log and remained there for a few moments, and then crawled to a thicket near by without being perceived by the Indians, who, thinking they had killed her, were after the old lady in the yard, who had come around the house at the call of her daughter, instead of running the other way into the brush, which she could have done and made her escape, as evidently the Indians did not know where she was until she came among them around the corner of the house. The daughter did not remain long in her hiding place, but made her way three miles down the river to where her brother, Wren, and a negro were in camp making shingles. Wren came on back, but ascended a mountain where he could overlook the valley to see if anything could be seen of the Indians. No signs of them were visible, but he made the discovery that the house was burned.

Now in the meantime, between this event and the last one narrated, Mr. Fessenden had moved from Blanco County and settled in ten miles of the Alexander place. Thither a messenger was sent to notify him and other scattered settlers, and he and others came to the scene. The house was reduced to ashes, and in the yard near it were the remains of Mrs. Alexander, partly consumed by the intense heat of the burning house. Her clothing had burned off, and Mr. Fessenden and others had to handle the remains carefully to keep the arms and legs from coming off, but which they did finally as they went to place her in a box that had been prepared for reception of the remains. Mr. Fessenden and others followed the Indians, but a snowstorm soon came on and they were forced to return. Others were sent to notify the absent men, and they were met coming back.

FOUR OF THE DOWDY FAMILY KILLED.

In 1878 a man named James Dowdy moved to Kerr County and settled on the Johnston fork of the Guadalupe River, two miles from the home of Mr. Fessenden, who lived on Stockman's Creek, near the Johnston fork.

Mr. Dowdy had a large flock of sheep, and had only been in his new home a short time when the fearful tragedy occurred which we now relate. On that day four of his children, three girls and one boy, went out with the sheep to keep them together while they grazed about a half a mile from home on a hillside. The oldest girl, named Fanny, was 20 years of age. The next was Alice, aged 18, Rilla 15, and the boy James 12. There was a grown son named Richard at the house. Before noon a band of Indians came upon the unfortunate children and killed every one of them. At the house that day it was the intention to eat an early dinner, and Richard and another young man present, who was engaged to Fanny, were to go and relieve the girls and the boy while they came to the house for their dinner. The meal was partaken of at 11 o'clock by the young men, and then they set out to hunt the flock of sheep. They soon returned, however, somewhat alarmed, and said they could not find the children, and that the sheep were badly scattered. The mother then hurried to the hills, and soon found her murdered children. Two of the girls, Alice and Rilla, were lying together, Fanny 200 yards from them, and James some distance from her. All were in a horrible condition from bullet, lance, and arrow wounds, but none were scalped. A runner was sent for Mr. Fessenden, and he and Louis Nelson came with a wagon and team and hauled the bodies home. Mrs. Fessenden also went up there and helped to wash and dress the girls and comb out their hair, and then sat up all night with them. All were buried the next day. Many arrows were lying around on the hillside where the victims ran and were pursued and shot at. The Indians had a drove of horses, and came from towards the Pedernales and went towards the head of the Guadalupe. Mr. Fessenden and others followed the Indians, but so much time had been consumed in getting in and burying the bodies that they were not overtaken. Some are of the opinion that it was not Indians who did the murder, but Mr. Fessenden was an old Indian trailer, and pronounced them such from the sign they left. The Dowdy family were from Goliad County.

Mr. Fessenden died in Bee County in 1897, and was buried at Beeville. He was in bad health and had gone on a trip down there to see if he could not be benefited.

Mrs. Fessenden still lives on the old place near Johnston fork, with some of her children.

FIGHT BETWEEN SETTLERS AND INDIANS.

1855.

In the above named year the Indians made a raid in the vicinity of Selma, on the Cibolo Creek, near the line of Guadalupe and Bexar counties, and carried off a large drove of horses, mostly belonging to Johnny B. Brown and Capt. William Davenport. The latter was in command of a small company of minute men for frontier protection. Among the men who belonged to this company was William Hale, second in command, George Murchason, Hood Murchason, William Turner, J. W. Smith, and others. Captain Davenport soon got nine of his men together and set out on the trail of the Indians. Those who are known to have been along were William Hale, George Murchason and his brother Hood, and J. W. Smith. The trail led northwest towards the mountains, and was followed as rapidly as possible, Captain Davenport himself being the trailer. Soon after starting it commenced to rain and continued to do so for several days, greatly to the hindrance of the pursuers, who had no way of keeping their guns and pistols dry, which was very essential in the days of muzzle-loaders. The tubes, however, were protected by keeping something tightly bound around them. The hard showers of rain would almost put out the trail, which caused slow progress until a point was reached where the Indians had traveled after the rain. They passed out near the new settlement at Boerne, and then took to the mountains over the roughest country they could find. So many of the horses were cut and locerated by the sharp rocks in the mountains that a trail of blood was left behind them. They were driving a hundred head, and would force them down places where they could not keep their feet without bracing themselves and sliding down stiff-legged. It was down these long, rugged mountain slants that the trails of blood were left. The white men had a like difficulty; their horses suffered very much, and the one ridden by Hood Murchason gave out and he had to walk and lead him. The trail finally came out into the Medina valley and passed north of where Bandera is now. There was a small

Mormon settlement there then, and likely a few other American settlers. The Indians went out onto the divide after leaving the valleys, and went into camp on a creek somewhere near the head of Paint Creek. The camp was in a thicket, but the white men located it by the smoke from an elevated position on a mountain, and also the large drove of horses which were grazing near. The pursuit had now lasted nine days and the Indians were resting in fancied security, thinking the white men were not coming on account of such long delay. They were making moccasins to put on the feet of the crippled horses that were the worst hurt in their desperate drive across the mountains. The settlers hid themselves from view as soon as possible and advanced upon them, but the Indians did not discover them until a charge was made into camp and rifles were cracking. There were only six Indians in camp, two of whom fell at the first volley and the others ran, not having time to string their bows. The white men followed them. The Indians went over the bank into the creek and took shelter under the bluff, which was of solid rock and sloped under. Here they strung their bows and made ready to fight, while the white men dismounted, tied their horses, and advanced to assault their position. It was a most admirable place to make a stand, as the assailants could not see them without advancing close and looking over. There was no chance to cross the creek and take them in the rear, on account of the bluff banks on both sides. After the first charge the white men saw that it was going to be difficult and dangerous to dislodge them. The Indians were on the watch, and as soon as they appeared on the bank over them they shot arrows at them, and one of the men was wounded in the arm. The men would shoot quick, and then dodge back and load. This was repeated until another man was wounded in the stomach, and still some of the Indians survived. They now resorted to strategy. The men that were not hurt advanced, crawling, with loaded rifles and their hats on sticks above their heads. As soon as the Indians saw the hats they let fly their arrows, and before they could adjust more the white men sprang to their feet over them and fired. This volley settled all of the Indians save one, and he left the position and crossed the creek, and commenced the difficult ascent of the bluff on the opposite side. Guns were quickly loaded and fired at him, but he hung on and slowly pulled himself up, although several times hit, and succeeded in getting up and disappearing in the brake beyond. On a return to camp it was found that one of the Indians who had fallen at the first fire was gone, but he was soon found about fifty yards away and still alive, only having been shot through the hips. Another shot finished him, and he was found to be the chief. Hood Murchason cut his long hair off, which was profusely decorated with thin silver plates. There was a feathered ornament on his shield which, when loosened and the wind allowed to blow it out, was eighteen feet in length. The other Indian was scalped, but the three dead ones in the water were not molested. The water where they stood and fought was as red as blood itself. The horses were all collected and the slow return commenced, the wounded men being taken care of as best they could under the circumstances. At the Mormon camp on the Medina all of the crippled horses were left, to be brought in later. Two days were consumed in getting to this place, but the balance of the trip was easier. Both wounded men recovered. The scalp of the Indian warrior and the shield and ornaments of the chief were given to the Rev. John S. McGee, who had lost a son a short time before, killed by Indians on the Cibolo. Rev. McGee carried these trophies a short time afterwards to Kentucky.

We often read about Indians being surprised and not having time to string their bows, and being put to great disadvantage in consequence, and some might ask why they did not keep them strung at all times and be ready for a fight at any moment. For the information of those who have had no experience in such things or taken no thought in regard to the matter, we will say that if a bow was kept strung at a high tension all the time the stick would become weakened, and the arrow could not be sent with much force. It is only when a party of men so completely surprise Indians and are among them before their presence is known, that they are unable to string their bows to meet the charge, for they can do so very quickly.

CHARLES PETERS.

Mr. Charles Peters was born in Hanover, Germany, in 1842, and came to America in 1855. When the Civil war broke out he joined the Confederate army at Savannah, Ga. The command he belonged to was called the Georgia Hussars, an old organization of a hundred years standing. At this time it was commanded by Capt. Fred Waring, and they were sent to Virginia. After the first battle of Manassas Mr. Peters joined the Jeff Davis Legion, which was composed of three companies of Mississippians, two of Alabamians, and the Hussars. This organization was commanded by Lieut.-Col. W. E. Martin, in the brigade of Gen. Wade Hampton, and all under the command of the famous cavalry leader, Gen. J. E. B. Stuart. Mr. Peters was in the Peninsula campaign and in many small battles and skirmishes; also at Williamsburg and the seven days' fight around Richmond, second battle of Manassas, Chancellorsville, Sharpsburg, South Mountain, and the Maryland campaign. In 1862, at the Blue Ridge, Virginia, near Salem, in a cavalry fight, he was wounded in the left thigh, the ball stopping against the bone, and was cut out by a surgeon. At the time the wound was received, Mr. Peters and a lieutenant were about to be cut off in a lane and were running to get out, being fired on from both sides. The lieutenant was killed and fell from his horse, shot through the head. After being wounded Mr. Peters stuck to his horse and ran through this terrible gauntlet of fire, with the balls whistling on every side, and succeeded in getting clear. At Gettysburg he was captured by General Custer's cavalry. He arrived during the last day's battle, their command having been delayed capturing wagon trains. When captured he was riding in company with a colonel, who escaped, but Mr. Peters was on a slow horse and was overtaken. He was bugler at the time, and was carried to Fort Delaware and kept until the war was over, being liberated on the 13th of June, 1865. He took transportation for New York, where he had two brothers, Louis and Nicholas, and came on from there to Texas in 1867. During the years 1868 and 1869 he drifted towards the frontier, and in the latter date was at Ben Fickland, when that place was just starting. During this time the stage driver from Fickland, or Fort Concho, a man named Melon, was killed by the Indians, and Mr. Peters took his place. This route was across the plains to a point further west, and was one of extreme peril and hazard both from Indians and stage robbers, but Mr. Peters was lucky in his trips, and for six months never failed to deliver his mail. By that time, however, he was tired of the business and gave up the contract, which was at once filled by a man called "Dutch Jake," and in ten days he not only lost his mail but the stage also. On one trip out the coach was overhauled by a band of Mexicans, Indians, and one white man. The latter was riding a fine black horse, and he rode along by the side of the vehicle and told Jake and his one guard to jump out and run and they would not be killed. This was acted upon as soon as a favorable place was reached, where there was protection of brush, not wishing to leap out into the open ground for fear of the Indians, who were coming close in the rear, while the white outlaw was advising them to abandon the stage and run. No attempt was made to follow them, and they arrived safely back at the fort and reported the disaster to the military. A squad of soldiers was sent out, and on arriving at the scene of the hold-up the stage and mules were gone. The Indians had carried the stage away, and at this time were riding about in it over the plains and having a fine time. The soldiers found them, but their force was not sufficient to make an attack with any chances of success, and they had to return without accomplishing anything, except as to finding out where the coach was carried to. The stage was full of Indians, yelling and making the mules gallop over the prairie, followed by a numerous band on horseback, also yelling, when the soldiers saw them. A stronger party was sent back, and after considerable search and trailing the stage was found in a gully with the tongue and part of the spokes cut out. The team of four mules had been carried away by these gay and festive Comanches when they tired of the sport and novelty of riding in a United States mail coach across the grassy plains.

The dilapidated vehicle was carried back to Ben Fickland and repaired by Mr. Peters, who was at that time working in a shop.

Mr. Peters was very lucky during his experience on the frontier in never coming into serious contact with the Indians During one winter he and some companions, among whom was Chas. Hank, stayed for months along the western streams killing buffalo, deer, and antelope, and also gathering pecans, without meeting any Indians, who at that time were numerous along the edge of the plains, and from there made their incursions upon the settlers further east. Hank was an old stage-driver, and had arrows shot into the stage on some of his trips. On one occasion during the winter hunt above mentioned he and Mr. Peters became lost while out and spent twenty-four hours on the plains without water, but finally struck the Concho River. Mr. Peters was so hot and thirsty that he waded into the water and lay down, and as he expressed it, "let the water run into him." When he got up he was as big as a barrel, and could hardly walk. He sat down for some time, thinking he had overdone the business, and that it would kill him, but finally came around all right and they made their way back to camp.

One night in Ben Fickland he saw a man killed named William Thompson. Peters and others, among whom was Sam Ragland, were in a shanty playing cards for amusement, when Thompson came, under the influence of liquor, and asked if Ragland was in there, the door being shut. No satisfactory reply was given him, and he went away, but soon returned and said he was going to smash the door and come in there and kill Ragland. The latter now said to his companions to open the door and let him in, and as they did so Thompson stepped in, pistol in hand, and Ragland shot him dead in his tracks. During another row one night old man Ben Fickland, for whom the place was named, had his boot heel shot off.

After Mr. Peters left Ben Fickland he worked four years for the same company, on a line from San Antonio to Eagle Pass. Two years of this time were spent on the Nueces, keeping the stage stand, attending to the teams, etc. From there he came down to the Sabinal River and kept the stage stand there for the same company, and remained there two years, and then, quitting this business in 1874, he went into camp alone in the Blanco Canyon, near his present home, about twenty miles northwest from the present Sabinal station. This was an exposed place for a lone man to remain, but Mr. Peters had made up his mind to settle down, and was willing and fearless enough to brave all the dangers and inconveniences of a frontier life to carve out the valuable home and ranch which he now occupies and enjoys. One night the Indians passed so near his little cabin he could plainly hear them talking, and at once blew out his light and awaited developments. His dog barked and showed signs of uneasiness, but the Indians passed on, either not locating the cabin or else afraid to make an attack. Mr. Peters had his horse staked out not far away, and arming himself with shotgun and pistol, brought him up and tied him near the cabin door, and there sat with gun and pistol ready for instant use until daylight. The shotgun once belonged to John Bowles, and was the same with which he killed two Indians and crippled another at his ranch on the Sabinal in 1859. After daylight came Mr. Peters went out to investigate, and found the trail of the Indians in 150 yards of his cabin.

After Mr. Peters commenced his settlement here others come in, among whom was Frank Jones, who settled and lived alone one mile above Mr. Peters. Sometimes Jones would have the companionship of a hired hand, as would also Mr. Peters. On January 12, 1875, Jones, Ben Brown, and Josh. Hastings went up the left prong of the creek about two miles, bear hunting. Hastings lived with Peters, and Brown with Jones. After rambling and hunting for some time unsuccessfully Brown and Hastings returned, but Jones said he would go on to a certain bluff and hunt for bees which he had been coursing. When night came and he did not return, no especial uneasiness was felt, as it was supposed he had joined a party of Frio hunters. Next day, however, a man came over from the Little Blanco east and reported that Indians were in the country. The impression now was that the Indians had killed Jones, and a search was instituted for him. This was kept up unsuccessfully for three days, but at the expiration of that time the body of the unfortunate man was found by Mr. Peters, William Garrett, and others. The body was found on the bluff, whither he had gone in search of bees in a low depression of the hills. It was entirely nude and lying face down. The marks of violence on the body were one bullet hole clear through it, breaking both arms in its passage, and one arrow in the back, which penetrated four inches. Mr. Peters drew this out, and so firmly was it fixed that the body was raised clear of the ground in doing so, and the spike then was detached from the shaft and remained in the body. The man met his death at the hands of Indians, as was verified by their tracks. Evidently they were on the bluff and saw Jones coming up the creek and laid an ambush for him, concealing themselves in different places so as to be certain of him, not knowing at what point he would make the ascent. Jones came up between two of them, and the one who lay behind a bunch of soto with a gun was the one who did the work. His imprint was seen in the rank grass where he lay, and the top of the soto stalk was cut off by the bullet when he fired at Jones, not more than a few yards distant, and in line with the body where it fell. Jones had his side towards the Indian, as the ball hit one arm, broke it, went through the body, and broke the other arm in its exit. Beyond, in various places, was the imprint of other Indians where they lay in the grass. Mr. Peters and Ben Brown were the first to discover the body, and Mr. Peters said they had evidently seen the body several times in their search before they ascended the bluff, as it lay in plain view, but being naked, resembled the white rocks which lay around it. One of Mr. Jones' dogs was the cause of them finally ascending the bluff, for he repeatedly went up to the body, but would return again when they failed to follow him. The men had lost the trail of Jones, and were trying to locate it again in the rocks and ravines below. Mr. Peters finally noticed the action of the dog and suggested a search on the bluff. The Indians had not entirely stripped the body, but, as was their strange custom, had left one sock, which had not been removed from the foot. The arrow was shot into the back after he was dead and stripped. The searchers were all called in now, and some of them went back to the cabin of Jones and there found some planks, which they converted into a rude box, and returned and placed the body in it. Near the spot was a sink or wide crack between solid walls of rock, and on cleaning out the trash and small stones from this fissure it presented a natural grave in width, depth, and length, and into this the body was placed and covered up carefully, and a mound of rocks heaped over it.

These same Indians had killed a paint mare belonging to Ed. Meyers and cooked and eaten her in 150 yards from the spot where they killed Jones, and had evidently been here several days before the unfortunate settler came upon them, and it was from their elevated camp that they discovered him and laid the scattered ambush to intercept him as before described. While in this camp the Indians had made ropes from the mane and tail of the animal which they had killed. They also stole sixteen head of horses belonging to Ed. Meyers, and carried them away. His ranch was at the foot of the mountains, near the Frio. Jones had a fine Springfield rifle and plenty of cartridges when killed, but being shot from ambush, had no chance to use it, and the Indians got possession of it. Jones had no connection in this country, and but little was known about him. There was nothing among his few effects that gave a clew as to where he came from. He had five or six dogs with him when murdered, but none of these were molested by the Indians, and they all came back home. Mr. Peters remained alone with the body while the others were gone to make a coffin, and they tried to get him to leave also, expressing a fear that the Indians would kill him, but he said, "No; lightning does not strike twice in the same place."

During his lonely life in the hills, surrounded by dense cedar-brakes and dark canyons, Mr. Peters killed many bear, panther, deer, turkey, and other game, and really enjoyed himself. He was a man of education and intelligence, and had the company of books and papers with which to pass away the time when tired of hunting and rambling, and was also raising cattle and hogs, having an unlimited range for both and plenty of water from the bold mountain streams. He finally changed his state of single blessedness and married the widow Allison, a lady from Mississippi, with whom he has lived a quiet and contented life. He was engaged in the mercantile business for twenty years at

Sabinal, in partnership with his brother Louis, under the firm name of Peters Brothers, but lived here on his ranch all the while and attended to the stock interests, and has been very successful in all of these things.

Mr. Peters relates a very sad incident which occurred while he was at Ben Fickland. A young man named Murray Mason came there from Virginia, and on one occasion, being on a trip up the country, intended to board the stage at Lipan Springs, which was about twenty miles from Fort Concho, and come on to Ben Fickland. There was a ranch near the springs but no stage stand, and the stage passed that place in the night. Mason intercepted it, but the driver, not hearing his hail on account of the rattling of the coach, he attempted to climb into it, not wishing to be left. The guard who sat on the seat with the driver, seeing his action, supposed he was a robber, and at once drew his pistol and fired at him. The ball entered the right breast, inflicting a mortal wound, and Mason turned loose and fell to the ground. The driver whipped up rapidly, thinking a band of robbers might be on hand, and when he arrived at Fickland reported killing or shooting a man at Lipan Springs who was attempting to climb onto the stage. Mr. Peters and others knew that Mason intended coming back in the stage on that trip, and at once said they would bet the guard had killed him. A party was at once made up and went back and found it to be so. The people at the ranch had found him, and said he lived an hour and a half after being shot. The body was then brought to Ben Fickland and buried. Mason was a fine young man, and well liked by all who knew him.

Mr. Peters showed the writer the famous gun which killed two Indians at one shot in the hands of John Bowles. It seems to have been a very dangerous kind of a gun, and generally killed things by the wholesale when turned loose. Mrs. Peters let it go off accidentally on one occasion while trying to shoot a rattlesnake, and killed two dogs.

PAUL VOGHT.

Mr. Paul Voght was born in Germany in 1844, came to Texas in 1854, and first settled on the Cibolo, eighteen miles east of Boerne. At that time the following settlers were there, all in a radius of four miles: A. Piper, Henry Voges, John Kabelmacher, William Gerfers, Peter Poss, R. Kürtzer, Sr., G. Obst, all in Bexar County. As a matter of course the Indians made raids, killed people, and stole stock as they did in all parts of the Texas frontier as soon as a settlement was commenced by the pioneers of those days. During one of these raids the Indians shot a horse belonging to Mr. Kabelmacher, and the animal ran home with the arrow in him. The intelligence of this raid was carried to San Antonio and reported to the military there, and a squad of United States soldiers was sent out, who scouted all over the country but failed to locate the hostiles. The old man Voght, father of Paul, had one favorite mare called Minnie, and the Indians passed her by several times without molesting her; the old man said the Indians did not want her, and that she was safe. Paul said, however, that the Indians would get her some time. Next time the Indians came the nag was missed, and the elder Voght, after a diligent search, was compelled to own that the Comanches had undoubtedly got off with Minnie this time. Paul said, "I told you so," but also went and took a look for the missing favorite, and to his surprise, after getting out in the range, heard the familiar sound of Minnie's bell. Arriving near the spot from which the sound emanated, he was sorely puzzled. The country was open, the bell still rattling, but no animal in sight. The mystery was soon solved. The Indians had taken off the bell when they caught the mare and hung it on a bush, and the wind was rattling it. Paul took it home and the old man said, "Yes, Minnie is gone," when he saw it and learned of the circumstance of finding it. Minnie, however, was not gone for good; the Indians rode her and rounded up horses all over the country, and when ready to commence their retreat back to the west, turned her loose and she came back home, to the great joy of the family, especially the old man, who said to Paul, "I knew the Indians did not want Minnie."

On one occasion, when the old man and Paul were out in the woods and without firearms, they suddenly came upon an Indian who had a gun in his hand. He looked at the white man and boy a few moments without saying anything or making any demonstrations of a hostile nature towards them, and then turned and walked slowly off through the forest. Paul now ran home and procured a shotgun, and came back with the intention of hunting the Indian and having a battle with him. He met the old man, however, who took the gun away from him and told him to go home; that if he followed that Indian he would stop behind a tree somewhere and kill him.

On a Sunday morning, when the Indians captured the two Smith brothers, Jeff and Clint, Paul saw them go out across the hills towards Spring Creek. The Indians were followed by the Gorley boys, Sam Patton and one of his brothers, John Lawhon, and August Knippe. In a dense cedarbrake near Curry's Creek the Indians ambushed the party and fired on them, and they were unable to do any damage to them on account of not being able to see them, and finally gave up the pursuit. When the Indians fired on the white men one ball struck the stirrup of August Knippe, split it open, and drove a splinter into his ankle, wounding him severely.

In 1867 the Indians attacked the ranch of George W. Kendall, for whom the county was named, and killed two men there, Schlosser and Baptiste.

In 1868 suspicion rested on Mexicans who lived in the country that they were committing some of the murders and depredations laid to the charge of Indians, and this was almost verified when a man named William Smith unexpectedly walked into a Mexican's house and found him making arrows. He quickly pushed them under the bed, but Smith pulled them out and examined them, and the maker gave no explanation of why he was making them. Not long after this the Bickle family were killed, supposed to be by Indians, and also a man named Spanneberg, at the same time and place, making four people in all. One boy made his escape, but ran so far and exerted himself to such an extent, being closely pursued by a Mexican or Indian, that his lungs were affected, from which he never entirely recovered, although he is living yet, but speaks with a wheezing noise. This wholesale murder occurred five miles east of Boerne. The boy who made his escape came first to old man Zoeller's place and told the news. Many people gathered around the place where the slain people were, and after they were buried a party was made up on the spot to take the trail of the murderers and punish them, whoever they might be, as soon as found. There were men from Kendall and Comal counties, and two or three from Bexar, sixteen in all who went in pursuit. The trail from the scene of the murder was so conflicting, and scattered in so many different directions, that the avengers were more than ever satisfied now that it was Mexicans, and at once commenced rounding up and capturing all of that race then living in the country. Arrows and many other things found in their possession fastened the guilt on them, and their captors had no scruples in executing them, and accordingly seven of them were put to death. Texas at that time was under military rule, and many of the men concerned in the raid on the Mexicans were arrested on affidavits, furnished it is supposed by Mexican women, none of whom were killed. A squad of United States soldiers came out from San Antonio and arrested the men, and they were taken back and confined about two weeks; but when the trial came up there was so much conflicting testimony among the witnesses against the men that they were all turned loose and allowed to go back home.

There is also a noted place in this county, called "Robbers' Camp." Here three horse-thieves were captured in their camp by the settlers and hung. "Dead Man's Hollow," another noted place, is where a horse-thief was killed and his body left there during the Civil war. It is fifteen miles below Boerne, on the Cibolo River, and is now included in the property and pasture of Mr. Chris. Pfeuffer.

Before this, in 1855, the Indians made a raid eight miles east of where Mr. Voght lived, and attacked the Hill ranch, in which they killed four persons—two men, one woman, and one child. One negro woman on the place made her escape.

The Indians made their last raid in Kendall County in 1872, and sixty men gathered under Lieut. Charles Rompel to follow them. The trail led through a dense cedarbrake, and when they were in the midst of it one of the men commenced blowing a bugle which he had with him. The men commenced laughing, and said the man was blowing up the Indians like a man with a horn calling hogs, as they used to do in the olden time! Captain Rompel was a soldier, and wore a sword, which he drew and rushed back furiously on the man and made him desist, and asked him if he was letting the Indians know they were coming. This scout was fruitless of results as far as catching Indians was concerned, for they made their escape.

About the same time a party of Indians made a raid above Boerne, and went out towards the Medina and stole one horse from Mr. Chris. Anderson, on Red Bluff Creek. The horse, however, was recovered. He gave out on the trip, and was left near Castroville.

In 1864 Mr. Voght was in the hills near where Sisterdale is now, late in the evening. He had eaten nothing since morning, and was very hungry. Seeing a deer, he dismounted, put the foot of his horse through the bridle reins, so that he could not run off, and taking cover, slipped upon the deer, thinking if he could kill it he would cook some and eat. When he arrived at a point from which he supposed he would be in gunshot of the game, he cautiously raised his head to look, but the deer was gone, and instead were five or six horses. He kept concealed and peeped, and soon discovered an Indian on one of the horses, lying low on the opposite side, but his hair visible under the horse's neck. Turning now, he ran back towards his own horse, followed by the Indians, who all straightened up in pursuit, yelling as they came. Mr. Voght had no time to throw the reins back over his horse's neck after disengaging the foot, but mounted and fled. The Indians followed in two parties, cut him off on Black Creek, and ran him in on a bluff of the creek. The distance down was ten feet, and the Indians thought sure they had him, but now was the time to take all chances, and he forced his horse over the bluff. His forefeet went into deep gravel as he struck, which kept him from falling or getting hurt. He now rode fifty yards and dismounted, tied his horse, and went back to the protection of the bluff to fight the Indians. They rode close along the bluff over his head and looked at the horse, but were afraid to go to him, for they knew the white man was was near with his gun, but they could not see him and finally went away, and he came out, mounted his horse, and went to a ranch.

Two old bachelors lived for many years in Kendall and Bexar counties, and were among the first settlers. Their names were Hermann and Bartenstein. Their cabins were five miles apart, and the latter lived just across the line in Bexar County. They often visited one another, but neither ever married. Hermann was engaged to a young lady once, but before the wedding day the Indians killed her, and the young man lived to be old and gray alone. Both are now dead.

During the Civil war Mr. Voght belonged to the Third infantry, company of Capt. Hermann Kampmann of San Antonio.

In 1871 Mr. Voght went to Fort Concho with Mr. Hartberger, who had a contract with the government to haul hay, and here he had some more Indian experience. An ox was lost, and the two men went down the river, one on each side, to hunt for him. Hartberger came in contact with an Indian. Voght saw him lay his hand on his six-shooter, and knowing that it was an Indian from his actions that he was about to shoot, commenced trying to disengage a Spencer carbine which was fastened to the pommel of his saddle, but it hung, and was with difficulty released. The Indian in question was on Mr. Voght's side of the river, but under the bank from him, and he could not see him. He ran from the man on the other side and came up the bluff onto the open prairie near Mr. Voght, not knowing he was there, and then dashed passed him at a rapid rate before he got his gun ready. He followed, however, and commenced shooting as soon as he could. His companion dashed across the narrow river and followed, and being on a fast horse soon came in range and also joined in shooting at the Indian with a revolver. In this way a mile or more of country was covered, and finally the Indian disappeared in a thicket. The motion of the running horses spoiled the aim of the white men, and this was one reason they failed to bring the Comanche down. They now rode around the thicket he was in and discovered a large band of Indians and a drove of horses in a valley, and at once went to the fort and reported to the commandant. A force of twenty-five United States cavalry was at once sent out and got on their trail. The Indians had a good start, and before the troops could overhaul them they captured a Mexican train on the El Paso road, killed the drivers, and burned the carts. The cavalry finally rounded them up in a canyon as it was getting dark and stationed guards around, but during the night they escaped, a few at a time, by crawling out and leaving the horses, which the soldiers rounded up when daylight came and carried them back to the fort.

In 1869 Mr. Voght went up the trail to Kansas, and had another experience with Indians. On the way back, and when near Belton, the Indians made a raid in five miles of that place and carried off about sixty head of horses. One very fine one was taken from a man named Blevins. Mr. Voght and about twenty other men took the trail, but soon divided. Part of them kept up the divide between the Colorado and Brazos and the others came up the river, each following different trails, as the Indians had also divided. The first party going up the divide overtook their Indians and got all the horses back except what they rode off, and got back without a fight. The other party also came up with their Indians on Pecan Bayou, but had a battle. The Indians had halted at noon and were shoeing horses with raw hide. A man named Williams was along who had a dog that would trail Indians, and there was no difficulty in following them, whether the trail was plain in places or not. There was one negro along named Ben, who was very brave and a good Indian fighter. The battle soon commenced and was hot for a few minutes, but the Indians were defeated and ran, leaving two dead on the ground and having some wounded. All of the Indians' horses were taken except one, and he was killed in the fight. The negro Ben was wounded in the shoulder with a bullet. He ran in among the Indians and charged one who was on his (Ben's) horse, which had been taken in the raid below, and while firing at the Indian killed his own horse, shooting him through the head with a pistol ball. There were twenty-nine Indians in the fight, and all went off on foot. On the San Saba River, as the men came back, an Indian was discovered sitting on a large rock on the bluff and watching them, but out of range. Voght dismounted and took cover, approaching a tree that was in range, but when he peered around it to shoot, the Indian was gone and could not be found, although a search was made for him. The return trip was very slow on account of the condition of the recaptured horses, which had been badly treated by the Indians. Bread gave out, and the men had to subsist on meat alone. On the Colorado many wild turkeys were seen and several of them killed and carried to a ranch, where the men tried to swap them for meal, but the people there did not have any. The men were four days on the trail of the Indians and much longer in returning, but finally arrived all right, and their wounded negro got medical attention.

Mr. Voght was on this cattle driving trip with Capt. James Ellison. In the Indian Territory, beyond the Washita River, a wagon broke down, and Mr. Voght volunteered to go back to a trading post twenty-three miles distant after an auger to use in fixing it. He went in the night, so as to better avoid Indians, and arrived there about daylight. Several Indians were there, and also two tramps who were traveling across the country on foot. Five dollars was paid for an anger, and Mr. Voght started back on the return trip. He had remained long enough to get breakfast, but the two footmen had started on, going in the same direction, and he calculated to soon overtake them, but before doing so heard two shots ahead and at once left the road and went into a ravine, where he remained concealed all day, and then went on again in the road at night. He soon met a herd coming, and the men with it reported finding the dead bodies of two men on the road. There were the two footmen who had been killed by the Indians, just as Mr. Voght had expected would be their end.

He arrived all right at their camp. He came near being

drowned crossing the Canadian River. A small boat he was in turned over, drifted down the river, and hung up on a poplar tree. Here his foot caught in the fork of a limb, and not being able to release it he was about to drown, when a negro came to him and, diving down, succeeded in getting the foot out, and he made it to shore.

Mr. Voght has a nice place about five miles south of Boerne, and seems to very much enjoy life.

JAMES C. CARR.

COL. J. C. CARR.

Col. James C. Carr was born in Fayette County, Tennessee, and came to Texas January 1, 1845.

Colonel Carr has lived fifty years on the frontiers of Texas, and is an old-time Indian fighter, not only in Texas, but in Oregon and California. In every position and condition of life, whether as a friend, a soldier, or a civilian, Colonel Carr has been equal to the emergencies, and conducted himself in such a manner as to win the respect and approbation of his fellow-citizens. During his long experience on the frontiers of Texas he has exhibited all those qualities of prudence and manhood that are so characteristic of the pioneers of civilization. Colonel Carr, being a newspaper correspondent, is well and favorably known throughout the Rio Grande counties as "Locomotive," "Buckskin," or "Leather Breeches."

Colonel Carr was in the prime of manhood when the tocsin of war sounded in the South in 1861, and with that readiness which has always distinguished his patriotism and love of his adopted State, he immediately enlisted in defense of the homes and altars of the South. He was soon appreciated as a soldier, and elected lieutenant of Company I, Thirty-second Texas cavalry, commanded by Col. P. C. Woods, De Bray's brigade. He participated in all the battles throughout that brilliant campaign, opening at Pleasant Hill and closing at Yellow Bayou.

The following is an extract from Colonel Carr's graphic description of the dedication of the new State capitol, published on the twelfth anniversary of that most interesting occasion to all Texans:

"Twelfth anniversary of the dedication of the new State capitol of Texas. Twelve years ago to-day, May 16, 1888, the broad avenue, well named Congress avenue, in Austin, was filled from sidewalk to sidewalk with gaily caparisoned bands of music, filling the air with sweet sounds and martial notes, preceding in line of march the State officials, invited guests, and military companies with banners waving, marching up and performing military evolutions en route to the capitol building. The sidewalks, the doors and windows of the business houses and offices, were filled with the beauty of Texas, waving handkerchiefs and clapping their hands in applause of some intricate movement of some favorite company, and standing at the head of this avenue, upon which the procession and massing crowds were congregating, the new, graceful, and magnificient capitol building, like a young bride waiting for her lover, and truly were lovers and admirers gathering about her to do her honor in dedicating her a temple—a monument to the magnitude and grandeur of Texas. The building itself and the capitol grounds were filled with the hardy citizens of Texas, mingling with the utmost freedom of our manners with faculties of colleges, members of the learned professions, representative men and women from every part of the State.

"They came from the region of the whispering pines of the East; from the classic banks of the Rio Grande; from the flowery, grass-covered plains, the Panhandle, the Gulf, the interior, the snowy waters of Canada, the tropical Florida and the golden sands of California, to witness the dedication of the new Texas capitol. With its imposing grandeur, elegant design, and beautiful finish—the wonder, astonishment, and admiration of all—this building is mammoth, massive, magnificent, and sublime. That is, it is mammoth in size, massive in structure, magnificent in appearance, and sublime in conception. All combined, with other attractions on that occasion, has made the 16th of May a day long to be held in proud remembrance by every true patriot within our borders,—a day that will ever be commemorated as one of the grandest and most eventful in the history of our State; a day in which the chain of unity that binds the east and the west and the north and the south of our empire State was forged anew, and its binding links of love, pride, patriotism, and mutual interest united and blended all in one might whole. Texas undivided, now and forever.

"Texans who are proud of the immensity of their State can with true justice to themselves be prouder of their beautiful solid granite and marble capitol, which rivals the grandest capitols of the ancient or modern worlds. Yes, it was on the 16th day of May, 1888, in the city of Austin, that the grand pageant of honor commenced to move in beautiful order up Congress Avenue towards the new capitol, preceded by the Masonic fraternity of Sir Knights and members of the grand lodge in brilliant regalia. Then next came the military, fifty-two companies, in gay uniform, martialed in all the pride, pomp, and circumstance of glorious war, the whole being led by the following bands: The famous Mexican National, the celebrated Gilmore, and fourteen others, with over seven hundred instruments, all discoursing the most enlivening martial music. The procession moved up the avenue to the grand stand at 9:30 a. m., where stood in waiting the speakers, Gov. L. S. Ross, Judge A. W. Terrell, Col. Abner Taylor, Hon. Temple Houston, and other orators of the day. This, together with the dedication ceremonies by the assembled members of the Masonic Grand Lodge of Texas, the military, with bands playing and colors flying, made complete a most magnificent scene—the grand dedication of the Lone Star State capitol."

We extract the following from the San Antonio Express in regard to the fair held in San Antonio in November, 1899:

"Col. J. C. Carr ('Locomotive') was boiling over with enthusiasm yesterday over the success of the Fair, and when a reporter for the Express ran across him he was perfectly willing to talk.

"'Yes, sir, she's a success from start to finish; a great, big, rip-roaring, all torn-up success.' That is the way he put it, by way of introduction. Continuing, he said:

"'It was grand in all its departments, representing the various resources of southwest Texas and Mexico. There were the long-horn and improved short-horn; the mustang pony and thoroughbred race horse; primitive and improved machinery; everything from a wooden-axle wheelbarrow to a steam engine.

"'The fair grounds composed a real live city, attractive and instructive. The pictures in the art department were many and varied, not only the one bought by Col. George W. West, entitled "Cattle Drifting," but others, showing beautiful valleys, lakes, foothills, mountains, distant and towering trees appearing to be tossing and bending with the wind, their evergreen branches outlined in a golden mist formed by rain following through the shining sun. There were other pictures of stock of all kinds, not drifting in a snowstorm, but grazing in pastures green. In fact, so real were the paintings that you could almost hear the singing of the birds and see the conquetting butterflies moving among the flowers from bloom to bloom. From the first entrance on the first day, October 28th, to the closing of the gates to-day, the thousands of visitors were all satisfied.

"'Due to what? The management, the committee, and others of this city; to the press; railways, especially the Aransas Pass, International & Great Northern, and Southern Pacific, including the splendid service of our street car lines and the patronage of San Antonio and the people of southwestern Texas generally. I met at the fair and talked with farmers and stockraisers from every county in the southwestern portion of our State, and many told me that at our next fair they would be on hand with exhibits competing for blue ribbons and prize money.

"'On ranger day it afforded me great pleasure to meet so many old veteran rangers whose service dates back into the 40's and 50's,—men who in years gone by protected our frontier settlers from the wild Comanche and other depredating Indians; men whose markmanship settled the warwhoop of the depredators and stayed the tomahawk and scalping knife that had caused cries of murder from women and children. I was also pleased to meet and hear Lanham, Chilton, and Bailey; and to say that the old Confeds enjoyed the talk of that distinguished comrade, Hon. S. W. T. Lanham, does not sorter express it.

"'I must mention and recommend that the Sons of Veterans of this city adopt as a member the Hon. Theo. Harris.

"'On with the San Antonio and Brownsville Railroad, and our International Fair in October, 1900.'"

Colonel Carr resides in the Alamo city, ripe in years and reminiscences of the past.

In the next chapter read Colonel Carr's courtship in Arkansaw.

COL. J. C. ("LOCOMOTIVE") CARR'S FIRST COURT-SHIP IN "ARKANSAW."

It was in the early 40's, when just in my teens, I left my native State, Tennessee, with my father and family, for Texas, by way of Arkansaw, where we were water-bound a few years, and lived up to the time of our departure for this State. All our household goods, on leaving Tennessee, were shipped from Memphis by steamboat down the Mississippi River to be delivered at Alexandria, on Red River. The steamboat was sunk, and in her we lost all we had, save and except a few wagons and ox teams by means of which the Carr family were trying to pull overland through to Texas.

Being delayed in Arkansaw by high water and other things, the Carr family stopped, built houses, bridges, rolled logs, and tried to cultivate the soil and live as others of that section and time did, shut off from the outside world. There were but few people in that country, but neighbors would gather from ten to fifteen miles around to help at a log rolling, house raising, or bridge building. Lived! you bet we did, on hog and hominy, bear meet, deer, turkey, etc. We made our own "licker;" tanned our own leather to make shoes, dressed skins for clothing, used herbs for medicine, made our tar, wagons, trucks, hats (of oat straw), coonskin caps; in fact, produced and made about everything we used. We ground corn for meal on old fashioned steel hand mills, and hand-picked our cotton to make cloth on old fashioned hand-made looms. We made our own furniture, bedsteads, chairs, buckets, baskets, and dishes. We raised our own lard cans,—fat gourds,—from which were made cups, dippers, and a great many things, including gourd-covered buttons for all purposes, which were put on old time hand-made clothing. Socks, stockings, and underwear, such as drawers and other things, were never seen,—that is, we never had such things. What few were had were used only by the very old people. Yet notwithstanding all these primitive conditions, there lived in the State of Arkansaw at that time some of the best people that ever blowed a horn or paddled a canoe.

It was here at a log-rolling and quilting that I met my first love, Miss Peggy Roarer, a handsome young lady about five years my senior. I was only a little up in my teens, while Miss Peggy was just passing out of hers. She was tall and her complexion resembled turkey eggs, a hue of which I was a great admirer. It was at night, and when the log-rolling and quilting were over, when the house was cleared, the fiddle started and the dancing in full blast, I was standing outside the door, like a poor boy at a corn shucking, looking wistfully on, too bashful to go in or say anything after going in. Miss Peggy, who sat on the end of a bench near the door, observed me for some time, and making room for me, said, "Sit down on the bench." After a little while she asked me if I could dance. Greatly embarrassed and stammering somewhat, I finally replied, "Yes'm." So the next cotillion was a "Piny Wood Reel," and she said, "Let's dance," and we did, after which we took our same seat on the end of the bench.

We—I mean myself and Miss Peggy—talked a little and danced again and again; talked and talked, danced and talked, neither Miss Peggy nor myself dancing with anyone else but each other from start to finish, from dark to daylight. Of course we told each other our names and where we lived. She lived ten miles west and I lived ten miles east from where we had on that occasion met.

This was about the middle of December, 1844, and I told her before parting that if I did not come to see her the following Sunday I would Christmas, sure. She kinder put her head over on my shoulder and said, "Oh, that's so long." Bidding each other good-by we parted, one going east, one west.

Think of it! A poor, bashful boy, who only learned to dance with nigger boys in the kitchen after such music as the Arkansas Traveler, Nigger in the Woodpile, Dinah Had a Wooden Leg, Great Big Taters in the Sandy Land, for the first time ten miles from home, for the first time going home after dancing all night with a ringing in his ears, "Oh, that's so long," the last words spoken by his first sweetheart.

Well, long before reaching my home I, too, wanted to put my head up against Miss Peggy's shoulder and whisper, "Yes, yes, any time is too long." My thoughts ran thus, soliloquizing with myself: "Our tan leather is just out and my dressed buckskins are about ready to be made into breeches, and I can have ma plat me a new oat straw hat, and wash my white cotton coat, and well, that's all,—shoes, hat, coat, breeches." I forgot my shirt, apron-checked and nearly new, and a white cotton coat that had only been washed once. That was all, and more than I ever had at one time before in all my life, and when I got them on, and washed and combed back my long hair, placing my new straw hat up and a little to one side on my head, I walked to and fro in front of the glass and fancied myself the best dressed and best looking boy in all that neck o' the woods. True, my naked ankles showed just a little, and I have since that time thought if I only had socks, my pants would have made connection—but I had none. Being accustomed to the old long plow shirt, which was only doffed on Sundays, in this instance a little naked show of ankles didn't amount to much.

I then got my traveling rig together, getting the plow gear and old Charlie (the horse) hitched to an old buggy that had been standing under a tree for six months or more. I assure you it took not only work, but rope and rawhide. However, I made it, and all was ready to start west at 10 a. m. The weather was dark and threatening, and after proceeding a few miles a cold north wind and rain was on me. It grew stronger and finally took away my buggy top, leaving me without any protection. I was not only wet and cold, but hungry, but the thought of Miss Peggy and a good warm supper at least was consoling, and for the time supplied the vacuum in my stomach. Continuing my journey, at about 2 p. m., and a little off my route, I found a house where I stopped and for several hours warmed. Of course I was too late for dinner, but, as before stated, the thought of my loved one and those last words, "Oh, that's so long," and the short end of my day's travel still being westward, I struck out in the rain for Mr. Roarer's, where I arrived about sundown.

On nearing the house I got a glimpse of Miss Peggy. I struck old Charlie with the whip, ran over a hog pen, turned over the buggy, broke off two wheels, and spilt myself out in the mud. The old gentleman, old lady, a little boy, and Miss Peggy, and all the dogs, something less than a dozen in all, got around me. Old man Roarer poured water over me and washed and scraped off the mud, and it was found that I was not otherwise hurt.

The old horse was caught, and of course Miss Peggy introduced me to her father and mother, and we all went into the house. It was still raining and a cold north wind was blowing. Mr. Roarer was from Missouri, and he too, a few years previous, like the other settlers, had got waterbound on his way to Texas.

Mr. Roarer's house was a one-story, one-room log cabin. The chimney and fireplace were of the old style, built with jams or hobs on either side, the fireplace to be used by the women to put cooking utensils on when not in use, such as skillets, ovens, coffee pots, etc. I was seated on one side of said fireplace and Mr. Roarer on the other, with the little boy on his knee, while Miss Peggy and her mother were cooking supper. I was not only wet and cold but hungry, and the old gentleman, appreciating the situation and to make me feel at home, was quite talkative. I was a very bashful boy, and boy-like sat silent. To break somewhat my timidity I got to fumbling with my fingers at the end of an old long-handle frying pan that projected near me from the jam of the fireplace, sticking my finger in and out of the hole in the pan handle. Finally I got my finger in over the joint and couldn't get it out, so there I was.

Of course the old gentleman nor anyone else knew I was fastened to the pan handle, but sure I was, and to make my predicament still worse, about that time the old lady announced supper. Great goodness, what a fix I was in. However, as luck had it, the chair in which I was seated, not being needed at the table, I was made happy by being told. "Well, if you won't have supper, keep your seat." My finger getting worse and worse, what should I do? There was only one remedy—pull it out—and while the family was at supper, with a determined twist, bringing off all the hide, out it came. I carelessly wrapped my hand in my handkerchief so as not to attract attention. The table was then cleared, and the old gentleman resumed his corner with the ladies and little boy in front. Time passed on, and finally the little boy and the two old people went to bed, leaving Miss Peggy and myself up at the fire, all in the same room, as it was a one-room house. There we sat, Miss Peggy and me, she on one side of the fireplace and I in my same seat on the other. I kept thinking what to say and how to say it without the old folks hearing it. On and on the time passed in perfect silence, until finally Miss Peggy ask me what I was thinking about. I told her nothing, and then she said she was thinking of going to bed, and that I could sleep in the back room, she at the same time opening a side door and pointing to a little house out in the field some fifty yeards distant. Said she. "You will find a bed in that room. Good night."

Away I went through the cold north wind. I found the door shut with a wooden pin about a foot long, with a string tied to one end and the other end sticking in a hole. I found that the "back room" was built for a shuck pen or cotton house, and that it was built of round logs, leaving large open cracks. The bed was of a one-legged pattern, a sort of corner scaffold with grass mattress, cotton pillow, and with one thin cover. Nevertheless Miss Peggy called it a back room where I slept. My, but it was cold, cold out there, and my teeth fairly rattled as I got off my cotton coat, hat, and shoes, and lastly, my partly wet and partly dry buckskin breeches. Thinking to break off some of the cold wind, I stuck my breeches in a large crack near my head and bounded into the rude bed, with nothing on but a short, thin, apron-check shirt. Winding up in the aforesaid thin cover, it was with me a stand-off whether I would starve or freeze. However, I lived through the night, and on the following morning, seeing everybody but me up, out of bed I jumped. I looked at the crack first for my breeches, and much to my dismay I found them gone. Upon second thought, I fancied they had fallen through the crack on the outside.

Watching my chance, as the door of my room fronted toward the house, out I went around the corner, with the cold north wind making the tail of my shirt flutter breezily around my waist. I looked hurriedly around for my breeches, but nowhere were they to be found. There I was. What a fix I was in. Presently

I discovered all that remained of my missing breeches, to wit, a few pieces of buckskin, with here and there a button sewed to it, evidence conclusive that my breeches had been chewed up by the cows. Great drops of water larger than blue whistlers came out of my eyes and rolled down my cheecks as I watched back around the corner for another opportunity to get back into my aforesaid back room, which I did, and again got to bed. To my seeming it was "Oh, so long," that dreary time rolled heedlessly on, until finally that same little boy was sent down to wake me up. I told him I was sick. Of course the little boy went back to the house and reported, when the old gentleman Mr. Roarer, a 260-pounder, with a stomach on him like a bass drum, came waddling down and remarked as he got to the door. "Say, young man, get up. I am satisfied you are sick, but get up and come up to the house and drink some coffee."

I sorter turned over, and in a sniffling, stuttering, cold kind of voice, told him I was not only sick, but the cows last night had eaten my breeches.

Of course the old gentleman promptly took in the situation. He got a pair of his own breeches to put on me. It was my only show to get out of bed. The breeches Mr. Roarer gave me were brought from Missouri. They were old-timers, hand-made cotton jeans, dyed with walnut bark and snakeberries, and were built with open barn-door front, or buttoned-up flap. This flap buttoned up on either side, where the pockets went in, and they had galluses. Imagine such a garment on me, a body weighing ninety pounds. When I put them on they reminded me of the first breeches my mother ever made me, even in the bosom, only the opening here was too great. So I about-faced. In other words, I took them off, changed fronts, and put them on again, buttoned up the aforesaid flap around my waist, rolled up the legs, put on my shoes, hat, and coat, and went to the house. Hungry? You bet I was, but too sick and mortified to eat.

Mr. Roarer was out in the horse lot, and Miss Peggy and her mother had just come from the cow pen and set on the table two large buckets of milk. These buckets, like nearly everything else about the place, were doubtless made by Mr. Roarer. They were made of cedar, with large, tall, broad handles put on with wooden peg fastenings, and when these buckets were carried by the handles and set down, the handles would stand erect. In this instance the buckets of milk sat on the table with the tall handles erect. Just about this time some one—a traveler on horseback—was passing in front of the house. All the dogs went barking after the traveler, and the old lady, Miss Peggy, the old gentleman, who was in the yard, and the little boy, all went out hollering at the dogs and looking to see if they could recognize the traveler. Being left alone in the house, and being nearly famished, I stealthily stuck my head under one of said bucket handles and begun drinking milk. Just at that moment the big bucket handle fell, from some cause, striking me on the back of the neck. The blow startled me, and my first thought was that Mrs. Roarer had hit me with a stick. Quickly straightening up, in my excitement I brought the bucket and milk all over my head and face. Blinded by the milk and bucket I fell over a chair, turned over the table, and with it spilt more milk, all amidst a crash of breakfast dishes. The general uproar brought Miss Peggy, the old lady, and the little boy, all slapping their hands and crying. When I did finally extricate myself and get loose from the bucket, there was Mr. Roarer, that old 260-pounder, chasing me around in the house. I verily believe he thought I was an escaped lunatic. But the old gentleman never succeeded in capturing me. I made for the fence, jumped clean over it, mounted old Charley, and cut out.

Taking Greeley's advice, I started west, and never stopped until I was safely on the west side of the Sabine River in Texas, where I have lived on the frontier to this day, June 1, 1900.

J. C. CARR.

Toast of Col. James C. Carr at the reunion of the San Jacinto Veterans, in the Alamo city, April 21, 1900.

"Here is to Texas. Looked upon by all christendom as the largest and grandest State and garden spot of the universe, and to-day throughout our broad land, and even beyond the blue and briny waters, she attracts more attention than any other portion of the habitable globe. Made so by what? The heroes of the Alamo, San Jacinto, and the fairest of God's creation—the ladies—a chivalrous, patriotic, liberty-loving people, and the Press."

THE SIEGE AND FALL OF THE ALAMO.

BY IDA RAND WILSON, ABBOTT, TEXAS.

Kindness of COL. J. C. CARR, *of the Alamo City.*

Eloquent indeed was the letter that Colonel Travis sent;
He had waited, watched and hoped, 'till his strength was nearly spent.
"Compatriots," he had written, "Come, our force is very small,
The enemy are all around us—nothing now divides us but a wall.
They have asked us to surrender, surrender at Santa Anna's will;
We have answered with a cannon shot and our flag waves proudly still.
Though our call may be neglected, as long as we have life and breath,
We'll fight for our country and honor, and it shall be victory or death."
Day after day within the fort in vain for hope they watch and wait,
The Mexican forces increase, and they soon shall know their fate;
The god of day, descending, sank slowly in the west,
Santa Anna's troops cease firing, the Texans pause to rest.
Brave Travis stood among his men, with low-bowed head and folded arm,
For to him had come the knowledge that 'twas the lull before the storm.
Then followed there the grandest scene that our history doth record:
It was one to inspire a poet, it was one to thrill a bard!
"Death is inevitable!" Travis cried. "In vain I've waited day by day,
The reinforcements will never, never come, and help is very far away;
Forgive me if I've raised false hopes; I knew not this should be our fate,
In deceiving you I deceived myself, and see my mistake now all too late!
But we can die but once, my boys," and his voice rang clearly then,
"Who will cross the sword line, boys; who will die with me like men?"
One by one they cross the sword line—even the wounded, all save one.
"Lift me over, too!" cried Bowie, and Travis answered "Boys, well done!"
Against four thousand human fiends what could they hope to do?
It was the hour of midnight, and the great struggle was at hand
That was to bring the Mexicans victory and death to the Texas band.
Hark! Listen! What is the terrible sound they hear?
'Tis the dreadful duello, ringing so loud and clear.
Closer they come and closer, now trying in vain to scale the wall,
But before the Texans' steady fire the advancing soldiers fall.
"Kill them!" ordered Santa Anna, "all who shirk the fight,"
As from the Texans' volleys they try to turn and run in flight.
Again they come, again they slowly try to scale the wall,
But the Texans fight like demons, and the enemy swiftly fall.
The fury of despair had nerved them, and they fight with might and main;
The Mexicans almost falter, and they hesitate to renew the fight again.

But Santa Anna's voice rebuked them. "Advance! Advance!" he cried,
Until the dead numbered hundreds, and the ground with blood was dyed,
But there's a limit to human endurance, and the noble Travis falls.
The Texans' strength is exhausted, and the enemy scale the walls.
One by one they fall, those heroes, and the spark of life has fled—
The last of that brave, gallant band is numbered with the dead.
Oh, God! What pen could picture the sight the sun shone on?
The brave hearts, stilled and silent, would never greet the dawn!
It shone on sights to wring the heart, and cast its golden flood
Across the silent battlefield bathed in life's crimson blood.
One feels a start of horror, it was so like some fearful dream,
The Mexicans won the victory—death and Santa Anna reigned supreme.
And thirsting still for vengeance, did they build a funeral pyre
And consign the brave Texans' bodies to the cruel tongues of fire.
The smoke ascended heavenward as the Sabbath sun sank slowly,
And from that sacred fire arose a smoke both bright and holy,
'Twas a flame that burned in every heart, and for it hundreds died.
It cost the Mexicans many a battle, and humbled Santa Anna's pride,
And this is written to their memory, whoever they may be,
Who gave their lives, their precious lives, that Texas might be free.

COL. T. F. SEVIER.

Came to Texas in 1848.

Theodore Francis Sevier was born February 22, 1832, in the town of Russellville, Logan County, Kentucky, and was related to the famous Col. John Sevier, one of the heroes of King's Mountain, commanding a regiment there on that occasion when the men of Sevier, Shelby, and others routed the British troops with great slaughter and killed their commander, Colonel Ferguson. Colonel Sevier was afterwards elected Governor of Tennessee, and served with distinction and honor in that capacity.

William Peter Sevier, father of Col. T. F. Sevier, served as second officer on the famous privateer Fox, which rendered such valuable and meritorious service during the war of 1812.

The subject of our sketch came to Texas in 1848, when but 16 years of age, and joined the United States army, which was then doing service on the Texas frontier. Young Sevier was an active soldier and did a great deal of hard scouting service, and was in most of the principal Indian battles of that time, in the late 40's and early 50's. In one Indian battle near Laredo fifteen soldiers engaged forty Indians and a most desperate fight took place, in which the Indians were finally driven off, but the troops were terribly cut to pieces, Sevier and two others alone escaping without injury. After this young Sevier became attached to the commissary department of the army, and in 1856 returned to the States and located in Nashville, Tenn., and in 1859 married Miss Mary Benton Douglas, daughter of Gen. Kelsey Harris Douglas, who served with such distinction in the Indian wars of the later 30's, holding his commission as brigadier general from the Republic of Texas. It was he, in conjunction with Gen. Thomas J. Rusk, who fought the decisive battle with the Cherokees in eastern Texas in 1839, in which both of the principal chiefs, Bowles and Big Mush, were killed, and which put an end to the war and forever crushed the power of the great Cherokee nation.

At the outbreak of the Civil war for State's rights Colonel

AFTER THE LAST GUN WAS FIRED AT THE ALAMO.

Sevier was captain of the Rock City Guards, of the Confederate forces, who so often distinguished themselves on hotly contested fields of slaughter, especially at Perryville, Ky. This company was the nucleus for the First Tennessee regiment, being divided into three companies, and Sevier was elected lieutenant-colonel, but was virtually its commander, and served with it until the spring of 1862, when he was made inspector general of Gen. Leonidas Polk's corps. After the death of General Polk he held the same position under Gen. A. P. Stewart, who succeeded Polk. Colonel Sevier participated in most of the battles of the war except Shiloh, and was wounded at Caswell, Ga., while on a tour of inspection.

After the war he was a member of the faculty of the University of the South, at Sewanee, Tenn., remaining with that institution for ten years.

He returned to Texas in 1889, and now resides at Sabinal station, in Uvalde County, and in consort with his son Hal publishes the Sabinal Sentinel.

CAPT. FRED METZGER.

Came to Texas in 1844.

The subject of this sketch was born in Germany, on the Rhine, in 1833, at a place called Nassau, then a dukedom but now belonging to the German empire. William Metzger, great uncle of Frederick, was a rear admiral in the navy of Holland under Prince Orleans.

Mr. Metzger came to Texas with his parents in 1844, as part of Castro's colony. His father had a brewing outfit which he intended to bring on to Castroville or San Antonio, but as transportation was not readily obtained, the family had to remain some time in tents, and all became sick at Port Lavaca, and they left there and went to Galveston, and there the elder Metzger died, and in 1846 Frederick enlisted in the army of the United States to fight Mexico, in the company of Captain Hornsby, Colonel Bonham commanding the regiment and General Lally the brigade. He went through the war and was in many battles and skirmishes, the hardest being at the village of Huamantla, where Lieut.-Col. Sam Walker of the Texas troops was killed. Metzger was near him when he fell, and says that he had a canteen hanging over his shoulder, and the ball went through this first and then through his body, and that he fell in his tracks and died at once. The body of the gallant officer was brought back to Texas and buried at San Antonio. Another hard fight was at the National Bridge, where Captain Hornsby had twenty-five men out of his company killed. One sergeant was shot in the knee by a brass ball while resting on one knee to fire, and blood poison set in and killed him. Another man was shot in the right eye, the ball passing through the side of the head and coming out of the ear. Lally's brigade captured the National Bridge fort.

While in Mexico Mr. Metzger visited the prison of Perote, where Big Foot Wallace and other Texans were confined a few years before, and says it was a very strong place, and at the corners of the prison were large mortars for throwing shells that a man could crawl into. He also examined the place where some of the captive Texans dug under the walls and made their escape.

Mr. Metzger came back to Galveston after the war was over, and in 1849 set out for California, but was taken sick at Fort Leavenworth and all of his outfit was stolen, as he had no one to take care of it for him. After many reverses, in 1851 Mr. Metzger was back at Galveston and sailed for the West Indies, and at Martinique saw some of Walker's men who went on the ill-fated expedition to South America, where the "gray-eyed man of destiny" met his fate and his men scattered. This party claimed French protection to save themselves and remained there some time, but finally went aboard of the United States sloop-of-war Portsmouth and sailed away, Metzger going on the same ship. He made the acquaintance of one of Walker's men named John Ecker, and they afterwards served in the same cavalry troop on the Texas frontier.

They enlisted in the United States service in Company D, Captain Enos. The regiment was commanded by Colonel Parmer, and was ordered to Texas. Hardee was lieutenant-colonel, Pap Thomas major, Robert E. Lee captain, Earl Van Dorn captain, Kirby Smith brevet major. Oaks was captain of Company C. Eagle lieutenant, John B. Hood adjutant, and Menter quartermaster. These were some of the distinguished men who served on both sides in the Civil war with whom Mr. Metzger served on the Texas frontier. Part of these troops went to Fort Mason and others to Camp Verde, in Kerr County, Metzger coming to the latter place. Captain Whiting also cammanded a company in this consignment of troops to Texas.

Soon after arriving at their Camp Verde quarters a runner came and informed them that the Indians were in the country, and thirty men were at once sent out under the command of Lieutenant Van Camp, with Polly Rodrigues as guide and trailer. The Indian raid was in the Medina valley, fifteen miles south of the post, and when the troops arrived on the scene a band of settlers led by F. L. Hicks was already on the trail and had fought the Indians at the head of the Medina and defeated them, Mr. Hicks killing the chief in the skirmish. Rodrigues found the body of this chief and scalped him and took his head dress, and afterwards let the scalp hang attached to his bridle. The soldiers followed on after the Indians three days, but could not overtake them. This was in 1857.

Lieutenant Van Camp afterwards went on the expedition with Major Van Dorn to the northwest, and was killed in the great Indian battle at the Wichita village.

In 1857 the Indians again came down on a raid, this time southeast from the post in the Guadalupe valley, and again a runner was sent to notify the soldiers. A detachment of twenty-five men was sent out under Sergt. William McDonald, Polly Rodrigues again being guide and trailer. The settlers, as before, were on the trail, among whom was Dr. J. C. Nowlin and a man named Moore. Among the soldiers a strange thing occurred just before they got the news of the raid. A man named John Martin said to Metzger, "I had a vision last night, in which I saw my sister, who lives in Baltimore, come to my tent door and beckon to me with her hand, and begged me to come home." Metzger said, "You get a furlough and go home."

When the news of the Indian raid came Metzger said to Martin, "You had better not go. Something will happen to you. Go home." Martin, however, said he would go this time, and then go home. The soldiers and citizens got together and followed the Indians in a northwest direction towards Kickapoo Springs, which was in the Fort McKavett country, and came upon them near the springs. The guide was ahead, and when he gave the alarm the men all rushed in and captured the mules and horses of the Indians, but the latter met the whites bravely, and although being surprised in camp and largely outnumbered, gave them a sharp fight, and the horse ridden by Dr. Nowlin was soon killed. Part of the men dismounted, among whom was Metzger, and opened fire from their horses. Jim Lafoyo, bugler, ran his horse to the left and engaged an Indian at close quarters and attempted to fire at him with a pistol, but it failed several times, and the Indian shot him in the stomach with an arrow, which would have killed him but for the intervention of an overcoat which was rolled up and in front of him, and the wound was only slight. The bugler after receiving the wound threw his pistol at the Indian's head and left him. Metzger now ran around on that side, and seeing an Indian, fired at him and he fell, but could not tell whether he killed him or not, and he then ran back past the dead horse of Dr. Nowlin and saw Sergeant McDonald fighting an Indian with his gun empty and trying to keep him off by pointing the empty weapon at him. Metzger went to his assistance and killed the Indian, who was the chief. John Martin fell mortally wounded to the right of where Dr. Nowlin's dead horse lay. The 'fight was soon over, and the Indians ran and scattered. Metzger picked up the pistol of the bugler, and also secured the scalp and fine head dress of the chief, which was covered with silver plates, one of which he afterwards had adjusted to the handle of a walking stick with his name engraved on it.

After the fight the wounded man Martin was carried to Fort McKavett, where Dr. Nowlin and the post surgeon there did all they could for him, but he died and was buried there. On the way to the fort Jim Lafoyo rode behind the wounded man and held him on his horse, as he was shot in the stomach and could not lie on a stretcher.

About two months after this Mr. Metzger was in another fight with Indians in the Guadalupe mountains. Three Indians were killed, one of whom was a squaw. One man named McKeen was shot in the back with an arrow, and Metzger's horse was wounded in the neck with an arrow.

When the Civil war broke out Mr. Metzger was captain of a frontier company commissioned by General Huffman. When these were disbanded Captain Metzger joined Colonel Duff's regiment, and was elected orderly sergeant in Capt. Frank Robinson's company, John C. Ware being lieutenant.

Captain Robinson is now county judge of Uvalde county. John C. Ware lives in Sabinal Canyon, and Captain Metzger lives in Hondo City, Medina County.

THE GILLELAND CHILDREN CAPTURED BY INDIANS.

1837.

In 1837 Johnston Gilleland and his wife, Mary Gilleland, came from Pennsylvania and settled in Refugio County, near the Don Carlos ranch. They had two children, Rebecca and William. Mr. Gilleland soon joined a ranging company commanded by Captain Tumlinson, and materially aided in protecting the frontier from hostile Indians.

One evening in 1840 Mr. Gilleland and his wife and children were a short distance from the house, about sunset, when suddenly a band of Indians with a loud warwhoop dashed upon them. The father and husband made a run for the house to get his gun with which to protect his family, the others following, but he and his wife were killed before they could get there, and the children captured and placed on horses and carried off, screaming. The Indians did not like this crying, and said they would cut off their hands and feet if they did not stop it, but an old Indian woman took their part and made the other Indians let them alone. The Comanches did not stop, but pushed on through the settlement all night, and the first halt they made was after daylight. During their flight, however, a band of soldiers and a squad of rangers, among whom was "Mustang" Grey, had struck their trail and were in hot pursuit of them, and came upon them during this halt and a furious battle commenced. The Indians soon ran and went into a dense forest, and here lanced the boy and knocked the girl in the head and left them both for dead; but they soon returned to consciousness. They had been taught to ask God to help them when in trouble, and now prayed for that deliverance. They knew that white men were not far off, for they saw them fighting some of the Indians while others were running into the bottom with them. The girl was the oldest, being eight years, while her brother was only six, and badly wounded and unable to walk, but the brave child took him in her arms and made an attempt to get out of the timber so that the white men could see them. Her strength soon failed and she sank down, but after resting she renewed the effort and kept on in this way until she came to the edge of the prairie, and saw many horsemen on it, riding about. Thinking they were Indians, she took up her little brother again and ran back into the brush and hid. The soldiers and rangers knew the Indians had the two children, for they had been informed by special courier of the killing and capture. The company of soldiers was commanded by Capt. Albert Sidney Johnston, afterwards the famous Confederate general, and he had sent out this squad under Lieut. Hannum to follow the Indians, and they had met Mustang Grey and some of Captain Price's rangers, who had seen the Indians, but were not strong enough to warrant an attack upon them, and were coming to Johnston's camp, but all now went together, and the battle above narrated was the consequence. The scattered men on the prairie were hunting for the children and calling them, not knowing what the Indians had done with them. When they came to the edge of the woods and called them loudly by name the little girl, knowing now it was friends, arose from the ground where she was lying hid, and lifting her little weak and badly wounded brother in her arms, carried him out to the men, many of whom shed tears at the sight as they raised them to their saddles and hurried them back to camp. Here they were kept until the following day and then carried to the Don Carlos ranch, and the little boy placed under the treatment of Drs. Axsom and Hammond. The girl was conveyed by General Johnston to Victoria, and was there joined by her brother when he recovered, and both placed in the care of a Presbyterian minister, Dr. Blair, and his good wife. They were like a father and mother to them.

Many years after this the boy accidentally shot himself in the hip, badly shattering it, but recovered from it and survived both wounds many years, but was always a sufferer.

The girl married a man named Fisher, and has relatives in Sabinal Canyon—the family of Orceneth Fisher, who was a Methodist preacher, and died there about 1880.

THE ETTER FAMILY.

Came to Texas in 1851.

Samuel Etter, Sr., was born in Switzerland in 1801, and started from Bremen, Germany, to Texas in 1851, in the fall of that year. His wife was Elizabeth Rocbei, and they had five sons and five daughters, namely: Samuel, Jr., John, Peter, Jacob, Gottlieb, Mary, Elizabeth, Anna, Rosina, and Magdalena. Mr. Etter was first under a contract to settle in the highlands of Illinois, a man named Grossniklaus being the head agent for that colony, but another agent advised him to settle at San Felipe, and Peter Heinerman, who was on the same ship, advised a different locality, which was Castro's colony in southwest Texas, whither he was himself bound. Mr. Etter decided on the latter suggestion, and came on to Galveston in a two-masted ship, the Herschel, having been on the ocean seven weeks, and landing on Christmas day. The trip to San Antonio was uneventful, and here Mr. Etter remained for some time and rented nine acres of land from Mr. Groesbeck, on Garden Street, and cleared it and planted a crop on it. There was a new house on this tract of land at the time, and all of it could have been bought for $400.

After the crop was planted Mr. Etter left the boys to cultivate it, and came on out to Castroville and bought, for $1.50 per acre, 350 acres of land from Charles Montel, which was situated five miles east of Castroville, north of the San Antonio road. Here he built a house out of elm planks, cutting the logs and hauling them to the sawmill of Mr. Montel on the Medina River, and having them converted into lumber. The family came out from San Antonio when it was finished, and occupied the new home, which was pleasantly situated and in a very desirable locality, and a farm was soon opened up in the black, rich prairie soil.

Mr. Etter was not bothered much by Indians, but had to keep on the lookout, and lost one horse during a raid. In this settlement on the east side of the river, but badly scattered, were James Brown, Mr. Woodward, who lived back towards Castroville, but below the road, old man Adams, who lived on Medio, towards San Antonio, and Sam Lytle, who lived low down on the Medina at the mouth of Protrancko Creek, and these were the nearest neighbors. Big Foot Wallace and Jeff Bond at this time had left their place down on the west bank of the Medina and settled on the Chicon, still further west. Jacob Droitcourt lived on the east bank of the Medina, opposite Castroville, and this was the only house between Mr. Etter and town. A battle with Indians took place seven miles north of Mr. Etter's place, in which a young lad named Jac Huffman killed two, but Mr. Etter was in no fights with them. He stayed close about home and attended to his farm, and he and his wife both died there at a good old age. Mr. Samuel Etter, Jr., the oldest son, now lives on the old place, and his wife, who was Augusta Tschoepe, was born in Prussia in 1833, and had four brothers—Louis, William, Rudolf, and Henry. Her sisters were Agatha, Louise, Lena, and Bertha, the latter dying in Germany six months before the balance of the family left the old home for Texas. She was a grown young lady, and cried all the time when the decision was made to hunt a new home across the water, and continually said that she would never go to Texas, and pined away and died. There were ten of the family on board the ship Von Fink when the start was made, which was in 1852, and they were nine weeks crossing the ocean. Among the passengers two children died and one was born on board the ship, and one great storm was encountered. Mrs. Etter liked sailing on the ocean, and was sorry when land was made, and would like to have gone on nine weeks more. The ship anchored in front of Indianola, on the coast of Texas, on the 14th of December, 1852, but could not come nearer than five miles on account of its size and lack of deep water, and had to unload passengers and freight on two schooners and convey them into port.

The trip from the coast was made in ox wagons to New Braunfels, in Comal County, and they arrived there on the 1st of January, 1853, and stayed three months, and then moved down into Guadalupe County, where Mr. Tschoepe was employed by Colonel Young to make furniture. Some time after this he bought land on Long Creek, two miles from Schumanville, in Guadalupe County, at $2 per acre, and moved the family out there, about 1884, but the old man and his son Louis, who was also a good wood workman, stayed in Seguin about three years off and on, from 1884 to 1887, and during this time did a good deal of carpenter work for General Jefferson, and Louis built the Faust mill in New Braunfels, but died just before it was completed, and the father and mother of Mrs. Etter died on the farm near Schumanville.

Before Louis died, however, the Civil war came on, and he and his brother Rudolf joined Sibley's brigade and were in nearly all of the battles in which it was engaged during the campaign in New Mexico and Louisiana, Rudolf being in twenty-two engagements and Louis in nineteen. Louis had his horse wounded badly once and himself twice slightly, and Rudolf, who belonged to the Val Verde battery, which he helped to capture, had two horses killed under him.

Lieutenant Sayers was adjutant to General Green and Rudolf was assistant, and he and Louis were held in high estimation by the adjutant, the former staying in the tent with him and General Green. When provisions became very scarce, and only one piece of bread was in the general's part of the commissary, he divided it into four parts, for himself, Sayers, Rudolf, and the negro cook.

Rudolf still lives in Guadalupe County, as also does Louise, who married Mr. Wolfort. Lena, who married Mr. Lindeman, died in Guadalupe County, and her children are there now. Agatha lives in Victoria; she married Mr. Schadwitz. Mrs. Etter first married Mr. Blum, and he died in Lockhart. She married Mr. Etter in Medina County.

Jacob Etter married Katy Keller, and she was the first child baptized in Castroville and the second one born. The first one born died in a few days. When Castroville had its fiftieth anniversary Mrs. Jacob Etter was placed in a wagon in the procession with the godmothers around her, and another wagon was for the oldest men. Judge Herman Haas made a speech in nice form showing the difference in the early settlement and the present,—the hostile Indians, rude shelters and wagons, farm implements, etc.

THEODORE THE SHEPHERD KILLED BY INDIANS.

During the first settlements on the Sabinal, near where the station is now, but in what year we are not able to find out, a young man named Theodore was killed by Indians. His other name also is not now remembered, but his taking off was very sad, and some of the old settlers remember the circumstance. At this time James Davenport lived at what was afterwards known as the Thompson place, about four miles north of the present station of Sabinal, on the road to Sabinal Canyon. This young man Theodore was hired to Mr. Davenport to herd sheep, and on the day that he met his death was up the Sabinal River several miles, and there came in contact with a band of Indians. The circumstance of his killing is not known, only by signs afterwards discovered. When he failed to come in at the proper time with the sheep a search was made for him, and he was finally found sitting against a hackberry tree, dead. His trail from the tree led back up the river nearly a mile, marked in many places by blood spots, to the place where the Indians had chased and shot him with arrows. Why they did not pursue and finish him on the spot is not known, for the country was tolerably open. He evidently traveled as long as his strength would permit down the river towards the Davenport ranch, and then, sitting down, leaned his back against the tree and died. His people lived on the Medina, and were notified of his death and the body buried under the tree where he was found. His people, however, soon came and removed the remains to his home and reinterred them.

At the time Theodore was killed Mr. George Dillard and his father-in-law, Mr. Chris. Kelley, had hauled a load of cypress lumber from Sabinal Canyon, where at that time was a sawmill, and unloaded it in a liveoak grove on the opposite side of the river lower down, but not a great ways from the spot where Theodore died, and narrowly escaped coming in contact with the Indians themselves. After finding out the circumstance of this

THE TREE UNDER WHICH THEODORE THE SHEPHERD DIED.
From Photo by Miss Edith Dillard.

raid and killing of the young man they abandoned the idea of settling where they had unloaded the lumber, which was at first their intention, and moved it back to the canyon, where it was more thickly settled. Mr. Dillard afterwards settled on the spot where Theodore died, his house being about one hundred yards north of the hackberry tree. In the picture the view is east towards the barn and hay stack, and the dwelling not visible. Mr. Dillard sold this place and now lives further out in the prairie, where he runs a farm and ranch.

WATKINS AND RICHARDSON KILLED BY INDIANS.

1860.

In August, 1860, B. F. Watkins and J. H. Richardson started from the mountains in the Frio and Sabinal country to Uvalde for the purpose of taking the oath of allegiance to the Confederate government. After crossing the Frio River they went into camp for the night about eight miles from Uvalde, and during the night or early next morning they were attacked and killed by Indians. Some time during the day after the killing a man named George Robinson, also on his way to Uvalde, came upon the bodies. They were most horribly mutilated and stripped and fifteen arrows were scattered around, besides what were in the slain men, showing a stand-off was made with the Indians for some time. Robinson galloped on to town with the news, and a party came out and brought the remains of the unfortunate settlers in and buried them in the cemetery at Uvalde. The stone which marks the spot was put there by friends and relatives of the deceased.

George Robinson, mentioned above, was the son of Henry Robinson, Sr., the famous scout and Indian fighter of the Southwest, and who was finally killed by the Indians in Nueces Canyon. The same Indians who killed him and Henry Adams at the same time attacked the Robinson ranch and were fought and kept off by George Robinson, then a boy, who succeeded in shooting two of them and was himself wounded in the arm by an arrow. A family named Kelsey was in a camp near by and one of the girls was wounded and scalped by the Indians, but was carried to Fort Inge and by careful attention recovered. Judge James McCormick, who still lives in Uvalde County, helped to remove the unfortunate girl to the fort and then helped to wait upon her until she recovered. Henry Robinson, Jr., another son of Henry, Sr., was killed by Indians near where the ranch of Joe Richarz now is, at the foot of the mountains on the Frio. This party of Indians was pursued by a squad of men from Sabinal

THIS STONE MARKS THE SPOT WHERE WATKINS AND RICHARDSON WERE KILLED BY THE INDIANS.

Canyon under command of Capt. John C. Ware, who overtook them and had a fight, in which the horse of Demp Fenley was killed. Among others along was Joe Kelley, Jack Kelley, and Wilson O'Brien.

ANCESTORS OF THE AUTHOR.

The name of Sowell, or Sewell proper, is of Celtic origin, and originated in the highlands of Scotland many centuries ago. In the Scottish war against King Edward of England they followed the fortunes of Sir William Wallace, and when he was taken and executed they espoused the cause (in an humble way as private soldiers) of Robert the Bruce, and helped to retain the crown to him on the bloody field of Bannockburn. When Oliver Cromwell broke up the British Parliament and raised an army to oppose King Charles, the Scottish Sewells joined his standard, and seven of them distinguished themselves in the charge of the highlanders at the great English battle of Lynn.

They came to the colonies of America at an early day, and two brothers settled on the Yadkin River in North Carolina, and their descendants moved to Virginia and Tennessee. The Virginians retained the original name of Sewell, while the Tennesseeans, by some cause, in after years spelled it Sowell. When the war of the Revolution broke out in 1776 our branch of the family were in North Carolina, and many of them joined the army of Washington. John Sowell, great-grandfather of the writer, was severely beaten by the Tories on account of a speech he made on one occasion at a country schoolhouse, in which he denounced them in most bitter terms.

We were also related to the Champes of Virginia, one of whom, John Champe, was a noted patriot soldier and warm friend of "Light Horse" Harry Lee, under whom he served. On one occasion Champe penetrated the British lines and undertook to capture Benedict Arnold after his treason and bring him back to the American lines, but failed on account of a violent storm which set in just as he had all of his plans laid.

John Sowell, grandfather of the writer, was born in Rutherford County, Tennessee, and when the war of 1812 broke out joined the army of Gen. Andrew Jackson and fought the Indians at the "Horseshoe Bend." There were many other Sowells in the army, one of whom, Shadrach, a powerful man physically, with long arms, killed three Indians with his clubbed rifle at the

ASA J. L. SOWELL.

breastwork of logs. William and Louis were both killed in battle with the Indians, the latter at Mackinaw Island and William under General Harrison, probably at Tippecanoe, for many of the Sowells fought in that battle. Joe Sowell, a captain of rangers, was killed in a fight with Indians in Fannin County, Texas, and his son John captured by the Indians and kept three years.

When the army of General Jackson went to New Orleans, grandfather John and others of the connection went with it and fought in the battle there. Grandfather was a gunsmith and made thirty rifles to arm a Tennessee company, and they were used at New Orleans.

My father, Asa J. L. Sowell, was born in Davidson County, Tennessee, in 1821, near the home of General Jackson, called "The Hermitage." Also four of my uncles was born there,— Andrew Jackson, William, Lewis, and John. Andrew was the oldest and was named by the wife of General Jackson after her distinguished husband, who was a warm friend of our family. This is where we get the family name of Andrew Jackson. I was named for my uncle, and have nephews named for me. My father's middle name was Lee, named for "Light Horse" Harry Lee, who was the father of Robert E. Lee, the great leader of the armies of the Confederacy in the Civil War.

From Tennessee grandfather moved to Missouri, and from there to Texas as part of the colonists of Green De Witt, arriving at Gonzales, Texas, in 1829. Here he put up a shop and made and mended guns, and also made a knife for James Bowie, which took his name.

When the Texas revolution broke out in 1835 and the battle of Gonzales was fought, grandfather made slugs of bits of iron to load the cannon with. His sons, Andrew, William, Lewis, and John, were in the fight, my father being too young to go. In the war with Mexico and the Indians Andrew became a noted scout and trailer, and was a companion of "Kit" Carson, with whom he swapped hats on one occasion. He served under Hays, Burleson, Caldwell, McCulloch, Mason, and Calahan, and was in the battles of Gonzales, Plum Creek, Blanco, Sabinal, Nueces, Mission Conception, Powder House, Grass fight, Council House, and Salado. In the Civil War he served in the Confederate army.

A. J. SOWELL AS A RANGER, 1870.

THE WRITER IN 1900. LAID DOWN THE WINCHESTER
AND TOOK UP THE PEN.

The Sowell league was located in the bend of the Guadalupe River below the present town of Seguin, and they helped to build that place in 1838. My father served as a ranger under Hays, McCulloch, and Calahan, and was the orderly sergeant of Capt. Henry McCulloch's company. He was the first district clerk of Guadalupe County, and afterwards at various times held every office in the county,—assessor, sheriff, mayor, county judge, etc.

My great-grandfather on the side of father's mother was John Carpenter, who was one of Francis Marion's men, and was killed in a fight with the Indians and Tories in the war of the Revolution. His daughter, my grandmother, was the fifth white woman to cross the San Marcos River in Texas.

My mother was Mary Mildred Turner, born in Nashville, Tennessee, and daughter of Major William S. Turner, who served on General Jackson's staff in the militia, and served under him in the war with the Creek Indians, participating in the battles of Talladega, Tallahassee, Horseshoe, and New Orleans. In the battle of Talladega he was twice wounded with arrows in the neck and head. His wife was Elizabeth Smith, and among her people were noted lawyers and doctors; of the former was Calvin Smith and the latter Dr. Goodlow Smith. Among the Turners were also noted lawyers, one of these being Jack Turner, of Nashville, Tennessee. My mother's brothers were William, Calvin, Hardin, and John, and one sister, Lucinda. They came to Texas in 1840. My father's sisters were Sarah and Rachel. My mother's great-grandfather, James Turner, was Governor of North Carolina in the early days, and one of her ancestors, John Turner, came over to America in the Mayflower.

There were nine children of our family, four boys and five girls, as follows: Andrew Jackson (myself, eldest), Leroy Polk, Pleaman Smith, and John; sisters, Adaline (older than myself), Lucy, Isabel, Laura, and Molly.

I was born on the 2d day of August, 1848, near Seguin, and when quite young father moved to the Blanco, in Hays County, and here in 1853 I came near being captured by an Indian. Five of us children,—my sister Adaline and three of Uncle Andrew's children, Asa, Elizabeth, and Mary,—were on a small hill near uncle's house getting cedar wax and pulling the bark from a slippery elm tree, when suddenly my sister says, "Look there;

what an ugly man," and ran. We all took one look and started, too. The Indian was coming out of a cedar brake very near, and almost got his hands on me, as I was the youngest and short-legged, and fell several times while running across an open glade on top of the hill. Our screams soon brought father and uncle Andrew with their guns, and the Indian ran back into the brake before they could get a shot at him, but they trailed him about a mile.

I served the State of Texas as a ranger in the Wichita campaign of 1870-71, and experienced some hard service in the northwest, almost freezing on several occasions in sudden blizzards while scouting in the Panhandle. On one occasion we spent three days and nights in a draw or depression of the prairie while a fierce storm of snow and sleet swept across the plain. Our only chance for fire was a few stunted mesquites, which we burned to the last twig and root. On another occasion we were caught and spent a fearful night in a sleet that cut and stung almost like shot, and our blankets and slickers were a sheet of ice. When daylight came my horse had succumbed to the blast, and I was a dismounted ranger. At another time I lay on the frozen ground with pneumonia, and sleet falling constantly all over me, and my hair frozen fast to my blanket; but I had true and brave companions with me who carried me 100 miles across the ice-covered prairies to Big Sandy Creek, where we went into camp in the heavy timber.

In 1871 I was detailed with fifteen others as scouts and was sent to the outside limit to watch along the spurs of the Wichitas for the Kiowas and Comanches, who were trying to beat back the settlers in Montague, Wise, and Jack counties, and it was while on this service that we had that terrible fight at the "Keep Ranch" in Wise County, ten rangers and one citizen from Montague County fighting forty-one Kiowas and Comanches on the open prairie for more than an hour, and witnessed by terror-stricken women and screaming children. In the end we were the victors, killing and wounding more than one-third of their number, including two chiefs in the slain,—Sittanke and Oska Horseback,—who both died on the field fighting us at only a few yards distance. Nearly half of our men were stricken but none fatally, although the life of Billy Sowell hung long in the bal-

THE WOUNDED RANGER.
Helping a Comrade at the "Keep Ranch" Battle.

ance, he having been shot badly in the side with a bullet. Our gallant little sergeant in command of the scouts, Edward H. Cobb, had his horse shot from under him, but mounted the horse of the chief Sittanke, who had just been killed in our front, and his horse broke through our squad to the rear.

I was on the forty-four days' scout, and after the fight between the cowboys and Indians in Battle Creek Canyon, which we tried to get into but were overrun and forced back by 300 head of stampeded horses, myself and Dan Woodruff were sent out by Sergt. Joel R. Payne, who was in command of this scout, as spies, and were ambushed near the head of Foyle's Creek, I think likely not far from where Albany is now, either in Taylor or Shackleford County. I can not tell, as I have never been back there since. Anyway, we had to run and keep them off for six miles, and our horses almost died under us, but we finally got away. On this same scout one night we got torn up in a cyclone and four saddle horses and a pack mule got away, my horse being one of the four, and we had to walk 151 miles and live on game without salt until we got to camp, consuming fifteen days during the time. I was also one of the dozen scouts who rode all night facing a sleet to succor the Keenon ranch, but

TEXAS RANGERS TRAILING INDIANS.

when we arrived the Comanches had done their bloody work, and seven women and children lay scattered around, scalped and mutilated.

This family history I suppose will be of more interest to my numerous relatives than other people, but here it is.

My father died at Seguin, as did also my mother and sister Lucy. Brother John died in Parker County at sister Isabel's. Pleaman Smith is a lawyer and lives at Seguin, and served his district in the Twenty-fourth Legislature as a Democratic nominee. Leroy Polk lives in San Antonio and is engaged in the mercantile business. Laura and Molly live in the Panhandle. Laura married Lem Smithers; Molly, Cliff Abbott, sheriff of Dallam County; Isabel married Milford Nichols, now deceased; John married Ida Rogers; Leroy married Almedia Tinsley; the writer married her sister, Mary Lillian; Pleaman Smith married Henriette McLean; Adaline married James A. Sowell, now dead. He helped to capture the Harriet Lane at Galveston and was wounded in Louisiana, and was in many battles there.

Father was a Royal Arch Mason, and was buried by that order. It was the largest funeral procession that ever went out of Seguin.

THE LOST VALLEY FIGHT.

1874.

The following facts of one among the most desperate Indian battles ever engaged in on the Texas frontier were furnished the writer by Mr. Walter M. Robinson, one of the participants, and who still survives and distinctly remembers all of the terrible scenes through which he passed and witnessed on that day.

This battle was fought on July 12, 1874, in "Lost Valley," Jack County, between the Texas rangers, thirty-five in number, commanded by Maj. John B. Jones and Captain Stephens, and 200 Comanche and Kiowa Indians, as near as their number could be estimated during a five hours battle, the Indians being led by Chief "Lone Wolf." On the day before the battle Major Jones, who was in command of all the rangers on the frontier, and who went from post to post with an escort inspecting the different companies and paying them off or adjusting any other matters needing his attention along the border, arrived at the camp of Captain Stephens, in command of a ranger force stationed in Jack County, northwest from Jacksboro about fifty or sixty miles. On July the 12th a report came to Captain Stephens that Indians were in the country, and Lieutenant Wilson was detailed with six men by the captain to take a scout into the vicinity from which Indians were reported and make an investigation, Walter Robinson, a member of Capt. Rufe Perry's company, being one of the members of this scout. The detail proceeded about six miles and came upon a large Indian trail which denoted a raiding band of Indians of unusual large force, and a runner was sent back to camp by the lieutenant to inform Major Jones and Captain Stephens of the fact, and advising a force to be sent out of all the men that could be spared from camp to take up the trail of the Indians and give them battle in case they could be overtaken. In the meantime, while the messenger was speeding on his mission, Lieutenant Wilson and the other five men followed slowly on the trail, and in about twelve miles Major Jones and Captain Stephens with thirty men overtook them, making the ranger force now about thirty-five all told.

The combined force now kept on the trail rapidly until twenty minutes before 12 o'clock a. m., when they came upon the Indians in a timbered but rough and rocky country in the Lost Creek valley, where the Comanches and Kiowas had placed their force in ambush to try issues with the rangers whom they had discovered on their trail. Before doing this, however, the wily chief had divided his force into three bands and crossed and re-crossed Lost Creek several times on purpose to disconcert and bother the rangers and cause them to scatter their force in pursuit, following the meanderings of the different trails, but finally he consolidated his whole force in a mott of timber on the west side of the creek. Before locating the Indians Major Jones divided his force into three squads to follow as many different trails, but admonished each party to remain in touch with each other and be ready at any moment to reunite in case of an emergency. The major with thirteen men went to the right and skirted around the foot of some hills and came in close range of the timber in which the whole Indian force was concealed, and was fired on by them, which was the first intimation he had of their presence. This volley wounded some horses, and on the heels of it came the charge, the Indians leaving cover and attacking Major Jones with great fury in the open prairie, but he stood his ground and the gallant squad around him opened up a hot fire from their Winchesters into the very faces of the yelling and advancing savages. The other two parties of the ranger force were not long in rushing to the scene of the fierce fight which was now being inaugurated, and the main battle opened with terrific fury on both sides, the yelling of the Indians almost drowning the noise of the carbines, which popped and cracked like a canebrake afire, and in a few moments Lee Corn was badly wounded with a bullet and his horse killed, besides other horses being wounded. A sweeping charge was now made by the rangers on horseback almost in among the Indians, who were thickly massed, and such was their rapid and fatal fire both with revolvers and Winchesters that the Comanches and Kiowas gave way and started in rapid and disordered flight through open ground towards the hills, followed by the now yelling rangers, who killed them here and there as they were overtaken on slow horses, or having them killed or disabled under them. In about a mile another skirt of timber was passed through, in which was a ravine made by washings from the hills, but the Indians crossed this and kept on through an open glade for a hundred yards or more, and then made a stand on the side of the hill amid rocks and bushes and opened a severe fire on the rangers from cover, which checked them, and they wheeled back to the ravine and there dismounted. During this fire from the Indians the horse ridden by Walter Robinson was killed, being hit by five bullets, and he went back to the ditch on foot, and a gallant young ranger of Stephens' company named Glass was killed, falling in front before the turn back was made. Also another ranger named Moore was wounded. The ravine or ditch was shallow, and while the rangers to some extent could protect themselves by lying down, it was not sufficient to cover the horses, and they were hit repeatedly. The Indians fairly swarmed around on the sides of the hills yelling and shooting, and some of them gradually worked around the rangers and shot at them from various points. This gallant little band, however, worthy the name of Texas rangers, were not dismayed, but would raise their heads above the ravine, take aim at some particular target, fire, and down again to adjust another charge, at the same time shouting defiance to their dusky foes. In about twenty minutes after the ravine was reached Zack Waddell noticed that ranger Glass, whom they thought dead, was kicking about on the ground, and expressed his intention of making a run and bringing him into the ravine. This looked so much like a man throwing his life away and doing no good that even the officers tried to persuade him from the rash act, but Waddell had his eye on his friend, and all at once leaped out of the ditch and ran rapidly to him, gathered him up in his arms, and started back amid a perfect shower of bullets and demoniac yells of the Indians, and the rangers in the ditch sprang to their feet, regardless of exposure, returned yell for yell and shot for shot with the Indians, and loudly cheered their gallant comrade, who came staggering with wounds and his burden in among them. He was hit with five bullets, but none inflicted serious wounds, and one of his boots was nearly shot off of his foot, so much so that he could hardly keep it on. Poor Glass never spoke, but lay there and breathed awhile, and then died there in the ravine with his comrades around him, with the noise of cracking carbines, whistling bullets, and savage yells in his dying ears.

Here for five hours the battle was kept up with only short intermissions. The Indians had plenty of good guns and ammunition, and the balls were almost constantly kicking up the dust around the margin of the ravine or hitting rocks and sending showers of scattered lead among the rangers. As before stated, some of the Indians went around the head of the ravine, surrounding the rangers and cutting off Lee Corn and Wheeler and two others who had stayed with Corn when his horse was killed and himself wounded, and they were forced to retreat back to the creek and hide themselves in the rank grass and bushes and mud and water in the bed of the creek. The rangers fighting the battle in the dry ravine suffered greatly for water, remaining five hours with the hot July sun beaming down on them. Their tongues swelled, and such was their thirst that they dug in the bed of the ravine with their Bowie knives to moist earth and sucked it between their parched lips, which gave some relief. During all of this time Major Jones exposed himself greatly and made several narrow escapes. Once he left the ravine and went to a tree and was watching the chief Lone Wolf to see if he could tell from his actions what his intentions were or what his next move would be, and talking to the boys and telling them to be careful now of their cartridges and not shoot all of them away. Captain Stephens also encouraged the boys by word and example, and in fact neither officers nor men showed the white feather during this trying time. While Major Jones was watching Lone Wolf he sat down and leaned against the tree, with the balls occasionally skipping around him, and Walter Robinson and Flint Damon said, "Look out, major, they will hit you directly," and about this time a hissing ball came and struck the tree near the major's head, filling his eyes and face full of bark and splinters, and with such force that he fell backwards on the ground as if killed, but quickly recovered himself.

About one hour by sun some of the rangers expressed a determination to leave the ravine in spite of the Indians and go to Lost Creek after water, but all were persuaded out of this notion except two, Bailey and Porter, and they mounted their horses and rode off. Two hundred yards from the ravine the Indians ran upon them and killed Bailey in plain views of his companions, his mare, though fleet, failing to run when the Indians came close, on account of fright, and reared and plunged until they shot and lanced her unfortunate rider from her back. Porter had better luck, but had a narrow escape for his life. The Indians ran him so close that he was compelled to abandon his horse when near the creek and leap from the high bank into it, one Indian who was very close saying, "Me git you! Me git you!" in broken English as he went over. Now it happened that the place Porter went over was close to the spot where Lee Corn was in hiding, and thinking it was an Indian hunting for him, shot at him as he hit the mud and water a few yards away, but fortunately missed, as he had to aim his gun with one hand, having the other arm badly shattered. In throwing the cartridge from the magazine into the barrel he had to hold the gun between his knees to do so. When night came the rangers back at the ravine were in a terrible strait, and a council was held to determine what was best to do. They were nearly exhausted with thirst and strain and shock of the battle, ammunition nearly all gone, dead and wounded comrades scattered here and there, and fourteen dead horses besides the wounded lying around and in the ditch. The Indians had drawn off at dark and nothing now could be heard of them, and Major Jones asked the boys which they had rather do—remain there until daylight and renew the battle again if the Indians did not leave, or until soldiers could come from Jacksboro to their relief, for a ranger named John P. Holmes had ridden out of the ravine on a wounded horse in sight of the Indians before night, and gone to the fort where United States soldiers were quartered to ask for assistance. After canvassing the situation thoroughly, the rangers concluded to leave the ravine and make an attempt to get to Jacksboro or meet the soldiers. The dead ranger, Glass, was strapped to an Indian horse whose rider had been killed, and he dashed down among the rangers and stayed there. When all was ready they silently departed down the ravine, more than half of them on foot, and succeeded in quenching their thirst at a small spring they found, and then kept on fifteen miles to a ranch, and there remained until the following morning and buried their dead comrade, this sad rite being performed by Walter Robinson and others, who were then to return to the battleground with a ranch wagon to bring in the wounded, being preceded by some of the rangers and a squad of soldiers who had arrived at the ranch before daylight, having been informed of the situation by the gallant Holmes, who had got through safely. Uneasiness was felt for the boys who had been left scattered in the Lost Creek bottoms, and a hurried return was made to the place by the rangers and soldiers, but on arriving there they were all gone and could nowhere be found. The fact was developed later that they had left some time during the night and made their escape to Loving's ranch. The body of Bailey was found near where the fight commenced, badly mutilated, scalped, and full of arrows, besides numerous lance wounds. He was buried near the spot where he met his fate, and since the country has settled up in that locality, a schoolhouse and church stand near his grave, or near the spot where he was killed. It was afterwards learned that forty-two Indians were bullet-stricken during the battle, nineteen of them dying on the field.

The rangers went back to Jacksboro, bought horses to replace those killed, and then went on into the Llano country.

It is related of Lee Corn that when his horse was killed and himself down beside him, with his left arm shattered, he still continued to work the lever of his gun, holding the barrel between his knees to load, and firing with one hand at the Indians who were swarming around them and yelling most fearfully, and during this time Major Jones passed him and the young ranger looked up and says, "We're givin' 'em hell, major."

Mr. Walter Robinson, who was one of the escort of Major Jones, and who took a prominent part in this fearful battle, belonged to Capt. Rufe Perry's company, and was in the Salt Creek fight in Menard County, and several others. He was cousin to Major Jones and nephew of Mrs. Julia Lee Sinks, who has contributed so many interesting sketches of the early times on the Texas frontier, especially around Austin. Mr. Robinson was born in Austin, and comes from an old historic family of pioneers of the place. His wife was a Hornsby, another noted frontier family, among whom a braver or more gallant set of men never settled on a frontier.

CREED TAYLOR.

CREED TAYLOR.

Came to Texas in 1824.

Creed Taylor was born in Tennessee in 1820, on the 10th of April. His father, Josiah Taylor, was born and raised in Virginia, in James County, on the James River, and was related to Gen. Zachary Taylor, so the general himself said. The occasion of his saying this was during the Mexican war when Creed Taylor, as a dispatch-bearer, brought a message to the general, and he asked the young courier what his name was, and on being told it was Taylor he asked several questions as to where his people came from, and if his father had a brother named William, and on being told that he had to the latter question, said, "Well, I and you are kinfolks, then."

Capt. Josiah Taylor, father of Creed, came to Texas in 1811 on an exploring expedition with many others from the States at that time to look at the country, and many Americans had already settled in the eastern part of the State. In the following year a revolution was inaugurated by the Mexicans to throw off the Spanish yoke, and many Americans and Indians in Texas joined them. The army collected at Spanish Bluff, and after an organization set out for Goliad to attack the Spanish army there. The opposing force to Spain in this body of men were mostly Americans and commanded by American officers, of whom were McGee, Kemper, Ross, Gaines, McFarland, and Captain Josiah, who had joined the expedition and commanded a company. One of the Mexican commanders was Bernardo and another was Manchaca. The American force, as we will call it, for they largely predominated, numbered 800 when they left the bluff, and many battles were fought with the Spaniards with various successes until 1813, when the Spanish army retreated to San Antonio and the Americans followed. Reinforcements had been sent to the Spanish Governor of Texas, Salcedo, and he now sent his army to meet the advancing Americans. The Spanish army, which was at the mouth of Salado Creek where it empties into the San Antonio River, consisted of 1500 regulars and 1000 militia, all under the command of the officer who brought the reinforcements from Mexico. He had solicited this position, and pledged his head to the Governor that he would kill and capture the entire American army.

The American army consisted of 800 Americans led by Kemper, 180 Mexicans commanded by Gaines and Manchaca, and 325 Indians under McFarland. The Americans, expecting an ambush, marched slowly in order of battle. The left wing moved in front under Ross, in which was Capt. Josiah Taylor and his men, all good rifle shots. The right, under Kemper, was in the rear, and a company of riflemen under Captain Luckett acted as flankers on the right. Their left was protected by the San Antonio River. About nine miles from San Antonio there was a ridge which divided the river and creek and the side next to town was prairie, while the other side, bordering the Salado Creek, was covered with chaparral brush. Here in this place the Spanish army lay in ambush while the Americans were coming up the river on the east side of the creek, and were not aware of their presence until they crossed and began to enter the ambuscade. They were first discovered by Luckett's riflemen, who at once fired on them. The Spaniards then arose and formed in front of the Americans about 400 yards below, their line extending nearly a mile, and in their center was twelve cannons. The Indians were now placed in front of the Americans to receive the charge of the Spanish cavalry, but they all ran at the first onset except the Cooshattas and a few others, who stood firm and received two more charges. By this time the Americans had formed at the foot of the ridge, and orders were given to advance to within thirty yards of the Spaniards, fire three rounds, load the fourth, and then charge all along the line.

This order was obeyed in silence and with such coolness that it struck terror to the Spanish army, and the volleys they fired at the Americans went over their heads on account of the advance being up hill. They did not wait for the charge, but broke up into disordered squads all along their line and fled in terror towards San Antonio. They were hotly pursued and hundreds of them killed in the disordered rout, and the wounded were butchered by the Indians. When the Spanish commander saw his army flying from the field and realized that the day was lost, he drew his sword and, turning his horse, rushed upon the ranks of the pursuing Americans. He first attacked Major Ross and then Colonel Kemper, and as his sword was raised to strike the latter he was shot dead by William Owens, a private in the company of Capt. Josiah Taylor. In this great Southwest Texas battle one thousand of the Spaniards were killed and but few taken prisoners, on account of the Indians, who followed in the rear of the Americans during the disordered flight.

The American army then went on to San Antonio and demanded the surrender of the place, and the Governor and his staff came out to comply, and the first Americans they came in contact with was the company of Capt. Josiah Taylor, drawn up in their front, and to their leader Salcedo offered his sword, but Captain Taylor would not receive it and referred him to Colonel Kemper. He refused it and referred him to General Bernardo, the Mexican commander, whereupon the Governor stuck it in the ground and went off and left it, and Bernardo took it up.

It is not the intention to give a full history of these stirring events of that time, but only to mention them on account of the part taken by the father of the subject of this sketch. Suffice it to say, another Spanish army came from Mexico and was defeated by the Americans on the Alazan Creek with great loss, and then a second army came but stopped on the Medina, and the Americans went out there to fight them, but were drawn into an ambush and almost annihilated. The Americans fought like tigers, and continued the battle after the day was lost and everything in confusion. The Mexicans, commanded by Manchaca, fought well and were nearly all killed in the center of the deadly ambuscade. The Spanish cavalry pursued and fought the remnants until nearly all were killed. Capt. Josiah Taylor rode his horse and stayed on him during all of this fearful slaughter, and was wounded seven times, but made his escape with about ninety other Americans to eastern Texas, where he had two large musket balls cut out of his body, and as soon as he recovered he went back home to Virginia.

In 1824 Captain Taylor returned to Texas with his family, and died in the winter of 1830 on his ranch, below Cuero.

Creed Taylor, after the death of his father, was sent to Gonzales by his mother to attend school, and he boarded at the house of Almon Dickinson, who was afterwards killed in the Alamo. His schoolteacher was named Miller, and his schoolmates were the Sowell boys,—Andrew, John, and Asa,—Highsmiths, Pontons, John Gaston, Galba Fuqua, and Dave Darst. In 1835 when the Mexicans came to take the cannon, Creed was in the fight five miles above the town near Zeke Williams' place, since called the Dikes place. He says they loaded the cannon at John Sowell's shop and carried it with them, and fired it three times during the fight.

When Stephen F. Austin went on out to San Antonio with an army to continue the war, Creed Taylor was along in the company of Capt. John J. Tumlinson, and was in the battle of Mission Concepcion, the Grass fight, and storming of San Antonio, and was about one hundred yards from Ben Milam when he was killed. The company he belonged to was really that of John A. Coleman, but he was not present in any of the fighting on account of sickness, and his lieutenant, Tumlinson, commanded and was called captain by the men. Creed went back home to his mother on the Guadalupe after the surrender of the Mexican army, and was there when the Alamo was taken and Santa Anna came on down with an army after General Houston. He moved his mother to Kennard's prairie, and then in company with Joe Tumlinson took the trail of Houston's army and caught up with them in camp on Buffalo Bayou the night before the battle of San Jacinto, and went through the battle on the following day without being attached to any particular company. He fired many shots, and part of the time was mixed up close in among the Mexicans. After the battle he went back home and attended to the stock and farmed some until 1840, when the Indians burned Linnville. He was in the pursuit and battle with the Indians on Plum Creek in the company of Capt. D. B. Fryer. Among the men whom he remembers seeing in the battle was Robert Hall, French Smith, Zeke Smith, Andrew Sowell, James Nichols, Ben McCulloch and his brother Henry, and Matthew Caldwell. Mr. Taylor killed several Indians in personal combats during the long running fight.

In the fall of this same year he went on an Indian expedition commanded by Col. Tom Howard, and belonged to the company of Capt. Matthew Caldwell. There were 170 white men on this Indian hunt, and they located a large camp of them where Brackett is now. A considerable battle took place and a great deal of noise was made, but none of the white men were killed and but few wounded. Twenty Indians were killed and 700 head of mules and horses were captured. Among the men along from the Guadalupe were William Tumlinson, Dan Grady, Calvin Turner, and John Gattes. A great many of these mules and horses had been carried off by the Indians from below in the settlements along the rivers, and were returned to their owners.

After this expedition Mr. Taylor joined the rangers under Jack Hays and was in the fight at Bandera Pass. The men that he can remember who were in the fight were, besides Captain Hays and himself, two of his brothers, Josiah and Pipkin, Andrew Erskine, Peter Fore, Ad Gillespie, Kit Ackland, Sam Luckey, George Neill, James Dunn, Sam Walker, and George Jackson. His recollection is that the time was June of 1841, that twenty-five rangers were in the fight, and that it lasted more than an hour. The Indians fired on them first and soon showed themselves in large force and came close, and the rangers had all they could do to manage them. About 11 o'clock the Indians began to give back towards the north end of the pass, pursued by the rangers, who constantly mixed with them and hand to hand conflicts took place, in one of which, near the north end of the pass, Kit Ackland killed the chief, and many horses were killed and wounded. Among the rangers killed was Peter Fore and George Jackson. The latter was a son of Tom Jackson, who was killed in the Alamo. Peter Fore was shot through the body with an arrow, the spike being on one side and the feather on the other. Sam Walker was thrust through with a lance and Andrew Erskine was wounded in the thigh with an arrow. He charged the Indian with a five-shooter, but the barrel dropped off without his knowledge, and he almost touched the Indian trying to shoot, but failed. The Comanche had his bow-stick shot in two and was also unable to shoot, but noticing the condition of the ranger's pistol, grasped an arrow in his hand and tried to stab him with it, but was at this time shot and killed by Creed Taylor. Mr. Taylor says other rangers were wounded and had to be carried to San Antonio to be treated, but he does not remember their names. He can only remember two that died on the ground.

When Wall captured San Antonio in 1842 the rangers were quartered in San Antonio, but most of them were out on a scout with Jack Hays and made their escape. When the Texans were gathered on the Salado to fight them and Captain Hays drew them out, Lieut. Henry McCulloch covered the retreat with ten picked men, four of them Taylors,—Creed, Pipkin, Josiah and James. Towards the last of the race Creed Taylor and McCulloch were alone in the rear, and 200 shots or more were fired at them by the Mexican cavalry, but neither were hit.

In the main battle that came off on the creek Creed Taylor had his arm broke, shot in the middle of the elbow, and the ball split on the bone, half going out and the other remaining. As it would never permanently heal, years afterwards he had the other part of the ball taken out by Dr. Herff of San Antonio. After the battle Mr. Taylor went to Seguin and stayed until his arm apparently got well, staying with Tom Nichols during the time. On the way to Seguin he passed over Dawson's battle ground, and said he never saw such a sight of mangled men and horses. He says in the Salado battle Calvin Turner was glanced on the side of the head with a grape shot and knocked down, and that one of the Sowell boys was wounded in the hand. When the Mexican war of 1846 broke out Mr. Taylor joined the regiment of rangers commanded by Capt. Jack Hays, and passed through nearly all of the battles in Mexico, the last he was in being at Buena Vista. The first one he says was at Palo Alto, and there he saw more men together than he ever saw before, and it was a grand sight. Both armies met each other with all the regimental bands playing at once on both sides, and five hundred flags were in sight.

Mr. Taylor still survives at this writing (April 27, 1900), and lives at the head of James River, in Kimble County, and has been there about thirty years. His life is being written by a gentleman of Fort Mason, and no doubt will be very interesting when all of the facts are brought out of his eventful life, of which this article is only a shadow.

M. SAATOFF.

Came to Texas in 1846.

Among the first settlers in the town of Quihi, and who still resides there, is Mr. M. Saatoff. He was born in the province of Hanover, Germany, in 1839, and on April 15, 1846, came to Texas with his father, M. M. Saatoff, and other members of the family. The elder Saatoff had contracted with an immigration agent named G. D'Hanis, as part of the colony of Henry Castro. From this agent the town of D'Hanis derives its name.

They sailed from Bremen on the ship Leo with eighty passengers, and the time consumed in the voyage was nine weeks. One child was born and named Leo, after the ship.

Like most of the others, they first landed at Galveston and then took shipping for Port Lavaca, staying there three weeks, eating and resting being furnished by Castro. Here young Saatoff heard bullfrogs and thought they were buffalo bellowing, as they had heard of those animals before arriving. The family made it through in Mexican carts to Castroville in August, 1846, and soon after went on out to the Quihi Creek, where a new settlement was to be made, reaching there the same day they started, and went into camp on the spot where their future homes were to be built. That first night a hard rain fell and almost spoiled all of their bedding and clothing, and on the following morning the wagons which had conveyed them there went back and left them in this water-soaked condition in this wild, Indian-infested country, with their belongings piled up on the ground in the mud and water; but there were brave hearts there, and they made the best shift they could under the circumstances and looked with hope to the future. The first thing to be done was to build small, rude shelters covered with grass and try to open up farming land, but the following year no crop was made. Some corn was planted with hoes, but the deer ate it up. Game, honey, and fish were plentiful and there was no danger of starving, and the next year a good crop of corn was made on new land One ox team served five or six families to break land with. The elder Saatoff had one yoke of oxen, and he would lend these to his neighbors to help get their land ready for planting. The Delaware, Tonkaway, and Lipan Indians often came and traded with them before the latter became hostile. The Tonks lived on the Blanco, Delawares on Pedernales, and the Lipans further south.

Mr. Saatoff has an old document in his possession which stipulates that the settlers were, inside of three years, to put fifteen acres of land in cultivation, and to sell no intoxicating drinks or firearms to the Indians, and in case they did this their lands would be forfeited. The people suffered some before crops could be made, and would have suffered more if it had not been for the Texas rangers who were stationed there for their protection, and who divided their rations with them and killed game for them, as the settlers were poorly provided with guns and ammunition. It was fifty miles to mill and corn scarce at $2 per bushel. When the rangers were disbanded the Indians came and stole nearly all of the horses in the country, and being now thrown on their own resources they had to defend themselves and rely on their own exertions. All of Mr. Saatoff's horse stock was stolen in 1866 except one mule, and this was all he had to cultivate a crop with in 1867. Mr. Gerdes was killed by the Indians while out hunting horses which they had already carried off. It was a very cold day, and the Indians stripped the old man and carried him one mile in that condition and then killed him, inflicting twenty-eight wounds. Mr. Saatoff found the trail of the Indians while out and came back to report, and learned that Mr. Gerdes was lost, and said then he was sure the Indians had killed him. A party who were out soon came in with the body, and Mr. Saatoff helped to bury him. The farmers at first only raised corn, having a good market for it at Forts Inge, Clark, Duncan, and Lincoln. In 1858 wheat, oats, and rye were cultivated and did well, but during the progress of the Civil war farming was neglected, there being more money in freighting by those who remained at home, and in consequence of this the farms grew up in weeds, and in 1865 no crops of any kind were made, and the want of them was soon felt. In 1866 six families went down in to Guadalupe County and made a good crop of corn on the Wilcox farm, and took notice how the people worked down there, having clean crops.

They went back to Quihi in September and carried a good deal of corn with them and sold to the people who had failed, and told them, "When you work your farms like they do in Guadalupe County, you will make good crops here." Next year wheat, oats, corn, and sorgum were planted, and all made a good crop, cutting the small grain with scythes, and in this year (1867) the first threshing machine was brought into the country, and in the following year several more, as crops were still good, and it became an agricultural county. Cotton was tried and it did well, but they had to haul it to the Cibolo, forty-five miles, to a gin, and the farmers now agreed with their merchant, Mr. Fred Muennink, at New Fountain, only two miles from Quihi, that if he would put up a gin they would plant 200 acres in cotton. This was agreed to, and in 1870 more than a bale to the acre was made, one man saying he made two bales to the acre; and so cotton raising was an established fact and the acreage increased each year.

The last Indian raid was in 1874, and they carried off and killed together fifty head of horses in the Quihi settlement, and killed one boy on Black Creek. On one occasion Mr. Saatoff and others made a famous ride of eighty miles in one day after Indians, but the latter went one hundred and got away.

JOHN E. WILSON.

Come to Texas in 1832.

John Ewing Wilson was born in Wilson County, Tennessee, one mile east of Lebanon, on the 6th of July, 1828, and his father, Joseph Wilson, was born in the same county in 1799. The county was named for his grandfather James Wilson, a soldier of the revolution, and who was killed in battle during that long struggle. The father, Joseph, was in the battle of New Orleans and was wounded in the leg, being the only man in his company hit. The mother of our subject was Margaret Barton, and her father was killed in the battle of Horseshoe Bend, when General Jackson defeated the Indians there. When young Sam Houston called for volunteers to storm a log fort where a number of Indians had collected near the river, Mr. Barton was one of the men that responded and went with the charge, and was killed with many others, and Houston was desperately wounded. Mr. Wilson's grandmother was Anna Bradley.

Joseph Wilson came to Texas with his family in 1832 and first settled four miles from San Augustine, but later, in 1837, moved to Bastrop. While en route on the main road from San Augustine to the settlements on the Colorado Mr. Wilson, then a boy, saw his first Indian, and he was a dead one. There was a log fort on the route where Anderson is now, called Fort Lacy, after the man who built it, and here the elder Wilson put up for the night on arriving there with his wagons and family. The fort was inclosed and Lacy told Mr. Wilson to come inside with his family, as there was danger from Indians. He also placed two young men in a fodder house to watch the horses, which were tied outside. Late in the night the Indians came and made an attempt to carry off the stock, but were discovered and fired on by the guards, and one was killed and another wounded. Joseph Wilson and Mr. Lacy ran out with their guns when the shots were heard and also fired on the Indians, but without effect, as they were making off in the moonlight across the prairie. When morning came the body of a large dead Indian was found near by, and Mr. Lacy told one of his negroes to bring a yoke of oxen and a log chain and drag him off. When the team came they were afraid of the Indian, and could not be driven near enough to fasten the chain to the body until they were blindfolded. The chain had a ring in one end, and a loop was made and slipped over the Indian's head and then drawn up. The blinds were now taken from the oxen's eyes, but as soon as they caught sight of the Indian close behind them they gave a loud snort, and, jerking loose from the negro, dashed off across the prairie with the Indian bouncing in the air behind them, and did not stop until exhausted. Suffice to say they carried the body as far from the fort as was necessary. Mr. John Wilson can distinctly remember how the Indian looked as he bobbed up and down behind the oxen as they ran with him across the prairie.

When the Wilson family arrived at Bastrop the Perry family, Manloves, Wilbargers, and others, and a German named Dietze, were there. General Burleson lived fifteen miles below and John H. Moore above La Grange. He and the mother of Mr. Wilson graduated at the same school at Lebanon, Tenn. One night shortly after getting here, while John Wilson and one of his brothers and two negroes belonging to their father were sleeping in their wagons a short distance from the balance of the family, who were in a small house, they had an Indian alarm. The horses had been tied to the wheels of the wagon, and in the night they began to snort and pull on the ropes, which caused the wagon to rock violently, and young John Wilson raised the wagon sheet and looked out and saw a big Indian standing very close who "shooed" at him and ran off, and John then jumped out of the wagon and ran to the house. This was in 1840, and was part of the large force of Comanches who were going on a big raid down the country which culminated in the burning and sacking of Linnville on the coast, and the battle of Plum Creek on their return. The Wilson family had before this gone out to San Antonio and tried to settle, but Indians and Mexican robbers and raiding bands from Mexico had caused all of the Americans and some of the Mexican settlers to vacate the place and move back east.

On one occasion, about the time of getting back from San

Antonio, in May of 1840, John Wilson and his brother James and one of their negroes were planting corn for a man named Johnson, three miles from home. After night the two brothers saddled their horses and started home across the prairie, although warned by Johnson not to do so, as he had been out that day and saw Indians. While riding across the bright moonlit prairie their horses suddenly stopped and threw up their heads, and about thirty men were seen running on horses, but soon disappeared from view. Next day it was learned the horsemen were Indians and that they were running Gen. Ed. Burleson, and made him lose his hat and saddlebags, but he recovered them by searching the ground next day. Had General Burleson not been ahead of the boys and the Indians came in contact with him first they would have had a race for life, and likely been caught.

When the Indians were coming back from Linnville nearly all of the men were collecting from the Colorado, Guadalupe, and other places to fight them. A large company left the Colorado under Burleson, and another composed of old men and boys were concentrated on Buckner's Creek, eighteen miles above Bastrop, as a reserve in case the first men that went out got whipped. Of this party were three boys—John Wilson, Jasper Berry, and Leander Herrill—who wanted to go with the first party and be in the battle, but were restrained by the older men. They, however, made up their minds to go, and hid their saddles and horses out that evening, and when night came mounted and started. From what they heard the men say they knew about where the Indians would be intercepted, and made rapidly for that point on Plum Creek, about twenty miles distant. It being night, however, and having no road to guide them, they became lost and wandered all night in the sand hills between Plum Creek and the Colorado, and when they finally arrived on the scene the battle was over. Mr. Wilson says that large crowds of men were scattered all over the country coming back from the battle, which was quite extended, covering many miles of country. The boys got to see some of the dead Indians.

Shortly after this many Americans settled at San Antonio, and Jack Hays was commissioned by General Houston to raise a company of rangers for their protection, and John Wilson and

Leander Herrill, hearing of this, mounted their horses and set out for San Antonio, and from there to the camp of Hays, on the Medina, and offered themselves as rangers. Herrill was accepted, but Wilson was too young and could not be enlisted, but he would not leave, and stayed three months with the rangers and went on many scouts with them, killed deer and buffalo, and had a good time generally.

In 1842, when Wall captured San Antonio and men were hurrying to the front to repel the invader, young Wilson again mounted his horse and offered his services to Gen. Matthew Caldwell, who used him as a messenger or express rider, and placed him on the San Antonio and Gonzales road at the crossing of Nash's Creek, to give information to all who came along and tell them what to do as to the concentration of the forces at the Salado Creek, near San Antonio. He was the first to carry the news of Dawson's defeat and the victory of Caldwell to La Grange, and as soon as that was accomplished started back for his post, but met Gonzalvo Woods, who made his escape from Dawson's massacre, and was badly wounded. He was shot in the shoulder and wounded in three places on the head with a saber. His horse was killed in the fight and himself hit with a bullet and badly sabered, and he tried to surrender, but a Mexican lancer dashed upon him with leveled lance, and Woods caught it and gave such a quick, strong pull that it jerked the Mexican from his horse to the ground, and he wrenched the lance from his grasp and ran it through his body and pinned him to the earth, and then, pulling it out, mounted the Mexican trooper's horse and made his escape, carrying the lance with him, which he still had, and which was very bloody. His wounds had not been dressed, and young Wilson at once washed all the blood from his head and poulticed the wounds with prickly pear, and then went back with Woods to La Grange. Norman Woods, a brother, was also in the fight and had his back broken and was carried a prisoner to Mexico, and died in the Perote prison. Zadock Woods, father of the boys mentioned, was also in the battle and was killed. The lance which Gonzalvo brought back is now in the possession of some of the Woods family near Yorktown, and is highly prized by them, as it should be.

In 1848 John Wilson was living with his father and family

on Peach Creek, in Gonzales County, where Waelder is now, and in that year Henry E. McCulloch raised a company of rangers and he joined. Their station was in Hamilton's valley, on Hamilton Creek, sixty miles from Austin, near where Burnet is now. Their officers, besides the captain, were First Lieutenant John King, Second Lieutenant Calvin S. Turner, Orderly Sergeant Asa J. L. Sowell. They did a good deal of scouting, but had no battles with Indians. Mr. Wilson says that while here Sergeant Sowell and Joe Williams caught the largest catfish he ever saw, and that it took both of them to hold it and get it out. He speaks in high praise of their orderly, and says he was the best man he ever saw, and covered all of the ground he stood on at all times and under all circumstances. The company was mustered out December 23, 1848.

In 1849, on the 23d day of August, Mr. Wilson joined a company of rangers commanded by Capt. John S. Ford, at Austin, and they went south and were stationed between Brownsville and San Patricio, near King's ranch, on the Santa Gertrudes Creek.

In November of the same year Mr. Wilson, Dave Steel, Charles Wiedenmiller, and John Dickens were on their way back to camp with a wagonload of supplies, and one evening camped and Wiedenmiller went to water the wagon horses in a little creek not far away, and they soon heard him scream for help. Wilson and Steel ran to him and found him surrounded by Indians, but drove them away by a well-directed fire, and all made their way quickly back to the wagon with the horses. The Indians rallied, and seeing that only two men had put them to flight, made a charge and the rangers went into a thicket. Here the Indians kept them all night, charging around, yelling, and shooting arrows and bullets into the brush. Occasionally the rangers would slip to the edge and shoot, and the Indians would run. Dickens left and went to camp at the commencement of the trouble and told Captain Ford that he thought the other three men were killed, and next morning the captain came to them with fifty men. The trail of the Indians was taken up and Captain Ford had a fight with them and killed several, but none of his men were hurt. Of this company Andrew Walker and Ed. Burleson were lieutenants.

During this term of service Mr. Wilson and James, his brother, and Ed. Stevens got on the trail of a band of Indians and followed them to the Rio Grande, stripped and swam over to see what discoveries they could make on the other side, and were arrested by the Mexican soldiers and confined in an old Mexican hut made out of poles. Here they remained until night, naked, and then Wilson and Stevens began to plan an escape. The soldiers all went to sleep except one guard, and he walked to and fro in front of the harcal with his musket, and it was agreed to kill him if they could. Each armed himself with a heavy hard stick, pulled out of the old house, and as the guard passed the door Wilson hit him a terrible blow on the back of the neck and killed him in his tracks. All three then made a run for the river, Wilson carrying the soldier's gun to make a fight with if pursued. It was all done so silently that none of the soldiers were aroused, and they gained the river without any signs of pursuit, and all plunged in and swam over to the Texas side, Wilson throwing the gun away as they entered the water. Their camp was six miles below on the river, and they soon made their way back. Captain Ford had sent them out to trail these Indians and see where they went to. This was in 1850.

In the same year the rangers followed another band of Indians and overtook them where Campbellton is now. They had been two days on the trail without anything to eat, and by this time were getting very hungry. There were fourteen rangers and thirty Indians. The Indians were in camp about daylight, roasting a colt which they had killed, and had 200 head of horses. They made no fight when the rangers charged them, but scattered, and all of the stock was retaken. It was about forty miles to Fort Merrill on the Nueces, and to that place the rangers went to get something to eat, and carried the horses with them. After getting all they wanted to eat they went into camp and concluded to rest until morning, and John Wilson, Jack Taylor, Mat Nowlin, and Lieutenant Burleson stayed among the horses to guard them. To pass away the time a blanket was spread and a deck of cards produced, and the party played by moonshine while the balance of the men lay near by asleep. Before any one was aware of it two Indians slipped up and got a horse apiece and started off, but at this time were discovered by Wilson, and he and others 'fired at them, killing one and wounding the other. The wounded one got into the brush and lay down, badly wounded in the body and in the hand, and his bowstick shot in two. The rangers had a Mexican guide and interpreter with them called "Old Roka," who had been a prisoner among the Indians nearly all of his life and could speak several Indian dialects, and when the wounded Indian was found "Old Roka" was told to converse with him in Comanche and see what he had to say, but being badly wounded he made but little reply, and soon died. This occurred outside of the fort limits, and at the time a whole regiment of dragoons were stationed there. They heard the firing at the ranger camp, but thought they had got up a row among themselves and paid no attention to it, but on the following morning, when some of them came down there and found a dead Indian in camp, they cut his head off and placed it on a pole. This made the rangers mad, and some of them went to the colonel and got him to order some of his men to take the head down and put it and the body together and bury them, which he did.

After the return to camp Captain Ford sent Mr. Wilson and Jack Taylor to see if any Indians could be found in force, and they soon located forty of them in ambush on the Nueces River, being the same the rangers had taken the horses from, and the Indians had followed them back. As soon as this was reported Captain Ford took fifteen men and went to fight them, and arrived there at 4 o'clock p. m., but the Indians were gone, the trail bearing south, which was followed rapidly until dark and then camp was made. On the following morning it was resumed, and in three miles came upon the camp of the Indians where they had stayed the night before in the edge of some timber. The trail still tended south and the rangers followed and shortly came in sight of them, but held back until the Indians got out on the prairie, as there was too much brush and timber to make a good fight. They finally, however, entered a more open country, and the rangers spurred up and came close upon them near the Agua Dulce Creek. The Indians were all on foot except a few, their horses having been taken by the rangers as before stated. Two mounted ones were in the rear to watch for the rangers, and these were charged but made their escape to the main body, and all of them came out into open ground and formed for battle. The rangers went in among them at a charge and several were killed at the first volley, but the Indians fought well and rapidly both with guns and bows. In the second round Dave Steel shot a chief in the head and killed him, and the balance began to get into confusion, and many personal combats took place. Captain Ford pursued one who was on horseback and aimed his pistol at him, but the Comanche leaned low down behind his horse to avoid the shot and his girth broke and he fell to the ground, but he was on his feet in an instant and aimed an arrow, but the captain shot him in the head and he fell, sending his arrow straight up as he went down. When the fight was over William Gillespie was found to be killed and Jack Spencer and one other ranger wounded. Gillespie was a nephew of Ad. Gillespie, a famous ranger under Hays, who was killed in Mexico. This was "Old Yellow Wolf's" band, and was in charge of a sub-chief. His son was also in the fight and was wounded and captured. Eight dead Indians were found on the ground and many were wounded. Gillespie killed one Indian, and a wounded Indian killed him. This fellow was on the ground and nearly dead, but bent his bow with his feet and shot the ranger through the heart, who was close and coming towards him. The rangers buried their gallant comrade on the banks of the Agua Dulce Creek. Mr. Wilson passed all through this hotly contested fight but was not hurt. In about two weeks after the rangers got back to camp Mr. Wilson was on guard one morning about daylight, and saw a white rag held up on a stick by two Indian squaws. He put his handkerchief on the end of his gun and held it up and they came in. They were the mother and aunt of the young Yellow Wolf, who was a captive, and the old chief, his father, had sent them to exchange all the captives he had, thirteen in all, for his son. Captain Ford agreed to this, and they were brought in and the exchange made. Most of their prisoners were Mexicans, one negro, and two or three whites. One of the latter was James Hart, captured near Refugio.

In 1851 Mr. Wilson, Andrew Wheeler, Andrew Walker, and two Mexicans were sent out by Captain Ford to capture wild cattle for beef for the company, and on a creek south of the Nueces called La Garta, in a very brushy place, a bunch of hobbled horses were discovered which belonged to a band of Indians. Lieutenant Walker told Wheeler to take the two Mexicans and round up the horses and unhobble them, and he and Wilson would watch for the Indians and protect them if any were near and should make a charge upon them. The horses were hobbled with strips of buffalo hide, and were all taken, thirty-five head in all, and no Indians put in an appearance. A trail, however, was discovered leading into a thicket, and Walker and Wilson followed it and found the saddles, ropes, and lances of the Indians who had gone off on foot to get some more horses. A runner was now sent back to camp for more men, and Captain Ford sent a squad and they lay there in ambush to await the return of the Indians, all the rangers being under the command of Lieut. A. J. Walker. On the fifth day John Wilson and Andrew Wheeler were on guard watching for the approach of the Indians, and discovered one coming down a draw at full speed on a horse. Lieutenant Walker was now notified of the approach of this Indian, and he said to let him pass and then cut him off so that he could not get back and notify the others, as no doubt they were near. The balance of the Indians, forty in number, soon came along, driving 200 head of horses, and the rangers got out of their ambush and charged them, greatly to their surprise. They split in two and rallied in two bunches to fight. Lieutenant Walker and part of the men attacked one party, and John Wilson, D. M. Level, Robert Rankin, Andrew Wheeler, and another ranger named Good wheeled to the left and attacked the balance, fifteen in number. These, seeing the small force assailing them, charged fiercely, and one of the rangers ran, and a doubtful battle now took place on this part of the ground. Wilson's horse was soon shot down and he had to abandon him, and Level's horse was killed and fell on him. He called to the ranger who ran to help him and not let an Indian lance him, who, seeing his condition, was coming to him for that purpose, but the ranger went on. John Wilson, who had just got clear of his fallen horse, heard the call and at once charged the Indian and killed him, having a repeating gun and several loads left. He then pulled the horse off of Level and he got on his feet and once more took part in the fight, although himself wounded in the thigh. Mr. Wilson

COL. JOHN S. FORD.

killed one more Indian during the fight and Wheeler killed one, and Walker's party killed five. Wheeler and an Indian faced each other a few yards apart and the ranger shot the Comanche in the mouth, knocking his teeth all out, the ball going out at the jaw. The Indian had quit his horse and this shot knocked him down, but he turned his head in time to partly escape a second shot from Wheeler, but the ball took his nose off in a side shot, but he raised to a sitting position and sat there until the fight was over. Lieutenant Walker then told John Wilson to finish him, but he refused, and the lieutenant threatened to put him under arrest, but still he would not comply and told him to arrest and be d——d. Wheeler was then told to shoot him, but he said he had shot him as many times as he wanted to or was going to. The lieutenant then handed a large holster pistol to a Mexican who was along and told him to go and finish that Indian, as he did not want to leave him in that condition. The Mexican took the pistol and rode up close to the Indian, who looked up, and, seeing the pistol in the Mexican's hand, knew what his fate was, and dropped his head down on his breast and the Mexican sent a ball into the crown of his head. These Indians when the fight commenced had a Mexican boy tied naked on a mule, and the mule loose without anything on him but the boy, and was running here and there, and the captive yelled manfully for the rangers not to shot him, that he was not an Indian. The rangers had to rope the mule and then cut the strings loose before he could be taken from the back of the animal. Years afterwards an Indian skull was found near this battleground and carried to San Antonio by Mr. E. R. Lane, and on being shown to Mr. Wilson he recognized it as that of the Indian whom Wheeler shot and the Mexican finished by order of Lieutenant Walker, by the bullet hole being in the crown of the skull.

The horses which were retaken from the Indians in this battle, 197 in number, belonged to a wealthy Mexican in Mexico, and this was the reason they were gone so long from their camp, and how they came by the Mexican captive. Captain Ford notified the Mexican that the rangers had recaptured his horses and for him to send after them. Three of the rangers had lost horses in the fight—Wilson, Level, and Roundtree. (The latter fought with Walker's party.) Captain Ford told these three men to select three of the best horses in the captured lot and appropriate them to their own use, and they did so, selecting the best they could find. The rich old Mexican came in person to receive his horses, and although there were no charges for getting them back and keeping them under herd, he made a great fuss about the rangers taking three of them. This made Captain Ford mad, and he told the old Mexican to take the balance of his horses and get back into Mexico as soon as he could or he would let his men hang him, which they were anxious to do, anyway. No use to say he did so, and did not stand on the order of his going.

At this time or the time of the fight Lieutenant Burleson had been sent to San Antonio by Captain Ford with ten men to bring $13,000 up to El Vacas, commissary money for the use of the rangers for supplies, pay, etc. The trip there was made all right and they got back to a point twenty-five miles west of where Walker had his fight west of the Nueces, in a salt marsh. Here they met trouble and fought one of the most desperate battles that is recorded on the Texas border, with the same Indians that Walker and his men had fought and whipped the day before. The men with Burleson were James Carr, Jack Spencer, Baker Barton, Warren Lyons, William Lackey, Alf. Tom, a German named Miller, and Givens, known in camp among the rangers as "washtub." Lyons had been a captive among the Indians and almost raised by them, and knew all about them, and had been in many fights with other Indians. When these Indians were first discovered they were in full retreat from Walker's fight, but stopped and began to make demonstrations toward Burleson's men, and Lyons, who was closely observing them, said to Burleson, "These Indians have been in a fight, mad, and are going to give us hell." Lyons then got down from his horse and pulled off his boots and Burleson thought he was fixing to run, but he was only making preparations for the fight, as the Indians were coming at a charge and yelling fiercely. They made no halt, and engaged the rangers hand to hand, and a most sanguinary battle took place. Wounds were received and given at close quarters on all parts of the ground, but finally the shattered remnants of the Indian braves drew off and quit the field, half of their number being killed and nearly all of the balance wounded. The first man killed of the rangers was Baker Barton. James Carr was wounded in two places, one with an arrow which cut out his bowels. William Lackey was badly wounded in the lungs with an arrow, and died at Laredo. Alf Tom was shot in the leg with an arrow, and Lieutenant Burleson was wounded three times in the head and arms. Spencer and Lyons were also wounded, the latter slightly. He knew how to duck and dodge among the Indians from his experience in fighting with Indians against Indians, and escaped many arrows that were aimed at him, and the wounds he received were glancing, and his hat was shot from his head. The most of the wounded rangers were so badly hurt they had to remain on the ground until a runner could be sent to Captain Ford, and he sent ambulances and conveyed them away.

Some time after this another scout was sent out under Lieutenant Burleson along the Rio Grande. Mexicans reported that the Indians had made a raid and killed two families below and carried off two women and a boy. The Indians were overtaken and a running fight commenced. One of them, who had been acting as a spy in the rear, was behind on a fine horse, and was crowded close by Burleson and John Wilson. Finally the lieutenant told Wilson if he could to kill the horse, and then they would be sure of the Indian. This he succeeded in doing and Burleson wounded the Indian, but he got into the brush and they could not find him. The balance of the Indians were caught up with and rapid firing commenced, and they tried to kill the prisoners but only succeeded in wounding the boy, and all were retaken. The Indians got into a big thicket and most of them escaped across the Rio Grande.

In 1852, when the rangers were discharged, Mr. Wilson went on an expedition into Mexico under Carabahal, mostly Mexicans, and they had a battle in which he was badly wounded in the arm by a bullet. Mr. Wilson's mother died in Gonzales County in 1848, and his father in the same county in 1855. He ranched in Bee County and then in the Panhandle, and has ranches up there yet in Brewster County, but lives on Beacon Hill, San Antonio, Bexar County.

Colonel Ford had many more battles with the Indians, one of

which, in 1858, occurred in the northwest part of the State, on the South Canadian River, in which a large number of Indians were killed. During the Civil war he commanded a regiment on the Rio Grande and fought the last battle of that great struggle. He was a native of North Carolina, and died at his home in San Antonio in 1898. On account of his vim and quick actions he was called "Old Rip" by the rangers.

JACK HUFFMAN.

Came to Texas in 1845.

Jacob Huffman, or Jack as he is called by those who know him, was born in Prussia, in the town of Hilbringin, near the Saar River, in 1838, and came to Texas in 1845. Many storms occurred during the passage and the vessel leaked badly, and finally a great storm drove them back 300 miles onto the coast of England, and they stayed there ten days for repairs near a great chalk bluff. Jack became very expert during the voyage, climbing ropes and masts, and the captain wanted to keep him, but his parents would not consent, so he became a pioneer and Indian fighter on the Texas frontier instead of a sailor.

The landing on Texas soil was made at Port Lavaca, and they found Prince Solms there waiting for them, and he took charge of them in the name of Henry Castro, whose colonists they were, and brought them out to Castroville in carts. The prince wore a uniform and sword, and amused himself and the people by the way killing tarantulas with his sword, they being very numerous along the route, and their bite was very poisonous. He would pin them to the ground with the keen point of the blade, or toss them up and cut them in two in the air.

The carts were covered with raw hides in lieu of wagon sheets, and being repeatedly drenched with rain, a most disagreable smell emanated from them. When it thundered loud the Mexican cart drivers would yell, and Mrs. Huffman would cry and wish she was back in Germany. When they arrived in Castroville the elder Huffman had $5 in money, with which he bought provisions and went three miles above town and planted corn, living in a picket hut covered with grass. His small farm of a few acres produced abundantly of corn, melons, and pumpkins, and he had plenty to live on, trading for meat from the Indians, 500 of whom were camped on the Medina River near by.

Jack remained at home until he was 14 years of age, and then worked around at anything he could find to do. He made one trip to Camp Verde with corn for the soldiers there, and returned by way of Bandera to load with lumber at Montel's sawmill, and when five miles below town on the way home his team stalled at a steep hill, and two Polanders came along and told him

HIS BROTHER JOHN WAS KILLED BY THE INDIANS,

And then helped him to get his wagon up, and he came on home with a heavy heart, for he was greatly attached to his brother. John was older than Jack and was married, and at the time he was killed was building a house on the Medina at the foot of the mountains in a very exposed place, as the Indians were now hostile. The walls of the house were up and John was on the roof nailing on boards, when six Comanche Indians suddenly appeared and attacked him and shot one arrow through his body before he could descend and get his gun, which was in the house. He made the attempt and got to the door, but here he received another arrow in the temple and fell. His gun was an eight-shooting rifle which he had purchased from Big Foot Wallace, and had he carried this on the house with him no doubt he could have kept off the Indians. A man named Dan Turner was helping him to build the house and at this time was bringing an armful of boards from the river bottom, and when he came into view some of the Indians made a charge on him, but he threw the boards down and ran back to the board tree and secured his gun, which he had left there, and then made his escape, intending to go to the Haby settlement below, but they lived on the opposite side of the river, and it was up from recent rains. Turner could not swim but made the attempt to cross anyhow, and came near being drowned, and lost his gun. He only saved himself by catching the limb of a cypress tree as he went down, and climbed up into it above the water. Here he stayed two days and nights waiting for the river to fall, and then tore up his clothing, and twisting them into a rope broke off a limb, fastened it to one end, and threw it repeatedly to the bank until it fastened in some bushes, and then drew himself over and again set out for the settlement. In about a mile he met a party of men going to see about John, who was in the habit of coming home on Sunday, and it was now Monday, and his wife and others were very uneasy about him. When they met Turner and heard his story they knew almost beyond a doubt that John was killed, for he said he saw John down when he turned to run from the Indians. On arriving at the cabin the body was found near where it fell, stripped and scalped, and the fine gun and Hoffman's mule gone. The body was now taken up and carried to Castroville and buried. The mule got away from the Indians and came back home in a few days.

JACK KILLS TWO INDIANS.

There were a great many mustangs in the country and Jack tried many times to catch one, and while out on this business one day rode up on two Comanche Indians lying down in the grass asleep, with their bows and arrows beside them. He was at a loss at first as to what action he would take, thinking at first to shoot one, but finally backed off quietly, as he only had one shot in a muzzle-loading gun, and the other Indian might get him with his arrows before he could run out of range of him. He now started to Castroville after help, but on the way found the horses of Dr. Bimm, whom he had been working for, and drove them in for fear the Indians would get them. When the alarm was raised four men mounted their horses and started back with young Huffman, but without carrying any ammunition except the loads in their rifles. The men were Chipman, Reinhart Swartz, Turpie, and Tom Outer. Jack was still a boy in his fifteenth year. When they arrived near the place the Indians had waked up but were still lying in the grass, and discovered the white men just as Jack waved his hand indicating to his companions the spot in the prairie where he had seen the Indians, and they, supposing this meant their discovery, sprang up and made a run for a thicket 200 yards away and a lively chase commenced, the men all firing their guns except Jack and Chipman. The latter was a Mormon, and seemed to have some scruples about taking human life, but said, "Jack, you shoot them and I will keep them cut off from the thicket." Young Huffman knew the value of a shot now, and running close to an Indian, dismounted so as to take better aim, and fired, and the

Indian fell, but sprang to his feet again and went on, making a fearfully curious noise. Chipman tried to cut the Indians off from cover, but one of them shot him twice with arrows, inflicting only slight wounds, but which caused him to lose his scruples about shooting Indians, and he fired at one but missed. In the meantime Huffman was reloading his gun as fast as he could, and as soon as he got it ready fired again at the Indian whom he first shot and badly wounded, and this time he killed him, the Indian falling with his face in a thorny bush. The other men with empty guns were idle spectators of the battle which young Huffman was now making, and he shouted to them to catch his horse, which, becoming frightened, was running off across the prairie, and he again commenced loading his gun for a third shot, and yelled to Swartz to charge the other Indian, who was about to get into the thicket, and shoot him with a little self-cocking pistol which he had. The man said the pistol was no good; he had tried it and it would not shoot. "Keep in sight of him then," said Jack, "until I get my gun loaded." Swartz now took off after the Indian, but soon ran over a big rattlesnake and turned back, telling Huffman, who was coming in a run with loaded gun, there was the biggest snake he ever saw. "Let the snake go to the devil," said Jack; "follow the Indian." Again he did so, but as he rode under a tree the Indian shot two arrows at him almost as quick as lightning, both of which would have struck his body had they not hit a small limb first and glanced upward. Jack now came up and fired and hit the Indian, but he succeeded in getting into the thicket out of sight. The white men now all got together again, one of them having Huffman's horse in charge, and they went back to the dead Indian and got his bow and arrows and other things, and went back to town, where the people gathered around them, and young Jacob was quite a hero in their eyes. Next morning a party went back to the scene of the fight and a diligent search was made for the other Indian, but he could not be found, but his buckskin leggings were, and covered with blood, proving he was badly wounded. Several days after this Captain Beck came out from San Antonio to buy cattle, and while riding over the range and through the thickets in the vicinity of the fight found the dead body of the other Indian not far from where Huffman last saw him, and brought his bow and arrows and rope to Castroville.

After this Jack went on many scouts after Indians and acted as guide and trailer for the soldiers from San Antonio, but got into no fights while with them, as they were too slow, and had sergeants with them who did not wish to catch Indians, preferring to stop at ranches and drink buttermilk. During one full moon, however, Jack had his

SECOND BATTLE WITH INDIANS.

On this occasion he found a dead cow at a place called "Government Canyon," deriving its name from Gen. Albert Sidney Johnston, who made a government road through it out towards Fredericksburg. The cow had not been long killed, and by Indians, he knew from their trail, and at once hurried to his ranch on the Helotes and told his neighbors the Indians were in and to tie up their horses and come to his house at daylight, and they would take an Indian hunt. They were on hand at the time designated and the start was made, the trail being found out in the prairie, and which led back past where the cow was killed and then on towards Verde Creek. The Indians had a large drove of horses, and the settlers in pursuit were Jack Huffman, John Green, Frank Heibner, Christian Aves, John Huffman, Jr., Ed. Galagher, Chris. Schuhart, and Garland Odum. The trail was followed rapidly and they came upon the Indians at 4 o'clock in the evening, who, when they saw the white men, stopped on the side of a hill 400 yards away and prepared to give them battle. The charge of the settlers was led by Huffman and Green, and they advanced to within eighty yards of the Indians, and, dismounting, commenced the battle, expecting the balance of the men to come up to where they were, but the others stopped too soon and commenced firing at long range. The Indians saw this advantage and came yelling and firing at close quarters, and Green was soon badly wounded, having his arm shattered by a ball while loading his gun and could do nothing more, and Huffman had to meet them alone. To add further to his discomfiture his gun snapped twice when he had a good aim on the foremost Indian, but at this time the other men began to come near and one of them ran to Huffman with a gun, which he took and snapped in an Indian's face, and as he turned to run snapped it again at his back. This gun was not loaded. Green was down by a tree and the Indians charged again, thinking they had the whites whipped, but this time Huffman's gun began to fire and he opened up on them right, his gun being a repeating Henry rifle, and soon had one of them down badly wounded, but he got up presently and ran. The cause of his gun failing at first to fire was an empty shell in the barrel, which, as soon as he discovered it, he threw out and it worked all right. Schuhart and Odum now came to his side and opened fire, and the Indians ran, with four more of their number wounded, which could be ascertained by them throwing their things away and running to the brush when the balls would strike them. There were two squaws in the band, and when the fight commenced they screamed and squealed like pigs and ran away over the mountain, both being mounted on horses, one of which belonged to old man Gillis, a white man, and the other to Toras, a Mexican. Jack shot twice at them as they ran away up the mountain, but failed to bring either down, and they all collected in a ravine beyond the mountain. One ball glanced Huffman's head, but he was not injured. The Indians made the fight with guns instead of bows, and made some close shots considering the excitement that prevailed and the bullets which were whistling around their own ears. Only ten Indians were seen, including the two squaws, and they left all of their horses, sixty-three, and some of their own, saddled. Green was very weak and sick, but came to Huffman during the fight and asked him to load his gun for him, but on turning around to do so discovered the man had left his gun at the tree that he had been leaning against. One Indian had left his horse with saddle and a canteen of water on him, and Huffman caught him and led him as they started to leave the ground, Green riding close beside him and very sick. Suddenly he said, "Catch me!" and commenced falling from his horse, but Huffman got hold of him and eased him to the ground, where he lay and called for water. Jack told him there was no water except that on the Indian's horse, and it might be poisoned. "I don't care if it is," said the wounded man; "I will die anyhow if I do not get some water." It was given to him and he soon revived, the water being all right. At this time the other men were rounding up the horses and getting them down the mountain, and some of the Indians still in sight.

Green recovered from his wound, but was afterwards killed by a Mexican.

For want of space we can not go through all of the frontier incidents of Mr. Huffman's life, but can say he was ever on the alert and was a typical border man, and now lives twenty miles west of San Antonio, where he owns a fine ranch, and says here he has killed many mustangs for their tallow to grease wagons, lariats, etc.

He knew Big Foot Wallace well, and often hunted with him and his famous dog Rock, and says when the dog died Wallace buried him and covered his grave with the skins of wild animals. Mr. Huffman married Miss Caroline Ernst, who was also a Castro colonist, and passed through many stirring scenes. On one occasion she watched a band of Indians rounding up horses near their ranch while her husband was away.

MRS. AMANDA L. SCULL.

Came to Texas in 1825.

Mrs. Amanda Scull was born in Jackson County, Mississippi, November 4, 1822, and was the daughter of Capt. Theodore Dorsett. She came to Texas with her father in 1825, and first settled in the Red lands on Irish Bayou, near Nacogdoches. Mrs. Scull is one of the few who still survive and can tell of the times of W. B. Travis, Patrick Jack, and Monroe Edwards, and of San Jacinto—a connecting link between the past and present. The writer had the pleasure of meeting and conversing with Mrs. Scull in April, 1900, at the house of her son, Mr. Gambia Scull, near Lavernia, Wilson County, but the residence of Mr. Scull was in Guadalupe County.

Mrs. Scull passed through those troublesome times in eastern Texas called the Fredonian war, and the Regulators and Moderators. Her father, Captain Dorsett, commanded a company in the Fredonian war.

The American settlers in east Texas and the Mexican population in the years from 1830 to 1835 were not on the best terms with each other and often open ruptures occurred, and during these times three prominent Americans, namely, W. B. Travis, Patrick Jack, and Monroe Edwards, were placed in prison at Anahuac. Now, at the time of their arrest they were boarding with Captain Dorsett, and he obtained the contract of feeding them while in confinement. Also in prison at the time was a man called "Jawbone Morris," and it seems that one particular Mexican guard had charge of him, and Morris finally commenced negotiations with him in the way of a bribe for escape. The price of $10 was agreed upon for the guard to let Morris escape, but he was not possessed of that amount of money in the prison, but had an empty pocketbook of well-dressed leather. In the town at this time Morris had a friend named W. D. Scull, whom the subject of this sketch afterwards married, and he was allowed to converse with the prisoners, but no notes were allowed to pass between them, nor were the guards allowed to carry anything but verbal messages to anyone. Mr.

Scull and Morris, however, had an agreement that in case the Mexican guard brought the pocketbook to Mr. Scull he was to pay him $10 and keep the book. This was all accomplished a few days after, and Morris escaped and was never seen or heard of by Mr. Scull afterwards, but he kept the pocketbook and wrote on it the date of the transaction, which was the 5th day of April, 1832. It is now in possession of his son, Mr. Gambia Scull, and was shown to the writer, and the writing, which was with ink, is still very plainly visible.

Mr. Scull during these times acted in the capacity of messenger from place to place, going most of the time in a boat from point to point around Galveston Bay, and was a member of a company commanded by Captain Erskine. Colonel Travis and Mr. Scull were schoolmates at Mobile, Ala., and he said that Travis was the brightest boy in school, was tall and manly in appearance, and had no difficulty in getting his lessons; even Latin was easy for him. Mrs. Scull says she can remember him as a very handsome man,—tall, well proportioned, light hair, blue, smiling eyes, broad white forehead, nice rounded chin and mouth, and it seemed to her like he ought to have been a woman. Their families were acquainted before they came to Texas, and Travis used to wait on her sister Ellen. He married in Alabama but his wife did not accompany him to Texas, and he often spoke tenderly and with great solicitude about a little son he had back there, saying he hoped some day to be able to do something for him in the way of lands and property. When he and the others were released from prison they came direct to Captain Dorsett's house, where they had formerly boarded, and greatly surprised the family, and at the same time rejoiced them, as they were very popular among all of the American settlers.

Mrs. Scull, then a girl, saw them approaching the house and exclaimed, "Oh, mamma! Yonder comes Mr. Travis, and Mr. Jack, and Mr. Edwards." The mother, not having any idea the Mexicans had released them, or were going to do so, soon replied, "Amanda, hush; what makes you want to talk that way?" In a few moments the three distinguished gentlemen entered the door and were warmly welcomed, and ate their first meal with the family after getting out of the prison. They remained here several days, and William Jack, brother to Patrick, came and carried him to his home on the Brazos. Travis and Edwards also went away, and that was the last time Mrs. Scull saw Travis, and all grieved sincerely when they heard of his tragic death in the Alamo. Monroe Edwards went to New Orleans and she saw him no more.

During the retreat of the families from Santa Anna Captain Dorsett went to Galveston, and Mrs. Scull says there was no town there then, only one house on the island, but many people in tents, and a brig anchored near by was a boardinghouse. The Dorsett family, with their tent, occupied some mounds that were thrown up by the pirate Lafitte and his men, and one of them named Campbell was still there. When rumors came of the near approach of the Mexicans, Captain Dorsett took his family in a boat and went out into the bay and plainly heard the cannon when the battle of San Jacinto was being fought, and Mrs. Scull can remember how the artillery sounded, and with what great anxiety they listened to it, for they knew that the fate of Texas was at issue, and that before the sun went down Texas would be free or lost. Next morning the news of the great victory was announced to all the people, and loud shouts and great rejoicing was heard.

Captain Dorsett went to the battleground and viewed the scene of the terrible slaughter, and then went to Gen. Houston's camp in the timber on Buffalo Bayou. Mrs. Scull says that a widow named McCormick lived near the battleground, and a little boggy branch over which the Mexicans had to pass, and in which so many of them mired and were killed in the retreat, was called McCormick's Creek.

While Captain Dorsett was in the camp of the Texans he learned a strange and unique feature of the war. The Mexican prisoners, 700 in number, were being given away to anyone that wanted them to work for them, and the captain took three. Their names were Hosea, Martines, and Bibee. This one was called "Baby" by the Dorsett family. Martines was wounded in the leg, the leaders being cut by a ball so that he could not walk, and Captain Dorsett did not want to take him, but he cried and begged until he did so for pity. He said he could do a great many things on the place if he was hurt in the leg;

that he could shell corn and feed chickens, etc. When the Mexicans were brought home Mrs. Dorsett told the captain that he ought not to have brought the wounded one, but he said, "If you had been there and heard him cry and beg to be taken, you would have done as I did."

Captain Dorsett moved from Galveston Island when things began to be settled again and went to Liberty County, and the Mexicans worked for him there on a farm. Martines died there on the 19th of August, 1843, of fever.

Miss Amanda Dorsett married Mr. W. D. Scull on the 8th of January, 1840, at her father's farm on the Trinity. Colonel Bradburn acted as goodfather to Mrs. Scull when she was baptized.

Mrs. Scull says that in 1835, when hostilities commenced with Mexico and men were concentrating and marching upon San Antonio, three Taylor brothers, all boys or youths, were picking cotton for her father, and as soon as they finished the job made preparations to go to the war, and many neighbors came in to see them off. Their names and ages are as follows: Edward, 21; James, 17; George, 15. These gallant boys died with Travis in the Alamo.

The mother of Mrs. Scull died in Liberty County in 1843, and in 1851 Mr. Scull came to Guadalupe County and settled on the Cibolo. In the following year Captain Dorsett came and lived with them until he died.

In 1855 the Indians made a raid down the Cibolo valley and killed Lewis McGee, young son of Rev. John S. McGee, and a negro girl 14 years old, named Lucy, who belonged to Mr. W. R. Elam. All this occurred in about two and a half miles of Mr. Scull's house, and the news was brought to them by Ed. Tarver. Most of the people in the settlement were gone to a barbecue at Seguin and but few men could be raised to follow the Indians, and great excitement prevailed. Mr. Scull, Jim Umphreys, and Silas Harmon loaded their guns and went to hunt the Indians, and Mr. Scull's family and others started to Seguin on foot. In this party were Mrs. Scull and her family, William, Mary, Sarah, Gambia, and Charley, Mr. Patton's negroes and his wife, Julia Shaw, her sister, Monroe Dorsett and his wife and four children, and three or four negroes.

The word had come that a large body of Indians were coming down the valley and for the people to leave their homes. Mrs. Scull and her party only went about one half mile from the house, and then all entered a deep gully at the head of a ravine and hid. Captain Dorsett had remained behind to get the horses, and joined them here with a negro boy named Homer and another negro, bringing the horses along. Guns were heard while here, and the people thought sure the Indians were close upon them. A messenger now arrived and told the people to fort up at the house of Mr. James Newton, and many of them went there and spent a wakeful, uneasy night. Major Montgomery loaded his wagon that night with the intention of starting back to Mississippi when daylight came, but changed his notion, and is here yet. On the following morning Mrs. Scull brought her family back home, and in a few days Mr. Scull came back and said the Indians were all gone out of the country and there was no more danger. They had followed the Indians to the Sabinal River, in Uvalde County.

The negro girl who was killed was a house girl and had been raised by Mrs. Elam, who thought a great deal of her. At the time that she met her death at the hands of the savages she was carrying water to work hands in the field of Robert Floyd. There was a small stream near by called Lipan Creek, near the Cibolo, and it was from this place she was coming with a bucket of water on her head when the Indians came upon her. She thought they were cowboys and stopped to look at them, and they at once surrounded her. The first thing the painted rescals did was to rope the bucket and jerk it off of her head. They then began to rope at her, but she threw the rope off several times, but they finally succeeded in fastening her, and her screams was answered by the men in the field. The Indians then lanced her and cut her across the bowels, and left. It was evident they intended to capture and carry her along, but her resistance and screams caused them to fatally wound her. She lived several hours, was perfectly conscious, and told all about the circumstance, but Mrs. Elam, her mistress, never saw her alive any more, but gave her a nice burial. Mr. Elam was at Floyd's, and was soon upon the scene and assisted the poor unfortunate as best he could, and sent young Tarver to warn the people below.

In 1859 Mr. Scull moved to the San Antonio River and settled five miles below Floresville. On the 13th day of July, 1861, the Indians made a raid and killed one of Captain Wayman's negroes and carried off another. Mr. Gambia Scull saw the dead negro and helped to bury him. He had four or five arrows in him. One had struck a joint of the back bone, and was the one that killed him. The others were in the shoulders. All of the horse stock in the country had been rounded up by the Indians, but they had stampeded and many of them were shot with arrows and some recaptured and carried off. Among these were the entire lot of John Peters. This was the last bad raid made in that part of the country. West of there, on the Lucas, the cow hands, among whom was Gambia Scull, were nearly rounded up by a large body of Indians, but the boys scattered and got away.

When the Civil war broke out William Scull, brother of Gambia, joined the regiment of Terry rangers in the company of Capt. William Houston, and was killed in the battle of Murfreesboro.

The elder Scull, father of Gambia, died on the 4th day of January, 1886. Mrs. Amanda Scull now lives with her daughter, Mrs. Emma Mattox, two miles from Lavernia, and near her son Gambia. There are four boys and two girls still living, all married, and all near by. Mrs. Mary Ellen Richardson, a daughter, lives in Lavernia. Mr. Gambia Scull has a fine farm near the old road along which marched the army of Santa Anna after the fall of the Alamo, when he was marching to the conquest of the balance of Texas. They encamped on the Cibolo River, near the present home of Mr. Scull, and many things have been found there from time to time, among which was a large chunk of lead weighing several pounds.

R. H. BURNEY.

The name of Burney has been closely connected with the history of Kerr County since a very early date. They passed through the frontier days and were used to Indian alarms, scouts, trails, and battles with the red men, and materially aided in settling and developing the country.

Robert H. Burney, one of the representative men of the large connection of the family of Burney, was born October 22, 1854, in McNary County, Tenn. His father, Judge H. M. Burney, came to Texas and settled in Kerr County in 1856, when Robert was but two years of age, and has passed the most of his life on the Texas frontier. His first schooling was of course only such as could be afforded in a sparsely settled country on the border, but he finally entered the Southwestern University at Georgetown, Texas, in 1875 and received medals for proficiency in mathematics and oratory. He graduated in 1879, with the degree of bachelor of arts, at the Southwestern University, and also in 1879 was made bachelor of laws after a course of lectures in the law department of Vanderbilt University, at Nashville, Tenn.

In 1874 Judge Burney joined a company of Texas rangers commanded by Capt. Neal Caldwell, and made many scouts after hostile Indians over the rough mountain country, and in all kinds of weather, suffering alike with heat and cold—sometimes almost scorching on the desert plains, suffering with thirst and hunger, and at other seasons of the year almost perishing in some sudden, driving blizzard far out in the open country of the plains and divides. With the money earned as a ranger he paid his tuition fees and part of his other college expenses. His experience as a ranger enabled him to gain an intimate knowledge of frontier life and the needs of the west, which has been of great service to him as a State senator. He was nominated by the Democracy and elected to represent the Twenty-eighth senatorial district in the Twentieth and Twenty-first Legislatures, and in 1890 was re-elected for a term of four years. His district was composed of sixteen counties, embracing an area of over 63,000 square miles. In the Twentieth Legislature he was chairman of the select joint committee of the senate and house charged with an examination into the conduct of the Comptroller's office. This thorough examination and exhaustive report was due largely to his labors and direction. It was the openly expressed opinion of the highest State officials that this report was most important and beneficial to the State.

He was the author in the Twentieth Legislature of the measure under which the geological department is operated. In the consideration of the vexed school land question he was considered by his colleagues an eminent authority, his opinion were listened to with marked respect and carried with them great weight, and he was finally placed upon the free conference committee of the two houses to adjust conflicting opinions and formulate a State policy.

In the Twenty-first Legislature he was chairman of the senate committee on education, and in the Twenty-second Legislature chairman of the senate committee on State asylums. He took an active part in the leading debates and important legislative work of these bodies, and added further strength to his well earned reputation as an able legislator.

On one occasion Judge Burney met with an accident which came near rendering him a cripple for life, and which few men under like circumstances survive. On this occasion he and others were out turkey-hunting in the mountains, and Judge Burney arose before daylight and repaired to a turkey roost alone, and unfortunately stepped off into a deep, rocky gorge and fell many feet, landing on the solid rock bottom below. His hip was crushed and other parts of his body badly bruised, so much so that he was unable to arise and was compelled to remain there for many hours until his calls for help finally attracted his companions, and it was then with great difficulty that he was rescued, on account of the steepness and ruggedness of the cliff over which he fell, and it was years before he recovered. Senator Burney married Miss Mattie Prather, of Palestine. He is a member of the Masonic fraternity, a good lawyer, and still resides in Kerr County, in the town of Kerrville, county seat.

CONCLUSION.

Owing to the size this present work has assumed, many worthy sketches have to be cut short, but the writer hopes at some future time to write them up at length. Among these are the following:

Hon. B. F. Cocke, who came from Tennessee to Texas with his family and settled in Kerr County in 1857, near Comfort, in the Guadalupe valley. His sons were Jack, Foster, James, Fred, and William. They were good frontiersmen, and had many scrapes with the Indians. On one occasion Foster and Fred ran fourteen Indians by waving their hats and calling to an imaginary force in the valley below, and at the same time boldly charging the Indians, who at once beat a hasty retreat. William was also closely pursued by three Indians about dusk between Center Point and Comfort, but he outran them, keeping his pistol in hand ready to shoot if they overhauled him. In 1872 he was ordained to the ministry by the Methodist church, and has been serving in that capacity since, and resides at Center Point, Kerr County, Texas.

Dr. J. Clark Ridley, who still survives at a very advanced age, at Center Point, was one of the first settlers in this country, and did as much to develop and settle up the country as anyone who came here at that early day.

John Tedford, one of the early settlers on the Verde Creek, near Center Point, was wounded and his horse and saddle captured by an Indians as he was going from his home to that of his sister, Mrs. Reese, wife of Sidney Reese, who lived on the Guadalupe above Center Point.

Capt. Charles Schrenier, one of the most successful business men of Kerrville, came at an early day and passed through some stirring scenes during the frontier days, serving as a Texas ranger part of the time along the border.

Capt. L. P. Sieker, now of Austin, spent nearly all of his young manhood days on the Texas border, trailing, scouting, and fighting Indians. He was captain of a company of rangers and was ever on the alert after the hostiles, following them with a tenacity and endurance that was most remarkable. On one occasion he pursued a band so fiercely across the plains for seven days that when finally the chase was abandoned it took the captain and his men three weeks to retrace their steps with their played-out horses and pack mules, but he had driven the Indians beyond the Pecos River. Many interesting incidents in the life of Captain Sieker will be written later. He is now captain and quartermaster of the frontier battalion.

Capt. Robert Hall, who spent more than half a century on the Texas frontier, is well known to the people of southwest Texas, and whose history has already been written in book form.

Capt. William Pitts, who now resides at Austin, is one of the old-time Indian fighters who served under Gen. Ed. Burleson and Capt. James H. Calahan, and is widely and favorably known in the west.

Thurlow Weed, who resides in Austin, was a gallant Texas ranger, serving as sergeant in Capt. Rufe Perry's company. He participated in the second Lost Valley fight and also in the long battle and chase of Comanches in Menard County, in which he killed an Indian at close quarters during a stand made by the Indians in a desperate attempt to drive back the rangers. Mr. Weed also has the honor and distinction of being one of the pallbearers in the reinterment of Big Foot Wallace at Austin, when his remains were moved from Devine by an act of the Legislature.

Ben and Henry McCulloch, the two brothers whose names are interwoven in nearly every chapter of the book, as others told of their heroic deeds along the border for more than fifty years. They were natives of Tennessee, and in their young days hunted and frolicked with David Crockett.

Among others who can not now be written, who deserve a chapter, are Wm. Davis Drown, Milford Day, Jr., Braxton Nicholson, Louis Oge, Judge P. D. Saner, R. H. Hunter (one of the old three hundred), Mr. Cole, veteran of the Mexican war, and Mrs. Bracn, one of the old-time pioneers. Also some other incidents in the life of Col. James C. Carr while in California and Oregon, where he got the name of "Buckskin."

Hoping that my efforts to perpetuate the name and fame of these heroes of the border will be appreciated by my readers, I remain, yours truly,

A. J. SOWELL.

www.ingramcontent.com/pod-product-compliance
Lightning Source LLC
Chambersburg PA
CBHW030539080526
44585CB00012B/197